Ultimate TypeScript Handbook

Build, scale and maintain Modern Web Applications with TypeScript

by

Dan Wellman

First published: July 2023
Published by: Orange Education Pvt Ltd, AVA™
Address: 9, Daryaganj, Delhi, 110002

ISBN: 978-93-88590-78-5
www.orangeava.com

Dedicated to

My beloved wife Tammy

And my children - Bethany, Matthew, James, and Jessica

About the Author

Dan Wellman is an author and a proficient web developer from the United Kingdom, with over 15 years of experience in the front-end realm. He has written extensively on JavaScript both online and offline and has created numerous videos for prominent organizations in the digital education sector, such as Envato and PluralSight. He is currently working as a senior developer for a global financial services company.

Technical Reviewers

- **Deeksha Kusuma** has a remarkable blend of expertise and practical experience, managing multiple teams and researching technical work. Deeksha has established herself as a trusted figure in leading teams and marking technical work. Her meticulous attention to detail, analytical prowess, and dedication to advancing knowledge make her an invaluable asset to any author seeking to refine their work. Her commitment to raising the bar in technical writing sets a standard that inspires both seasoned and aspiring authors alike.

  Along with technical research in her spare time, she loves travelling, cooking, spending time with her 11-year-old and having a steaming hot cup of coffee. Yes, she is an ardent lover of coffee. She is determined to travel to every country in the world!

- **Chris** is a Senior Software Engineer and qualified teacher of Mathematics who lives on the South coast of the UK with his wife, two sons, a cat and a dog. While he has experience with a variety of technologies across the stack, in recent years he has focused his attention specialising in the frontend. He's been an avid user of TypeScript since it was introduced to him via Angular, which he has been using since it was in beta.

  He is particularly passionate about unit testing and often takes time to mentor junior engineers in how to approach testing with best practices that can yield a robust suite of tests.

  In his spare time, Chris enjoys walking the dog, sipping South American Malbec and playing World of Warcraft. He loves to read, preferring anything either with dragons in it, or modern horror inspired by the works of H.P. Lovecraft.

Acknowledgements

First and foremost, I would like to express my gratitude to the editorial team at Orange AVA for their continued assistance and guidance throughout the process of writing this book. Without their support, this book would not have been possible.

I would also like to extend my special thanks to the technical reviewers, Chris Ford and Deeksha Prakash, and my esteemed colleague, Oleg Bevz, for their thorough review of the initial drafts of this book. It would not be the same without their insight and technical mastery in TypeScript. I am indebted to each of them.

Lastly, while too numerous to name individually, I want to thank the giants on whose shoulders I stand, the countless authors of the many TypeScript and front-end development blogs and tutorials I've read, and the inestimable number of articles and videos from which I have learned, throughout my development career. Thank you to the community I am proud to be a part of.

Preface

Welcome to Ultimate Typescript Handbook. Over the course of this book, I hope to share with you my passion and excitement for using TypeScript to produce maintainable and functional web applications.

Don't worry if you don't yet have this burning desire to use TypeScript, although I would expect some degree of curiosity at least given that you have chosen this book. I too was initially skeptical about the benefits that TypeScript would bring, the cost of switching development, and whether it would even last or fade into obscurity following an initial but waning popularity like CoffeeScript did in years gone by.

After discovering the safety that TypeScript brings to any JavaScript project and the ease with which it can be adopted, my fears were soon alleviated, and I started on the path that I continue to follow to this day. Once I made the switch, I never looked back, and I am confident that you too will feel the same. After writing TypeScript for just a short amount of time, you'll shudder at the thought an old piece of code you need to work on which is written in JavaScript and not TypeScript.

Over the course of this book, I will take you on a guided tour of all TypeScript's major aspects. You may be starting this journey with absolutely no prior experience with TypeScript, or you may have some level of knowledge already; it doesn't matter. Having some knowledge and experience of working with JavaScript would be beneficial, as this will allow a deeper appreciation of the benefits that TypeScript brings.

Regardless of where you start, by the end of the book, you will have mastered the fundamentals of the language and be ready and confident to begin using it on a day-to-day basis. If you're an existing JavaScript developer on the fence about whether to make the jump to TypeScript, then this is the book for you.

Chapter 1 will provide a gentle introduction to the world of TypeScript and provide some information on the type system it uses, some advantages and disadvantages to using the language, and how it works to prevent bugs and help you to write better applications.

Chapter 2 will show you how to set up a development environment so that you can begin using TypeScript. You'll see how to download and install it, how to create a new TypeScript project, and how to configure TypeScript using its main configuration file to best cater to the requirements of your project.

Chapter 3 will start to look at some of the most fundamental aspects of developing with TypeScript including primitive types, union types, and literal types. Among other things, you'll learn about type aliases, which are the bread-and-butter of TypeScript development, and the special any, unknown, and never types.

Chapter 4 will focus on using the TypeScript compiler and show how TypeScript is compiled, what the compiled files look like, and some of the CLI flags that we can pass to the compiler to control its behavior. You'll see how to use 3rd party libraries with TypeScript, and how to generate declaration files.

Chapter 5 is a deep dive into enums, interfaces, and namespaces in TypeScript, which focuses on how to work with these very common entities. The knowledge you'll gain here will include merging and extending interfaces and namespaces, and how to use the varied types of enums available in TypeScript.

Chapter 6 shows how to work with some of the different data structures that you'll use most often - objects, arrays, and tuples. You'll learn about read-only arrays, optional and rest elements in tuples, and index signatures and property modifiers in objects. You'll also be introduced to the topic of generics in the context of objects, and see one of TypeScript's utility types in action.

Chapter 7 is dedicated to the all-important function in TypeScript and will cover a range of topics including basic function type annotations, optional and rest parameters, generator functions, and generic functions. You'll also see how to make function overloads, how to work with this parameters, and how type inference works with functions.

Chapter 8 will focus entirely on classes in TypeScript, covering topics including class declarations and expressions, constructors and access modifiers, and generic classes. You'll see how to add getters and setters, how to deal with inheritance, and look at a classic design pattern implemented with TypeScript.

Chapter 9 will look at how we can use narrowing and type guards to safely work with values that may be one of several different types, as well as show how to use the in and satisfies operators.

Chapter 10 will show you how to work with and manipulate types. You'll learn how to use conditional types, indexed access types, and mapped types, as well as look at TypeScript's wide variety of built-in utility types.

Chapter 11 is all about modules in TypeScript and will show you how to create modular code which imports and exports code as needed by your application. You'll see some of the TypeScript configuration options related to modules, how modules are resolved by the compiler, and how existing modules can be augmented.

Chapter 12 will focus solely on creating declaration files in TypeScript, which may be necessary for working with older JavaScript libraries that do not already have existing declarations. You'll see how to create declarations for global libraries and modular libraries, how to add living documentation with JSDoc, and how to publish your declarations so that other developers can use them too.

Chapter 13 is a final practical chapter which will see you build your first complete TypeScript application using the Angular framework, to help cement the knowledge you've gained throughout the book into a firm foundation for building upon in future.

Downloading the code bundles and colored images

Please follow the link to download the
Code Bundles of the book:

https://github.com/OrangeAVA/Ultimate-Typescript-Handbook

The code bundles and images of the book are also hosted on
https://rebrand.ly/5caab9

In case there's an update to the code, it will be updated on the existing GitHub repository.

Errata

We take immense pride in our work at Orange Education Pvt Ltd and follow best practices to ensure the accuracy of our content to provide an indulging reading experience to our subscribers. Our readers are our mirrors, and we use their inputs to reflect and improve upon human errors, if any, that may have occurred during the publishing processes involved. To let us maintain the quality and help us reach out to any readers who might be having difficulties due to any unforeseen errors, please write to us at :

errata@orangeava.com

Your support, suggestions, and feedback are highly appreciated.

DID YOU KNOW

Did you know that Orange Education Pvt Ltd offers eBook versions of every book published, with PDF and ePub files available? You can upgrade to the eBook version at www.orangeava.com and as a print book customer, you are entitled to a discount on the eBook copy. Get in touch with us at: **info@orangeava.com** for more details.

At **www.orangeava.com**, you can also read a collection of free technical articles, sign up for a range of free newsletters, and receive exclusive discounts and offers on AVA™ Books and eBooks.

Piracy

If you come across any illegal copies of our works in any form on the internet, we would be grateful if you would provide us with the location address or website name. Please contact us at **info@orangeava.com** with a link to the material.

Are you interested in authoring with us?

If there is a topic that you have expertise in, and you are interested in either writing or contributing to a book, please write to us at **business@orangeava.com**. We are on a journey to help developers and tech professionals to gain insights on the present technological advancements and innovations happening across the globe and build a community that believes Knowledge is best acquired by sharing and learning with others. Please reach out to us to learn what our audience demands and how you can be part of this educational reform. We also welcome ideas from tech experts and help them build learning and development content for their domains.

Reviews

Please leave a review. Once you have read and used this book, why not leave a review on the site that you purchased it from? Potential readers can then see and use your unbiased opinion to make purchase decisions. We at Orange Education would love to know what you think about our products, and our authors can learn from your feedback. Thank you!

For more information about Orange Education, please visit **www.orangeava.com**.

Table of Contents

CHAPTER 1

Introduction to TypeScript and its Benefits

Introduction

In this first chapter of the book, we will focus on the reasons why one should consider using TypeScript, the benefits it can offer to developers, and how it can reduce the number of bugs in an application. We will also delve into the type system used by TypeScript, its various aspects, and how designing applications while considering the different types in use in our program can lead to a better application. Let's get started!

Structure

In this chapter, we will cover the following subjects:

- Introduction to TypeScript
- TypeScript's type system
- Advantages of using TypeScript
- The ways in which TypeScript prevents bugs
- Steps to begin using TypeScript
- Type-driven development

Introduction to TypeScript

TypeScript is one of the most popular programming languages on the planet, as well as one of the fastest-growing languages. It was originally released by Microsoft in 2012, and although it took some time to build momentum, by

2017 it had exploded in popularity. It spawned a whole ecosystem of tooling and frameworks, and some say it was instrumental in causing the full-stack revolution currently in full swing.

A short history of TypeScript

TypeScript was created by Microsoft as an internal project at some point in 2010, and was in development until its public release in 2012, when it was at version 0.8. Development has continued at a rapid pace since its public release, and the version 5 milestone was reached shortly before this book was published.

TypeScript was initially created in response to the demands of both internal developers and external clients who wished for a front-end language that was safer to use than existing JavaScript, and just as easy to implement and start using-TypeScript was Microsoft's response to these demands

By the post-millennial era of web development, JavaScript had already earned itself a reputation as a buggy and difficult language to work with. Back-end developers were happy to stay away from it, allowing the rise of front-end development as a distinct career choice in its own right. But TypeScript offered the promise of a safer, more familiar, and less buggy language to work with on the front-end, which enticed back-end developers to again take an interest in the front-end, allowing the concept of full-stack development to blossom.

As of 2022, TypeScript enjoys the position of fourth most popular programming language in use according to Stack Overflow, behind only Java, Python, and the king of programming languages itself of course - JavaScript and looks set to continue its meteoric rise in the coming years.

TypeScript is a superset of JavaScript; it contains everything that JavaScript contains, and then a little more on top. TypeScript isn't just a static type system. It isn't just a library, a framework, or a set of utilities. It is a programming language in its own right. Everything that can be done in JavaScript can also be done in TypeScript.

Main components of TypeScript

TypeScript consists of three main parts; first, there is the syntax and if you already know JavaScript to a relatively good level, you already know most of TypeScript, because as I just mentioned, TypeScript contains all of JavaScript.

On top of this, TypeScript adds some new syntax to express types and some new keywords. We'll cover all of this in more detail as we progress through the book.

The second component is the compiler. TypeScript itself isn't supported by any browser; it can't be run natively on the internet. Instead, it is one of a number of different languages that are compiled into JavaScript so that it can be run by any regular browser. The TypeScript compiler is known as TSC and is included when TypeScript is installed. It is run from the command line and can be configured to be run as a build step in a CI/CD pipeline. We'll learn more about the compiler and how to use it later in the book.

The final aspect is that of editor integration. TypeScript was created by Microsoft and is fully integrated with the popular Microsoft suite of IDEs Visual Studio by default, without any additional configuration. It can also be installed in many of today's most popular development tools and editors. This component of TypeScript turbo-charges local development, giving you type information and code completion right there as you're developing.

In case you're wondering exactly how capable TypeScript is, and exactly what kinds of application can be created using TypeScript, take a moment to appreciate that Visual Studio Code itself is written in TypeScript. Visual Studio Code is one of today's most popular and capable IDEs and is used daily by millions of developers globally. In light of this, I believe that there is no application too big or too complex to create using TypeScript.

TypeScript's type system

There are many different kinds of type systems that are used to enforce the types of values, and the operations that may be performed on them, used by different programming languages. One common category of the type system is called a **nominal type system**, where it is the name of a value, or the place in which it is used, which determines its type.

Conversely, TypeScript uses what's known as a **structural type system** to enforce types - it is the structure of a value that determines the value's type. This kind of type system is colloquially known as duck typing-if it looks like a duck, walks like a duck, and quacks like a duck, it's a duck!

TypeScript is able to infer the types of some values based on how we use them. For example, if we assign a string to a variable without explicitly stating that the variable has the type `string`, TypeScript will go ahead and assign the type `string` to that value and warn us if we later try to store a number in that variable or try to perform an operation on the value that doesn't make sense for strings.

TypeScript can also infer the types of values based on the construct they are used in. When using an array with a `for` loop for example, TypeScript knows that the type of the first parameter passed to the callback function will be the same type as the original value in the array on which the loop is used because that's how `for` loops work in JavaScript and TypeScript fully understands how JavaScript works.

TypeScript's type system is also a static type system, which means that the types are checked statically during compile time by TypeScript's compiler. This is opposed to a dynamic type system, which checks types at runtime. This would not be possible for TypeScript given that TypeScript is never run directly, it is the resulting JavaScript that the compiler emits which is ultimately run.

JavaScript itself uses a dynamic type system and infers types during program execution depending on the type of value that is in use. This is why JavaScript performs its infamous type coercion; in JavaScript, if one variable contains an integer, and another variable contains a string, if you try to add these two variables together, JavaScript will coerce the numeric value silently to a string and concatenate the two values instead of adding them, which often leads to unexpected results.

This kind of silent bug is exactly the motivation for using a safer type-system, where bugs and incorrect usage of the language can be caught and addressed during compilation, before making it into production and potentially crippling your application.

Advantages of using TypeScript

Using TypeScript as the development language of choice in place of JavaScript comes with a number of benefits, hence the popularity of the language. Let's take a moment to look at some of these advantages.

Catching bugs

One of the main advantages of TypeScript is its ability to catch bugs before they reach production, which ultimately saves time and money. The actual number of bugs that can be prevented by TypeScript is the subject of some debate, but I've seen estimates that range from 10% all the way up to 38%.

Of course, these figures only capture what is known as public bugs; bugs that have been committed to source control and, in some cases, actually deployed to a production environment.

This kind of bug represents only the tip of the iceberg in that most of the bugs that TypeScript will catch will never be committed to source control or publicly deployed because the developer will have been alerted to them by TypeScript and will have fixed them before they ever make it into source control. This kind of bug is sometimes called a private bug because it remains private to the individual developer that caused it.

Even the lower estimate of 10% of public bugs, when combined with the incalculable number of private bugs, alone makes a compelling case for the adoption of TypeScript over raw JavaScript. Fixing bugs in development as opposed to production is both quicker and cheaper by a considerable margin. But TypeScript offers more than just early bug discovery and resolution.

TypeScript considerably enhances the development experience by bringing advanced features like code completion or Intellisense, and a living, inline form of documentation that guides the developer as they are literally writing their code. With TypeScript, as soon as you type the name of an object, it pops up a menu that shows all the properties and methods that are available from that object:

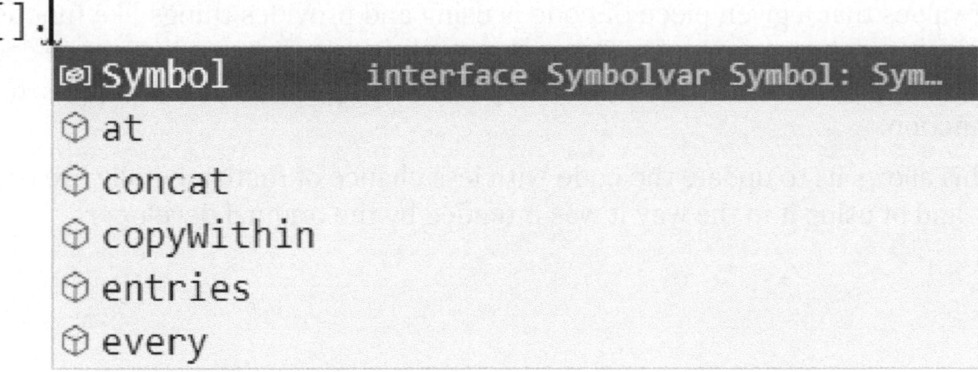

Figure 1.1: *Code-completion menu for an array literal in Visual Studio Code*

Readability

So, TypeScript makes writing functional and correct code easier, but I find that it also makes reading code easier as well, and reading code written by other developers, or even by ourselves many weeks or months earlier, is a significant part of any developer's workload.

Some developers I've spoken to in the past insist that developers spend more time reading code than they do writing it, especially for more senior developers, or those involved with the maintenance of a more mature piece of software. This is especially true when considering the often-mandatory code review, or pull request, stage of professional or open-source software development.

It is important that developers reviewing code before it is checked-in can get a good idea of how the code works and what it is supposed to do in as quick a time as possible, and the additional information and intent that can be expressed with TypeScript goes a long way in making code self-documented and vastly more readable.

Refactoring

Refactoring code, or taking old code and improving it, while retaining broadly the same functionality as before, perhaps with some additional, new functionality, is another task that is made easier with TypeScript.

A comprehensive suite of unit tests will also help in this regard, but the additional safety that TypeScript brings can help to increase developer confidence when changing the existing code, and the two paradigms of test-first and TypeScript development complement each other perfectly

TypeScript takes the mystery out of unfamiliar code and signposts the types of values that a given piece of code is using and provides things like function parameter and return types. This makes it a lot easier to not only use the code as a consumer, but to infer what the code is doing and how it is supposed to function.

This allows us to update the code with less chance of fundamentally breaking it, and of using it in the way it was intended by the original developer.

Future language features

TypeScript has traditionally had faster release cycles than JavaScript itself, and so has tended to implement new features in TypeScript before they appear in JavaScript, so using TypeScript gives us a heads-up on new features coming into our development toolbox and allows us to start working with future features sooner. This may seem like a small benefit, but you show me a developer that doesn't like working with shiny new features of their language of choice!

A classic example is classes, which could be used in TypeScript for a long time before they were fully supported in JavaScript, making TypeScript the obvious choice for heavily object-oriented projects.

Disadvantages of TypeScript

TypeScript isn't all sunshine and rainbows, it does have some drawbacks of its own, however small and overstated those may be. Let's take a moment to explore these too, for balance.

One of the biggest criticisms of TypeScript is that it leads to more code being written for a given piece of functionality when compared to JavaScript, and this is no doubt true. But the additional code that is written with TypeScript I feel is minimal, and the benefits that this small amount of code brings far outweigh the cost of some additional keystrokes.

Of course, this scales with the size of the project, so applications with hundreds of thousands of lines of code are going to contain far more additional TypeScript than smaller projects containing merely hundreds or thousands of lines. But larger applications will likely be developed by many, many developers, so the additional load for an individual developer tends to even out.

Another disadvantage is that it introduces an additional compilation step that JavaScript itself does not have. This can increase build times and add additional complexity to any build pipeline, although these issues are generally easily managed.

The TypeScript compiler itself is pretty fast, so compilation times are minimal for everything but the largest of projects, and most professionally produced web applications are almost certainly using a build pipeline already to produce the artefacts needed to deploy the application, so TypeScript will likely be a small addition to an existing process, rather than an entirely new process in its own right, and many modern frameworks already come with built-in TypeScript out of the box.

Lastly, TypeScript requires additional learning to master, on top of any knowledge one might already have of JavaScript, and new skills to work with the tooling are also required. This new knowledge takes time to acquire, but this really is no different from learning any new programming language, and the fact that it builds on top of an already known language (for developers that already know JavaScript) helps to flatten the learning curve.

The ways in which TypeScript prevents bugs

TypeScript adds a static type system to JavaScript, enforcing a much higher level of security that the values we are working with or operating on are of the correct, or expected, types. Calling a `string` method on a `number`, such a trivial but all too easy to make mistake, will crash your application, stopping a user from doing whatever it is they were trying to do.

TypeScript makes this kind of error almost impossible because it forces you to check that the value you are working with really is a `string` before allowing you to call `string` methods on it. You can avoid this whole class of errors caused by trying to access properties or methods that don't exist on the current value, and due to the tight integration between the editor and the code, the editor will warn you if you make this mistake, long before your code ever reaches production.

For example, consider the case where you have a value which you expect to be a `number`, but for some reason is a `string`. The editor will warn you as soon as you try to work with the value as if it were a number:

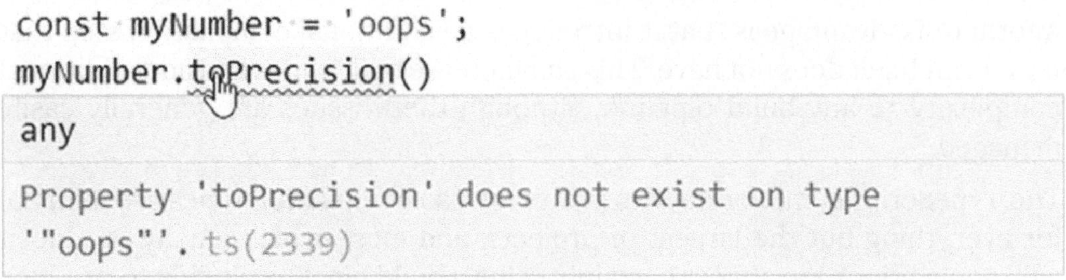

```
const myNumber = 'oops';
myNumber.toPrecision()
any
Property 'toPrecision' does not exist on type
'"oops"'. ts(2339)
```

Figure 1.2: *Method does not exist on type error in Visual Studio Code*

Another place where bugs may be found before they can cause carnage is in the compiler when compiling TypeScript into JavaScript, which is a necessary step that must be completed before your code will run in a browser. Consider a small utility function that counts the number of properties an object has:

```
function countProps(obj) {
  return Object.keys(obj).length;
}
```

If we try to compile code that contains a call to this function without passing the required object as a parameter, the compiler will spot the error and warn us, and we can even instruct the compiler not to generate any output if the input contains errors such as this:

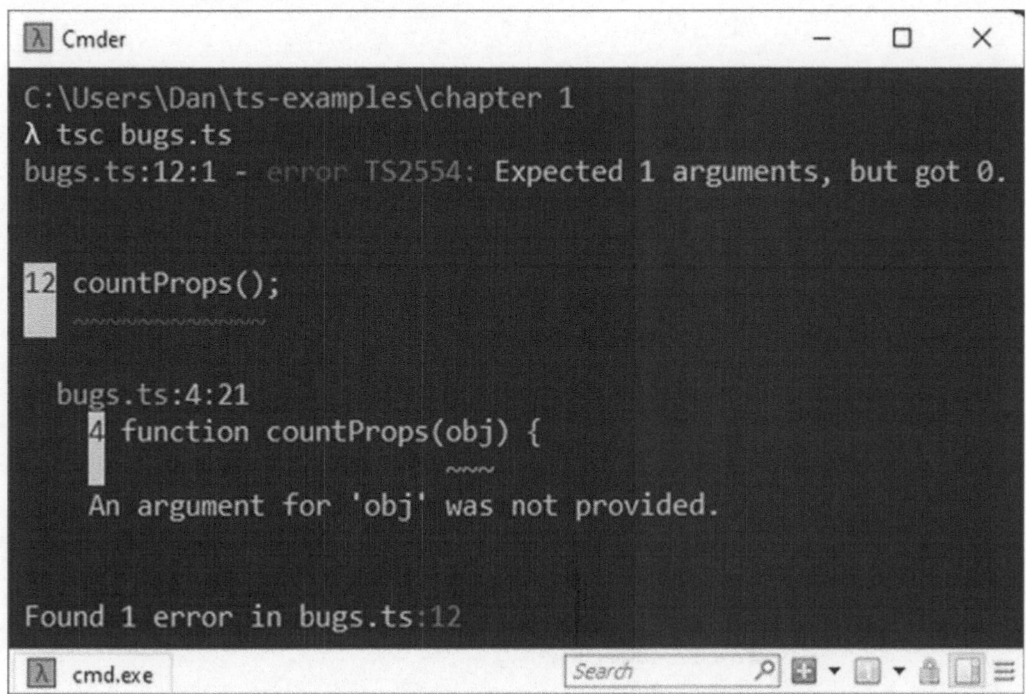

Figure 1.3: *TypeScript compiler error in a Windows terminal application*

Steps to begin using TypeScript

TypeScript is entirely optional, and we can opt into it as slowly as we want. Migrating an existing JavaScript project to TypeScript is extremely easy. Consider a small JavaScript file that handles creating `Person` objects:

JS original.js ×

chapter 1 > JS original.js > ...

```
class Person {
  constructor(attrs) {
    for (let prop in attrs) {
      this[prop] = attrs[prop];
    }
  }
}

const bob = new Person({
  name: 'Bob',
  age: 44,
});
```

Figure 1.4: *A small example of a JavaScript file*

To convert this file to valid TypeScript, simply change the file extension from **.js** to **.ts:**

TS converted.ts ×

chapter 1 > TS converted.ts > ...

```
class Person {
  constructor(attrs) {
    for (let prop in attrs) {
      this[prop] = attrs[prop];
    }
  }
}

const bob = new Person({
  name: 'Bob',
  age: 44,
});
```

Figure 1.5: *JavaScript converted to a TypeScript file with no additional changes*

Now that we have a TypeScript file, we can begin to add types to it at the speed which is comfortable for us; for example, rather than allowing any named properties and values in the `attrs` object passed to the `Person` constructor, we can specify an `interface` which details exactly which properties can be used and what their value types should be, for example:

```
interface PersonAttrs {
  name: string;
  age: number;
}

class Person {
  constructor(attrs: PersonAttrs) {
    for (let prop in attrs) {
      this[prop] = attrs[prop];
    }
  }
}
```

Don't worry too much about the exact syntax used in the above code snippet. We'll cover what all of it means later in the book. The point is that we can begin to add type information as slowly as we want to, a single type at a time if necessary, and perhaps days, weeks or at any point after converting the original JavaScript file to TypeScript. We can add each new piece of type information by itself if we want to, and slowly migrate the original code to fully-fledged TypeScript.

> **NOTE: Not all JavaScript can be converted to TypeScript without making any additional changes–sometimes small issues will need to be fixed, but these are often as simple as declaring the type of particular value.**

Using TypeScript in a brand-new project is even easier as we can build in support from the very beginning by designing a build process that includes the TypeScript compilation step, and we can even initialize a new TypeScript configuration file with sensible defaults using the TypeScript compiler itself.

Type-driven development

There have been numerous popular development paradigms that are intended to make the software development process more straightforward, such as test-driven development, where the unit tests are written before the actual functional code and can guide the development of the application so that all use cases are accounted for up-front.

Type-driven development is a paradigm where the types are created first; we can design our application by considering the types that will be needed to represent the different elements of our system and the attributes that those elements will have.

We can also design the signatures of the methods or functions that will be used to operate on the values in our system, what the types of the parameters will be, and what type of data the functions or methods will return.

For example, instead of writing a full function declaration initially, we can instead use TypeScript's **`declare`** keyword and just specify the function signature, without the full implementation. For example, imagine we are creating a small helper function that can create HTML elements:

```
declare function createHtmlElement(tagName: string): HTMLElement;
```

The **`declare`** keyword tells the TypeScript compiler that at runtime, there will be a function called **`createHtmlElement`**, which will accept a single **`string`** parameter, and return an object of the type **`HtmlElement`**. Consider this the contract of the function, a clear specification of the type of input it receives, and the type of value it should return.

The function in the previous code snippet has no implementation, and the declare keyword basically disallows the actual function declaration to exist at this point. For this to be a true TypeScript declaration, it would need to be in a special TypeScript declaration file, with the extension **d.ts** instead of just **.ts**. We'll look at the different ways to create these files later in the book.

In order to define the actual implementation of the function, we can remove the **`declare`** keyword and add the function declaration after the return type. Working in this way forces us to think about our code, the inputs and outputs that it will be working with, and how it should behave up-front before we even write a single line of production code.

Starting with a declaration like this, even if it is later removed, is useful because the editor will guide us as we are writing the code. In this case, until the **`createHtmlElement`** function actually returns an object of the type **`HtmlElement`**, the editor will warn us that the function is not behaving in the way that it should–it's breaking the contract:

```
interface HTMLElement

Any HTML element. Some elements directly implement this
interface, while others implement it via an interface that
inherits it.

A function whose declared type is neither 'void' nor
'any' must return a value. ts(2355)
function createHtmlElement(tagName: string): HTMLElement {

}
```

Figure 1.6: *Function must return a value error in Visual Studio Code*

The idea behind type-driven development is similar to that of test-driven development, where the tests are written before the actual code, which again forces the developer to fully consider the code before actually writing it.

Type-driven development and test-driven development are not mutually exclusive, they can and should be used together for maximum benefit to the design of your code.

Conclusion

This chapter has served as a gentle introduction to the world of TypeScript and hopefully has motivated you to read on and continue your journey into the language and its uses. We looked at where TypeScript came from and how it can help you to write more scalable, maintainable, and safer-to-refactor applications.

In the next chapter, let's move on and set up a development environment ready to start writing TypeScript.

References

- **https://css-tricks.com/the-relevance-of-typescript-in-2022/**
- **https://blog.acolyer.org/2017/09/19/to-type-or-not-to-type-quantifying-detectable-bugs-in-javascript/**
- **https://www.securityjourney.com/post/typescript-doesnt-suck-you-just-dont-care-about-security**

CHAPTER 2

Setting up a Development Environment

Introduction

In this chapter, we will learn how to get started with developing in TypeScript and take that first step into building commercial-grade, maintainable and bug-minimal web applications. To do that, we'll need to learn how to set up a development environment suited to writing TypeScript, and that's what we'll be learning here.

In order to use TypeScript, we will need to install a few things including TypeScript itself, and a compatible IDE (Integrated Development Environment) which understands TypeScript and can provide us with the great tooling which makes working with TypeScript both productive and pleasurable.

We'll also learn a little about the things we'll be installing, how to install TypeScript both globally to our system, and locally within a project, and how to generate a brand-new TypeScript project using the TypeScript compiler, as well as learn how TypeScript can be configured once it has been installed.

Structure

In this chapter, we will cover the following topics:

- Installing dependencies
- Installing TypeScript globally
- Creating a new TypeScript project
- Installing TypeScript locally in a project

- Configuring TypeScript using tsconfig.json
- Enabling TypeScript checking in JavaScript files

Installing dependencies

There are a couple of different things that as a bare minimum should be installed if we wish to write TypeScript. The first is the popular JavaScript runtime Node.js, which we will use to install and compile TypeScript itself.

The second thing that we need to install is an IDE that we can use to develop TypeScript applications, and which is able to understand and make use of the language to provide the development tooling for which TypeScript is so renowned.

Windows users may also benefit from installing a 3rd party terminal application in order to enhance the development experience. The default terminal application on Windows is called Command Prompt and supports only very basic commands. Fortunately, there are many more powerful alternatives available, including Bash (installed by default with Git), or PowerShell (included with Windows by default).

Here, I have used a third party wrapper for the command line on Windows called Cmder (available at **https://cmder.app/**); it is this application you will see in all subsequent figures showing a terminal application for the remainder of this book.

Version numbers

The world of software development is constantly evolving, with new tools, frameworks, and versions of existing tools and frameworks appearing on a near-constant basis. While exciting, this does mean that recommendations for which version of any particular piece of software to use quickly go out of date.

Any version numbers of any software, tools, or frameworks recommended or discussed in this book should be taken as correct at the time of writing, but subject to change as time passes.

Installing Node.js On Windows

Node.js has many different installation options and different versions that you may install, a detailed explanation of which is beyond the scope of this book. It is generally recommended to be using Node.js version 12 or above for modern TypeScript development.

The current LTS (Long Term Support) version of Node.js is version 16, so my recommendation would be to simply install the current LTS version of Node.js, which should be compatible with the latest version of TypeScript.

You can find full information on installation, and download the recommended package for your operating system, on the Node.js website by visiting the URL **https://node.js/org**. Once downloaded, run the executable installer, to install it (Refer *Figure 2.1*):

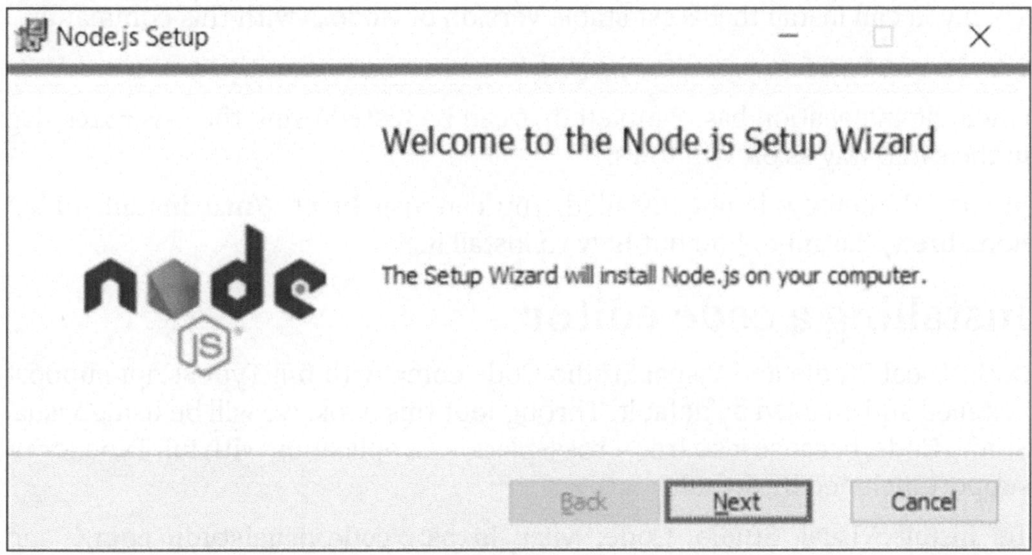

***Figure 2.1:** The Windows Node.js installer*

Once Node.js is installed, you will be able to use it from the command-line or terminal application (hereafter referred to simply as terminal) of your computer. To test that Node has been installed correctly, you can try running the following command in your terminal:

```
node --version
```

The output of this command, if Node.js has been installed correctly, should be a version string, such as v16.16.0.

The Node.js installation also installs Node's package manager NPM, which we can use to install TypeScript, and many other JavaScript and TypeScript-related packages from the online NPM repository.

Installing Node.js on Mac

The best way to install Node.js on a Mac is to use Homebrew, which will handle downloading, unpackaging and installing the application. It is recommended to update Homebrew before installing Node.js, so the first step is to run the following command in the Terminal:

```
brew update
```

Then you can install the latest stable version of Node.js with this command:

```
brew install node
```

Once the installation has completed, it can be tested using the `--version` flag in the same way as on Windows.

In case Homebrew is not installed, you can visit **https://mac.install.guide/homebrew/3.html** to find out how to install it.

Installing a code editor

Both Visual Studio and Visual Studio Code come with full TypeScript support installed and enabled by default. Throughout this book, we will be using Visual Studio Code, because it's a free, cross-platform application with full TypeScript support included by default.

To install Visual Studio Code, visit **https://code.visualstudio.com/** and download the applicable standard version for your operating system. Follow the installation instructions and, once complete, you should have the latest version installed and ready for use.

As well as TypeScript itself, Visual Studio Code has a rich ecosystem of TypeScript-related extensions that can be installed for free to further enhance your development experience.

Visual Studio comes with a "recent" stable version of TypeScript pre-installed, which the application uses to provide code-highlighting and other development tooling. We cannot use this version ourselves directly, we will still need to install it on our system to compile our TypeScript.

From this point forward, whenever I mention the editor, I will be referring specifically to Visual Studio Code. Any time I refer to an editor that is not Visual Studio Code, I will reference that editor by name.

Installing TypeScript globally

TypeScript may be installed as an NPM module globally on our system. This is advised because it will allow us to use the TypeScript compiler in our terminal application from any directory on our system, which is useful for generating new TypeScript projects. We'll see how to do this in just a moment.

First, we will need to install TypeScript, we can do that via NPM using the following command in our terminal application:

```
npm install -g typescript
```

This will install the current release version of TypeScript. The presence of the **-g** flag is what causes TypeScript to be installed globally. Once the package has been installed, you can test that it has been installed correctly by running the following command in your terminal:

```
tsc --v
```

The TypeScript compiler is called tsc, and this command will output a version string such as **Version 4.7.4** if TypeScript has been installed correctly. We'll be looking at the compiler in much more detail later in the book. If for some reason the version number is not displayed, you may need to restart your terminal or computer.

Creating a new TypeScript project

Now that TypeScript is installed globally, we can use the compiler to create a brand-new TypeScript project. First, we should create a new directory for our project, let's call it **ts-examples**. Once this is created, we should change our terminal application to this new folder, then we can run the following command:

```
tsc --init
```

Invoking the compiler with the **`--init`** flag will generate a new **tsconfig.json** file in the directory within which the command is run. Once the project has been generated, the compiler will output a list of the configuration options that it has enabled to the terminal window (Refer *Figure* 2.2).

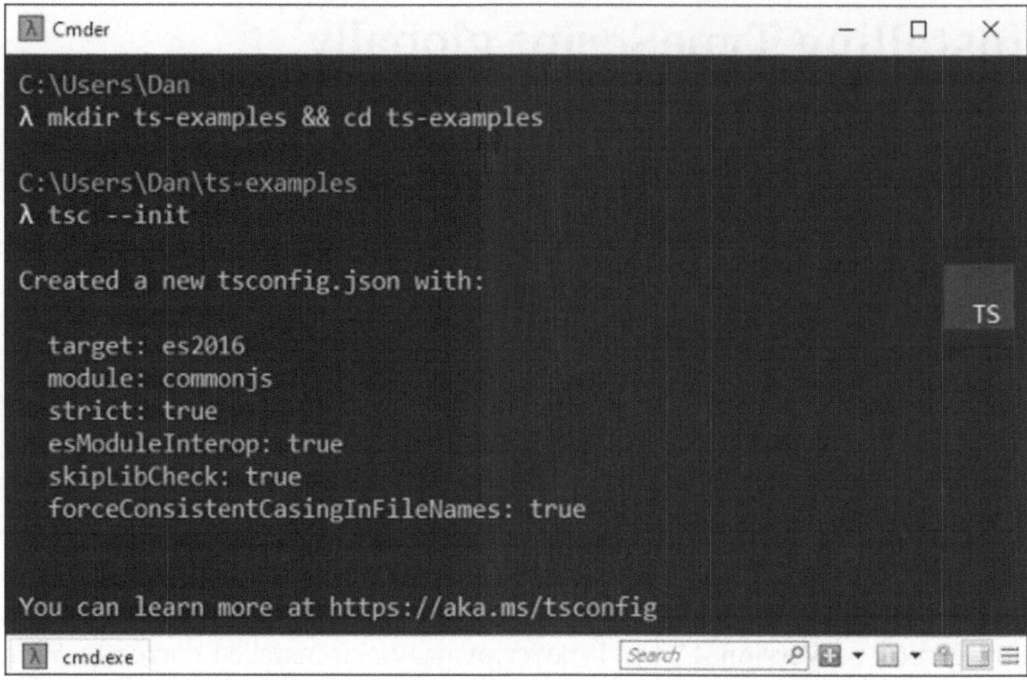

Figure 2.2: *Output from the compiler when using --init*

For the remainder of this book, this folder will be our TypeScript project directory and is where all of our TypeScript files and any related assets will be stored.

The tsconfig.json file

The `tsconfig.json` file is the main configuration file for TypeScript which controls how the compiler behaves when it compiles our TypeScript files into JavaScript, and to a limited degree, how our IDE provides tooling while we are developing. A directory that contains a **tsconfig.json** file is considered the root of a TypeScript project.

If you open up this new file in your text editor or IDE, you will see a selection of some of the more common configuration options that TypeScript supports.

By default, most of these options are commented out, but they also contain documenting comments that describe the effect that setting the configuration options will have, which makes this file a valuable built-in resource for learning a little bit about how to use TypeScript effectively. It also makes it easy to quickly enable common options by removing the comment at the start of the relevant line.

The options that are not commented out are the ones that are enabled, and these should match the list of options that were output to the terminal window after running the `--init` command with the compiler.

The configuration options that we set will usually be very project-specific and will vary even depending on whether we are compiling for development or production environments, as well as the exact nature of the application we are building. For now, we can go with the defaults enabled by the compiler.

Installing TypeScript locally to a project

Now that we have created a TypeScript project, we can install a local copy of TypeScript into the project itself. You may wonder why this is necessary given that we have already installed TypeScript globally on our system.

Generally, when we are building an application, we need to control the versions of any dependencies we use, even if those dependencies are used only for development purposes like TypeScript is.

While TypeScript tries to avoid making breaking changes, it is unavoidable that these may occur from time to time, so it is important that developers are using the same version of TypeScript denoted by the project whilst developing. Installing the package directly in the project gives us full control over exactly which version of TypeScript is used for the project, regardless of which version developers may have installed locally.

One way to think of it is that the global version is for us individually to use on our own system, but the local version belongs to the project itself and is for a larger number of developers to all use.

To install the latest release version of TypeScript into a project, we can use the following command in our terminal application, making sure the terminal is focused on the directory in which TypeScript is to be installed:

```
npm install typescript
```

Without the `-g` flag, the TypeScript package will be installed locally in the current directory. This will result in a new directory called **node_modules** being created in the current directory; this directory is where all of the NPM packages we install locally to this project will reside.

A **package.json** file and **package-lock.json** file will also be created as by-products of running the installation command. These two files are used to specify all of the NPM packages that the project requires in order to function in both development and production.

These two files are unrelated to TypeScript and can safely be ignored in the context of this book from this point on.

Another difference between installing TypeScript globally versus locally is that we will only install the global version once. Now that it's installed, we can run **tsc** commands from any directory on our system, but barring the occasional update, we can largely forget about this version. Conversely, we will be installing the local version much more often, depending on how frequently we create new TypeScript projects.

Configuring TypeScript with tsconfig.json

The `tsconfig.json` file is where we can set any of TypeScript's different configuration options. By default, inside this generated file they are broadly separated into groups of different categories of related options, which control how different aspects of TypeScript work. These categories are:

- Project-level options
- Language and environmental options
- Options related to modules
- Options related to JavaScript and code editor support
- Options to control what is emitted by the compiler
- Constraints on interoperability
- Type-checking options
- Completeness and output formatting options
- Backwards-compatibility options
- Options controlling how types are acquired
- Options related to watch mode

The generated **tsconfig.json** file does not contain the complete set of supported configuration options. For a complete list of all the configuration options that TypeScript supports, see the documentation at **https://www.typescriptlang.org/tsconfig**. It also does not contain all of the above groups of options.

All in all, there are a huge number of different configuration options that we can specify, and the exact configuration we use is likely to vary considerably between projects, depending on the specific nature of each project.

The frameworks we use for building applications will also have a bearing on the configuration that we use. React developers, for example, are likely to make more use of the JSX-related configuration options than Angular developers. Frameworks that use TypeScript are also likely to include a preconfigured **tsconfig.json** file that sets any options required by the framework.

Additionally, some of the configuration options are there to help transition older JavaScript projects to TypeScript, and as such, would not be required in brand-new projects created today.

There are however some common options that we will find we frequently configure in our projects. We'll take a quick look at some of these more common configurations in just a moment, but before we do that, let's just look at the configuration options that are enabled by default when we create a brand new TypeScript project using the compiler as we have done here.

Default enabled configuration options

The following options are configured by default when generating a new TypeScript project without passing any options on the command line.

target

This option specifies the ECMAScript version of JavaScript that is emitted when the project is compiled. By default, this option is set to `es2016`. This version is safe to use with modern browsers, but it may be necessary for you to lower the target version if legacy browser support is required.

This option also impacts the JavaScript that is emitted; setting this option to a value lower than `es2015/es6` for example, will result in things like arrow functions being converted to regular functions, and other syntactical changes to make sure the code can run in the target environment.

The minimum version of JavaScript that we can target with TypeScript is `ES3`, and the highest version is `es2023`. This latter value will certainly change in the future as ECMAScript continues to evolve.

There is one more value that we can specify for this option, and that is `esnext`. This value just tells the compiler to target whatever is the upcoming ECMAScript release, but the actual value that this option will match depends upon which version of TypeScript you have installed, which makes this option unpredictable and so you should avoid it where possible.

module

This configuration option allows us to specify the module format that is used when our project is compiled to JavaScript. By default, the value of this option is `commonjs`, which is the module format supported by Node.js.

Other values that we can specify for this configuration option include:

- `none`
- `amd`
- `umd`
- `system`
- `es2015/es2020/es2022/es2023/esnext`
- `node16/nodenext`

The `umd` option refers to Universal Module Definition, named as such because it works in both browsers and Node.js. It makes use of **IIFEs (Immediately Invoked Function Expressions)** and was often produced as a fallback by the popular resource-bundler Webpack.

The `amd` option refers to Asynchronous Module Definition, which was implemented in browsers by the once very popular **Require.js** library. This format is no longer used as commonly as it once was but may still be required for very old framework-less JavaScript projects.

The `system` option refers to System.js, a module loader that fully supported ES Modules before native support became widespread, and which is still commonly used.

The `es*` options refer to different versions of the official ES Modules specification. For example, the `es2015` option gives basic ES Module support, while the `es2020` option adds support for dynamic modules, and `es2022` includes top-level use of the `await` operator.

Traditionally Node.js supported only CommonJS, but beginning with Node.js version 16, ES Module support was added, which we can target with the `node16` option.

esModuleInterop

By default, this option is given the value `true` and is enabled to fix issues caused by early versions of TypeScript making what turned out to be false assumptions about how ES modules would work.

This option may need to be disabled (by setting it to `false`, commenting it out, or removing it from the **tsconfig.json** altogether) if your project uses libraries that define their API using inherited properties.

forceConsistentCasingInFileNames

This option is also given the default value of `true`. ES Modules rely on being able to locate modules using file names and paths to physical files on the file system. Some operating systems are case-sensitive, and others case-insensitive, so it is important that all developers on the project use the correct casing. This option will cause an error if a module file path is specified using the wrong casing.

strict

Strict mode is also set to `true` by default to enable thorough type-checking in our editor and when compiling TypeScript. It is a short-hand property that enables numerous individual strict checks for various options.

This configuration gives us the most strict type-checking, without the burden of a complex and repetitious configuration that needs to be enabled each time we begin a new TypeScript project.

It can be useful to disable or remove this option and instead enable each of the strictness options that it encompasses individually. This makes it easier to fine-tune our strictness configuration based on the needs of the current project, or to focus on fixing one category of strictness issues at a time when converting JavaScript to TypeScript.

The most commonly-used individual options that fall under the `strict` umbrella are as follows:

- `strictBindCallApply`
- `strictFunctionTypes`
- `strictNullChecks`
- `strictPropertyInitialization`
- `useUnknownInCatchVariables`
- `noImplicitAny`
- `noImplicitThis`

Let's take a quick look at each of these in turn as they are all enabled by default (under the umbrella option `strict`) when initializing a new TypeScript project from the terminal.

The **`strictBindCallApply`** option enforces that when any of **`bind`**, **`call`** or **`apply`** are used, they are invoked with the correct argument types for the underlying function they are called on.

The **`strictFunctionTypes`** option ensures that when a function is invoked, the parameters passed to it exactly match the type that the function expects. Without this, TypeScript is somewhat lenient in this area.

The **`strictNullChecks`** option strictly enforces **`null`** and **`undefined`** as distinct types. If this option is disabled, TypeScript is much more lenient with values that might possibly be **`null`** or **`undefined`**.

The **`strictPropertyInitialization`** option ensures that any properties of a class that are defined are initialized with values in the class's constructor.

The **`useUnknownInCatchVariables`** option, automatically sets the type of parameters passed to the **`catch`** clause in a try/catch statement as **`unknown`**, which leads to more expressive error handling as the type of the parameter must be manually checked before it is used.

In situations where a type is not provided for a value, and the type for a value cannot be inferred from the value's usage, TypeScript will implicitly set the type to **`any`**. This effectively disables type checking for that value so may allow the value to be used in such a way that will cause errors at runtime. The **`noImplicitAny`** option causes an error to be shown whenever TypeScript would implicitly treat a value as **`any`**, allowing us to provide the correct type information for the value.

The **`noImplicitThis`** option is similar to **`noImplicitAny`**, but only shows an error when the value of **`this`** is implicitly **`any`**.

NOTE: For a complete list of all strictness-related configuration options, see the documentation at https://www.typescriptlang.org/tsconfig#strict.

skipLibCheck

This option is set to **`true`** by default and is used to avoid type-checking declaration files (files with the file extension **.d.ts**) in the application. This is a performance-related issue that speeds up compilation time as it reduces the number of files that are checked by the compiler.

Commonly used configuration options

As I mentioned earlier, exactly which configuration options you enable is likely to vary between projects, there are however numerous additional options that we will use often. We will look at a selection of these common options below. Note that none of the following options are configured or enabled by default. Some of them, but not all, are included in the generated **tsconfig.json** file but are commented out.

files

It is common to tell TypeScript the main files of your application using a glob pattern (see the **include** section below), which is a way to match files using a special path such as `app/**/*.ts - this` path would match any file with a `.ts` extension inside any sub-directory inside a directory called `app`.

Nevertheless, there may still be a small selection of files that are important to your application, but which do not reside in the same directory structure as the main files that you want to compile. In this scenario, we can use the files option, which takes an array of specific file paths that should be included in the compilation process.

Smaller applications may not need to use glob patterns at all and can rely solely on specific file references passed to the `files` configuration option. Larger applications may rely only on file globs, or some combination of both specific files and files matched by a glob.

include

Leading on from the `files` option above is the `include` configuration, the option which allows us to specify the glob patterns that TypeScript should use to find all of the necessary files for our application during compilation.

This configuration option also takes an array, so multiple glob patterns can be provided, if necessary, to match groups of files held in different locations. As specified above, our application configuration may contain either `include`, `files`, or both depending on its complexity and size.

exclude

While the `include` option allows us to specifically mention files that should always be included in the compilation of TypeScript to JavaScript, the `exclude` option allows us to specify any files that should never be compiled.

baseUrl

The `baseUrl` option is used to specify the root directory that non-absolute file paths are resolved relative to. It is usually configured to `./` which matches the same directory in which the **tsconfig.json** file itself is within.

rootDir

The `rootDir` option allows us to specify the root directory for the files in the compiled output. By default, TypeScript will automatically match the directory structure of the input files in the emitted JavaScript, but depending on the complexity of the input structure, or on other configurations you may have set, this inferred output structure may not be exactly what you require.

The `rootDir` option allows us to specifically dictate what the top-level directory of the files inside the root of the compiled output should be.

paths

The paths configuration allows us to remap imports inside TypeScript files to locations relative to the `baseUrl`. This allows us to create short alias paths for importing third party libraries from deep within the **node_modules** directory, for example, to make importing these libraries less verbose inside the TypeScript files in which they are used.

This means that instead of having to type something like `node_modules/some-library/app/dist/some-lib` in every file that we want to import `some-lib` into, we could create a simpler import by adding a configuration like this:

```
'path': {
  'some-lib': ['node_modules/some-library/app/dist/some-lib'],
}
```

In this case, we would then be able to import the file from the full path specified inside the array, using the short path specified by the property name.

The `paths` option takes an object, where each key in the object is an alias, and each value is the corresponding path for that alias. We can provide as many of these as we wish, and each value takes an array in order to map multiple locations to a single alias if necessary. It also supports the use of wild cards within alias names, for example, the following configuration

```
'some-lib/*': ['app/some-lib/*'],
```

Means any import for a path in a folder under **some-lib** should be sourced from **app/some-lib**.

outDir

By default, the compiler emits JavaScript files to the same directory that the original TypeScript file was contained in. This may be acceptable for smaller applications, or those with a simplified directory structure, but for larger applications, or those containing a more complex internal file structure, it may be necessary to specify an alternative directory into which all emitted JavaScript files should be output.

We use the `outDir` configuration option to specify where the compiled files should be emitted. This option is often used in conjunction with the `rootDir` option described above.

resolveJsonModule

By default, TypeScript does not allow JSON files to be loaded and imported into TypeScript files as if they were TypeScript. This is a very useful feature because we can use simple JSON files to hold local data used for developing the application without the need for a local database.

It's also very useful for storing mock data that can be used for unit testing to make tests more isolated, and so `resolveJsonModule` is a very commonly used configuration option.

To enable it, we just need to uncomment it in the **tsconfig.json** file as it is one of the ones that is included in the generated file but commented out.

While this is far from a comprehensive list of all the available configurations, this list contains a sensible foundation on which you can build your knowledge of TypeScript configuration. Other configuration options not covered here will be discussed in this book as and when they become relevant.

Top-level configuration options

Many of the configuration options that we've looked at are compiler options, and therefore reside within the `compilerOptions` object in the **tsconfig.json** file. There are some configuration options however that are known as top-level options which are used outside of the `compilerOptions` object. The `compilerOptions` option itself is a top-level option, as are the `include`, `exclude` and `files` options that we looked at earlier in this section.

Take care when adding configuration options that do not appear in the file generated by the compiler that you are adding them inside or outside of the `compilerOptions` object as appropriate.

Updating the project configuration

As we progress through this book, we will use certain features of TypeScript that will rely on a certain configuration. Some configuration options will be discussed as they become relevant, but there are also some additional configuration changes that we want to make now.

We should make the following configuration changes to the **tsconfig.json** file; uncomment or add them as applicable:

```
"module": "es2022",
```

```
"outDir": "./dist",
```

We set the **module** option to `es2022` to enable the latest support for ES Modules. We can also configure an `outDir` to avoid warnings about not being able to overwrite the plain JavaScript file that we are just about to create in the following section. We will also need to exclude the Chapter 1 directory from our compilation as the example project will not compile correctly if it is included due to the files it contains. We should add a new top-level option called `exclude` to the **tsconfig.json** file and specify **chapter 1** as an ignored directory:

```
"exclude": ["chapter 1"]
```

This option should be added outside of the `compilerOptions` section of the file because it is a top-level configuration option.

Enabling TypeScript checking in JavaScript

Before we dive fully into the nuts and bolts of using TypeScript, I just want to mention the fact that we can still leverage the benefits of TypeScript, even if we aren't using TypeScript at all. If we have a project that for whatever reason can't be converted to TypeScript, we can still enable a basic level of type-checking even in regular JavaScript files. To do this, we need to use a third party tool called **JSDoc**.

JSDoc defines a micro-syntax that uses a special format of regular JavaScript comments which can be used to add documentation to JavaScript files. This can then be used to provide tooling in supporting editors or to generate rich API documentation that describes how your application should be used by other developers.

JSDoc uses special tags inside comments to document specific features of JavaScript, and some of those tags can be used to document types. In turn, Visual Studio Code can understand these tags and use them to enforce types in plain JavaScript.

Find out more information about all of the tags supported by JSDoc at **https://jsdoc.app**.

Default behavior

To test the examples in this section, you can create a JavaScript file (not a TypeScript file yet) and see how the editor behaves as code is added to the file. For reference, the file can be found in the code archive accompanying this book; it is located in the **chapter 2** folder and is called **javascript-typing.js.** I'd recommend creating a blank JavaScript file and opening it in Visual Studio Code to get the most from this section.

By default, Visual Studio Code provides a very low-level of type-related information. For example, if we declare and initialize a variable with a value, the editor will infer that the type of that variable is the type of the value we have assigned it:

```
let a = 1;
```

In this case, wherever we use the value **a** the editor will tell us that this variable is a number if we hover the mouse pointer over it:

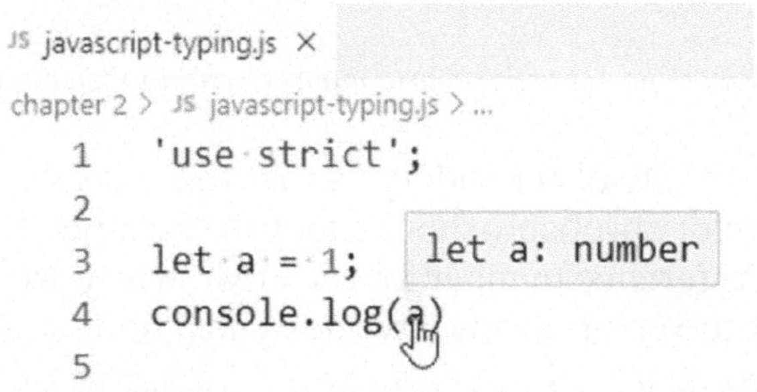

JS javascript-typing.js ×

chapter 2 > JS javascript-typing.js > ...

```
'use strict';

let a = 1;   let a: number
console.log(a)
```

Figure 2.3: *Variable description tooltip in Visual Studio Code*

However, it will not warn us if we reassign the variable to another type of value, or try to do something illegal, like trying to access a property of it if for some reason it happened to be **`null`**.

We would see this error manifest in a browser as an **`Uncaught TypeError`** of course, but we don't get a warning in our tooling, and that is where it gives us the most benefit. The development phase is the easiest and cheapest place to fix bugs.

Enabling type checking

To enable a more useful level of type-checking, we can set the **`checkJs`** configuration option to **`true`**. This is one of the properties added to the generated **tsconfig.json** file but commented out, so all we have to do is uncomment it and the option will be enabled.

Once we have enabled this option, the editor should be ready to begin type-checking in any JavaScript file inside the project. Let's try to reassign **`a`** to a different type, say a string:

```
a = 'oops';
```

Immediately, the editor should add a red, wavy underline to the variable **`a`** to let us know there is a potential problem here. If we hover the mouse pointer over the variable, we should see a warning:

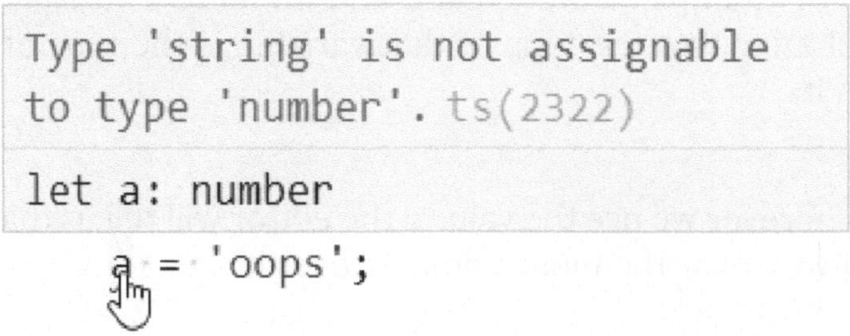

```
Type 'string' is not assignable
to type 'number'. ts(2322)
let a: number
a = 'oops';
```

Figure 2.4 *String not assignable to number error in Visual Studio Code*

This is TypeScript's way of reminding us that the variable was initialized as a number, and therefore probably should not be reassigned to a string value. We should also see a reference number for the error, which we can use to find out more about what the error means if we need help understanding it.

This type-checking will work across files or modules, so if we initialize a value as a particular type in one file, and then reassign it to a different type in another file, the editor will still helpfully show this as an error.

But what if this variable actually should be a string, because later on in our program we try to manipulate it as a string, and it was the initialization that was wrong? This is where we can use JS Doc to specifically tell TypeScript the type that the variable should be.

Adding JSDoc annotations

JSDoc supports many tags that we can use to describe and document our code, but one of the primary JSDoc tags that we'll want to use when we specifically want to make use of Visual Studio Code's type tooling is the `@type` tag.

We can add the following JSDoc immediately above the initialization of the `a` variable:

```
/**
 * @type {string} An optional description
 */
```

A regular JavaScript block comment begins with a forward slash and is followed by a single asterisk. The JSDoc micro-syntax uses a forward slash followed by two asterisks, making all valid JSDocs also valid JavaScript comments. JSDocs should always immediately precede the line they are referring to.

So, we begin with the JSDoc opening, and then each line inside the block begins with an asterisk. We use one line here but could use as many as necessary to adequately convey the intent of our code. We use the `@type` tag followed by the type we want to set in curly brackets.

Following the type, we can optionally provide a description of what the variable is for or how it should be used - anything that will help other developers, and even ourselves, understand the code better.

Now, the red line should move from the reassignment of the variable to its initialization, although the error message presented when we hover the mouse pointer over it should largely be the same, except that the terms 'string' and 'number' should be reversed now (Refer Figure 2.5):

```
JS javascript-typing.js > ...
'use let a: string

/**  @type — {string} An optional description
 * @ Type 'number' is not assignable to type 'string'. ts(2322)
 */  View Problem  Quick Fix... (Ctrl+.)
let a = 1;
a = 'oops';
```

Figure 2.5: *VSCode warning in a JavaScript file*

This is how we can annotate any variable declaration in a plain JavaScript file to give the editor information about the type of value that the variable may contain, and as well as annotating variable declarations, we can also annotate things like functions and classes.

For example, let's imagine we have the following simple function declaration:

```
function addNums(num1, num2) {
  return num1 + num2;
}
```

We have a simple function that accepts two arguments and returns the sum of them. Now let's say that we call this function at some later point in our code, but forget to pass the second argument:

```
exampleFn(1);
```

At this point, we do have some error lines under the two parameters in the function declaration. If we hover over the first one with the mouse pointer, we should see the following warning:

Parameter 'arg1' implicitly has 'any' type.

We'll be looking at the `any` type in much more detail later in the book. The point here is that the warning we are being given doesn't correspond particularly well to the actual problem in our code.

We can use JSDoc to clarify exactly what the function does, what type the arguments passed to it should be, and the type of the return value to expect when invoking it by using the following:

```
/**
 * sum two numbers
 * @param {number} num1
 * @param {number} num2
 * @returns {number} The sum of the parameters
 */
```

This time after the JSDoc opening line, we have a simple description of the function, again this is optional but is good practice to include. We then have an individual line for each parameter the function accepts; in this case, we have two parameters so have two lines utilizing the **`@param`** tag, which is used to describe the function parameters.

This uses the same format as the **`@type`** tag that we used earlier; the tag we want to use, followed by the type the parameter should be within curly brackets, followed by an optional description - in this case, that is just the name of the parameter.

The last line before the JSDoc closing line uses the **`@returns`** tag to specify that the function will return a number and that number is the sum of the parameters. Now we should find that the red underline has moved under the expression invoking the function, which is better because that is where the actual problem is.

If we hover on this with the mouse pointer now, we should see a pop-up containing quite a lot of information about the function including the description of the function we set on the first line of the JSDoc, the types of all the parameters, and its return type and description. This kind of information is very useful when we are working in a completely different file than the one the function is declared in.

Below the information from the JSDoc, we should also see this warning message:

Expected 2 arguments, but got 1.

This is much more useful than the default message that the parameters could be any type, but we should remember that this level of type-checking is still fairly rudimentary; if we add a second argument to the invocation of the **`exampleFn`** function, but use a string, say, instead of a number, then we get no warning at all, as the expression inside the function where the parameters are added together will succeed for numbers and strings, it will just concatenate them instead of performing addition.

If we do try to pass an argument of a type other than a number or a string, however, such as passing `null` as the second argument, then we will see a warning that the argument is not of the expected type:

The argument of type 'null' is not assignable to the parameter of type 'number'.

Example project structure and use

All of the code featured in this book is available in the accompanying code download for the book and is contained within a directory called **ts-examples.** Within this folder is a series of sub-directories, one for each chapter in the book. Within each subdirectory are one or more mostly TypeScript files, which show the corresponding code examples for each chapter respectively.

Where logical, each file may be further broken down into commented sections that align with sub-headings within each chapter, to make it clear which examples to consult when reading any part of the book.

These files are provided as a point of reference, and I would urge you to create your own files when working through the examples in this book to maximise your understanding of each of the topics we will cover. If you find that an example is not working as described in the book, the example files may help to pinpoint what the issue is.

As you work through the examples in the book, it may be helpful to segregate your own working files into a directory structure similar to the accompanying files, and to name each file you create after the concept being described, for example, when we are looking at primitive types in the next chapter, calling your own working file **primitives.ts** may help you to locate particular examples in the future.

Of course, this is not strictly necessary; TypeScript will happily compile any TypeScript files in your project into JavaScript files that can be run in a browser whatever the original TypeScript files are called, and whatever subdirectories they may be contained within, but for the book to be most effective, being able to come back and find a particular code example weeks or months after it is written will help.

Conclusion

In this chapter, we have seen how we can set up a basic development environment that will allow us to write TypeScript applications. We first saw that we should install some dependencies, namely Node.js and a TypeScript-enabled editor, such as VSCode (although there are other IDEs that support it natively or via user-installed extensions).

We then moved on to see how to use NPM to install TypeScript both globally on our system so that we can run TypeScript compiler commands from any directory on our system, as well as how to install it locally inside a TypeScript project.

Once TypeScript was installed, we saw how to use the compiler to create a new TypeScript project, which basically creates a copy of TypeScript's configuration file **tsconfig.json** and enables a selection of basic configuration options.

We spent some time examining the configuration options that the compiler enables by default when we create a new TypeScript project, as well as looking at some of the more commonly used configurations that we will often need to use in our projects.

Next, we saw how to configure our TypeScript project to enable type-checking inside JavaScript files, and saw that by default, variable types are inferred by the editor from the type that they are initialized with, which may or may not be acceptable depending on how we intend to use the variable in our code.

Lastly, we saw how to use the popular third party tool JSDoc to add annotations to things like variable and function declarations to describe exactly what the types of variables or function parameters are, which allows us to document the expected behavior of our code and provide information to the editor on how we intend to use it.

Now that we have an environment ready to develop TypeScript, and an editor that understands it, let's move on to look at the basic types that we can add using TypeScript.

References

- **https://node.js/org**
- **https://code.visualstudio.com/**
- **https://jsdoc.app**
- **https://www.typescriptlang.org/tsconfig**

CHAPTER 3

Basic Type Annotations

Introduction

In this chapter, we are going to dive straight in and start looking at the basic types that TypeScript supports. We looked at some basic JavaScript examples in the last chapter, but from this point on, we'll be working solely with TypeScript files.

The aim of this chapter is to give a thorough introduction to the use of some of the most fundamental aspects of TypeScript. This will give you a solid foundation for moving forward in your learning and which subsequent chapters will build upon.

Structure

In this chapter, we will discuss the following topics:

- Primitive types
- The `any` type
- The `unknown` type
- The `never` type
- The `as` operator
- Union types
- Literal types
- Type aliases
- The non-null assertion operator

All the code examples in this chapter have corresponding TypeScript files in the downloadable companion content for this book. For example, any example code shown in the *BigInt* section can be found in a folder called **Chapter 3** at the root of the project, in a file called **bigint.ts**, while examples in the *Union Types* section will be found in the **Chapter 3** folder in a file called **union.ts**.

These files are provided as a reference aid, and I would encourage you to actively try out all of the examples in an editor in order to get a good feel for TypeScript development.

Primitive types

TypeScript supports all of the same primitives that JavaScript itself supports, so variables, function parameters, and class members can be described as being of one of these fundamental types:

- **`bigint`**
- **`boolean`**
- **`number`**
- **`null`**
- **`string`**
- **`symbol`**
- **`undefined`**

Unlike JavaScript, TypeScript has primitive types as well as primitive values. Primitive values behave the same way in TypeScript as they do in JavaScript, but for each primitive value in TypeScript, there is a corresponding primitive type.

Let's take a quick look at each of these different types in turn.

BigInt

The **`bigint`** type is used to create and work with very large or very small numbers that are considered *unsafe* to use as regular integers in JavaScript due to the limitations of JavaScript's numerical support.

To specify that a variable is of the type **`bigint`**, we add a colon after the variable's identifier on the left-hand side of the declaration followed by the type **`bigint`**:

```
let bignum: bigint = BigInt(0);
```

The variable **`bignum`** will now have the type **`bigint`** associated with it. Note that we use the lowercase type **`bigint`** as opposed to the Camel Cased **`BigInt`**. We should always ensure that we use the lowercase versions of all of the primitive types when adding type annotations because the Camel Cased versions are the constructors.

Note that the **`bigint`** type is only available in environments supporting ECMAScript 2020 or later and will produce errors in TypeScript files when the target option in the **`tsconfig.json`** file is set to a lower version than es2020.

> **NOTE: Usually, it is not necessary to explicitly specify the type of a variable when we are assigning it a primitive value as TypeScript will be able to infer the correct type from the assignment itself. It is common for commercial projects to mandate that specifying types for simple assignments is forbidden.**

If we now try to do something illegal with the **`bignum`** variable, something prohibited by JavaScript itself, like multiplying it with a number, we'll see an error for it right there in the editor, before we even try to compile the file:

```
const result = bignum * 1;
```

If we hover the mouse pointer over the left-hand part of the above expression, we'll see a warning that:

Operator * cannot be applied to types 'bigint' and 'number'.

If we do try to compile the file, we'll see the same errors in the terminal output, but note that the compiler will still compile the file into JavaScript and emit it to the output directory by default.

It's very common for projects to disable this default behavior of still compiling invalid TypeScript into JavaScript - failing the compilation when the TypeScript is invalid is one of the best tools we have for creating bug-free applications. So, for production applications, it is almost always recommended to configure this behavior.

To fail the compiler when the TypeScript contains errors, we can enable the **`noEmitOnError`** option in the **tsconfig.json** file. Once this option has been enabled, output files will no longer be emitted if any TypeScript file inside the project contains errors, although we can still compile individual files that do not contain errors.

We'll be looking at the compiler and how to use it in much more detail later in the book; so, don't worry too much about it at this point.

Boolean

As in JavaScript, the **boolean** type in TypeScript is a primitive that may have only one of the two values **true** or **false**. We use the same colon followed by type syntax when declaring any of the primitive types including Booleans:

```
let isEnabled: boolean = true;
```

In this format, we are free to change the value to **false** at some point later in our program, and even back again to **true** later on if we choose. Note that as well as supplying the type **boolean**, we can also specify that the type should be one of the literal values **true** or **false**:

```
let legacySupport: false = false;
```

The variable **legacySupport** now has the immutable value of **false**, and this value cannot be changed to **true** later on in the application, even though we declared the variable using let as opposed to **const**.

Aside from the explicit literal **true** and **false** types described above, Booleans in TypeScript work exactly the same way as they do in regular JavaScript, and there should be no surprises for anyone with anything but the most basic of JavaScript experience.

Number

In TypeScript - exactly as in JavaScript - numbers may be either integer or floating-point values and have a "safe" range of -253 to +235 – anything outside of this range needs to be used with **bigint** instead. Although in fairness, it does represent quite a wide range of values and bigint is a relatively recent addition to the ECMAScipt specification.

To specify a value of the type **number**, we use the same format as with other primitive types – a colon, followed by the type in lowercase:

```
let num: number;
```

In this case, the variable **num** is declared but not initialized with the type **number**. The usual JavaScript variable declaration rules apply when using TypeScript, so only **const** values must be initialized with a value at declaration time. This is true for all variable declarations in TypeScript.

One common problem in JavaScript is the misuse of **NaN** in comparisons. **NaN** is a special numerical value that can be the result of performing impossible numerical operations, like dividing by zero, or trying to multiply a string.

Because nothing is equal to **`NaN`**, not even **`NaN`** itself, comparing a value to **`NaN`** directly will always return **`false`**. As this is such a common mistake, TypeScript will automatically warn against direct comparisons to **`NaN`** with an error and advise to use the **`Number.isNaN`** method instead:

```
This condition will always return 'false'. ts(2845)

number.ts(6, 5): Did you mean 'Number.isNaN(num)'?
if (num === NaN) {
  // ...
}
```

Figure 3.1: *Condition will always return false error in Visual Studio Code*

Null

In JavaScript, everything is either a primitive, or an object, and just like in JavaScript, in TypeScript the value **`null`** is used to signify that an object explicitly does not exist, or intentionally has no value.

For example, imagine that a user logged into our application is represented using an object. If the user logs out, we can set their user object to **`null`** to signify that it intentionally no longer exists.

How **`null`** is treated in TypeScript depends on the configuration in use, although by default the strictest level of type-checking for **`null`** (and **`undefined`**) is enabled when creating a new project using the TypeScript compiler; so, both **`null`** (and **`undefined`**) are fully type-checked by default when generating a **tsconfig.json** file with the compiler.

Syntactically, we can specify that a value has the type **`null`** in exactly the same format as we have with other primitives:

```
let nothing: null = null;
```

This is perfectly valid TypeScript, however, doing this is incredibly unhelpful in almost all situations because, with the **`strictNullChecks`** configuration enabled, we will not be able to change the value of the variable to anything else later on, so the value is effectively locked to **`null`** forever. For example:

```
let nothing: null = null;

// later...

nothing = 1; // Type '1' is not assignable to type 'null'
```

We will see an error in our editor here that '1' cannot be assigned to 'null'. Due to this, we will almost never see the `null` type used in this way in a variable declaration.

Similarly, if we specify a variable is of one particular type, say a `string`, we cannot then set this value to `null` later on – in that case, we will see a similar message that null cannot be assigned to a string.

In light of these facts, the `null` type is much more commonly used as part of a union type to say that a value may be, for example, a number or the value `null`. We'll be looking at union types in much more detail later in this chapter.

String

Strings in TypeScript have no special meaning or functionality beyond that found in JavaScript. We can denote that a value is of the type `string` in the same way as we can with other primitive types:

```
let greeting: string = 'Hello';
```

The same guideline of avoiding such overly-verbose declarations apply also to strings; commonly we would denote the types of class members or parameters using this format, but rarely simple variable declarations like this.

It is common in ESLint to have a lint rule that forbids unnecessary type declarations such as in the above example.

Symbol

The symbol primitive was added to JavaScript in the ES2015/ES6 release, and as such, must be used with the target option of the **tsconfig.json** file set to es2015 or above.

TypeScript gives us both a primitive type of `symbol`, and a sub-type of this type called `unique symbol`. Both can be used in an expected way:

```
let aSym: symbol = Symbol();

const otherSym: unique symbol = Symbol();
```

The difference between them is that **`unique symbol`** may only be used with **`const`** declarations as opposed to **`var`** or **`let`**, while **`symbol`** can be used with **`const`**, **`var`** or **`let`** declarations.

A symbol is a globally unique primitive value, so strict comparisons between them will always return **`false`**, and if we try to compare two values annotated with **`unique symbol`**, then we will see an error that there is no overlap between the two values.

Symbols are often used to create unique keys for objects, like this:

```
const unique = Symbol();

const obj = { [unique]: 'unique value' };
```

This offers a form of weak information hiding, as the **`unique value`** string is only accessible using the reference to the symbol, stored in the **`unique`** variable. Symbol-keyed properties are not revealed in for loops so without a reference to the symbol, the value of the property cannot be read.

Undefined

Similar to **`null`**, **`undefined`** is a special primitive in JavaScript for a variable that exists but has not been assigned a value, or for the value of an object property that has not been defined. Of course, **`undefined`** is also a value itself and can be directly set as the value of a variable, object property, or class member.

TypeScript has a corresponding **`undefined`** type that technically could be used as a type annotation for a variable declaration:

```
let notYet: undefined = undefined;
```

Although legal code, we would probably not want to do this for the simple fact that now the **`notYet`** variable can only ever contain the value **`undefined`**. Like the **`null`** type, this is a primitive type that we will rarely use ourselves directly outside of union types.

Also like the **`null`** type, how **`undefined`** is treated in TypeScript is also determined by whether either the **`strict`** or **`strictNullChecks`** configuration options are enabled, these are often handled in the same way by TypeScript.

With either of these configuration options enabled, TypeScript will strictly require us to check whether something is **`undefined`** before we attempt to access any of its properties or methods.

We'll look at this topic in more detail later in this chapter when we discuss type assertions.

The any type

TypeScript adds a special type, that is not a part of JavaScript at all, called **any**; this type means that the value in question could literally be of any supported type, with the implication that the value may be called like a function, or have its properties read like an object, or treated like any primitive.

Values of this type may be used in TypeScript in any way that is legal in JavaScript.

We can set values to this type ourselves manually, just like any of the primitive types we have already looked at:

```
let anything: any = 'still any';
```

Our type annotation will override TypeScript's inference mechanism. So, in this case, the variable **anything** will be of type **any**, and we will have no restrictions on the types of values that may be assigned to the variable at any future point, or how the value is used later in the code.

When we use the **any** type, we basically tell the compiler not to do any further type-checking on this value at all. We will use the **any** type in our applications from time to time. There are some valid use cases for it, including simply wishing to disable type-checking on a particularly complex object in order to avoid having to write an overly descriptive type for it.

The **any** type is also used by TypeScript itself, and values may be marked as **any** when TypeScript is unable to infer what their type should be.

Consider the following code:

```
function len(a) {

  return a.length;

}

let test = 'a';

len(test);
```

We declare a simple function called **len**, which accepts a single argument called **a** and returns the **length** property of this argument. Immediately we should see some error underlining in the editor, and when we hover the mouse pointer over it, we should see the following error description:

Parameter 'a' implicitly has an 'any' type.

This is an error because there is no way for TypeScript to correctly infer what the parameter's type is and so it can't check that the value is being used correctly – the value may not even have a `length` property. When we use `any` explicitly, we should know exactly which type a value is and are hopefully using it in a limited and controlled way, the implications of which we fully understand.

But when TypeScript implicitly treats a value as `any`, it needs to warn us that no type-checking will occur on this value at all from this point on because we haven't explicitly told it not to check this value's type by intentionally setting it to the `any` type. We may therefore use the value incorrectly and TypeScript wouldn't be able to warn us, which is sort of the whole point of TypeScript.

Even though we call the function with a string immediately after declaring it, TypeScript still cannot infer that the parameter's type will always be `string`, even though we pass it a string on the next line, so we may not be able to return its `length` property. As the function may not be able to return the object's `length` property, it will also have its return type set to `any`.

We'll be looking at functions in much more detail later in the book, including how to annotate them to let TypeScript know what types the function should accept as arguments and return.

> **NOTE: We are able to switch off the error for the implicit any in our code if we wish to use the tsconfig.json configuration file by disabling either the strict or noImplicitAny options, depending on which of them is enabled.**

You should also note that if we declare a variable without initializing it, TypeScript will infer the type `any` for that variable too, which effectively turns off type-checking in the editor for the variable anywhere:

```
let later;
```

Even if we set the value of the `later` variable to, say, a string value, the editor will continue to see the variable as having the type `any`:

```
let later;
let later: any
later = 'test';
```

Figure 3.2: *Inferred any type*

In this case, we should specifically add the type of the `later` variable with a type annotation, as a `string` in this example, to avoid this.

The `any` type can be useful if we are converting JavaScript to TypeScript and can't, or don't want to, specify all of the type information immediately – setting types to `any` can be a useful interim measure in this case, but usages of it should be temporary and be replaced with proper types as soon as possible to gain the maximum benefit from using TypeScript.

The unknown type

Another special TypeScript type that is not familiar to us already from JavaScript is the `unknown` type. This can be thought of as a kind of polar opposite to `any`; whereas the `any` type allows us to do anything at all with a value, such as assign to it, invoke methods on it, or read its properties, the `unknown` type restricts the operations we can do on it.

We can specify a value that has an `unknown` type using a colon as expected:

```
let notKnown: unknown;
```

At this point, the only thing we can do is assign a primitive value to the `notKnown` variable. Even if we assign an object to the variable and give it a property and corresponding value, like this:

```
notKnown = { test: 'test' };
```

Typescript still won't let us access the `test` property due to it being of the type `unknown`. Similarly, if we assign a function as the value of the `notKnown` variable, like this:

```
notKnown = () => 'test';
```

Then, TypeScript will not let us invoke the variable as a function. Additionally, we may assign an array to a variable with the type `unknown`:

```
notKnown = [1, 2, 3];
```

But in this case, we won't be able to access any of the elements inside it.

We are able to assign any type of primitive value to it, however, and simple equality comparisons will work as expected:

```
notKnown = 'test';
if (notKnown === 'test') {
  console.log('we will see this log message');
}
```

The `unknown` type is considered safer to use than the `any` type because it prevents us from using values in ways that were not intended for them to be used. Conversely, the `any` type does nothing to prevent us from using a value entirely incorrectly, which could cause our application to fail.

The never type

One more TypeScript type without a corresponding JavaScript equivalent is the `never` type. This type represents a state that should never exist and may be inferred by TypeScript in certain situations, such as for the return value of a function that never stops executing, in the case that the function throws an error, for example.

It is also commonly used with `switch` statements to ensure that the case checking carried out by the switch is exhaustive. A switch statement is exhaustive if it covers all possible cases.

We can use the `never` type to make sure that a `switch` expression handles all of the types in a union type with case statements, and it is commonly used as the `return` type of a function invoked in the `switch` statement's default clause. We'll see a full example of this later in the book once we have finished covering the basics of TypeScript.

The as operator

So far, we have added all of our type information using a colon followed by the type that we want to use, like this:

```
let myVar: string;
```

This is the most common way of specifying type information when using TypeScript, but it's not the only way; we can also use the **`as`** operator as a form of type-casting to specify that a value is of a particular type:

```
let anotherVar = 'another' as string;
```

This time, the annotation appears on the right-hand side of the expression, following the value rather than the variable declaration. We use the **`as`** keyword followed by the type that we want to cast the value to. This is known as a **type-assertion** - we are specifically asserting to TypeScript what the type of this value is.

Although valid, the previous example is something we would almost never see in actual day-to-day TypeScript. Instead, we would most likely use the **`as`** operator to down-cast from a less-specific to a more-specific type, or as a compound cast where we cast a value from one type immediately to another type. Let's see what both of these techniques look like in real code.

Down-casting

Down-casting is a useful technique where we have an object of a general type, and we want to cast it down to a more specific type in order to use a property that only specific sub-classes of that object have.

A good example is when working with an event object inside a handler method attached to a DOM element. Consider the following code:

```
function clickHandler(event: Event) {

  const childElement = event.target.querySelector('#child');

}
```

The event parameter of the **`clickHandler`** function above will be of the built-in type **`Event`**.

The **`Event`** object passed to handler functions by browsers *will* have a **`target`** property, and this property *will* be a reference to the HTML element that the handler is attached to, and as it is an element, it *will* have a **`querySelector`** method.

However, the **`event.target`** has its own special type, which is **`EventTarget`**, and the declaration of this type does not include a **`querySelector`** method - this method is found on the **`HTMLElement`** type instead. The preceding code will produce the following TypeScript error:

Property 'querySelector' does not exist on type 'EventTarget'.

To tell TypeScript that the **event.target** will actually be a HTML element, and therefore will have a **querySelector** method, we can down-cast the property to the desired sub-type:

```
const childElement = (event.target as HTMLElement).querySelector('#child');
```

This is allowed because in JavaScript **HTMLElement** is a subclass of **EventTarget**, and correspondingly, in TypeScript the **HTMLElement** type is a sub-type of the **EventTarget** type.

In this case, we also need to wrap the part of the expression where we use the **as** operator in parentheses. Now, the TypeScript compiler will know our intentions and the error will disappear.

As well as down-casting, the opposite of this is up-casting, where a type is broadened from a more specific type to a less specific type. Up-casting is less commonly used than down-casting, but may still be required occasionally.

Compound casting

Another type-casting technique using the **as** operator is called compound casting, or double assertion; this is where we use multiple **as** operators in a single statement and is usually used in conjunction with the **unknown** type to create objects that have some but not all of the required properties of another type.

As an example, imagine that we want to use a fake **Event** object in a unit test to test the **clickHandler** function from the previous example. We will have to pass this function a parameter of the type **Event** when we call it. Let's try to create one with a **target** property, (otherwise, the function will simply return immediately, and we won't be able to test it):

```
const testEvent: Event = { target: document.createElement('div') };
```

Immediately, we should see an error in the editor, with TypeScript complaining that the **testEvent** object is missing many properties that belong to objects of the type **Event**.

There are 21 properties in total missing from our fake event object, it would be extremely arduous to create them all manually, especially when we are really only interested in testing the **target** property anyway.

To fix this situation, we can use a compound cast that first casts our object to the special **unknown** type, and then to the desired type, **Event** in this case:

```
const testEvent = { target: document.createElement('div') } as unknown
as Event;
```

Now, the error should be gone. In this case, TypeScript will treat the **testEvent** object as if it really were an object of the **Event** type and simply ignores the missing properties.

This is safer than simply casting our **testEvent** object to the **any** type, which would also solve our problem, but would leave us open to, for example, trying to invoke methods that real **Event** objects don't have. In our case, if we try to call a method that **Event** objects don't have, TypeScript will produce an error:

```
testEvent.banana(); // Property 'banana' does not exist on 'Event'
```

If we had used the **any** type instead, that error would not appear and TypeScript would allow the code to run and crash our application.

Note that TypeScript will prevent us from making an impossible assertion:

```
let boolean = 1 as boolean;
```

In this case, TypeScript will show the following error message in the editor:

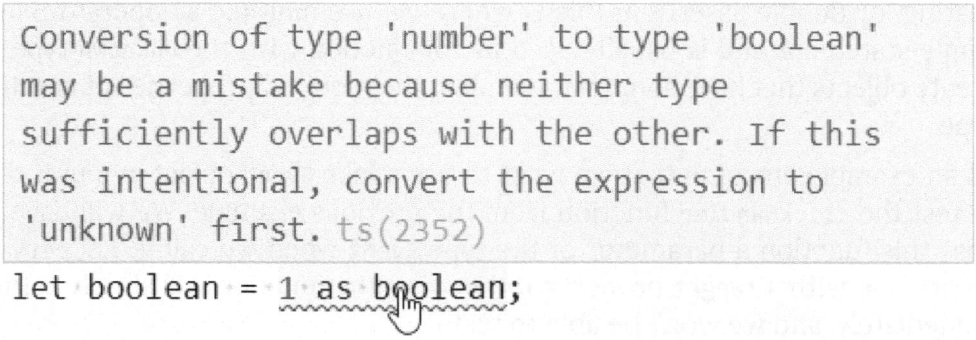

```
Conversion of type 'number' to type 'boolean'
may be a mistake because neither type
sufficiently overlaps with the other. If this
was intentional, convert the expression to
'unknown' first. ts(2352)
let boolean = 1 as boolean;
```

Figure 3.3: *Type conversion error on Visual Studio Code*

Helpfully, TypeScript hints at the end of the error message to use compound casting to first cast the value to the **unknown** type, before casting it to the desired type.

Older type-casting syntax

There is also an older form of type-casting in TypeScript which uses a different syntax entirely from the **`as`** operator. This form uses angle brackets to surround the type, and like the **`as`** operator, appears on the right-hand side of assignment expressions, although in this format, it precedes the value being cast:

```
let myNum = <number>1;
```

This expression will set the type of the **`myNum`** variable to the type **`number`** in exactly the same way that using the **`as`** operator would. This syntax is now deprecated since TypeScript added support for TSX files. TSX is TypeScript for JSX, and JSX is an embeddable XML syntax that compiles to JavaScript, and which is commonly used with the popular React framework. JSX syntax looks like a combination of JavaScript and HTML and this is the reason that the older angle-bracket syntax for type-casting cannot be used – TSX would interpret it as an HTML element instead of a type assertion.

This older type-casting could be used in plain TypeScript files, or when using frameworks that don't use JSX, such as Angular, but as this syntax is now deprecated, it is recommended to use the **`as`** operator always instead, regardless of whether JSX/TSX is actually in use.

Union types

A union type in TypeScript is where a value may be one of a predefined set of distinct types – we use it to tell the compiler that a value might be this type or it might be that type. The syntax is straight-forward – we separate each of the types in our union with the pipe character:

```
let either: string | number = 1;
```

Here, we're saying that the **`either`** variable may be of the type **`string`** or the type **`number`**, and then initializing it with the numerical value 1.

Note that we could also initialize it with a string, but if we try to set it to any other type, either now during initialization, or later in our application, TypeScript will show us an error, like this:

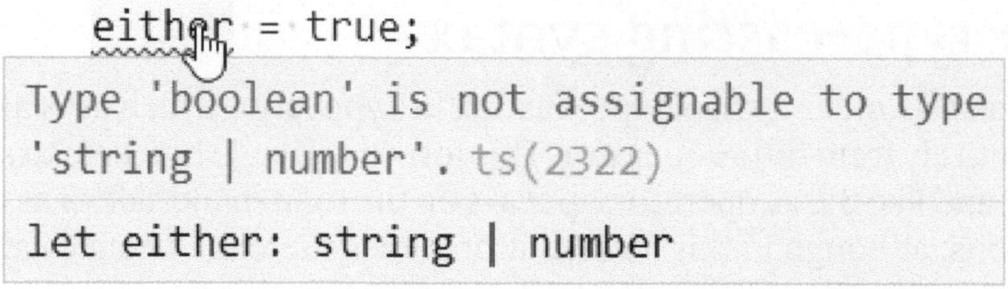

```
either = true;

Type 'boolean' is not assignable to type
'string | number'. ts(2322)

let either: string | number
```

Figure 3.4: *Type not assignable to type error in Visual Studio Code*

When working with the **`either`** variable, or any other union type, we will only be able to call methods or access properties that are available to all members of the union – so strings or numbers in this case. There is very little overlap between these two types, so we will need to know more about which type it actually is in order to do something useful with it.

Using the example above, we could have a value that might be of the type **`string`** if it's coming from the value of an HTML input element, or it could be of the type **`number`** if it's coming from somewhere else in our application.

Let's say we have a function that is passed a value as either a **`string`** or a **`number`**:

```
function getRefNumber(refNumber: string | number) {
  if (typeof refNumber === 'string') {
    refNumber = parseInt(refNumber, 10);
  }

  return refNumber;
}
```

We declare a function called **`getRefNumber`** that is passed a parameter called **`refNumber`**, and this parameter is a union of the types **`string`** and **`number`**. Inside the function, we need to check what the **`typeof`** operator reports the type of the parameter to be, so we check to see if it's **`string`**. If it is, we can safely work with it as if the parameter had been defined with only the **`string`** type. This is known as a type guard – we'll be looking at these in more detail later in the book.

In this example, we just convert the value to a number using the **`parseInt`** method, and from this point on inside the function, we know that **`refNumber`** will always be of the type **`number`**. Here, we just return the number, but we could do any other numerical operations on that value that we wanted to in a real-world application.

This process of determining the actual type from a union of types is known as **narrowing**, and this is another topic we'll be looking at in much greater detail later in the book.

There are no restrictions on the number of types that we can include in a union type, we just need to separate each type in the union with the pipe symbol.

Union types are flexible and allow us to work with values that could logically be one of several different types, possibly depending on the context in which the value is used. But using them also means that we ourselves need to be sure of exactly which type it actually is when we want to work with it.

Literal types

A literal type is a primitive sub-type that takes a specific value; we saw this briefly earlier when we looked at the Boolean type, and in that case, the literal sub-type of a Boolean type is when the specific values **`true`** or **`false`** are specified as the type.

Just like Booleans, the primitive types of **`number`**, **`bigint`**, and **`string`** also support literal sub-types, in these cases to specifically set a value to a particular number or string respectively.

When we looked at the literal Boolean sub-type earlier, we told the compiler that we were using a literal type by specifically supplying the value in the type position (after the colon), like this:

```
let isEnabled: true = true;
```

Strictly speaking, we can do the same with numbers and strings, like:

```
let literalNum: 1 = 1;
```

Or:

```
let literalString: 'literal';
```

Or:

```
let literalBigInt: 1n = 1n;
```

The variable **`literalNum`** is locked to the literal sub-type and value **`1`**, **`literalBigInt`** is locked to the literal sub-type **`1n`**, and **`literalString`** is locked to the literal sub-type **`'literal'`**.

As well as explicitly typed variable declaration/initialization, TypeScript can also infer literal sub-types if we use **`const`** to declare a variable as opposed to **`let`** or **`var`**. For example, with the following code:

```
const inferredLiteral = 1;
```

In this case, because we specifically used **`const`** to declare the variable, TypeScript will set the type of **`inferredLiteral`** to the literal numerical sub-type **`1`**. The same behavior is seen with strings as well, as long as we use **`const`** in the declaration.

Literal union types

Literal types are most commonly seen when working with type unions. As we've seen, using literal types alone do not provide much value, and are rarely seen in day-to-day code.

But using them in union types is a great way of restricting values to one of a predefined range of different literals. Let's see how with a quick example.

Imagine that we have a function for moving an element on a web page in one dimension:

```
function move1D(direction: 'left' | 'right') {
  // move the element
}
```

This function takes a single parameter called **`direction`**, which we have specified is a union type of the literal string values **`left`** or **`right`**. The benefit of this is that when we come to invoke this function at a later time, we will get code completion for all of the different types in the union, making it clear exactly which values the function expects to be passed when it is invoked:

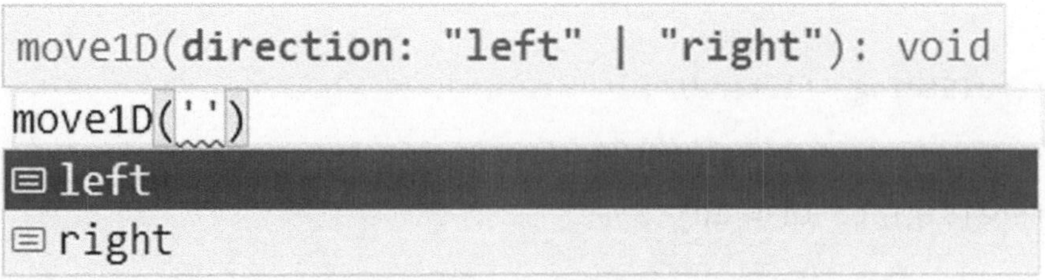

```
move1D(direction: "left" | "right"): void
move1D('')
left
right
```

***Figure 3.5:** Literal union function signature tooltip and type code-completion in Visual Studio Code*

This makes it almost impossible to use the function incorrectly and inadvertently introduce bugs into our application and is especially useful when working in larger teams of developers where the person invoking or using the function may not be the person who wrote it originally. It becomes a form of living inline documentation for using the function correctly.

We also get feedback in the editor or terminal when compiling if we supply a value that isn't one of the types in the union. For example, if we pass the string `up`, we'll see the error message:

Argument of the type 'up' is not assignable to parameter of type '"left" | "right"'.

Literal union types therefore represent an excellent way of leveraging TypeScript to guide others on how to use specific bits of code, for example, to ensure that a function is called with the correct arguments.

Type aliases

Type aliases are a way of declaring types in a reusable way using an identifier – like a variable declaration but for types. So far, we've added all of our example types as annotations directly after the thing they are used to describe. In the previous section, for example, we had a function that accepted a parameter with a union type:

```
function move1D(direction: 'left' | 'right') {

  // move the element

}
```

Here, the type annotation appears in line with the parameter declaration. Instead, we could add a type alias for it, like this:

```
type directions = 'left' | 'right';
```

To declare a type alias, we use the **`type`** keyword followed by a name for the alias, and its type as a value, very similar to a regular variable declaration but using **`type`** instead of **`var`**, **`let`** or **`const`**.

Now, we can use this type alias anywhere that we want to make use of this literal union type, like in the **`move1D`** function, for example:

```
function move1D(direction: directions) {

  // move the element

}
```

In this case, we get exactly the same code completion in the editor, exactly as if we had used an inline type annotation instead of the alias. We can of course reuse this type in other places too now that we have an identifier for it.

Note however that once the type is declared, we cannot modify it later on. If we try to extend it by adding some more types to the union for example:

```
directions = 'left' | 'right' | 'up' | 'down';
```

Then, we will see an error:

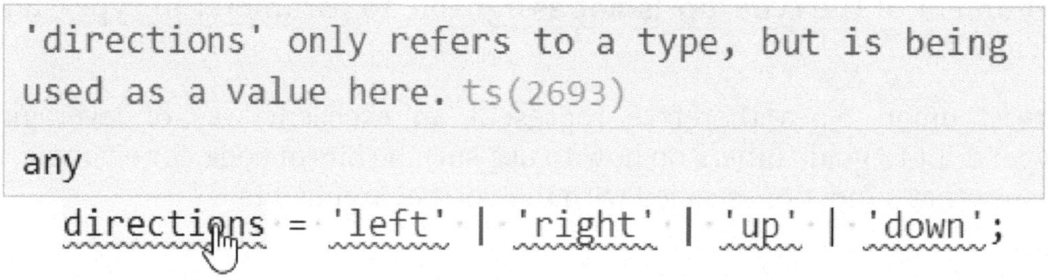

```
'directions' only refers to a type, but is being
used as a value here. ts(2693)
any
directions = 'left' | 'right' | 'up' | 'down';
```

Figure 3.6: *Type used as a value error in Visual Studio Code*

If we want to extend a type alias, we basically need to create a new one with a different identifier, and then include the type that we want to extend, like this:

```
type directions2D = directions | 'up' | 'down';
```

The new type, **directions2D**, will include all of the members from both the **directions** union and the new union members explicitly specified in the expression, the literal strings **up** and **down** in this case.

We could then set it as the type for a parameter in a **move2D** function, for example:

```
function move2D(direction: directions2D) {
  // move the element
}
```

Type aliases are a simple way to reuse a type declaration in multiple places, but they have no other special behavior; they are merely a way to refer to a type using an identifier. They also don't have to be union types – any type can be used with an alias.

Type assertion

We've looked briefly at the **null** and **undefined** primitive types, as well as union types, and we've also seen how to use the **as** operator to make type assertions. Let's take a moment to look at these topics together.

Consider the following function:

```
function splitString(str: string | null) {
  return str.split('');
}
```

We have a function called **splitString** which accepts a single parameter called **str** and this parameter is the union type **string | null**. The function simply returns the result of calling the **split** method on the **str** parameter.

The editor will immediately highlight an error on the line where we call the **split** method on **str** inside the function:

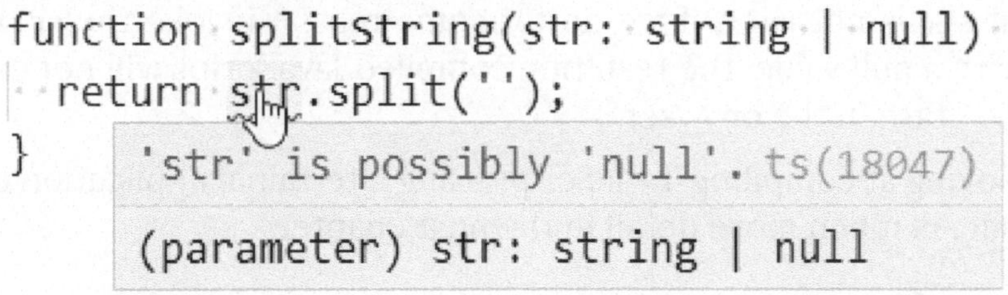

```
function splitString(str: string | null) {
  return str.split('');
}
'str' is possibly 'null'. ts(18047)
(parameter) str: string | null
```

***Figure 3.7:** Object is possibly 'null' warning in Visual Studio Code*

The correct way to fix this issue is to check that **str** is actually of the type **string** before trying to call string methods on it, for example, we could return earlier from the function if we detect that **str** is **null**:

```
function splitString(str: string | null) {
  if (str == null) return;
  return str.split('');
}
```

We can use a simple **if** statement to check **str** isn't equal to **null** and returns from the function if it is. Note that we can use the non-strict equality operator as a short hand to check for both **null** and **undefined** at the same time. This will remove the error in the editor.

We can also use a type assertion to fix the error in a different way:

```
function splitString(str: string | null) {
  return (str as string).split('');
}
```

This time instead of explicitly checking if **`str`** is **`null`**, we can use the **`as`** operator to assert that **`str`** definitely is a string. However, we should use this only where we are sure that the argument being passed when this function is invoked is definitely the expected type - if it is actually **`null`**, the code will happily compile without errors, but we definitely would see an error in the actual browser.

For example, this code will not produce any warnings in the editor or in the terminal when compiling the TypeScript into JavaScript:

```
splitString(null);
```

But it will cause an error in the browser when the JavaScript is executed. It is safer to avoid using type assertion in this way for this reason. With the explicit check that **`str`** is not **`null`**, if we do for some reason invoke the **`splitString`** method with a null value, the resulting compiled JavaScript will not cause our program to crash in the browser.

We'll be looking at compiling TypeScript using a terminal application or Visual Studio Code, in much more detail in the next chapter.

Non-null assertion operator

The non-null assertion operator is another way to specify that a value definitely isn't **`null`**. This will disable both **`null`** and **`undefined`** checks made by TypeScript for the value it is used on and prevent the editor displaying errors.

For example, instead of specifically casting the **`str`** parameter to a string using the **`as`** operator, we could instead use the non-null assertion operator to achieve the same outcome:

```
function splitString(str: string | null) {
  return str!.split('');
}
```

The non-null assertion operator is a postfix exclamation point - we use it directly after the value that we want to assert is not **`null`**.

This will disable any further **`null`** or **`undefined`** checking carried out by TypeScript. With the use of the **`as`** operator that we saw previously, if the value that we are asserting is not **`null`** does happen to actually be **`null`**, we will end up with errors in the compiled JavaScript, so take care when using it.

Conclusion

In this chapter, we've looked at some of the most fundamental aspects of TypeScript annotations - the kind of things that we'll be writing every time we code.

We've seen that for all of JavaScript's primitive values, TypeScript has a corresponding type that can be used to describe what different values in your program represent. This is true for JavaScript's commonly used primitives like **`string`** and **`number`**, and for lesser used ones like **`bigint`** or **`symbol`**.

We took a quick look at each of these primitives in turn and saw how to annotate values using a colon followed by the type we want to specify, like this:

```
let str: string = '';
```

We also looked at some special types that are found only in TypeScript and do not have corresponding JavaScript counterparts. These types are:

- The **`any`** type
- The **`unknown`** type
- The **`never`** type

We saw that the **`any`** type effectively disables any further type-checking on the value which is declared with it as its type. It can be useful in some situations to avoid having to add a very complex type description, but we should probably try to use it as sparingly as possible as it negates most of the benefits of using TypeScript in the first place.

We also learned about an implicit **`any`**, which is when we haven't specifically set a value to the **`any`** type, but TypeScript is unable to reliably determine what type the value is. We saw that this causes an error (when the configuration has either the **`strict`** or **`noImplicitAny`** options enabled) which we will need to fix by supplying the relevant type information.

We also covered TypeScript's **`unknown`** type, which can be considered as kind of the opposite of the **`any`** type. With the **`unknown`** type, we can't assume the value is an object and try to access its properties or assume it's an array and try to access its members, and we also can't treat it like a function and try to invoke it. The only thing we can do is assign a primitive value to it.

We also took a look at the `never` type, which is a special type used to describe a value that should never be set. TypeScript will sometimes set the return value of a function that never actually returns to this type.

Next, we looked at the `as` operator, which we can use to make type assertions and cast a value to a particular type. We looked at two techniques commonly used with type assertions - down-casting and compound casting.

Then we moved on to look at union types. We learned that these are types consisting of multiple types and are used to specify that a value may be one of several different types. The syntax for union types is to separate each type with the pipe character.

We also looked at literal types, which are sub-types of some primitive types like `boolean`, `number`, `bigint`, and `string`.

We then moved on to see that literal subtypes can also be used with union types, which is useful when we want a value to one of a predefined set of values.

Following this, we looked at type aliases and saw that these are ways to store a type using an identifier, which we can then later use where we wish to specify the type.

After this, we took a look at type assertions again in more detail, this time looking specifically at the different ways that we can handle `null` and `undefined` in union types.

We learned that we can use a type guard to avoid using the value if it is `null` (or `undefined`), or that we could do the same using the `as` operator to assert that the value is of the type that we expect it to be, but that using type guards is the safer choice unless we explicitly know that the value is definitely of the expected type.

Finally, we looked at the non-null assertion operator, which is used to tell TypeScript that a value is specifically not `null` or `undefined`.

In the next chapter, we will take an in-depth look at compiling our TypeScript into JavaScript using both the terminal application, and Visual Studio Code.

References

- **https://www.typescriptlang.org/docs/handbook/2/everyday-types.html**
- **https://www.typescripttutorial.net/typescript-tutorial/type-casting/**

CHAPTER 4

Using the TypeScript Compiler

Introduction

As well as creating a brand-new project, there are a number of other things that the TypeScript compiler can do, which we can enable using various flags; things such as setting the language used for TypeScript's errors and warnings, and listing all of the files included in the current compilation among others.

There is also a wide range of build-related options that we can enable to run different kinds of compilations, and we can also set any of typeScript's configuration options manually when invoking the compiler from a terminal application.

In this chapter, we'll explore some of the things we can do from a terminal using the many flags supported by the compiler, as well as cover related concepts like installing third-party types for third-party JavaScript libraries that we might want to use in our projects, or how we can generate our own definition files so that other developers may use our code.

Structure

In this chapter, we will cover the following topics:

- Compiling our TypeScript files
- Inspecting compiled files
- CLI flags
- Using watch mode

- Building projects
- Integrating with other build tools
- Using third-party libraries
- Generating **.d.ts** files

Compiling our TypeScript files

The main purpose of the TypeScript compiler is of course to compile our TypeScript files into JavaScript files ready to be run in a browser. Let's first look at the different ways that we can do that using a terminal.

By default, if we run the `tsc` command in a terminal by itself, the compiler will attempt to compile all of the TypeScript files that it can find in any sub-directory of the working directory, using the closest **tsconfig.json** file that it can find, recursively looking upwards in the directory tree. Any directory that contains a **tsconfig.json** file is considered the root of a TypeScript project.

The example project accompanying this book has a root directory called **ts-examples**, which contains the **tsconfig.json** configuration file, along with sub-directories for each chapter containing individual **.ts** files.

If we change the working directory in our terminal to one of these sub-directories and run the **tsc** command there, the compiler will not find a **tsconfig.json** file in the current directory, but it will then navigate up to the root directory and find the configuration file to use there instead.

If there are no errors in the code the compiler will compile all of the TypeScript files it finds, and for each one, it generates a **.js** file containing the compiled code alongside the **.ts** file. When the compilation succeeds, there is no output to the Terminal at all – the only output is the generated files in the file system.

If the compiler encounters any errors in any of the files included in the compilation, and if the `noEmitOnError` configuration is enabled, the compiler may fail to compile the project and instead output errors to the Terminal detailing any problem(s):

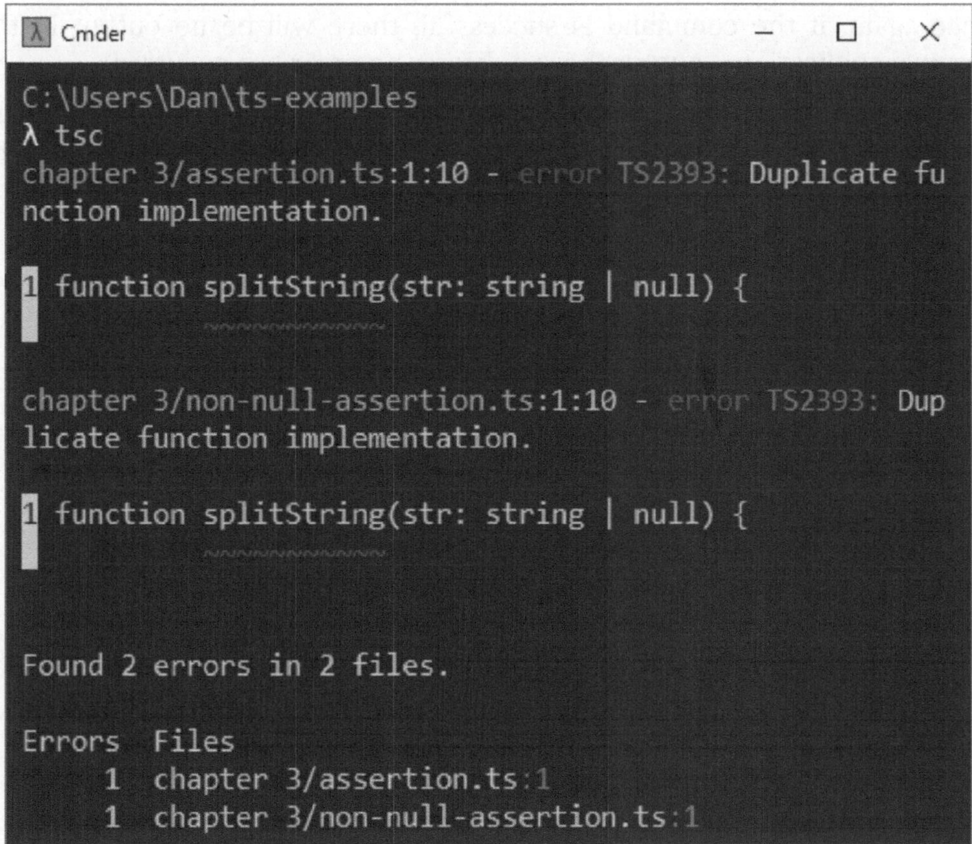

***Figure 4.1**: Error output when running tsc in the example project*

In this case, TypeScript is warning us that there is a duplicate function implementation and shows us which two files contain the duplication, which line it occurs on, and what the code on that line looks like.

Having the compiler output the compiled files alongside the original source files is less than optimal, however – when we want to deploy our application, we don't want to distribute the TypeScript files along with the JavaScript files, so any build process would need to discard, or otherwise exclude, the original TypeScript files when copying the application files to deploy, and there is no real reason to make a build process more complicated than it needs to be.

Instead, we can have the compiler emit all of the compiled files into a sub-directory of the project. We can do this for a single compilation by passing the **`--outDir`** option in the terminal, or we can do it permanently by updating the **tsconfig.json** configuration file. Let's do it from the terminal first:

```
tsc --outDir ./dist
```

Once again, if the command is successful, there will be no output in the terminal application – output there indicates an error has occurred.

The successful output will be the batch of generated JavaScript files, but this time, instead of being placed alongside the original source files, they will all be contained in a directory at the root of the project called **dist**:

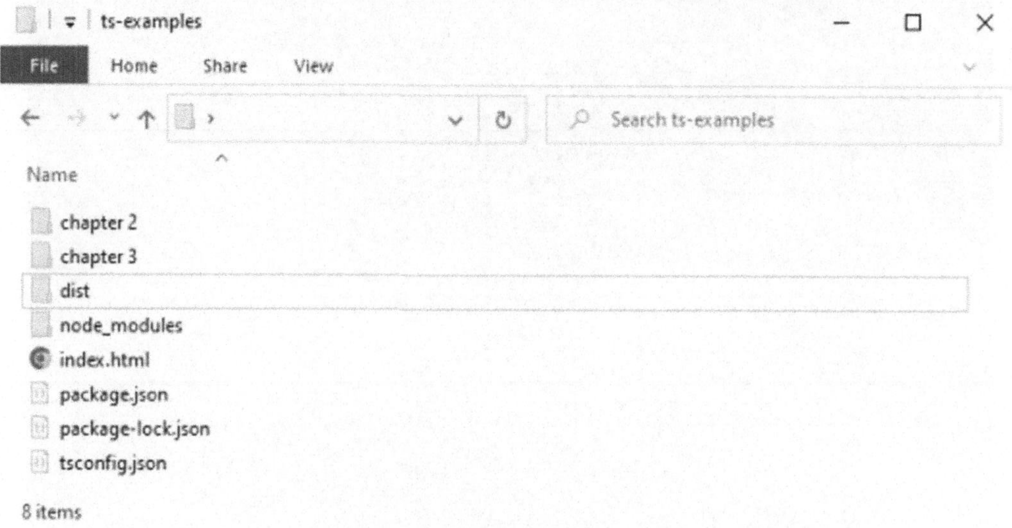

***Figure 4.2**: The emitted dist folder in Windows Explorer*

If you've been creating directories as recommended earlier in the book, your project directory should look similar to that shown in *Figure* 4.2.

Note that the **dist** folder will mirror the structure of the project being compiled, so in this case, the **dist** directory will contain a subdirectory called **`chapter 3`**, and the compiled JavaScript files will be inside that folder. For example, the structure of compiled files in the **ts-examples** project will appear like this:

```
dist
     |_ chapter 3
                  |_ aliases.js
```

Having the output generated in a separate folder is a much better choice for a typical web application, so we can go ahead and make this configuration change permanent by enabling the option in the **tsconfig.json** file:

```
"outDir": "./dist",
```

We can pass any TypeScript configuration option in the terminal in the same way, by prefixing the name of the option in the configuration file with a double hyphen `--`. Doing this will have the same effect as it would in the configuration file, except that it will only apply to the current compilation.

In addition to compiling all of the TypeScript files in the project, we can direct the compiler to compile a single file, by passing the path to the file after the `tsc` command, for example:

```
tsc "chapter 3/aliases.ts"
```

In this case, we can compile a file called **aliases.ts** in a directory called **chapter 3**, and we have to quote the path because it contains a space. One thing you should notice is that the compiler reverts to placing the compiled file alongside the source file when the file is emitted when running the command in the terminal.

The reason for this is that when we compile a single file, the compiler ignores any **tsconfig.json** configuration file that is present in the working directory. The compiler has no configuration options enabled by default in the terminal; it just does a basic compilation when used like this.

By default, the compiler will use the closest **tsconfig.json** file it can find navigating up through the file system, but we can also specify the path to the **tsconfig.json** file we wish to use in the terminal instead. We would use the **--project** flag to do that.

A **tsconfig.json** file placed in a subdirectory can extend another **tsconfig.json** file found higher up in the project directory structure. Let's create another **tsconfig.json** file to see this in action. You should create it inside the directory **chapter 4** in your project directory.

For reference, this file can also be found inside the **chapter 4** directory in the accompanying example project.

The new **tsconfig.json** file should contain the following configuration.

```
{
  "extends": "../tsconfig.json",
  "include": ["../**/*.ts"],
  "exclude": ["./webpack-integration", "my-lib"]
}
```

We also need to tell the compiler which files we would like to compile, which we do using the `include` option, because it will treat the **chapter 4** folder containing the **tsconfig.json** file we specify with `--project` as the root of the project. In this case, we tell the compiler to include all files in the parent of the current directory.

We can also make use of the `exclude` top-level option to exclude some of the files from later examples in this chapter – if we don't do this, we'll see errors in the terminal and we won't be able to compile using the **tsconfig.json** file in the root of the **chapter 4** directory.

The default value for the include configuration option is `**/*.ts` which is a special path known as a *file glob pattern*. This special path means find any file with a **.ts** extension in the current directory and all subdirectories of the current directory.

The **chapter 4** folder doesn't contain any TypeScript files, however, so without providing the `include` configuration, the compilation will fail with an error that there are no input files – the compiler can't compile if there are no files to compile.

We could also add any additional configuration options in this additional configuration file, and they would override the same configuration options in the base file that is being extended.

To use this **tsconfig.json** file instead of the top-level one in the root of the ts-examples project, we would use this command in the terminal:

```
tsc --project "chapter 4/tsconfig.json"
```

We use the `--project` flag to provide the path to the configuration file we wish to use. Again, the path is quoted in this example due to the space character in the directory name.

In this case, the project should compile as expected and emit a **dist** folder containing all of the compiled files. One thing you'll notice if you open up this directory in a file browser, or in Visual Studio Code, is that all of the files are placed into the dist folder directly with no deeper file tree within the folder. Sometimes it is preferable to have the dist folder match the internal folder structure of the project.

To do this, we can set the `rootDir` configuration option in the **tsconfig.json** file at the root of the project. We can use the commented-out default value in the configuration file, so all we need to do is uncomment it:

```
"rootDir": "./",
```

Now when we compile the project, inside the **dist** folder will be sub-directories mirroring the directory structure within the project. Remember, a TypeScript project is defined as the directory containing the **tsconfig.json** file in use.

Inspecting compiled files

Now that we've compiled some files, let's take a moment to open some up and take a look at the JavaScript emitted by the compiler.

The first file inside the **dist** folder (if there isn't a **dist** folder in your local copy of the example project, try running the `tsc` command from a terminal as described earlier) should be **aliases.js** – compare the contents of this emitted file with the original **aliases.ts** file:

TS aliases.ts ×

chapter 3 > TS aliases.ts > [@] directions2D

```
type directions = 'left' | 'right';
//directions = 'left' | 'right' | 'up' | 'down';
type directions2D = directions | 'up' | 'down';

function move2D(direction: directions2D) {
    // move the element
}
```

JS aliases.js ×

dist > JS aliases.js > ...

```
"use strict";
function move2D(direction) {
    // move the element
}
```

Figure 4.3: *The original TypeScript file (top) and emitted JavaScript file (bottom) in Visual Studio Code*

When the compiler processes a file, it will strip out all of the type annotations, and any type declarations; as you can see here, both the type declarations and the type annotations for the parameter accepted by the `move2D` function, are indeed removed in the resulting JavaScript file.

Additionally, the compiler has removed the first comment from the file, but not the comment inside the function. The reason for this is simple – the first comment does not have a space between the comment start delimiter and the text, whereas the second comment does. TypeScript distinguishes between these and by default, does not strip the second form out in the compiled code.

There is a compiler option we can use to strip out all comments, regardless of whether they have a space after the start delimiter or not. This is the **`removeComments`** option, and we can use it either in the main configuration file or by passing it as a flag in the terminal, for example:

```
tsc --removeComments
```

It's worth noting that the compiler also removes empty lines from the input file, even those inside functions.

Lastly, the compiler has inserted a **`"use strict";`** directive at the top of each file. This is because none of our files are modules and could therefore be run accidentally in non-strict mode, which would be bad news for our application, so to play it safe, TypeScript ensures that each file will be run in strict mode.

If we make one of our TypeScript files a module, by exporting something from it using the **`export`** keyword, then the **`"use strict"`** directive will not be inserted at the top of the file, because in JavaScript, modules are always evaluated in strict mode.

At this point, the example files are all quite basic, so there shouldn't be any surprises in any of the compiled files. The main points to take away are that all type annotations and type declarations are removed by the compiler in order to generate valid JavaScript.

CLI flags

We saw earlier in the book that we can create a new TypeScript project using the **`tsc`** command in conjunction with the **`--init`** flag.

There are a number of other general flags that we can use in conjunction with the standard **`tsc`** command. Let's take a quick look at each of them now. Make sure you have your terminal application at the ready and a copy of the example files if you want to follow along with the examples in this section.

--version

If we want to know the exact version of TypeScript we are using, we can use the `--version` flag:

Figure 4.4: The output of the --version flag in a terminal application

Note that this will output your global version of TypeScript, not the local version of TypeScript if you happen to be running the terminal application from within a TypeScript project (which in this case we are). We can also use a shortened variation of this flag `-v`.

There are several different ways to determine the local version of TypeScript that is installed within a particular project, depending on your **package.json** configuration. If you use a specific version of TypeScript in your project, like this:

```
"typescript": "4.8.2"
```

Then the specific version denoted in the **package.json** file will be the actual version in use in the project. However, if the project uses the hat (^) or tilde (~) symbol in the version number, like this:

```
"typescript": "^4.7.4"
```

Or this:

```
"typescript": "~4.7.4"
```

Then that will instead be the *minimum* version of TypeScript in use, but it may actually be using a higher version if there is a higher minor or patch version available in the NPM repository; in this case, to see which actual version is in use locally in the project, you can use NPM's `ls` command:

PROBLEMS OUTPUT DEBUG CONSOLE TERMINAL

```
PS C:\Users\Dan\ts-examples> npm ls typescript

ts-examples@ C:\Users\Dan\ts-examples
└── typescript@4.8.2

PS C:\Users\Dan\ts-examples>
```

***Figure 4.5**: Output from ls command in Visual Studio Code's integrated terminal*

The `ls` command is used to list information about packages in an NPM project. We specify the name of the package that we want to list, in this case, **`typescript`**, after the `ls` command. This will return the specific version of the specified package in use.

In the preceding figure, the actual version of the typescript package installed locally in the project is output on the third line and is version **`4.8.2`**.

For reference, the ~ symbol before a version number in the **`package.json`** file means that any higher patch version may be installed, for the version **`~1.0.0`**, this means that any version to **`1.0.n`** may be installed. On the other hand, for the version number **`^1.0.0`**, it means that any version to 1.n.n may be installed.

One additional place that we can see the exact installed version of a particular package is in the **package-lock.json** file, which NPM creates automatically alongside the **package.json** file whenever we run the **`npm install`** command. We can open this up in Visual Studio Code or another editor and search for the name of the package to see the exact version in use and some other meta-information about the package like the SHA hash for that version, which is sometimes used to verify the authenticity of NPM packages.

--listFilesOnly

It may not always be clear whether a particular file is being included in the compiled output of our program, especially when working with very large applications that may include thousands of individual source files.

For a complete list of every single source file, and the path it is located at, which is included in the compiled output, we can use the **`-listFilesOnly`** flag:

```
tsc -listFilesOnly
```

This flag can be very useful, as not only does the output of this flag show our own working TypeScript files that we have created and written ourselves, but it also includes all of TypeScript's own definition files, which give us types for things inherently part of JavaScript, like DOM access methods:

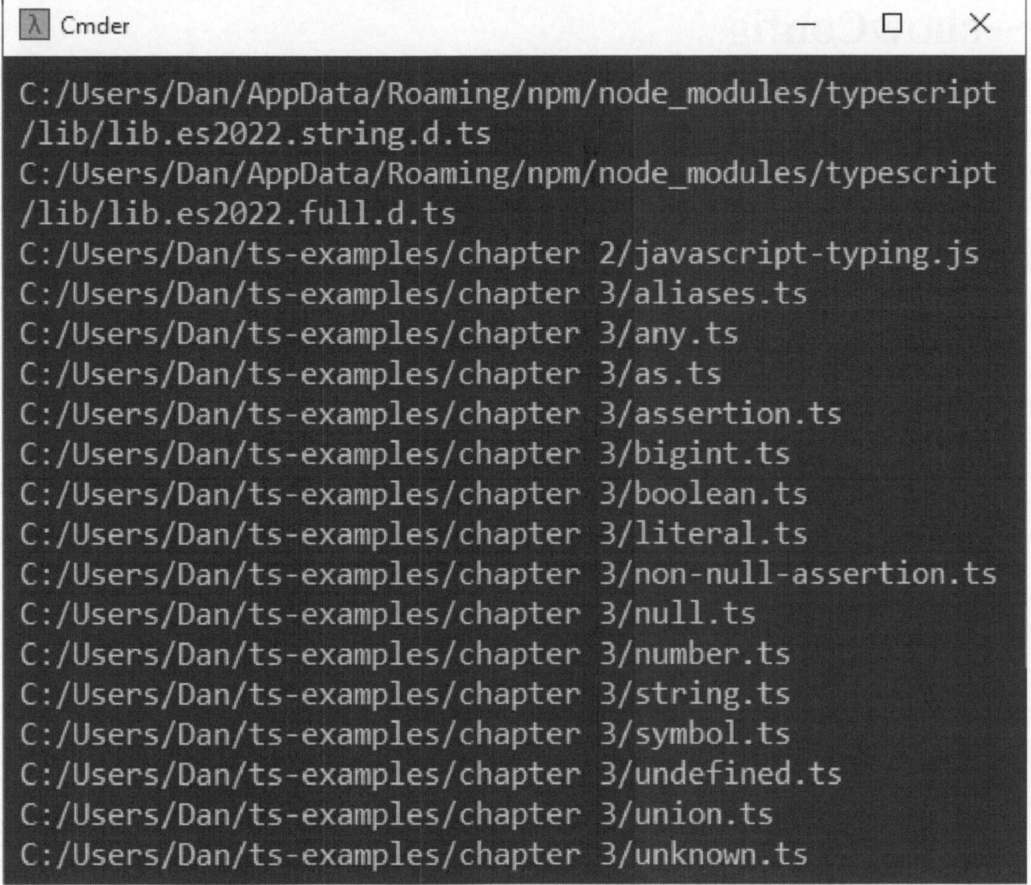

Figure 4.6: *Listing all TypeScript files in an application*

In the preceding example output, we can see all of the files we have created so far throughout the book at the bottom of the output, along with the path they were found at. The list of files at the end of the output is the files within the example project.

The first two lines in the preceding output shown however come from the global installation of the `typescript` NPM package on my system and represent types that are included by default with any TypeScript project on my machine and contain types for default JavaScript functionality.

Files with the extension ***.d.ts** are TypeScript declaration files, also known as ambient modules, or declarations, which are used to provide type information to the TypeScript compiler for third party code. We'll look at these in more detail shortly.

--showConfig

If we want to see the exact TypeScript configuration in use for the current compilation, we can add the `--showConfig` flag:

```
tsc --showConfig
```

This command is useful because it shows us the config from the **tsconfig.json** file merged with any defaults; for example, in the following output, the config also includes the list of files, which TypeScript has determined and added to the configuration automatically under the `files` configuration option:

```
Cmder
λ tsc --showConfig
{
    "compilerOptions": {
        "target": "es2022",
        "module": "es2022",
        "checkJs": true,
        "noEmitOnError": true,
        "esModuleInterop": true,
        "forceConsistentCasingInFileNames": true,
        "strict": true,
        "skipLibCheck": true
    },
    "files": [
        "./chapter 2/javascript-typing.js",
        "./chapter 3/aliases.ts",
        "./chapter 3/any.ts",
        "./chapter 3/as.ts",
        "./chapter 3/assertion.ts",
        "./chapter 3/bigint.ts",
        "./chapter 3/boolean.ts",
        "./chapter 3/literal.ts",
        "./chapter 3/non-null-assertion.ts",
        "./chapter 3/null.ts",
        "./chapter 3/number.ts",
        "./chapter 3/string.ts",
        "./chapter 3/symbol.ts",
        "./chapter 3/undefined.ts",
        "./chapter 3/union.ts",
        "./chapter 3/unknown.ts"
    ]
```

***Figure 4.7**: Output showing merged config for the current compilation*

The configuration for TypeScript can be extended by additional **tsconfig.json** files contained within sub-directories.

In a larger application, we may have a main **tsconfig.json** file in the root directory, with additional **tsconfig.spec.json**, **tsconfig.dev.json**, and **tsconfig.prod.json** files, any one of which may be in use, depending on whether we are running the unit tests, using a development build, or running a production build.

It can be useful to use the `--showConfig` flag to determine the exact configuration of the compilation if the project is very large, or complex, or contains numerous configuration files for different scenarios.

--help

Another useful command is the `--help` command:

```
tsc --help
```

This command will output a subset of information concerning the most commonly used command line flags we can pass, compiler options, and build commands, which can be useful as a quick reference point.

To see *all* of the compiler options and build commands, we can also append the `--all` flag to the end of the command:

```
tsc --help --all
```

This command lists all of the supported configuration flags, build flags, and compiler options that can be used. Here is an example of the output from this flag in a terminal application on Windows:

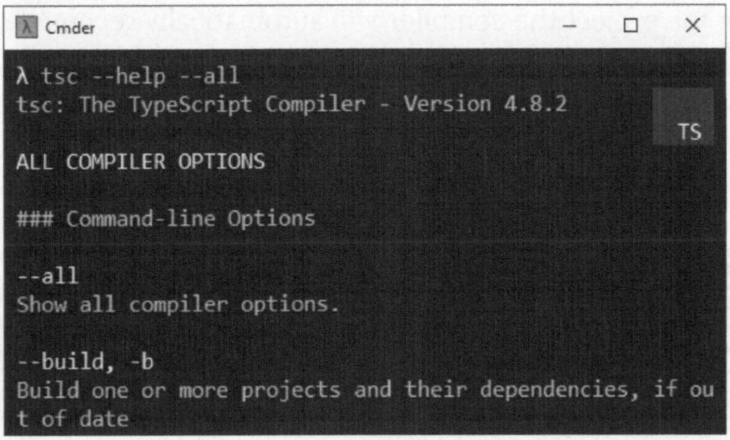

```
Cmder
λ tsc --help --all
tsc: The TypeScript Compiler - Version 4.8.2
                                                    TS
ALL COMPILER OPTIONS

### Command-line Options

--all
Show all compiler options.

--build, -b
Build one or more projects and their dependencies, if ou
t of date
```

Figure 4.8: *Output from the --help --all flags in a 3rd-party terminal application*

As you can see in the preceding screenshot, it lists all of the various flags we can use and gives a description of each option, and if it accepts values, the type of value, and the default value for each option.

Using watch mode

Watch mode is a useful development aid where we can have the compiler continuously watch a group of files, and as soon as any of those files are saved after being edited, or changed, the compiler will automatically recompile the project for us. While developing a TypeScript application, we will usually have watch mode running most of the time.

Enabling watch mode is extremely straight-forward, we just add the **`--watch`** flag when invoking the compiler in the terminal:

```
tsc --watch
```

This time we will see some output in the terminal:

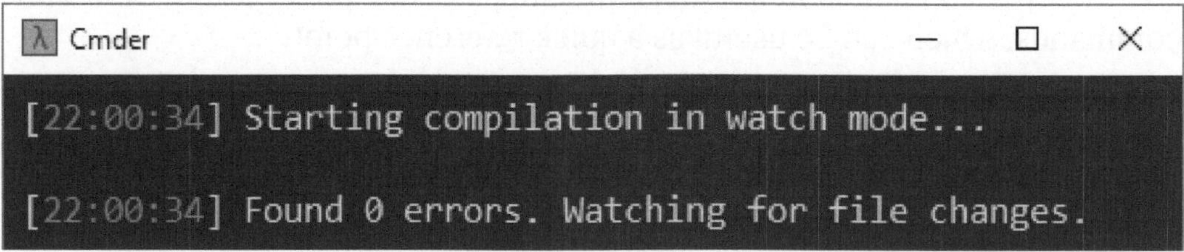

Figure 4.9: *Output of starting watch mode in a terminal application on Windows*

While this terminal remains open with the process running, any time we save a file within the project the compiler will automatically recompile the project for us.

The terminal output will update once a file change has been detected and the project has been recompiled:

```
[22:03:23] File change detected. Starting incremental co
mpilation...

[22:03:23] Found 0 errors. Watching for file changes.
```

Figure 4.10: *Output to the terminal after a file change detected*

Watch mode uses an incremental compilation mode after the initial compilation when it starts up, as you can see in the message shown in the *Figure 4.10*.

This means that TypeScript will only compile files that have actually changed, saving on resources, which can be useful if we are working on a large application with many source files – it would be a waste of time and resources to recompile files that have not changes since the last time the project was compiled.

As well as watching TypeScript files, the compiler also watches some other types of files, such as JSON files, meaning that if we change our configuration file to perhaps exclude some files or folders from the compilation, the watch process will detect that change as well and recompile the relevant parts of the project. It is worth noting that the **node_modules** folder is also watched by default, and this folder is usually very, very large and contains many, many files. This can have a negative impact on the performance of the compilation.

On Windows or Mac platforms, using the **`--watch`** flag will generally be all you need to do, but on Linux, some extra configuration is available due to how this operating system handles watching files and folders, which by all accounts is not as reliable as on Windows or Mac platforms.

TypeScript provides the top-level option **`watchOptions`** to allow us to provide extra configuration for the watch process on Linux platforms if necessary. As it's a top-level option, we specify it at the same level as **`compilerOptions`**, not inside **`compilerOptions`**.

Under **`watchOptions`** we have the following options available:

- `watchFile`
- `watchDirectory`
- `fallbackPolling`
- `synchronousWatchDirectory`
- `excludeDirectories`
- `excludeFiles`
- `assumeChangesOnlyAffectDirectDependencies`

The rest of this section is intended mostly for reference purposes, it will be useful mostly only to developers using Linux; feel free to skip the rest of this section if you do not intend to use this platform.

watchFile

The `watchFile` option controls how the watch process watches individual files. The default value is `useFsEvents`, which relies on events emitted by the file system when watched files change. Other values accepted by this option are:

- `fixedPollingInterval`: use an interval to poll every file in the compilation several times a second for changes.
- `priorityPollingInterval`: use an interval to poll every file in the compilation several times a second for changes but check some files less often than others depending on how frequently the compiler thinks they will change.
- `dynamicPriorityPolling`: poll every file in the compilation several times a second for changes but check some files less often than others depending on how frequently they do change.
- `useFsEventsOnParentDirectory`: similar to the default `useFsEvents`, but watches parent directories instead of individual files.
- `fixedChunkSizePolling`: whether the chunk size polling of watched files should be fixed.

watchDirectory

The `watchDirectory` option controls how the watch process watches folders. The default value for this option is also `useFsEvents`, which makes this option also rely on operating system events when watching folders by default. Other values accepted by this option are:

- `fixedPollingInterval`: use an interval to poll every folder in the compilation several times a second for changes to files.
- `dynamicPriorityPolling`: poll every folder in the compilation several times a second for changes but check some folders less often than others depending on how frequently the compiler thinks they will change using a dynamic queue.
- `fixedChunkSizePolling`: whether the chunk size polling of watched directories should be fixed.

fallbackPolling

When the watch process is using the default settings for the **`watchFile`** and **`watchDirectory`** options, the system may eventually run out of native file watchers. This could be a problem for a large application containing many TypeScript files, so the compiler has a fallback strategy in case this happens.

We can use the **`fallbackPolling`** option to configure that, it supports the following values:

- **`fixedPollingInterval`**: Use the **`fixedPollingInterval`** strategy for files (see the *watchFile* section on the previous page for a description of this strategy).
- **`priorityPollingInterval`**: Use the **`priorityPollingInterval`** strategy for files (see the *watchFile* section on the previous page for a description of this strategy).
- **`dynamicPriorityPolling`**: use the **`dynamicPriorityPolling`** strategy for files (see the *watchFile* section on the previous page for a description of this strategy).
- **`synchronousWatchDirectory`**: disable deferred watching on directories – this option is unlikely to be required unless using an unconventional application setup.
- **`dynamicPriority`**: files that are changed more frequently will have a higher priority than files that are changed less often.
- **`fixedChunkSize`**: polled chunk sizes are fixed.
- **`fixedInterval`**: the time interval between checks is fixed.
- **`priorityInterval`**: frequently updated files have a higher polling priority than files updated less often.

synchronousWatchDirectory

By default, the compiler will call callbacks synchronously and update the state of directory watchers when recursive watching isn't natively supported on the platform in use. To disable this, we can set this option to the value **`false`**.

As with the preceding few options, this is likely to be useful only on platforms that do not support native recursive folder watching.

excludeDirectories

To reduce the number of files that the compiler is watching, we can use the `excludeDirectories` option to specify an array of folders to exclude from the compilation. Because the **node_modules** folder in Node projects tends to be quite large and contains a significant number of files and folders, it is common to exclude this directory from the watch process:

```
"excludeDirectories": ["**/node_modules"]
```

Other folders, such as a **temp** folder, or build output folder, are also commonly excluded from the watch process to make it more efficient. This option supports glob patterns, such as the double star at the beginning of the path in the preceding example.

excludeFiles

As well as excluding directories from the compilation, we can also exclude individual files. This option also takes an array, and like `excludeDirectories`, it also supports file glob patterns as well as paths to specific files.

assumeChangesOnlyAffectDirectDependencies

This option can be enabled to reduce the amount of checking that is done for deep chains of dependencies - when a TypeScript file imports another file, which itself imports another file, and so on and so forth. By default, the compiler will check the entire chain of these dependencies.

When this option is enabled, however, the compiler will only check direct dependencies, rather than the whole chain of dependencies, so this option can be used to speed up the watch process for large applications with many imports.

Environment variables

TypeScript also provides three environment variables that can be used on platforms that don't support watching directories recursively, or support native file watching using file system events, such as Linux.

See the guide at **https://www.freecodecamp.org/news/how-to-set-an-environment-variable-in-linux** for more information on how to set environment variables on Linux platforms.

The available environment variables are:

- **`TSC_WATCHFILE`**
- **`TSC_WATCHDIRECTORY`**
- **`TSC_NONPOLLING_WATCHER`**

The **`TSC_WATCHFILE`** environment variable can be set to the following values:

- **`PriorityPollingInterval`**
- **`DynamicPriorityPolling`**
- **`UseFsEvents`**
- **`UseFsEventWithFallbackDynamicPolling`**
- **`UseFsEventsOnParentDirectory`**

The **`TSC_WATCHDIRECTORY`** environment variable can be set to the following values:

- `RecursiveDirectoryUsingFsWatchFile`
- `RecursiveDirectoryUsingDynamicPriorityPolling`

Note that on platforms that do support file-system events and recursive directory watching, such as Windows, or Mac platforms, these environment variables are ignored.

For full information on what these different values mean when used with the appropriate environment variables, you should consult the TypeScript handbook, which is available at **https://www.typescriptlang.org/docs/handbook/configuring-watch.html**.

Do also note that incorrectly updating the environment variables on your system can potentially result in a loss of data or irrecoverable system failure – take care to consult the relevant documentation for your platform to ensure that the process is carried out correctly.

Building projects

Sometimes the application we are building may be more complex than a directory containing a few sub-directories. In a mono-repo for example, there may be many projects and libraries grouped together, with numerous dependencies between them.

TypeScript supports both simple and complex application architectures, allows us to use a series of linked **tsconfig.json** files to specify the dependencies between projects, and makes sure that they are built together as required, depending on whether or not they are up to date.

Sub-projects that extend another project are known as referenced projects as the root tsconfig.json file uses the `references` configuration option to specify them

To build our TypeScript files instead of just compiling them, we just need to use the `--build` (or `-b`) flag when we invoke the compiler:

```
tsc --build
```

When we use the `--build` flag to compile a project, the compiler will also compile any dependent projects if they have changed since the last compilation. It keeps track of the state of each project using a special tsbuildinfo file; we'll look at these in more detail shortly.

The `--build` flag is an alternative way to compile TypeScript files that can offer faster build times, and which allows us to break up our application into smaller, more coherent pieces, which can also be an aid to development.

Let's look at an example in action. Inside the **chapter 4** directory in your own project directory, create a new folder called projects, and then inside this folder, create three subfolders, one called main-project, one called sub-project-1, and one called sub-project-2.

Inside all of these new folders create a subdirectory called src, and within this new src directory, create a single TypeScript file containing only a string variable:

```
const subExample1: string = 'This is an example!';
```

These typescript files should be called **main-source-file-1.ts**, **sub-source-file-1.ts**, and **sub-source-file-2.ts** respectively. Note that the name of the variable in each of these files will need to be unique.

Let's imagine that the main project is dependent on the two sub-projects; we can configure this using a new tsconfig.json file, which we should create in the root of the main-project directory (not inside the **src** subdirectory). It is recommended to use the `tsc --init` command in the Terminal to create the new tsconfig.json file so that the default options are added and enabled. Ensure the terminal is focused on the main-project directory when running the command.

In addition to the default options in the new tsconfig.json file, you will need to add a new top-level option called references to specify the **sub-project-1** and **sub-project-2** directories as dependencies:

```
"references": [
  { "path": "../sub-project-1" },
  { "path": "../sub-project-2" },
]
```

Take care to add the **references** option outside of the **compilerOptions** section, not inside it.

We should also set the **rootDir** option inside the **compilerOptions** section, to configure the projects folder, which contains the main and sub-projects, as the root directory – if we don't do this, the compiler won't include all of the source files correctly when we build the main project. It should have the following value:

```
"rootDir": "../",
```

As well as this main tsconfig.json file, each of the sub-projects will need to have their own tsconfig.json files in the root of each folder as well. These are much smaller, and both of them are identical, although that doesn't have to be the case.

They should both contain the following code:

```
{
  "extends": "../main-project/tsconfig.json",
  "include": ["**/*.ts"],
  "compilerOptions": {
    "composite": true
  }
}
```

All of these **sub-tsconfig.json** files need to extend the main **tsconfig.json** file – again, if we don't do this then the projects will not get built correctly. We also need to specify that this is a referenced project using the composite compiler option.

A side-effect of using this option is that the **rootDir** configuration option of the project will be automatically set to the directory containing the tsconfig.

json file. We should also ensure that TypeScript source files can be found by setting the `include` top-level option.

So, to recap, we have three folders:

- main-project
- sub-project-1
- sub-project-2

Each of these folders contains a folder called **src**, which itself contains a TypeScript file, and a **tsconfig.json** file. The main **tsconfig.json** file (the one inside the main-project directory) uses the `references` configuration option to specify **`sub-project-1`** and **`sub-project-2`** as dependencies.

The **tsconfig.json** files in the sub-projects both need to extend the main **tsconfig.json** file, and both specify that they are composite projects. At this point, everything should be in place – we can build the application using the **`--build`** flag in the terminal:

```
tsc --build
```

Any output in the terminal means an error occurred, but if everything goes according to plan, the main - project folder will gain a **dist** folder containing all of the compiled code from the main project and the sub-projects. This will be similar to the **dist** folder we created earlier using only the **`tsc`** command, with a couple of notable differences, as shown in the following figure:

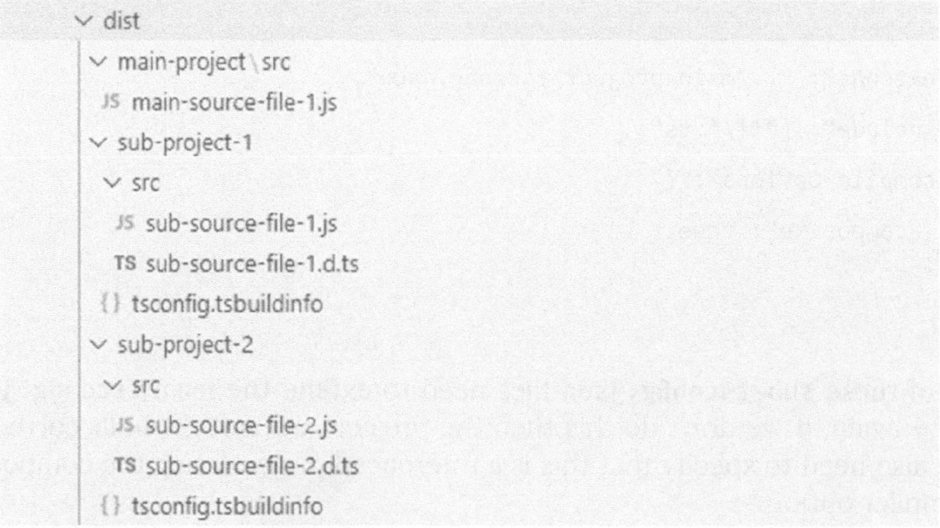

```
dist
  main-project\src
    main-source-file-1.js
  sub-project-1
    src
      sub-source-file-1.js
      sub-source-file-1.d.ts
    tsconfig.tsbuildinfo
  sub-project-2
    src
      sub-source-file-2.js
      sub-source-file-2.d.ts
    tsconfig.tsbuildinfo
```

***Figure 4.11**: The compiled output of the build command in Visual Studio Code*

Both of the dependent projects will be compiled, but as well as generating JavaScript files, it will also generate a declaration file for each TypeScript file within each sub-project. Declaration files are used with libraries to provide information to the compiler about the types used. We'll look at these files in more detail later in the book.

As well as a declaration file, we'll also find a single tsconfig.tsbuildinfo file generated in the root of each sub-project. These files are used by the compiler to determine which code needs to be compiled when running a subsequent build, so that only files which have changed since the last build are recompiled, and this is what helps make builds with the **`--build`** flag faster than a standard compile.

One point to note is that the build will fail if any of the TypeScript files in the compilation contain errors, which is probably for the best in a larger, more complex application composed of numerous projects.

Build-specific flags

There are a number of different flags that we can use in conjunction with the **`--build`** flag. These are as follows:

- `--clean`
- `--dry`
- `--force`
- `--verbose`
- `--watch`

The **`--clean`** flag is used to delete all of the files in the output directory, it doesn't actually build any projects. It only deletes files, it doesn't delete folders, so the dist directory itself, along with any sub-directories, will remain.

The **`--dry`** flag also doesn't actually build any projects or compile any files. Instead, this flag causes the compiler to output a report to the terminal which shows what it would have built had the flag not been used:

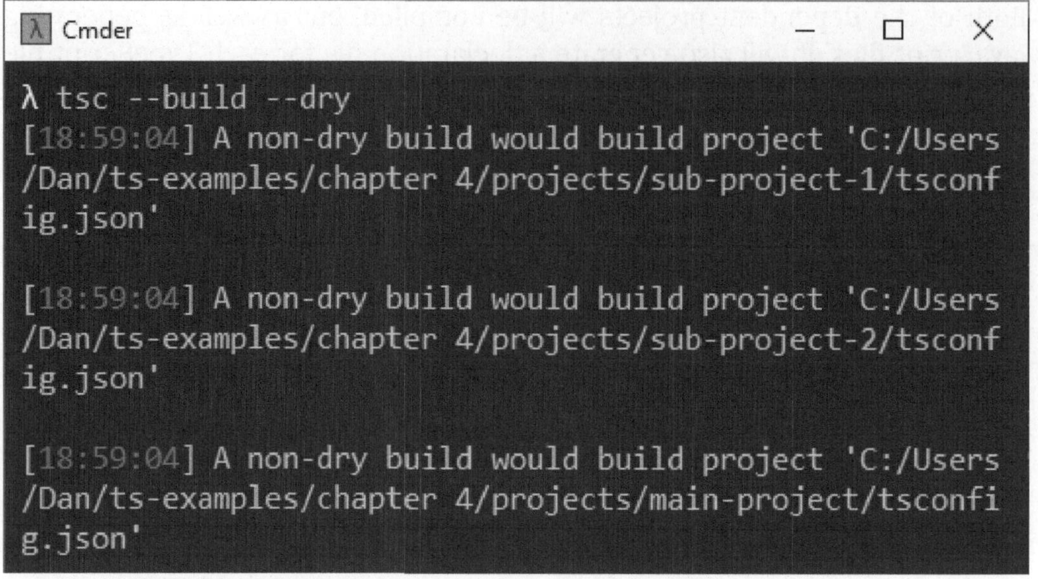

Figure 4.12: *Output of the --dry flag in a 3rd party terminal on Windows*

The **`--dry`** flag can also be used in conjunction with the **`--clean`** flag, to show what would be deleted had the flag not been used.

The **`--force`** flag is used to build all referenced projects, regardless of whether they have been updated or not.

The **`--verbose`** flag causes the compiler to emit information to the terminal regarding the projects that were built. There can be a lot of output depending on the size of the project; here is a snippet of the kind of information it outputs:

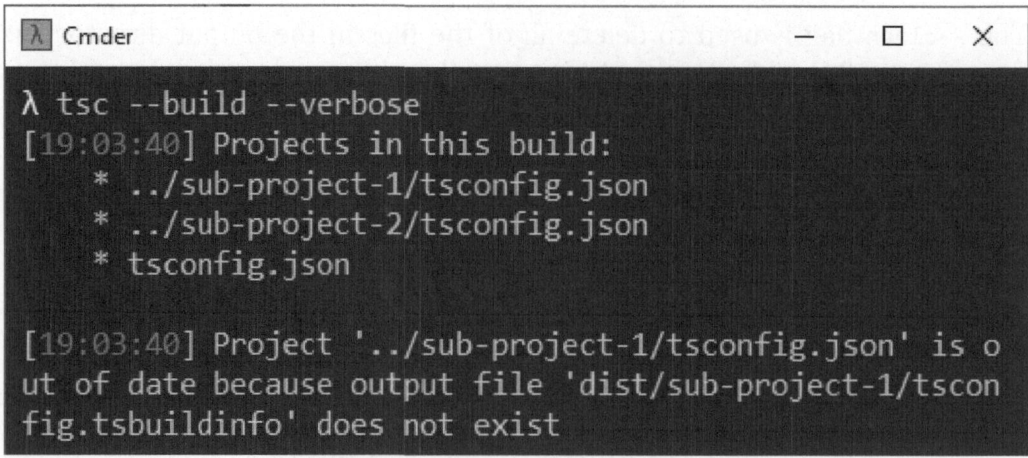

Figure 4.13: *Example output of the --verbose flag*

The `--watch` flag works in the same way as it does with the regular compiler; it watches files for changes and rebuilds any affected referenced projects as and when necessary.

Integrating with other build tools

Typescript compilation is very easily integrated with many of today and yesterday's most popular JavaScript build tools, I'm talking about things like Babel, Grunt, Gulp, and Webpack, as well as tools that may be more closely associated with back-end build systems like MSBuild and NuGet.

While some of these tools may spark a moment of fond remembrance, it would be outside of the scope of this book to describe each of them in detail.

The TypeScript documentation already does a very good job of showing how to integrate with the above and many more build systems, so for further information, do consult the information that can be found online at **https://www.typescriptlang.org/docs/handbook/integrating-with-build-tools.html**.

Instead of focusing on all of the different build tools, we will cover a basic example of integrating with just one of them, a build system that is very much still in use at the time of writing and looks set to continue to be a popular tool for TypeScript developers everywhere – Webpack.

Integrating with webpack

Webpack is a module bundling system that takes JavaScript modules with dependencies and bundles them into static assets for use in a browser. It's been around for a long time and can bundle a wide range of different types of files including JavaScript, SCSS or SASS, HTML, images, and fonts.

It also has a vast ecosystem of plugins, and as such the setup and configuration can be quite extensive. To minimize any setup and allow us to focus on the TypeScript aspect of the configuration, we will use a Webpack starter kit, which is included in the example project accompanying this book.

The starter kit that we will use can be found online at **https://github.com/wbkd/webpack-starter**, and is included in a directory in the **chapter 4** folder called **webpack-integration**. Although for this example, I would recommend you create a new folder outside of the example directory for the examples in this book.

The first thing we need to do is navigate into this directory in our terminal application and run `npm install` to install the dependencies. Once this is done, the directory will gain a **node_modules** folder, as is usual for an NPM project.

By default, the Webpack starter repo is a minimal Webpack application, which does not include TypeScript integration by default - this is what we will be adding ourselves. Webpack itself is like a foundation, upon which we add the plugins necessary for our project - these plugins are referred to as loaders as they are intended for loading (and processing) different types of files during the bundling process.

In order to have Webpack understand what to do with TypeScript files, we need to install the TypeScript loader for Webpack - `ts-loader`. We can do that by running the following command in the terminal:

npm install --save-dev ts-loader

Once the loader is installed, we can add the required configuration for it. Webpack is configured using regular JavaScript files, in the starter project they can be found in a sub-directory called **webpack**.

There are three files inside this directory; a base configuration file called **webpack.common.js**, and then **webpack.config.dev.js**, and **webpack.config.prod.js** which both extend the base configuration with settings suitable for their respective environments.

Each of these files contains varying amounts of configuration, most of it irrelevant to TypeScript and this discussion. In essence, these files load a series of plugins and utilities, provide configuration for Webpack itself, define the plugins, and then configure the plugins and utilities.

Let's run through the steps necessary to convert this project from JavaScript to TypeScript compilation and then bundling.

TypeScript webpack configuration

The example project contains a basic file in the **src** subdirectory called **index.ts**, which is the entry file for the application - the file that Webpack will load and which imports everything else necessary for the application to run.

In this example, the entry file is as follows:

```
import '../styles/index.scss';

import { app } from './app';

console.log('App running: ', app.name);
```

In this case, the file imports the styles and an **app** object and logs a message to the console showing the name of the app. The **app** object will be imported from another TypeScript file in the same directory called **app.ts**, but note that the extension is not specified in the import.

This **app.ts** file simply exports a basic **app** object containing the name of the app:

```
export const app = { name: 'my-app' };
```

The first thing we need to do is update the entry point for our application. In the base configuration file **webpack.common.js**, the entry point to the application is configured using the **entry** configuration option.

Currently, Webpack will be looking for a file called **index.js** in the scripts directory – we should update this to **index.ts** instead:

```
entry: {
  app: Path.resolve(__dirname, '../src/scripts/index.ts'),
},
```

Next, we need to tell Webpack how to process TypeScript files; we can do that by adding a rule which matches files with a **.ts** extension and tells Webpack to use **ts-loader** for those types of files.

By default, the starter project looks for any **.mjs** (Module JavaScript) files in the project. We aren't using these, so we can replace the existing rule on lines 36 through 40 in the **webpack.common.js** file with this configuration to avoid looking for files which we know beforehand will not exist in the current project:

```
{
  test: /\.ts$/,
  use: 'ts-loader',
  exclude: /node_modules/,
},
```

What this configuration says is to match any file that ends with a **.ts** extension, excluding any files in the **node_modules** directory, and process them with the **ts-loader** plugin.

Also, in the **webpack.common.js** configuration file, in the resolve configuration option on line 29, we need to tell Webpack to allow the importing of TypeScript modules in files:

```
extensions: ['.ts', '.js'],
```

These are the minimum configuration changes we need to make in order to convert this project to use TypeScript, but there is still one more thing we need to do.

Lastly, we need to add a **tsconfig.json** file to the root of the starter project. We can extend the main **tsconfig.json** file at the root of the **ts-examples** directory, and then limit the included files to only those TypeScript files found in the **src** sub-directory of the **webpack-integration** directory:

```
{
  "extends": "../../tsconfig.json",
  "include": ["./src/**/*.ts"],
}
```

At this point, we should have everything in place to be able to compile the example TypeScript files. We can run a production build using the following command in our terminal:

```
npm run build
```

This command will build the project and generate compiled JavaScript, CSS, and HTML static output in a folder in the root **webpack-integration** directory called **build**, which we could then deploy to some kind of production environment.

We can run also run a development build using the following command in the terminal instead:

```
npm start
```

This will compile and bundle the files and start up a local development server which we can use to preview the application in a browser and display the URL that we need to enter in the browser to view the **index.html** file, which will be something along the lines of **`http://192.168.1.136:8080/`**.

The resulting application should appear in the browser like this, and you should see the log message we added showing the name of the app in the developer tools console:

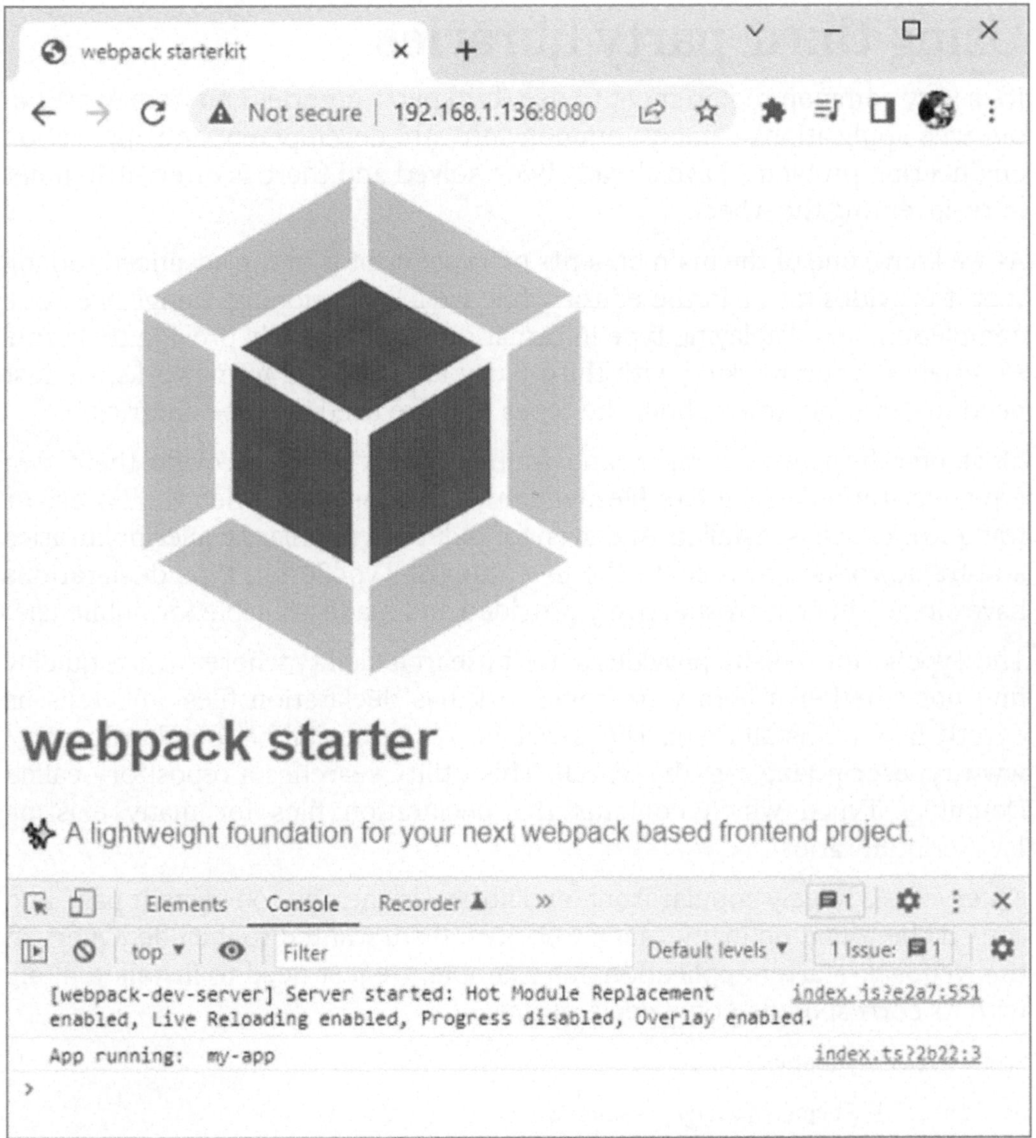

Figure 4.14: *Viewing the example application in Chrome on Windows*

The **`start`** command also has watch enabled by default, so any time we make changes to files in the **src** directory of the app, the relevant files will be recompiled. If we are viewing the application in a browser, the browser will be automatically reloaded.

Using third-party libraries

It's a very common requirement to use third party libraries and frameworks in our web applications - many common software development and application engineering problems have already been solved and there is often little point in re-inventing the wheel.

As we know, one of the main benefits of TypeScript is in the advanced tooling that it provides for us in the editor while we are developing, things like code completion, and displaying type information. We can easily provide this same experience when working with third party libraries and frameworks, we just need to get information about the types that are used in these libraries.

Most new front-end libraries and frameworks will now provide their own type declarations using **d.ts** files, which will be installed when the library or framework itself is installed. And even for older but popular JavaScript libraries and frameworks that predate the invention of TypeScript, type declarations have already been retrospectively provided and made available for public use.

The TypeScript website provides a useful search facility where we can quickly find out whether a library or framework has declaration files, and tells us exactly how to install them. This excellent resource can be found at **https://www.typescriptlang.org/dt/search**. This utility searches a repository called Definitely Typed which contains the declaration files for many existing JavaScript libraries.

jQuery was a hugely popular front-end library in the not-too-distant past, and can still be found on many, many websites. If we wanted to include jQuery in the webpack-starter application, for example, we just need to install it, along with its corresponding type declarations:

```
npm install jquery

npm install @types/jquery --save-dev
```

These two commands will install jQuery itself as a full application dependency, because it is required to actually run the application in a browser, and secondly, install the type declarations for jQuery as a development dependency because the types are not required by the browser and are only used for development purposes.

Third-party types are installed in the **node_modules** folder in a sub-directory called **@types** - any declaration files inside this folder are automatically visible to the TypeScript compiler and Visual Studio Code.

Once this has been done, we are free to import it into our application and use it, while getting the full type-information provided by the editor. We could change the **app.ts** file so that it includes the jQuery version in the app object for example:

```
import jquery from 'jquery';

export const app = { name: 'my-app', jqueryVersion: jquery.fn.jquery };
```

TypeScript makes it very easy to work with third party libraries or frameworks and still get a great tooling and development experience in the editor, which, after all, is what TypeScript is all about.

Generating .d.ts files

We saw earlier that **d.ts** files are generated from referenced projects when using the compiler with the `--build` flag, and that these are often provided by third party libraries in order to give the compiler information about the types used by the library and the functionality it exposes through its API.

We can generate **d.ts** files either from TypeScript files or even from basic JavaScript files if there is some reason why the JavaScript project that we're working with cannot be upgraded to a TypeScript project.

Let's see how we can create them for our own TypeScript libraries. As we learned when we looked at using the compiler in build mode a little earlier in this chapter, we can have the compiler generate declaration files (these files are sometimes also known as ambient modules) for us automatically when the TypeScript is compiled.

Inside the **chapter 4** directory, there is a folder called **my-lib**, which contains a simple TypeScript file that exports an object containing a single property and two methods:

```
export const myLib = {
  _version: '0.0.1',
  version: () => myLib._version,
  reverseString: (str: string) => str.split('').reverse().join('')
}
```

As this library is a TypeScript project in its own right, it also has its own **tsconfig.json** file, although, for simplicity, this file merely extends the main **tsconfig.json** file in the root of the **ts-examples** folder:

```
{
  "extends": "../../tsconfig.json",
}
```

In order to tell the compiler to emit declaration files alongside the compiled JavaScript files, we can add the `declaration` compiler option to this file also. As this is a compiler option, it needs to sit within the `compilerOptions` root option:

```
"compilerOptions": {
  "declaration": true,
  "outDir": "./dist"
}
```

We can also specify an output directory located inside the **my-lib** directory to avoid the output of this folder becoming mixed up with the output from other examples.

Now, with this simple configuration in place, the compiler will generate an accompanying **my-lib.d.ts** declaration file every time we compile the library.

To run this example, you can either change the working directory of the terminal application to the **my-lib** directory or keep the working directory as the top-level **ts-examples** directory and use the `--project` flag to point the compiler at the **tsconfig.json** file shown earlier, for example:

```
tsc --project "chapter 4/my-lib"
```

Note that we can use the basic compiler as we have set the `declaration` option in our configuration file; we don't have to do a full build (which wouldn't work in this case anyway as we aren't using a referenced project in this example) to get this behavior.

The generated declaration file should look like this:

TS my-lib.d.ts ×

chapter 4 > my-lib > dist > chapter 4 > my-lib > TS my-lib.d.ts > ...

```
export declare const myLib: {
    _version: string;
    version: () => string;
    reverseString: (str: string) => string;
};
```

Figure 4.15: *A generated declaration file in Visual Studio Code on Windows*

The resulting basic declaration file for this example looks very similar to the original TypeScript source file in that it retains all of the type information that we originally specified, but note that it also contains any type information that the compiler was able to infer - we do not need to specify every last type used in our source file manually.

For example, the compiler knows that the `_version` property is a string, and that the `version` method is an arrow function that returns a string, even though we did not explicitly specify this in the original **my-lib.ts** file.

Note that this file only describes the types that are used, it doesn't contain any actual runnable code itself - for example, it tells the compiler that the `reverseString` method returns a string, but it doesn't actually return a string itself, that, happens in the original TypeScript source file.

Using the `declaration` compiler option to generate declaration files is a useful and time-saving feature of the compiler that can make sharing our own libraries and utilities a much better experience for other developers consuming our code and provide a form of living documentation that travels around with our code.

> **Don't forget that the declaration compiler option, as well as many others, can be specified in the tsconfig.json configuration file, or passed on the command line in a Terminal in the format --declaration for one-off usage.**

Generating d.ts files from .js files

As well as generating declaration files when compiling a TypeScript project, we can also generate declaration files from JavaScript files, which is useful if we are working with a very old or uncommon library that doesn't already have a declaration file uploaded to the Definitely Typed repository, or if we're working with our own custom JavaScript project that for whatever reason, cannot be updated to TypeScript.

In the **chapter 4** directory in the example files accompanying this book, there is a sub-directory called **old-lib** which contains a sub-directory called **src**, within which a single JavaScript file resides. You should create this folder structure in your own example project and add a JavaScript file in the **src** directory.

This file contains a JavaScript file called **old-lib.js** containing the following code:

```
var oldLib = {
  /**
   * Reverse a string
   * @param {string} str The string to reverse
   * @returns {string} The reversed string
   */
  reverse: function(str) {
    return str.split('').reverse().join('');
  }
}
```

It simply creates a global object attached to the `window` which contains a method called `reverse`, which can be used to reverse a string, very similar to the example in the previous section except that it's a JavaScript file instead of a TypeScript file.

Note that for the compiler to be able to generate a **d.ts** file, the JavaScript source file needs to have JSDoc comments describing the types used in the file.

To have the compiler generate a declaration file for this code, we first need to add a new **tsconfig.json** file to this directory. This file should contain the following code:

```
{
  "compilerOptions": {
    "allowJs": true,
    "checkJs": true,
    "declaration": true,
    "emitDeclarationOnly": true
  }
}
```

This file will show as having an error in it, and theoretically, it does have an error – there are no TypeScript input files. However, the preceding configuration will still work when the input file is one or more JavaScript files.

We set the **allowJs** option to **true** because we want to include JavaScript files in the project. We also add the **checkJs** option so that the JavaScript can be checked when the compiler generates the declaration file. This isn't strictly necessary but it is good practice.

We use the declaration option to tell the compiler that we want to create declaration files, and we also set **emitDeclarationOnly** to **true** because we don't want to emit any JavaScript files – we already have those in this case.

We already have the typescript NPM package installed in the root **ts-examples** folder, but if we didn't, we would have to install that also.

At this point, we should have everything in place, so if we set the **old-lib** directory to the working directory in the terminal and run a standard **tsc** compile, we should end up with a new **old-lib.d.ts** file, which contains the following declaration:

TS old-lib.d.ts ×

chapter 4 > old-lib > src > TS old-lib.d.ts > ...

```
declare namespace oldLib {
    function reverse(str: string): string;
}
```

Figure 4.16: *A generated declaration file in Visual Studio Code on Windows*

We could then go ahead and add this declaration to another project. To do that, we should make sure the file is within the project and configured using the **`typeRoots`** configuration option, for example:

```
"compilerOptions": {
  "typeRoots": ["./node_modules/**", "old-lib.d.ts"]
}
```

We would then be able to get the full development experience when using this library.

Conclusion

In this chapter, we focused almost entirely on using the TypeScript compiler from our terminal application.

We first saw how to use the **`tsc`** command to perform a basic one-off compilation of our project and look at some of the common compiler options that we might want to use to emit all of our output files to a specific location, or configure which files are included, for example.

We learned that some options are root options specified at the top level of the object inside the **tsconfig.json** file and that other options are compiler options and thus sit inside the **`compilerOptions`** root option.

Once we had compiled some TypeScript files into JavaScript, we then took a moment to look at the kind of code that is emitted by the compiler and learned that it removes all of the type information in the resulting JavaScript output, and may or may not remove comments by default depending on the format of those comments.

We also looked at some of the more common general flags that we can use when running the **`tsc`** command, things like the **`--help`** flag for seeing a list of all of the various flags and options we can use, or the **`--version`** flag for getting the version of TypeScript in use.

We then moved on to look at watch mode, which is where the compiler watches files for changes and automatically recompiles the project when files are changed. We also looked at the various configuration options there are which are related to the **`--watch`** flag but noted that many of these are most commonly used on Linux platforms, due to the way in which it responds to file-system events.

Following this we looked at the `--build` flag, which is used to run the compiler in a slightly different way that may improve build times for larger more complex projects. We saw that the `build` flag will not only build our project, but also any referenced projects that the main project is dependent on.

We also took a look at how we can integrate TypeScript compilation with other build tools and looked at an example where we integrated with the popular Webpack bundling system.

As we will often want to use other libraries and frameworks in our projects, we also covered including third party libraries in our applications and saw how to install the declaration files for these libraries so that we can get the full development experience of TypeScript when using them.

Finally, we saw how to generate our own declaration files from either TypeScript or JavaScript projects in order to make sharing our code easier.

In the next chapter, let's move on to look at interfaces and enums in TypeScript.

References

- **https://www.typescriptlang.org/tsconfig**
- **https://webpack.js.org/guides/typescript/**
- **https://michaelsoolee.com/npm-package-tilde-caret/**

CHAPTER 5

Enums, Interfaces, and Namespaces

Introduction

Earlier in this book, we learned about type aliases and noted at the time that they are very similar to interfaces. In this chapter, we are going to come back and look at interfaces in more detail, as these are a very commonly used part of TypeScript.

Once we're done with interfaces, we'll then move on to look at namespaces in TypeScript. Namespaces are a great way to organize related code, and so are a construct that we are going to want to be familiar with when building commercial applications, although their use is less common than both interfaces and enums.

We'll also take a good look at enums in TypeScript. Enums are like a value that may contain one of several possible options. This feature of TypeScript is unusual in that enums remain in the compiled JavaScript output, albeit in a slightly different form.

Those developers coming to TypeScript from other programming languages may already be familiar with these types of constructs, but for those with a pure JavaScript experience, they may be somewhat esoteric, as none of them are found natively in JavaScript at all.

Structure

In this chapter we will cover the following topics:

- Interfaces
- Interface merging
- Extending interfaces
- Namespaces
- Namespace merging
- Enums
- Numeric enums
- Reverse mapping
- Exhaustiveness and the never type
- String enums
- Heterogenous enums
- Computed and constant enums
- Literal enums
- Inlining enums
- Using the keyof operator

Interfaces

In TypeScript, we can use an interface to describe what the shape of an object should look like – which properties and methods it has, what types the object's properties should be, and which types any methods it has should return.

Interfaces are very commonly used in TypeScript; every single commercial-grade application that I've worked on, certainly in the last 5 to 6 years or so, has made heavy use of them, so they are a feature of TypeScript that you'll likely encounter and use often.

NOTE: Interfaces are very similar to type aliases, which we looked at in *Chapter* 3, and the two can be used interchangeably in almost all situations.

To declare an interface, we use the `interface` keyword and supply a block wrapped in curly braces containing the named members and their types, like this:

```
interface Person {
  name: string;
  age: number;
};
```

We've defined an interface for **Person** objects and specified that objects of this type should have two properties, one called **name** which should be of the type **string**, and one called **age** which is of the type **number**. We can now use our interface as a type when creating variables, or in other places where type annotations are valid, such as on function parameters or function returns. For example:

```
const me: Person = {
  name: 'Dan',
  age: 44,
};
```

The objects we create must have all of the properties and methods specified by the interface, and they must have only those properties and methods specified by the interface.

If we fail to supply one of the required properties, the editor will tell us which property (or properties) we missed, and the type of value that it expects. For example, if we remove the **age** property from the **me** object, like this:

```
const me: Person = {
  name: 'Dan',
};
```

We'll then see the following error:

```
const me: Person
Property 'age' is missing in type '{ name: string; }'
but required in type 'Person'. ts(2741)
interfaces.ts(3, 3): 'age' is declared here.
```

Figure 5.1: *Missing property error in Visual Studio Code*

Conversely, if we add a property to our object which isn't in the interface, we'll see a different error in the editor instead. For example, if we add a property called **`interests`**, like this:

```
const me: Person = {
  name: 'Dan',
  age: 44,
  interests: ['TypeScript'],
};
```

Then we'll see this error:

```
(property) interests: string[]
Type '{ name: string; age: number;
interests: string[]; }' is not assignable to
type 'Person'.
  Object literal may only specify known
properties, and 'interests' does not exist
in type 'Person'. ts(2322)
```

Figure 5.2: *Object may only specify named properties error*

NOTE: It is possible to force an object to have a property or method not specified by the interface using the type-casting. We'll look at this later in the book.

Similarly, if we try to set the value of a property to the wrong type of value, like this:

```
const me: Person = {
  name: 'Dan',
  age: '44',
};
```

That will also cause an error in the editor:

```
(property) Person.age: number

Type 'string' is not assignable to type
'number'. ts(2322)

interfaces.ts(3, 3): The expected type comes
from property 'age' which is declared here on
type 'Person'
```

Figure 5.3: *Unexpected type error*

Interfaces are very prescriptive by default - we must specify all named members, and we can't specify members that are not named specifically in the interface definition. We do still have some flexibility, however.

We can very easily make a property in an interface optional simply by adding a question mark directly after the property identifier.

Let's go ahead and add an **interests** property to our **Person** interface, and mark it as optional:

```
interface Person {
  name: string;
  age: number;
  interests?: string[];
};
```

The **interests** property is an array containing any number of string elements; we haven't looked at arrays in TypeScript in much detail at all yet, but don't worry, we'll be covering them in much more detail a little later in the book. The main focus here is on making the property optional, not what type we give it.

Now we can create instances of the **Person** interface and it doesn't matter if those instances have the **interests** property or not, they will still be considered valid **Person** objects – specifying the **interests** property is completely optional. If we do specify it, it must of course be a string array.

As well as optional properties, we can also specify that properties are read-only, that is, once they are initialized, they cannot be changed. To do this, we use the **readonly** access modifier before the property identifier.

For example, we could make the **name** property in our **Person** interface a read-only property like this:

```
interface Person {
  readonly name: string;
  age: number;
  interests?: string[];
};
```

Now, if we try to reassign the value of the **name** property of **Person** instances after they have been created, like this:

```
const me: Person = {
  name: 'Dan',
  age: 44,
};
me.name = 'Bill';
```

Then we'll see the following error in the editor:

```
(property) Person.name: any
Cannot assign to 'name' because it is a
read-only property. ts(2540)
```

Figure 5.4: *Read-only assignment error*

We can create a very permissive interface for objects so that objects can have any named property using an index signature:

```
interface AnyProps {
  [key: string]: string;
}
```

An index signature takes the format of the name **key** and its type, in this case **string**, in square brackets, followed by a colon and the value type, which in this case is also **string**.

In this example, we can now create instances of the **AnyProps** type, and instances of this object will be able to have literally any **string** property identifiers, we just need to make sure that the value of any properties we do add is of the type **string**:

```
const random: AnyProps = {
  literallyAnything: 'Just has to be a string',
};
```

This is an interesting feature of TypeScript and can be useful in some situations where we don't know beforehand exactly which property names an object will have, but it somewhat negates the benefit of using an interface in the first place to control which members an object may have, so care should be taken when using this feature.

We can also use an interface as the type description for the member of another interface. For example, we might want to specify that the **name** property of **Person** objects, should be of the type of another interface called **PersonName**:

```
interface PersonName {
  firstName: string;
  familyName: string;
  otherNames?: string[];
};
```

The **PersonName** interface has mandatory **firstName** and **lastName** properties of the type **string** and can accept an optional array of other names, also in a **string** array. Now we can update the **name** property of the **Person** interface to be of the type **PersonName**:

```
interface Person {
  name: PersonName;
  age: number;
  interests?: string[];
};
```

Making this change will of course invalidate the **me** object instance we added earlier because the **name** property no longer conforms to the interface. Let's update it:

```
const me: Person = {
  name: {
    firstName: 'Dan',
    familyName: 'Wellman',
  },
  age: 44,
  interests: ['Swimming'],
};
```

Now, the `me` object conforms to the `Person` interface once again, TypeScript is satisfied, and the error in the editor (or compiler) goes away.

As interfaces are entirely a construct of TypeScript, they will be completely removed from the emitted JavaScript during compilation.

Interface merging

TypeScript makes it very easy for us to merge interface declarations, something that is not possible with type definitions, hence this is one of the main reasons to use interfaces as opposed to type definitions.

Merging an interface is exactly as it sounds – two declarations are merged together and all distinct properties from the individual interfaces will appear in the resulting interface after the merge. One point to note however is that existing members cannot be overwritten in order to change an existing property's type.

Interface merging can be useful when we don't have access to change the original interface, such as when using an interface imported from a third party library but wish to modify it in some way.

Continuing with the previous `Person` example, later in our application, we may want to add a new property to the `Person` interface in an ad-hoc way, perhaps based on the result of some other operation.

To do this, we can simply define the interface again using the `interface` keyword once again, with the same identifier, and specifying any new properties and their types that we would like to add:

```
interface Person {
  readonly name: PersonName;
  age: number;
  interests?: string[];
};

// later
interface Person {
  height?: number;
};
```

In this case, we redeclare the `Person` interface and add an optional property called `height`. We can redeclare the same interface multiple times, and TypeScript will merge all of the declarations together.

So now, when we create new object instances of the type `Person` or update existing instances, these may optionally contain a `height` property of the type `number`.

> **NOTE: Remember, only unique interface properties can be merged; if an existing property appears in both declarations, it must have exactly the same type or an error will occur.**

Extending interfaces

As well as interface merging, which happens when interfaces with the same identifiers are declared multiple times, we can also extend interfaces using the `extends` keyword, as if they were a class.

For example, we may have a more specialized type of `Person` called a `Developer`, which has an additional property called `languages` to specify which programming languages the developer is fluent in:

```
interface Developer extends Person {
  languages: string[];
};
```

In this case, the **Developer** interface extends the **Person** interface using the **extends** keyword and all instances of the **Developer** interface will need to include the mandatory properties of both **Person** and **Developer**:

```
const dev: Developer = {
  name: {
    firstName: 'Dan',
    familyName: 'Wellman',
  },
  age: 44,
  languages: ['TypeScript', 'JavaScript'],
}
```

There is no limit to the number of interfaces that can be merged in this way, we just need to separate them with a comma when declaring the interface.

For example, we may have another interface called **FirstAider**:

```
interface FirstAider {
  cprTrained: boolean;
};
```

As well as an **interface** called **DevManager** which **extends** both the **Developer** and **FirstAider** interfaces, like this:

```
interface DevManager extends Developer, FirstAider {
  // members from all Person, Developer, and FirstAider interfaces
};
```

Now the **DevManager** interface will be a combination of both of the interfaces being extended, and remember, the **Developer** interface already extended the **Person** interface, so **DevManager** will contain the members from all three of these interfaces.

Extending an interface with the **extends** keyword and interface merging triggered by redeclaring an interface with the same identifier both work in almost exactly the same way and really, we could pick either technique for handling the simple cases that we've looked at so far.

The main difference between the two is that when extending interfaces, we can still use the original interfaces separately, as they existed prior to extending. When merging interfaces, we can no longer use the original interfaces after merging has occurred.

There is another subtle difference between merging and extending interfaces, and that is in how methods are handled. As we saw with declaration merging, when redeclaring an interface, if we specify the same property in both interfaces, then the property in both interfaces must have the same type.

Similarly, if we declare the same method in a merged interface, then both methods must have the same signature - they must accept the same parameters, the parameters must be of the same type, and the methods must have the same return type.

This is true whether we are extending an interface with the **`extends`** keyword or relying on merging by TypeScript. For example, consider the following simple interface:

```
interface MethodTest {

  method: (arg0: string) => string;

};
```

The interface consists of a single method, which accepts one parameter of the type **`string`**, and has a return type also of **`string`**. If we redeclare this interface later, we might want to change the type of the parameter and the return type:

```
// later

interface MethodTest {

  method: (arg0: number) => number;

};
```

This is unacceptable, and the editor will show an error:

```
(property) methodTest.method: (arg0: string)
=> string

Subsequent property declarations must have
the same type.  Property 'method' must be of
type '(arg0: string) => string', but here
has type '(arg0: string) => number'. ts(2717)

interfaces.ts(51, 3): 'method' was also
declared here.
```

Figure 5.5: *Subsequent property declarations must have the same type error*

With declaration merging, we can get around this by creating a function overload instead, which uses a slightly different syntax:

```
interface MethodTest {
  method(arg0: string): string;
}
// later
interface MethodTest {
  method(arg0: number): number;
}
```

We move the parentheses directly after the identifier and remove the `=>` part of the arrow function. This will cause TypeScript to create an overload for the method, and the error that we originally saw in the editor will be gone.

This is not possible when using the `extends` keyword, however, so this represents really the main practical difference between merging interfaces and extending interfaces. We'll look at function overloading in much more detail later in this book.

Interfaces are a straightforward and powerful way of making sure that objects in our application conform to a particular specification and have the expected properties with the expected types of values.

Namespaces

In programming terms, a namespace is a container or scope where similar functionality or logic can be grouped together and where identifiers have less chance of colliding. JavaScript has no implicit support for namespaces, in that the term **namespace** is not a reserved word and has no inherent meaning or behavior.

However, creating the equivalent of a namespace in JavaScript is relatively easy – we simply use objects to represent namespaces, and store the required data or functionality inside them as properties or methods.

For example, we may wish to separate some simple utility methods into different namespaces for string utilities and number utilities.

We can do that easily using POJOs (Plain Old JavaScript Objects):

```
const stringUtils = {
  reverse: str => str.split('').reverse().join(''),
};
const numberUtils = {
  reverse: num => parseInt(num.toString().split('').reverse().join(''), 10),
};
```

We create two objects **stringUtils** and **numberUtils** and give each one a method called **reverse**, which reverses either a string or a number respectively. To use one of the **reverse** methods, we just target whichever container object, or namespace if you will, that we wish to use, with standard dot notation, for example:

```
stringUtils.reverse('abc'); // cba
numberUtils.reverse(123); // 321
```

Using namespaces in this way means that we can use the same identifier for the **reverse** method in both utility objects, which is useful because on the face of it, the methods both do essentially the same thing, just for a different type of value.

It may seem like a small thing, but as your application grows, the number of things that you the programmer have to personally name grows exponentially, and naming many things well, with useful names that clearly indicate intent and purpose, is extremely hard, as any seasoned developer will assert!

TypeScript does have baked-in support for namespaces, however, so we don't even need to use POJOs when using TypeScript, we can just use namespaces if that is our intention.

Let's reformulate the previous code snippet to TypeScript:

```
namespace StringUtils {

  export const reverse =
    (str: string) => str.split('').reverse().join('');

};

namespace NumberUtils {

  export const reverse =
    (num: number) => parseInt(num.toString().split('').reverse().
      join(''), 10);

};
```

To define a namespace, we use the **namespace** keyword followed by the identifier and then a pair of curly brackets.

Anything that we want to be available outside of the namespace needs to be exported, so in this case, we export an arrow function with the name **reverse** from both the **StringUtils** and **NumberUtils** namespaces. Note that again, by convention in TypeScript we use Pascal Case for namespace identifiers.

Any functionality that we want to remain private and only accessible within the namespace can just be defined normally without being exported. Historically, namespaces in TypeScript were known as internal modules, but this is a somewhat archaic term that is no longer used.

Using the **export** statement inside a namespace doesn't make it a true module, not in the sense of an ES Module in any case. Values that are exported from a namespace don't need to be imported, they are merely used via the namespace, like this:

```
StringUtils.reverse('abc'); // cba

NumberUtils.reverse(123); // 321
```

We use standard dot notation to invoke the methods, exactly as if we were interacting with regular objects.

Namespace merging

Just like interfaces, namespaces can also be merged, and this merging happens in exactly the same way as it does with interfaces; we simply redeclare the namespace using the same identifier as before, and add any new properties that we would like to include in the namespace:

```
namespace NsTest {
  export const str = 'abc'
};
namespace NsTest {
  export const num = 123;
};
NsTest.str; // abc
NsTest.num; // 123
```

In this case, both of the variables **str** and **num** will be available via the **NsTest** namespace. The reason for merging namespaces is similar to merging interfaces - it is useful if we don't have access to the original namespace, perhaps if it comes from a third party library, and wish to modify it in some way.

When merging namespaces, we cannot declare the same property twice at all. If we try to do this:

```
namespace NsTest {
  export const str = 'abc'
};
namespace NsTest {
  export const str = 123;
};
```

Then we'll see an error that we can't redeclare the variable because it's already scoped to the block:

```
const NsTest.str: 123
Cannot redeclare block-scoped variable 'str'. ts(2451)
```

Figure 5.6*: Cannot redeclare variable error in Visual Studio Code*

Namespaces in TypeScript are used less frequently than either interfaces or enums; personally, I've yet to work on a single commercial application that has employed them in any capacity.

Enums

An enum, or enumerated type, is like a static list of predefined values, one of which may be selected as the value of a variable or parameter at any given point in our application. They can be very useful for restricting the value that a variable may be to one of the enum's members.

They are a common feature of many popular programming languages, except JavaScript, which has no concept of them natively.

Enums are not removed from the compiled JavaScript entirely; instead, they become objects and so can be passed to functions and treated like regular values.

TypeScript supports a number of different types of enum, including numeric or string, and their values can be either constant or computed. There are some subtle differences in how these variations behave, so let's take a look at each of them.

Numeric enums

The default type of enum in TypeScript, if we don't explicitly specify any values for the members, is a numeric enum:

```
enum Fruit {
  Apple,
  Blackberry,
  Melon,
};
```

We use the **`enum`** keyword, followed by the identifier of the enum, in this case, that is **`Fruit`**. We then have an object containing the identifiers for all of the enum members, with each member separated by a comma; in this case, that's **`Apple`**, **`Blackberry`**, and **`Melon`**. It's a common convention to use Pascal Case for enum and member identifiers.

In this example, we haven't explicitly specified values for any of the enum members, only the identifiers, so TypeScript will allocate each of them an automatically incrementing numerical value, beginning with the value zero – like the indices of an array.

So, in this example, **`Apple`** has the value **`0`**, **`Blackberry`** has the value **`1`**, and **`Melon`** has the value **`2`**. This is what makes the enum a numerical enum – its members have numerical values.

If we were to log out the value of **`Fruit.Blackberry`**, for example, we would see 1 printed to the console:

```
console.log(Fruit.Blackberry); // 1
```

We can also use quotes around the member identifiers, it makes no difference to how they behave, therefore it's unusual to do this in practice.

One point to note is that, in this example, **`Fruit.Apple`** would be falsey in comparisons, as it has the value **`0`**. All other enum members (**`Fruit.Blackberry`** and **`Fruit.Melon`** in this example) would be truthy.

We can also explicitly define the numeric values for each enum member if we wish:

```
enum Fruit {

  Apple = 5,

  Blackberry = 6,

  Melon = 7,

};
```

This would make no difference to how the enum would be used, the members just have different values – **`Fruit.Apple`** is equal to **`Fruit.Apple`**, whatever the value of **`Fruit.Apple`** happens to be.

For example, consider the following code:

```
function determinePortionSize(fruit: Fruit) {
  switch (fruit) {

    case Fruit.Apple:

      return 1;

    case Fruit.Blackberry:

      return 10;

    case Fruit.Melon:
```

```
      return 0.5;
  }
}
```

Here we define a function called **determinePortionSize**, which accepts a parameter called **fruit**. This parameter is set to the enum **Fruit** as the type, which means that the function must be passed one of the values from the enum when it is invoked:

```
determinePortionSize(Fruit.Blackberry); // 10
```

After the **determinePortionSize** function declaration, we can then invoke the function and can pass it **Fruit.Blackberry** as an argument.

The editor will warn us if we try to invoke the function with an argument that does not match one of the members of the **Fruit** enum, such as the string **'oops'**. In this case, we'll see an error:

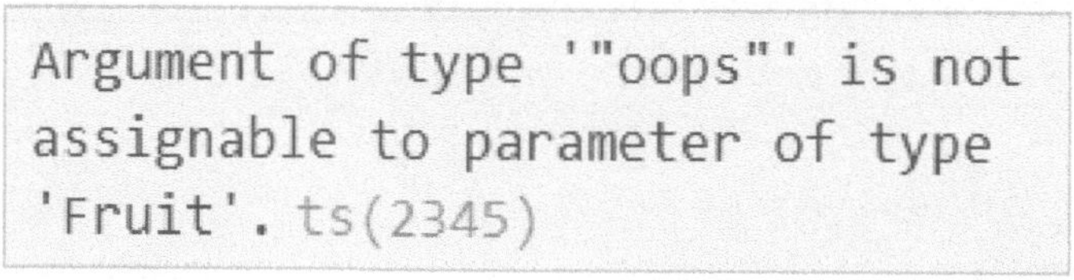

```
Argument of type '"oops"' is not
assignable to parameter of type
'Fruit'. ts(2345)
```

Figure 5.7: *Wrong parameter type error in Visual Studio Code*

Note that we could pass the value of the enum member we wanted to use directly, so we could have invoked it like this in the previous example and had the exact same result:

```
determinePortionSize(6); // 10
```

But personally, I feel it is far more readable and conveys the intent of the code much better to use the named enum member. One benefit of using enums is that the editor provides code-completion for all members of the enum in the editor when using them:

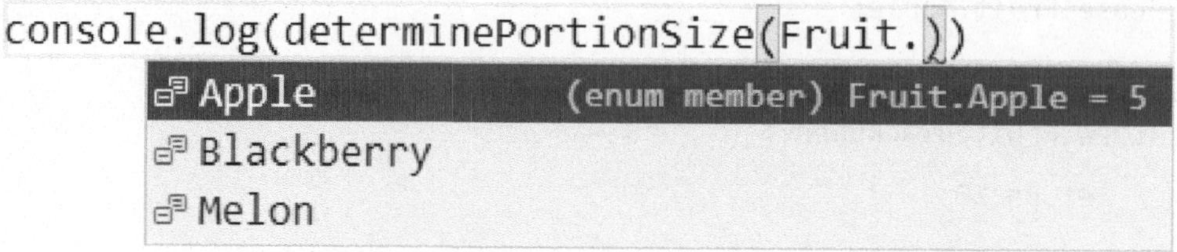

```
console.log(determinePortionSize(Fruit.))
    Apple                    (enum member) Fruit.Apple = 5
    Blackberry
    Melon
```

Figure 5.8: *Code completion for an enum in Visual Studio Code*

Note that TypeScript doesn't prevent us from passing numbers that do not exist as values of enum members, however, so we could pass a number that doesn't correspond to one of the values in our enum and the compiler won't consider this an error, the value would just be **`undefined`**, similar to accessing a property on an object that doesn't exist:

```
determinePortionSize(60); // undefined
```

Note that we can also specify only the value for the first enum member if we wish:

```
enum Fruit {

  Apple = 5,

  Blackberry,

  Melon,

};
```

Thanks to TypeScript's auto-incrementing, the value of **`Blackberry`** will still be **`6`**, and the value of **`Melon`** will still be **`7`**.

We can also set numeric enum members using unary or binary operators, so all of the following examples are also valid constant member values:

```
enum Fruit {

  Apple = -5,

  Blackberry = 6 * 2,

  Melon = 7 ^ 2,

};
```

We can also use the value of one enum member as the value of another enum member in a different enum:

```
enum TropicalFruit {

  Mango,

  Papaya,

  Melon = Fruit.Melon,

};
```

The **TropicalFruit** enum also has a member called **Melon** (although it doesn't have to have the same, identifier) and the value of this member is set to the value of the **Fruit.melon** member. With numeric enums, this is considered a constant value.

One point to note is that duplicated enum values are allowed in TypeScript, for example, the following enum is valid:

```
enum Drupes {

  Plum = 5,

  Peach = 5,

}
```

Both members have the numerical value **5**.

This models the behavior of some other programming languages, like C# for example, but it may cause confusion and provides no real benefit. Personally, I prefer to stay away from duplicated enum values. Some linters, such as ESLint, provide rules that disallows duplicates like this.

Reverse mapping

Another feature of numeric enums in TypeScript is that they get a reverse mapping from the value back to the member name. This means that we can see the identifier of the member using the value along with a square-bracket notation on the enum itself, like this:

```
console.log(Fruit[5]); // Apple
```

This can be useful in debugging scenarios to better determine which enum member was in use at a particular time.

Exhaustiveness and the never type

Earlier in the book, when we looked at the **never** type, I mentioned that the **never** type is frequently used to make sure a switch statement is exhaustive, that is, that it checks all possible cases.

I want to just return to this subject briefly in order to show a concrete example of this technique in practice, and the **determinePortionSize** example function that we saw earlier is a great place to do that.

First of all, let's add a new function to handle unknown enum members:

```
function handleUnknownMember(member: never): never {
  throw new Error('Unhandled enum member: ' + Fruit[member]);
}
```

We add a new function called **handleUnknownMember** which accepts a single parameter called **member**, which is of the type **never**. We can also specify the return type of the function by adding a colon directly after the closing bracket of the function's parameter list, followed by the type the function will return.

In this case, the function has a return type of **never**. Only functions that don't have a reachable endpoint, that is, they never return a value, can have a return type of **never**.

Inside the function, we can throw a new error with a simple message which shows the unhandled member's identifier as part of the error message.

Note that we can use reverse mapping to get the member's identifier rather than using the member's value, which in this case is just a number.

Now back inside the **determinePortionSize** function, we can add a **default** case to the existing **switch** statement:

```
function determinePortionSize(fruit: Fruit) {
  switch (fruit) {
    case Fruit.Apple:
      return 1;
    case Fruit.Blackberry:
      return 10;
    case Fruit.Melon:
      return 0.5;
    default:
      handleUnknownMember(fruit);
  }
}
```

The **default** case calls the new **handleUnknownMember** function we just added, passing it the **fruit** argument which will be passed to the **determinePortionSize** function when it gets invoked.

So, you may be wondering what the point of this is. What we've done here is implement protection against other developers (or ourselves at some future point once we've forgotten all about this code) adding new members to the **Fruit** enum and not adding cases to handle those members inside the **determinePortionSize** function.

Go ahead and try it, update the **Fruit** enum by adding a new member, like this for example:

```
enum Fruit {
  Apple = 5,
  Blackberry = 6,
  Melon = 7,
  Banana = 8,
};
```

Here, we've added a new member called **Banana** with the value **8**.

As soon as we add the new member, we should see an error in the editor where we invoke the **handleUnknownMember** function, like this:

```
(parameter) fruit: Fruit.Banana
Argument of type 'Fruit' is not
assignable to parameter of type
'never'. ts(2345)
```

Figure 5.9: *Unknown member error in Visual Studio Code*

What the error is telling us is that the new member is going to cause the **fruit** argument to fall into the default case in the **switch** statement, which will cause it to be cast to the **never** type when it is passed to the **handleUnknownMember** function, and as nothing can be assigned to **never**, this causes the error that we see.

This is already low-level protection, as the error will stop us from compiling the code, however, we can do better. If we cast the **fruit** argument to the **never** type in the function invocation this will satisfy the compiler and we will be able to compile the code to JavaScript and see it in a browser:

```
handleUnknownMember(fruit as never);
```

So now, we'll be able to compile the code, and if we run the compiled JavaScript in a browser, we'll see a much more useful error:

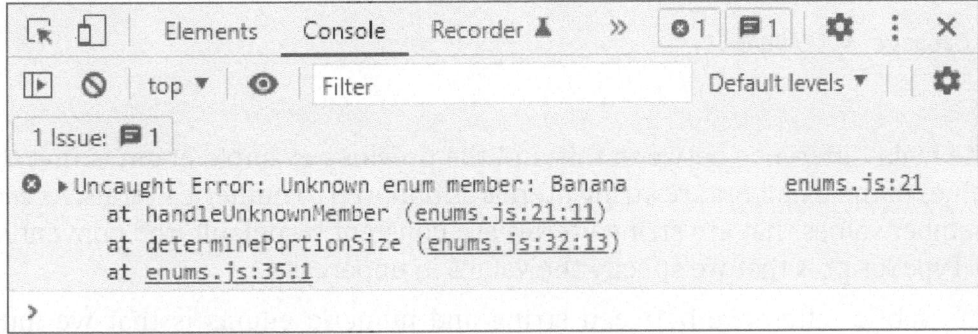

Figure 5.10: *Unknown enum error in the Chrome developer tools console*

This is more useful than TypeScript's esoteric message, because we get full information about the error, like the name of the enum member, and where in the code the error was thrown, which could be critical for debugging purposes. To fix the error, we can just add a case for the new enum member in the **determinePortionSize** function, perhaps like this:

```
case Fruit.Banana:

    return 1;
```

If we recompile the code and try again, the error in the browser will go away, because we are again handling all of the enum members. This is a great metaphor for the kinds of benefits that TypeScript brings – added safety when adding code to an existing application.

NOTE: Unlike types, enums are not removed in the compiled JavaScript, they are converted into objects instead.

String enums

As well as numerical enums, TypeScript also allows us to define string enums, where the values of each of the members are set to string literals instead of numeric literals, like in this example:

```
enum Vegetables {
  Pea = 'PEA',
  Potato = 'POTATO',
  Cabbage = 'CABBAGE',
};
```

The main difference between this and the previous example enum is that the values of the members are string literals as opposed to numeric literals. As **enum** member values that are string literals are constant by default, the convention in TypeScript is that we specify the values in uppercase.

One subtle difference between string and numeric enums is that we must specify values for all members in the enum.

For example, this would be illegal in TypeScript:

```
enum Vegetables {
  Pea = 'PEA',
  Potato = 'POTATO',
  Cabbage,
};
```

Indeed, the preceding code generates the following error in the editor:

```
(enum member) Vegetables.Cabbage
Enum member must have initializer. ts(1061)
```

Figure 5.11: *Enum member must have an initializer error in Visual Studio Code*

Another subtle difference between string and numerical enums is that with string enums if we set the type of a parameter to an enum when we invoke that function, we can't pass a string literal that matches one of the enum members like we can pass a plain number with numeric enums.

For example, the following code will generate an error:

```
function peelVegetable(vegetable: Vegetables) {
  // do something
}
peelVegetable('Potato'); // Error
```

Here, instead of passing the enum member in the format **Vegetables.Potato**, we instead pass the string literal **'Potato'**. This code will result in the error:

```
Argument of type '"Potato"' is
not assignable to parameter of
type 'Vegetables'. ts(2345)
```

Figure 5.12: *Argument is not an assignable error in Visual Studio Code*

To avoid this error, we must use an enum member explicitly when invoking the function, like this for example:

```
peelVegetable(Vegetables.Potato); // Fine
```

You should note that reverse mappings are not supported with string enums, and also that we cannot use the value of one string enum member as the value of another string member, so the following example is invalid TypeScript:

```
enum Tubers {
  Parsnip = 'Parsnip',
  Potato = Vegetables.Potato,
};
```

In string enums, this is considered a computed member, and computed members are not allowed in string enums, so this will generate the following error:

```
enum Vegetables

Computed values are not permitted in an
enum with string valued members. ts(2553)
```

Figure 5.13: *Computed values not permitted error in Visual Studio Code*

The main benefit of using string enums as opposed to numeric enums is mainly in debugging – it's far easier to know which enum member is in use when logging string enums to the console or sending them off to some back-end monitoring API.

Don't forget, however, that the reverse mapping feature of numeric enums can also provide a better debugging experience if numeric enums are strictly required and for some reason, we are not able to use a string enum.

Heterogeneous enums

TypeScript also supports heterogeneous enums, that is, enums where the member values are strings numbers, like this:

```
enum Vegetables {

  Pea = 'PEA',

  Potato = 'POTATO',

  Cabbage = 0,

};
```

While technically valid, and unlikely to cause any issues, there is no real benefit to mixing member value types in this way. Interestingly, if we do use a numeric value for a later member, TypeScript's automatic incrementing will kick in again for any sequential uninitialized members.

So, if we change the **Vegetables** enum to this:

```
enum Vegetables {

  Pea = 'PEA',

  Potato = 0,

  Cabbage,

};
```

In this case, the value of the uninitialized member **Cabbage** will automatically be set to 1 because we explicitly gave the preceding member a numeric value, which starts up the automatic incrementing.

If we revert to another string value for one of the members later, this will then stop the automatic incrementation for uninitialized members once again.

Consider the following code for example:

```
enum Vegetables {
  Pea = 'PEA',
  Potato = 0,
  Cabbage,
  Corn = 'CORN',
  Parsnip = 5,
  Spinach,
}
```

In this code snippet, after the member **Potato**, the automatic incrementing begins and assigns the value **1** to **Cabbage**. The automatic incrementing is then disabled for subsequent members when we assign a string value to the **Corn** member.

To restart the incrementing after this, we just need to assign a numeric value to a member, as we do with the member **Parsnip**. As **Spinach** is then uninitialized, it will then automatically be given the value **6**.

As you can see, the number we use does not need to be contiguous with the last numeric literal, we just need to assign any number as the initializer of a member, and it will be incremented automatically by one for any following contiguous members that are uninitialized.

As mentioned before, there is no real reason to mix numeric and string members in the same enum, so this is something you aren't likely to encounter when working on commercial applications. Consider this section a discussion on an interesting part of the language to be aware of as opposed to something that you'll want to use on a regular basis.

One final point to note about heterogenous enums is that reverse mappings will work for numerical members, but not for string members.

Computed and constant enums

All of the previous examples that we have looked at so far have involved enums with constant values – that is, values that are known at compile time. However, in TypeScript, we can also make use of computed enums, where the value is not known at compile time, only at runtime.

A member value that is set to the value returned by a function will be considered computed:

```
enum TropicalFruit {

  Mango,

  Papaya,

  Melon = Fruit.Melon,

  PassionFruit = returnTen(),

};

function returnTen() { return 10 }
```

In this case, both **Melon** and **PassionFruit** will be considered computed members.

If we try to use the member of another enum as the value of another enum member with string enums. TypeScript will see that member as computed.

For example, if we try to do that by creating a new **Vegetables2** string enum and using one of the members of the **Vegetables** string enum, like this:

```
enum Vegetables2 {

  Onion = ‘Onion’,

  Kale = Vegetables.Cabbage,

}
```

In this case, older versions of TypeScript (prior to version 5) will show an error warning that computed values may not be used with enums that have string members:

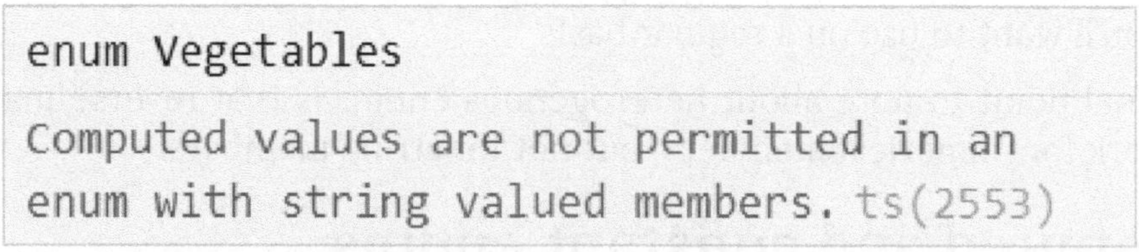

```
enum Vegetables

Computed values are not permitted in an
enum with string valued members. ts(2553)
```

Figure 5.14: *Computed values not permitted with string enums error*

Any expression that is not considered constant, such as those cases that we have looked at already, will be considered computed.

Note that this is no longer an error in TypeScript versions 5 and above.

Literal enums

As well as being constant, if all members in an enum are numeric (including negative number) or string literals, the enum is considered a literal enum. With literal enums the members themselves effectively become types. This means that we can specify that a value must be a specific enum member rather than just saying that the value must be one of the members.

For example, consider the following code:

```
interface Legume {
  vegetable: Vegetables.Pea;
};
interface Tuber {
  vegetable: Vegetables.Potato;
};
```

We can create two interfaces, one called **`Legume`** and one called **`Tuber`**, each has a member called **`vegetable`**. In the **`Legume`** interface this is specifically set to **`Vegetables.Pea`**, whereas in the **`Tuber`** interface, this member is set specifically to **`Vegetables.Potato`**.

This means that when we create objects that conform to one of these types, the **`vegetable`** property of the object must be the correct specific member of the **`Vegetable`** enum.

For example, if we try to set the **`vegetable`** property of a **`Tuber`** object to **`Vegetables.Pea`**, like this:

```
const myTuber: Tuber = {
  vegetable: Vegetables.Pea,
};
```

In that case we will see the following error in the editor:

```
(property) Tuber.vegetable: Vegetables.Potato

Type 'Vegetables.Pea' is not assignable to type
'Vegetables.Potato'. ts(2322)
enums.ts(73, 3): The expected type comes from
property 'vegetable' which is declared here on
type 'Tuber'
```

Figure 5.15: *Literal member-type enforcement error in Visual Studio Code*

Another aspect of literal enums is that they can be considered as if they were a union of the members within the enum. For this reason, they are also referred to as union enums. This is helpful because TypeScript will warn us if we try to compare members incorrectly.

For example, we may have a function to "grow" a vegetable, and we may wish to handle **`Vegetables.Potato`** differently than **`Vegetable.Pea`** or **`Vegetable.Cabbage`**. We may use an **`if`** statement to differentiate between these two groups, perhaps something like this:

```
function grow(seed: Vegetables) {

  if (seed !== Vegetables.Pea || seed !== Vegetables.Cabbage) {

    // plant Potato

  }

}
```

In this case, we've used the logical OR operator here when we should have used the logical AND operator; the comparison doesn't make sense. If **`seed`** is not equal to **`Vegetables.Pea`** then the **`if`** statement will short-circuit and the OR condition will not be evaluated.

But if **`seed`** is equal to **`Vegetables.Pea`** the OR condition will be evaluated and will always return **`true`** because if **`seed`** is equal to **`Vegetables.Pea`**, it can't also be equal to **`Vegetables.Cabbage`**, because they are different types.

TypeScript will warn us of this issue with the following error in the editor:

```
enum Vegetables

This condition will always return 'true' since
the types 'Vegetables.Pea' and
'Vegetables.Cabbage' have no overlap. ts(2367)
```

Figure 5.16: *No overlap between different types*

When TypeScript says that the two types have no overlap, it is basically saying that these are distinct types and something cannot be of both types. **`Vegetables`** is effectively the union type **`PEA | POTATO | CABBAGE`** therefore cannot be both **`PEA`** *and* **`CABBAGE`**.

Inlining enums

As we learned earlier in this section, enums exist at runtime, after compilation, in the form of objects. However, we can use a slightly different form of enum where the values of enum members are inlined in the places where the enum is used. In this case, the enums will not exist at run time.

Using this form of an enum can help to reduce the amount of compiled code that is output, however, we can only use this form of enum when all of the enum's members are constant values. Let's look at a basic example. Consider the following code:

```
enum Tools {
  Hammer,
  Drill,
};

function doItYourself(tool: Tools) {
  if (tool === Tools.Hammer) {
    console.log('Hammer time');
  }
}
```

```
doItYourself(Tools.Hammer); // Hammer time
```

We have a simple numeric enum called **`Tools`** with two members, **`Hammer`** and **`Drill`**, which have the values **`0`** and **`1`** respectively. We then define a function called **`doItYourself`** which takes a parameter with the type set to the enum.

Inside the function, we check whether the argument passed to the function is **`Tools.Hammer`** and if it is, we log a simple message to the console.

Lastly, we invoke the function, passing it **`Tools.Hammer`** as an argument.

This code will be compiled by TypeScript to this:

```
var Tools;
(function (Tools) {
    Tools[Tools["Hammer"] = 0] = "Hammer";
    Tools[Tools["Drill"] = 1] = "Drill";
})(Tools || (Tools = {}));
function doItYourself(tool) {
    if (tool === Tools.Hammer) {
        console.log('Hammer time');
    }
}
doItYourself(Tools.Hammer); // Hammer time
```

`Tools` is an object in the resulting code with the properties **`Hammer`** and **`Drill`**. These properties will have the values **`0`** and **`1`** respectively in the compiled object.

We can therefore use the object in comparisons, as inside the **`doItYourself`** function, and log the values to the console.

To inline the **`Tools`** enum, we prefix the declaration with **`const`**, like this:

```
const enum Tools {
  Hammer,
  Drill,
}
```

The rest of the example code remains the same.

Now, the compiled output will look like this:

```
function doItYourself(tool) {
    if (tool === 0 /* Tools.Hammer */) {
        console.log('Hammer time');
    }
}
doItYourself(0 /* Tools.Hammer */); // Hammer time
```

This time there is no **Tools** object - the values of the members are put in the places where the object references were previously, that is, in the **if** comparison and as an argument to the **doItYoutself** function invocation. There is noticeably less code generated in this case.

Note that TypeScript will helpfully put a comment at each place where an enum member is inlined, showing the identifier of the member that was inlined.

Note also that we can inline string enums as well. The only requirement for inlining is that the values of the enum are constant - we cannot inline computed enum members as the compiler doesn't know what the values will be when it compiles the TypeScript to JavaScript.

Using the keyof operator

The **keyof** type operator works slightly differently than usual when it comes to enums. For example, if we want to get the member names of the **Fruit** enum, we might think to use the **keyof** operator, perhaps like this:

```
type FruitKeys = keyof Fruit;
const fruits: FruitKeys = 'Apple';
```

In this case, the **FruitKeys** type will be a union type consisting of the members of the prototype of the value of the members of **Fruit**. These members are numbers, so the resulting union type consists of the methods from the **Number** prototype:

```
"toString" | "toFixed" | "toExponential" | "toPrecision" | "valueOf" |
"toLocaleString"
```

This will therefore result in an error on the **`fruits`** variable, because the string **`Apple`**, which we are trying to set as the value of the **`fruits`** variable, doesn't correspond to one of the union members above.

Instead, the **`keyof`** operator should be used in conjunction with the **`typeof`** operator to create a union type of the actual identifiers for an enum's members:

```
type FruitKeys = keyof typeof Fruit;

const fruits: FruitKeys = 'Apple';
```

Now there will be no error because the **`FruitKeys`** type will consist of the union of the enum's member values:

```
"Apple" | "Blackberry" | "Melon"
```

This technique can be useful to avoid having to create the union type manually and potentially forgetting to add one of the enum's members, or failing to update it if the enum is updated at some future point.

Conclusion

In this chapter, we looked at a couple of very commonly used TypeScript features, as well as a not-so-commonly used feature. These were interfaces and enums, and namespaces respectively.

Interfaces allow us to describe what the shape of an object should be; the properties and methods it should have, and the types or return types and parameter types of those properties and methods. Using them allows us to create a blueprint for what objects of this type should look like. We learned how to define interfaces, how to merge them, and how to extend them.

We learned that namespaces are a simple way to group related functionality together under a common identifier and that doing so can help us to avoid naming collisions when we have many similar things that we need to name. While not as commonly used as interfaces or enums, they do still have a place in TypeScript.

We also looked deeply at enums in TypeScript as these are commonly found in commercial-grade applications. Enums allow us to define an enumerated list of constant or computed string or numeric enums. When all members are constant, we learned that we can also reduce the size of our compiled files if necessary, by inlining them at usage sites.

We also saw a great example of exhaustiveness in `switch` statements to add protection against a developer adding a new member to an enum, but forgetting to handle it, and saw how to leverage the `never` type to produce a useful error message

In the next chapter, let's move on to look at objects and arrays in TypeScript.

References

- **https://www.typescriptlang.org/docs/handbook**
- **https://en.wikipedia.org/wiki/Enumerated_type**
- **https://2ality.com/2020/01/typescript-enums.html**

CHAPTER 6

Objects, Arrays, and Tuples in TypeScript

Introduction

Objects and arrays are some of the most commonly used data structures in JavaScript and will therefore be a significant part of all but the simplest web applications. As you've almost certainly heard before, almost everything in JavaScript is an object of some type, so we'll almost always be using them in one way or another.

We'll therefore take a good look at object types, building on what we learned about interfaces and type aliases earlier in the book in order to define types for custom objects to specify which properties objects of this type should have, whether they are read-only or optional, and what types of their values should have.

TypeScript also has full support for array types and allows us to declare them in two distinct ways, both of which we'll look at in depth. It also supports tuples, which are a special type of array which have a fixed number of elements of a specific type, in a specific sequence. We'll also be covering these.

Structure

In this chapter, we will cover the following topics:

- Arrays
- Array type inference
- Read-only arrays
- Tuples

- Optional elements
- Rest elements
- Read-only tuples
- Object types
- Property modifiers
- Index signatures
- Intersections
- Generic objects
- Readonly utility type

Arrays

As we saw briefly in the previous chapter, an array can be specified as a type using the type of the members that will be stored in the array, followed by a pair of square brackets, like this:

```
const strings: string[] = [];
```

In this case, the **strings** variable will be an array containing elements of the type **string**. This also works for other TypeScript entities like enums:

```
enum Status {
  Waiting,
  Complete,
}
const statuses: Status[] = [Status.Waiting];
```

In this case, **statuses** is an array of values that match one of the **Status** enum's members.

Or interfaces:

```
interface Process {
  name: string,
  status: Status,
}
const processes: Process[] = [{ name: 'Process 1', status: Status.Waiting }];
```

Here, **processes** is an array of objects that conform to the **Process** interface.

This is the literal form for specifying an array type, a sort of shorthand. As well as this form, there is also an alternative form known as generic syntax that we can use to provide an array type, which looks like this:

```
const strings: Array<string> = [];
```

This time we use the **Array** generic type followed by the type of member the array will contain, in this case, **string**, inside a pair of angle brackets.

TypeScript has a feature called generics, which are sort of like variables for types - we'll be looking at these in much more detail later in the book. For now, just remember that this is the generic form of specifying an array.

The generic syntax is directly equivalent to the literal syntax, there is almost no difference between the two, except when using the **readonly** access modifier to create a read-only array, which we'll be looking at shortly.

We can also say that a value will be of a mixed-type array. For example, to specify an array whose members may be either strings or numbers, we could do this:

```
const codes: (string | number)[] = [1, '2'];
```

In this case, we say that the **codes** variable is an array of the union type **string | number**. This has no impact on the number of elements the array can contain or the order of individual elements – we could specify any number of strings or numbers in any order, they just have to be either numbers or strings.

Note that the parentheses are needed around the union type in this example, otherwise, the compiler would think we were specifying a string, or a number array, like this: **string | number[]**, rather than the intended **string[] | number[]**.

The preceding example was the literal format; we can also use the generic format to specify a mixed-type array, for example:

```
const codes: Array<string|number> = [1, '2'];
```

Again, this is exactly equivalent to the literal form.

Array type inference

If we don't annotate an array with type information, TypeScript can infer the array type based on how it is declared and initialized. For example:

```
const ids = [‘1A’, ‘1B’]; // string[]
```

The array **ids** will be correctly inferred as **string[]** by TypeScript. This works for mixed arrays also:

```
const altIds = [1, ‘1a’]; // (string|number)[]
```

However, for types we have defined ourselves, it is better to explicitly declare the type to ensure that the correct type is used.

For example, using the same **Process** interface that we saw previously, consider the following code:

```
interface Process {

  name: string,

  status: Status,

}

const processes = [

  { name: ‘Process 1’, status: Status.Waiting }

]; // Process[]??
```

In this case, we would perhaps expect the compiler to infer **Process[]** at the type of the **processes** variable, but this is not the case. Instead, the type would be inferred as an array of object literals containing **name** and **status** properties:

```
const processes: {
    name: string;
    status: Status;
}[]
```

Figure 6.1: *How TypeScript sees the unannotated variable*

In this case, it is better to explicitly type the variable ourselves to give TypeScript, as well as anyone else reading our code, a better idea of what's going on:

```
const processes: Process[] = [
  { name: 'Process', status: Status.Waiting }
]; // Process[]
```

In this case, there is no ambiguity, the type is explicitly **`Process[]`**.

Read-only arrays

TypeScript allows us to define arrays that are read-only and cannot be modified in any way by using the **`readonly`** access modifier, like this:

```
const unmodifiable: readonly string[] = ['cannot be changed'];
```

Any operations that mutate the array, like **`push`**, **`pop`**, or **`splice`**, are now prohibited on the array in the **`unmodifiable`** variable.

For example, if we try to push a new element to the array, like this:

```
unmodifiable.push('oops'); // error
```

Then we'll see this error:

```
any
Property 'push' does not exist on type
'readonly string[]'. ts(2339)
```

Figure 6.2: *Error in Visual Studio Code when mutating a read-only array*

As well as the array being read-only, the elements within the array also become read-only, so we cannot modify any of the existing items either:

```
unmodifiable[0] = 'cannot do it'; // error
```

This would incur the following error:

```
const unmodifiable: readonly string[]
Index signature in type 'readonly string[]' only
permits reading. ts(2542)
```

Figure 6.3: *Error in Visual Studio Code when trying to change a read-only element*

When using the **readonly** modifier, we must use the literal syntax. If we try to use the generic format, like this for example:

```
const unmodifiable: readonly Array<string> = ['cannot be changed'];
```

Then we'll see a different error in the editor:

```
'readonly' type modifier is only
permitted on array and tuple literal
types. ts(1354)
```

Figure 6.4: *Modifier only permitted on literal types error in Visual Studio Code*

However, we can use the **ReadonlyArray** type instead to use the generic syntax, like this:

```
const unmodifiable2: ReadonlyArray<string> = ['immutable'];
```

This is exactly equivalent to using the literal syntax.

Aside from these features, arrays are used in the same way in TypeScript as they are in regular JavaScript, and support all of the same methods and features that we've come to know and love.

Tuples

In TypeScript, a tuple is a special type of array with a specific number of elements of a specific type, in a specific order. The syntax to declare a tuple is similar to that of declaring an array, except that we don't specify a type before the set of square brackets.

Instead, inside the square brackets, we specify the element types the array should contain, in the order that they should appear, like this:

```
const category: [number, string, boolean] = [1, '1A', true];
```

In this case, **category** is a tuple – an array with exactly three elements where the first element is of the type **number**, the second element is of the type **string**, and the third and final element is of the type **boolean**.

Note that a tuple can have any number of elements, we are not restricted to two, three, or any other arbitrary limit.

If we try to update any of the tuple's existing elements to the wrong type, like this for example:

```
category[0] = '1';
```

Then we will see an error warning us that we are not using the correct type:

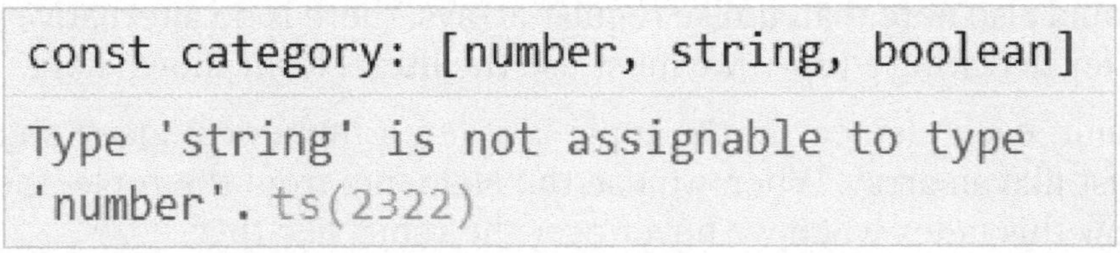

```
const category: [number, string, boolean]
Type 'string' is not assignable to type
'number'. ts(2322)
```

Figure 6.5: *Wrong type error in Visual Studio Code*

If we try to add a new element to the array using square-bracket notation, like this for example:

```
category[3] = false; // error
```

Then we'll see this error:

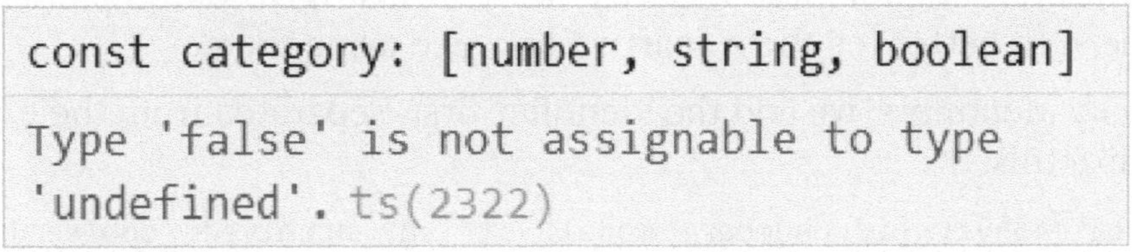

```
const category: [number, string, boolean]
Type 'false' is not assignable to type
'undefined'. ts(2322)
```

Figure 6.6: *Cannot assign to an undefined error in Visual Studio Code*

Additionally, tuples are given a numeric literal matching the number of types we provide as their **length** property, so we also cannot modify the length directly:

```
category.length = 4;
```

Doing this will cause the editor to show this error:

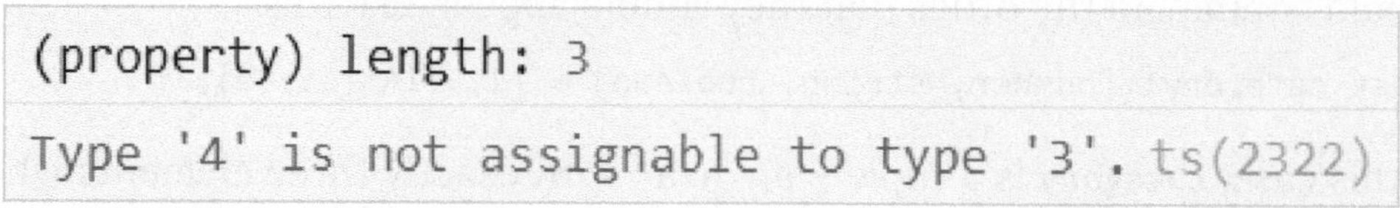

```
(property) length: 3
Type '4' is not assignable to type '3'. ts(2322)
```

Figure 6.7: *Cannot assign to a literal type error in Visual Studio Code*

However, we are not prevented from changing the tuple's elements using array methods like **push** for example:

```
category.push(1); // works
```

In this case, the push method will see the tuple as a regular array in which any of the elements may be of the type **number**, **string**, or **boolean**, as if we had declared it like this: **(number | string | boolean)[]**.

You should also note that, unlike regular arrays, there is no alternative generic syntax for declaring a tuple, we must use the literal form shown here.

By default, each element in the tuple is given a numerical index starting at zero, just like an array. When we use the elements from the tuple, the editor will show this index when we hover over the value, like this:

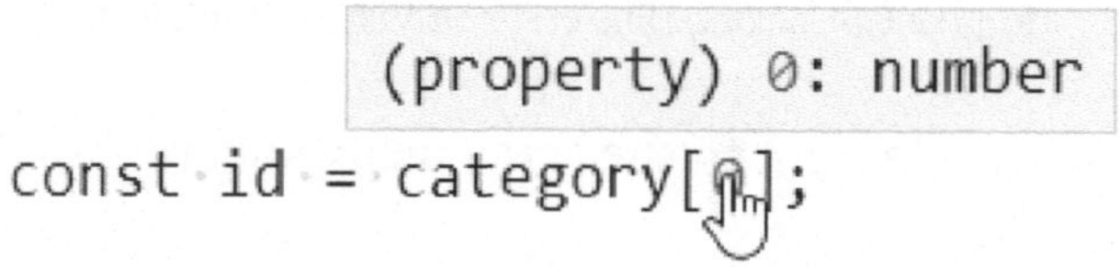

```
(property) 0: number
const id = category[0];
```

Figure 6.8: *Tooltip showing tuple index and type in Visual Studio Code*

This is useful, but for better clarity, we can also give our tuple elements identifiers, to better tell them apart when we're using them.

To specify identifiers, we add the identifier first, separated from the type by a colon, like this:

```
const category2: [id: number, model: string, archived: boolean] = [1,
'1A', true];
```

Now when we use the elements from the **category2** tuple and hover over them, the editor will show us the full identifier for the element:

```
(property) 0: number (id)
const id = category2[0];
```

***Figure 6.9**: Tooltip showing tuple index, type, and identifier in Visual Studio Code*

We still see the index and the type, but we will also see the identifier in brackets at the end of the tooltip, so this makes it much easier to ensure we are working with the intended element.

Optional elements in tuples

We can specify that an element in the tuple is optional by adding a question mark directly after the element type:

```
const category3: [number, string, boolean?] = [1, '1A', true];
```

This time, the element of type **boolean** at index 2 in the **category3** tuple will be optional.

Because the element is now optional, and may or may not be present, TypeScript will see the tuple as if we had declared it like this:

[number, string, boolean|undefined].

The element at index 2 is now the union type **boolean | undefined.**

Rest elements in tuples

Rest elements are used to say that a specific type may occur any number of times, including zero times. We define a rest element using the spread operator, like this:

```
let category4: [number, ...string[], boolean];
```

The element at index 2 now has the spread operator in front of it, and a pair of square brackets following it. We are telling the compiler that this tuple will contain a **number**, followed by zero or more **string** elements, and end with a **boolean**.

This means that values of this type could look like this:

```
category4 = [1, '1A', '1B', '1C', true];
```

Or equally, like this:

```
category4 = [1, true];
```

Both are completely valid.

NOTE: Optional elements cannot follow the rest elements in tuples.

Read-only tuples

Just like with arrays, we can also mark tuples as read-only using the **`readonly`** modifier. The syntax for this is as follows:

```
let category5: readonly [number, string, boolean] = [1, '1A', true];
```

The **`readonly`** access modifier should appear before the tuple's opening square bracket. Now, none of the tuple's elements may be assigned individually, and we cannot use array methods like **`push`** to add new elements.

For example, if we try to assign to the first element in the tuple, like this:

```
category5[0] = 5; // error
```

Then, we'll see an error like this in the editor:

```
(property) 0: number

Cannot assign to '0' because it
is a read-only property. ts(2540)
```

Figure 6.10: *Cannot assign to read-only property error in Visual Studio Code*

Object types

Objects are the beating heart of our front-end applications and will be commonly used in everything from the simplest standalone projects to the largest commercial applications. Objects are represented in TypeScript as object types:

```
let car: { doors: number, make: string };
```

In this case, we created a **car** variable and specified an anonymous object type with two properties **doors**, which should be a **number**, and **make**, which should be a **string**. We are now free to assign an object to the **car** variable which conforms to the object type we specified, like this:

```
car = { doors: 5, make: 'Tesla' };
```

Objects using this type must specify all the properties of the type, and only the properties of the type. If we skip a property that is specified in the type definition, like this:

```
car = { doors: 5 }; // error
```

Then, we'll see this error:

```
let car: {
    doors: number;
    make: string;
}

Property 'make' is missing in type '{
doors: number; }' but required in type '{
doors: number; make: string; }'. ts(2741)

objects.ts(1, 27): 'make' is declared
here.
```

Figure 6.11: *Missing property error in Visual Studio Code*

In this case, Visual Studio Code will highlight the object as being the source of the error. On the other hand, if we add a property that is not specified by the object type, like this:

```
car = { doors: 5, make: 'Tesla', oops: 'whoops' }; // error
```

Then, we'll see an error like this instead:

```
(property) oops: string
Type '{ doors: number; make: string;
oops: string; }' is not assignable to
type '{ doors: number; make: string; }'.
  Object literal may only specify known
properties, and 'oops' does not exist in
type '{ doors: number; make: string;
}'. ts(2322)
```

Figure 6.12: *Unknown property error in Visual Studio Code*

This time Visual Studio Code will highlight the extraneous property inside the object.

If we try to set an allowed property to the wrong type of value, like this:

```
car = { doors: 5, make: 2 }; // error
```

We'll also see an error, this time as follows:

```
(property) make: string
Type 'number' is not assignable to type
'string'. ts(2322)
objects.ts(1, 27): The expected type comes from
property 'make' which is declared here on type '{
doors: number; make: string; }'
```

Figure 6.13: *Wrong property type error in Visual Studio Code*

Anonymous object types, like the one we just used, are convenient and flexible in that we can use them anywhere that it is legal to provide type information – variable declarations, function parameters, and function return types, for example, and very often, the type information will be near the site at which it is used which can be helpful for readability.

But they cannot be shared or reused anywhere else, limiting their usefulness in larger applications. For maximum reusability, instead of using anonymous object types, we can use an interface or a type alias to describe the object type instead.

For example, we can convert our previous example to use an **interface** instead:

```
interface Car {

  doors: number;

  make: string;

};

const car2: Car = { doors: 3, make: 'Porsche' };
```

This is functionally equivalent to the anonymous type definition but has the added bonus that we can reuse the **Car** interface in other places. Don't forget, a type definition using the **type** keyword instead of **interface** would work equally as well here.

As well as specifying properties, we can also specify methods that the object should have. In this case, when adding the type, we should specify the signature of the method – the parameters it accepts and its return type:

```
let car: { drive: (arg0: string) => void };
```

Here we have specified that the type for this variable is an object containing a single method called **drive**. This method accepts a single parameter which should be of the type string. I've called this parameter **arg0** because it's the first argument and arguments have zero-based indexes, but this choice is entirely arbitrary; you can call the parameter(s) in a type definition whatever you deem appropriate.

The identifier we give in the signature here does not restrict the name of the parameter in the actual implementation, so giving the parameter an actual name here might suggest that the name of the parameter is mandatory. Therefore we will take this approach and use a general parameter name instead.

We've specified the return type as **void** here, but this is a bit of a special case. Usually, **void** is used to signal that a function doesn't return a value, but in JavaScript, a function without an explicit return statement still returns the value **undefined**.

When we specify **void** as a return type for a method in this way, we mean that it doesn't have a useful return, not that the function literally doesn't have a return type at all.

When we come to declare the value of the **car** variable this time, we must add a method that matches the signature we specified in the type:

```
car = {
  drive: (direction: string) => {
    // drive in the direction
  },
};
```

We assign an object to the **car** variable, and this object has a property called **drive**, the value of which is an arrow function that takes a single **string** parameter.

As mentioned earlier, the signature specified **arg0** as the first parameter, but here we are free to call that parameter what we want, in this case, **direction**. It's not important what the parameter is called, only that the function receives a single parameter, and that the parameter is of the type **string**.

If we try to pass the function a parameter of a different type, or we try to pass a different number of parameters, we'll see an error in the editor.

One point to note is that even though we have specified the return type of the **drive** method as **void**, technically we could still return a value from it if we wanted to. This is allowed because of the flexibility associated with **void** as a function return type – we are free to return any type of value and the compiler won't complain about the return statement, but it will cause an error if we try to use the return value of a function or method marked as **void**.

For example, the following code will produce an error:

```
const result = car.drive('forward');
if (result) {
  // error
}
```

In this case, the editor will highlight the use of result in the if statement and show the following error:

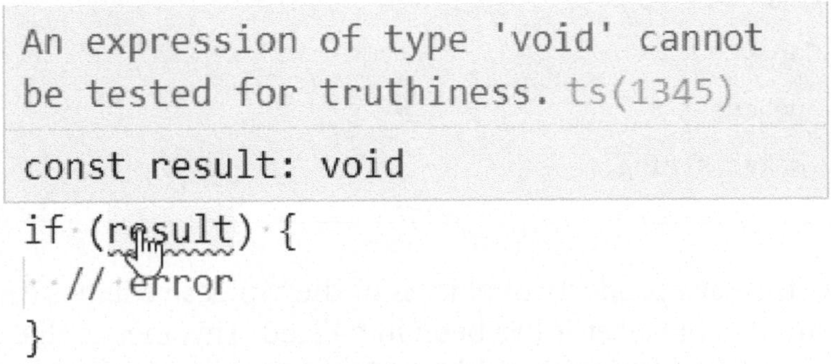

```
An expression of type 'void' cannot
be tested for truthiness. ts(1345)

const result: void

if (result) {
  // error
}
```

Figure 6.14: *Void cannot be tested for truthiness error in Visual Studio Code*

If we do specify a return type in the method signature, then the method in the implementation has to return that type.

We haven't covered functions in TypeScript yet so don't worry too much about this last example, the takeaway here is that we can add method signatures to object types.

Property modifiers

Like with arrays and tuples, we can easily make object type properties optional or read-only.

To specify that an object property is optional, we add a question mark directly after the property identifier, like this:

```
interface Car {
  doors?: number;
  make: string;
}
```

Now, objects of the type `Car` may or may not have a `doors` property. TypeScript will see the `doors` property type as if we had used the union type `number | undefined`.

Depending on the strictness of our configuration, this will usually mean that we will need to be thorough and check for `undefined` values before attempting to use any optional properties.

In addition to optional properties, we can also specify that a property should be read-only. We do this by prefixing the **readonly** modifier before the property name, like this:

```
interface Car {

  doors?: number;

  readonly make: string;

};
```

In this case, the **make** property of objects of the type **Car** will be read-only and will not be modifiable after it has been initialized. This means that we cannot assign a new value to the property, but it is possible to modify the property in some ways; if the property type is an array, we can add new items to that array. This is in contrast to the behavior of read-only arrays.

You should note that optional properties may also be read-only.

Index signatures

We saw index signatures briefly in the last chapter when we looked at interfaces. Let's just cover them again here.

An index signature is used when we want to specify that a property in an object type may have any key and a specific type of value. Like this, for example:

```
interface Car {

  [prop: string]: string | boolean;

};
```

The index signature is the part in square brackets. It has an identifier, followed by the familiar colon and type description. In this case, we need to use a union type if we want the properties of the object to be one of the multiple types, which for the purpose of this example we do.

Now we can create objects of the type **Car** which can have any named properties, as long as those properties are of the type **string** or **boolean**, like this for example:

```
const car3: Car = { make: 'Lotus', spoiler: true };
```

We can also provide multiple index signatures, like this:

```
interface Car {
  [prop: string]: string | boolean | number;
  [id: number]: number;
};
```

Now objects of the type **Car** may specify numerical keys as well as string keys, but we restrict the type of these properties to numbers in this example.

Note that we also need to add the type of the new **id** index signature to the union of the existing **prop** index signature to avoid an error in the editor.

Now we could have a **Car** object like this:

```
const car4: Car = { make: 'Lotus', 0: 168 };
```

Accessing the numerical index works as expected:

```
const topSpeedMph = car4[0]; // 168
```

Note that we must use square brackets to access or assign numerical keys, although in the background TypeScript will convert the numerical indexes to strings anyway, so we could use strings instead of numbers to access or assign to these, like **car['0']** in this case.

We can make an index signature read-only if we wish, again using the **readonly** modifier:

```
interface Car {
  [prop: string]: string | boolean | number;
  readonly [id: number]: number;
};
```

Now we will be unable to reassign the value of the property **0** once it has been initialized, so trying to do this will cause an error in the editor:

```
car4[0] = 200; // error
```

In this case, we will see this error:

```
const car4: Car
Index signature in type 'Car' only permits
reading. ts(2542)
```

Figure 6.15: *Read-only index signature error in Visual Studio Code*

Intersections

Intersections are another way of combining object types together in order to produce new object types. We can create intersections of types and interfaces using the `&` operator. Consider the following example; imagine we have an interface for `Vinyl` objects, and one for `Cd` objects:

```
interface Vinyl {
  rpm?: number;
  title: string;
};
interface Cd {
  trackNumber?: number;
  title: string;
};
```

Both interfaces have a `title` property of the type `string`, while `Vinyl` has an optional `rpm` property which is a number, and `Cd` has an optional `trackNumber` property, which is also a number.

If we wanted to combine these interfaces in order to create a new interface by extending them, we would have to define an intermediate interface, like this:

```
interface CircularMedia extends Vinyl, Cd {}
```

In this case, the new interface doesn't add any new properties, so it kind of feels a little overkill, especially if we're not interested in reusing this intermediate interface anywhere else in our code.

Using intersection, we can create a new type of object without the need for extending:

```
const album: Vinyl & Cd = {
  rpm: 45,
  title: 'Dark Side of the Moon'
};
```

In this case, we can create the intersection on the fly, without having to declare an intermediate version of the interface. Although flexible and convenient, it does mean of course that this particular intersection isn't reusable, so if this is important, we will need to define a type alias for the intersection, like this:

```
type CircularMedia = Vinyl & Cd;
```

Now we can go ahead and reuse this intersection type wherever else we need to.

As well as **`interface`** intersections, we can also create **`type`** intersections, that is, intersections of type aliases created using the **`type`** keyword, like this:

```
type mp3 = { bitrate?: number }
type mp4 = { encoding?: string }
type digitalMedia = mp3 & mp4;
```

The **`digitalMedia`** type is now a type intersection of the **`mp3`** and **`mp4`** types so values using that intersection will need to implement the required properties from each of the objects in the intersection, although that isn't an issue for this example as all of the properties involved are optional.

Generic object types

Generic object types are object types that can be used with a range of different types rather than a declaratively prescribed type.

TypeScript supports other forms of generics too, and we'll cover those in more detail in later chapters, here we'll just focus on generic object types.

Think of an array in TypeScript; arrays are generic because they can contain elements of many other types, like a string array, a numeric array, an array containing any other type, or mixed types even.

This is why arrays support both the literal and generic syntax, with the generic form appearing for a string array, for example, appearing like this:

```
Array<string>.
```

We can create generic object types that can be used in a similar way. Let's see how. Imagine we have some interfaces that represent different types of messages that might be displayed to a user of your application:

```
interface Warning {
  level: string;
  text: string;
};
interface Info {
  level: string;
  text: string;
};
```

Now, let's say that we want to display these different types of messages in a modal of some kind. We could create a bunch of different **`Modal`** interfaces for displaying the different types of messages, but if we have a lot of different types of messages, we could end up with a lot of different but very similar interfaces.

Or we could use a generic object type instead to work with any of the different types of messages:

```
interface Modal<Type> {
  message: Type;
}
```

We use the **`interface`** keyword and an identifier, **`Modal`** in this case, and then within angle brackets directly after the identifier, we supply a type parameter called **`Type`**. As this is an identifier, we don't strictly have to call it **`Type`**, but this is what is used conventionally, although it's often shortened to just **`T`**. like this: **`<T>`**.

Inside the interface, we add a property called **message** and say that its type will be whatever type the type parameter **Type** is.

We could then create some **Warning** and **Info** objects, like this perhaps:

```
const dataLoss: Warning = {
  level: 'error',
  text: 'Data may be lost, continue?',
};
const completed: Info = {
  level: 'info',
  text: 'Process complete',
};
```

Each of the two objects we create is of the types **Warning** and **Info** respectively, so each contains the required properties with values of the correct type as specified by the two example interfaces.

Finally, we could then create some **Modal** objects:

```
const dataLossModal: Modal<Warning> = { message: dataLoss };
const completedModal: Modal<Info> = { message: completed };
```

When we come to actually use the generic object type we defined, we need to pass the actual type we want to use as the type parameter between angle brackets; in the first line, we pass the **Warning** interface we created as the type, and in the second line we pass **Info**. The objects we create will need to conform to the **Modal** interface, so each has a message property containing the actual **message** object.

Thanks to generics, **Modal** is a flexible object type that can work with many other types without having to be modified each time we add a new type of message object to display in a modal, and we don't have a proliferation of very similar interfaces.

We'll come back and look at how to create generic functions that work with generic object types in the next chapter.

Note that while we have used interfaces in this example, type aliases also support generics, so the following code would also work in the same way:

```
type Modal<Type> = {
  message: Type;
};
type Warning = {
  level: string;
  text: string;
};
type Info = {
  level: string;
  text: string;
};
```

The rest of the previous example code would remain the same and the **dataLossModal** and **completedModal** objects would be declared in exactly the same way.

Readonly utility type

TypeScript provides a range of utility types to make it easier to perform some common type transformations – that is, transforming one type into another type. We'll be looking at these as a collection in more detail later in the book, but for now, we'll learn about the Readonly utility type, given that we've looked at read-only arrays and tuples, and read-only object properties.

We can use the **Readonly** utility type to create a type where all of the properties are automatically set to **readonly**. Let's say we have a simple interface called **ReadWrite**:

```
interface ReadWrite { prop: string };
```

The interface defines a single property called **prop**, which should take a **string** value. We can now initialize objects using this interface, set the **prop** property, and then later overwrite the property with a different value:

```
let writable: ReadWrite = { prop: 'init'};
writable.prop = 'can overwrite';
```

We won't see any errors in the editor here. But if we define a new type using the **Readonly** utility, we can easily make the **prop** property read-only:

```
let notWritable: Readonly<ReadWrite>;
```

We use angle brackets to pass the **Readonly** type the interface that we wish to make read-only, in this case the **ReadWrite** interface that we defined first. We'll now be able to initialize the **prop** property:

```
notWritable = { prop: 'init' };
```

But we won't be able to overwrite it later; if we try to do this for example:

```
notWritable.prop = 'nope'; // error
```

Then we'll see an error in the editor or compiler informing us that the property is read-only and cannot be modified.

Even though the **ReadWrite** interface did not specify that the **prop** property was read-only, using the **Readonly** utility type automatically created a new type in which all of the properties of the original type are read-only. If we're working with a larger interface that contains many properties, this can save us a significant amount of code that we need to write ourselves.

Conclusion

Arrays and objects are some of the most commonly used parts of JavaScript, so correspondingly, array types and object types will be some of the most common things you'll use in TypeScript.

We saw that we can use arrays or readonly array types, and that arrays have a generic syntax using angle brackets, or a short-hand literal syntax using square brackets, but that the two are functionally equivalent.

We also saw that we can use object types to specify exactly which properties an object should have, whether those properties are optional or read-only, and how to combine object types by intersecting them.

We finished by looking at generic object types which allow us to create custom object types that can work across a range of types, including those we might create ourselves, and also covered one of TypeScript's built-in utility types – the **Readonly** type.

In the next chapter, we're going to take good look at functions – another very heavily used aspect of JavaScript and something we'll want to master in TypeScript.

References

- **https://www.typescriptlang.org/docs/handbook**
- **https://www.damirscorner.com/blog/posts/20180601-ExtendingTypescriptTypeswithIntersection.html**

CHAPTER 7

Functions in TypeScript

Introduction

Functions are the general workhorses of both JavaScript and TypeScript – many of the expressions we write will be contained within functions so it's a good idea to be very familiar with them and all of their capabilities.

Functions have many features; they are callable of course but may also support use with the `new` keyword (although this is less common since the introduction of classes in ES2015), and can additionally have their own properties. In this chapter, we'll see how to support all of these features and more when working with function types.

We have used some basic functions in some of the previous examples in earlier chapters in this book, more so in the last few chapters, but in this chapter, we are going to focus exclusively on them and how they can be used in TypeScript.

Structure

In this chapter, we will look at the following topics:

- Parameter type and return type annotations
- Type Inference for functions
- Arrow functions
- Type inference for arrow functions
- Optional parameters
- Rest parameters and rest arguments

- Destructured Parameters
- Void return type
- Function type expressions
- Call signatures
- Function type interfaces
- Construct signatures
- This parameter
- Function overloads
- Generator functions
- Generic functions
- Generic function constraints

Parameter type and Return type Annotations

Let's take a moment to review the basics of the type annotations we can use with functions - parameter types and return types:

```
function sayHello(name: string): string {
  return `Hello ${name}`;
}
```

In this case, we have a function called **`sayHello`** which accepts a parameter called **`name`**, and this parameter should be of the type **`string`**. The type information for a parameter is provided after a colon immediately following the parameter name.

The return type for the function is added after a colon that follows the closing parenthesis of the parameter list, but before the opening curly bracket that denotes the function body. In this example, the function returns a **`string`**, but it could return any valid type.

Adding parameter type and return type annotations to a function, ensures the correct usage and implementation of the function. As soon as we've typed the function identifier and parentheses in the editor, a tooltip will appear showing the function's type signature – the names and types of the parameters, and the return type:

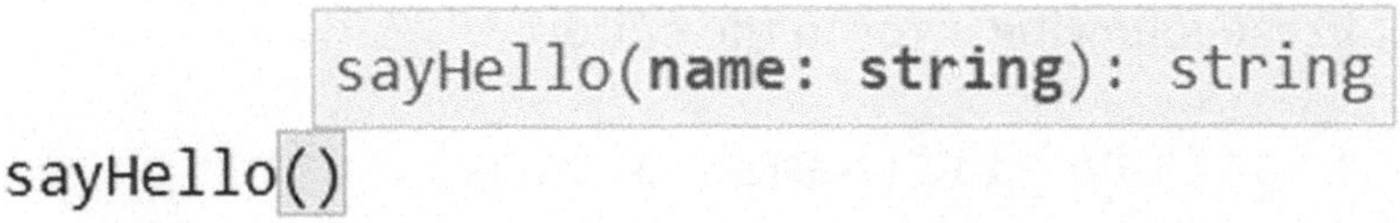

```
sayHello(name: string): string
sayHello()
```

***Figure 7.1**: Function signature tooltip in Visual Studio Code*

If we try to pass an argument with the wrong type, like passing a number to the **sayHello** function instead of a string, like this for example:

```
sayHello(123); // error
```

We will see this error in the editor:

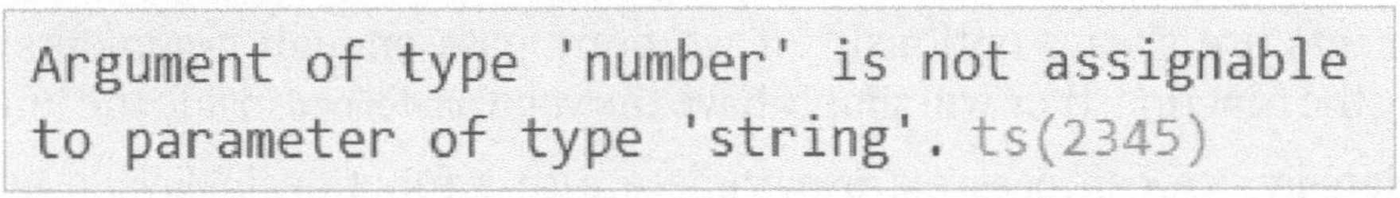

```
Argument of type 'number' is not assignable
to parameter of type 'string'. ts(2345)
```

***Figure 7.2**: Wrong parameter type error in Visual Studio Code*

As we are specifying the return type of the function, if we try to capture the return type in a variable and give that variable the wrong type, like this perhaps:

```
const myNumber: number = sayHello('oops'); // error
```

Then we'll see an error warning us that we are using the return type incorrectly – the function returns a string, but we're trying to assign the type **number**:

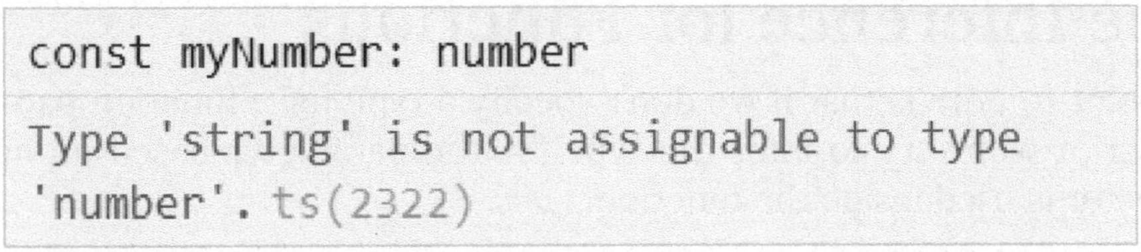

```
const myNumber: number

Type 'string' is not assignable to type
'number'. ts(2322)
```

***Figure 7.3**: String cannot be assigned to number error in Visual Studio Code*

If we don't pass any arguments at all, or pass too many arguments, we'll instead see an error telling us how many arguments were passed and how many were actually expected. For example, this function call:

```
sayHello(); // error
```

Will result in the following error in the editor:

```
function sayHello(name: string): string

Expected 1 arguments, but got 0. ts(2554)

functions.ts(1, 19): An argument for 'name'
was not provided.
```

Figure 7.4: *Wrong number of arguments error in Visual Studio Code*

This is an important difference with plain JavaScript; in JavaScript, all function arguments are always optional - if we don't pass enough arguments when calling the function, they will simply have the value `undefined` inside the function.

Additionally, we can pass extra parameters to a function in JavaScript, and while these will not be accessible as named parameters inside the function, they will still show up in the `arguments` array-like collection inside the function.

In TypeScript, as we have seen, we cannot call a function and pass it the wrong number of arguments; either too few or too many will cause errors in the editor or compiler, which may result in the TypeScript not being compiled in the strictest configurations. We can mark parameters as optional, however, which we'll look at this shortly.

Type Inference for Functions

One point to note is that if we don't specify a type for a function parameter, TypeScript won't try to infer the type for the parameter based on how the parameter is used inside the function.

Instead, it will simply set the parameter type to `any`. This will prevent errors in the editor but will disable all type-checking for that parameter inside the function, which could result in run-time errors in the browser which aren't caught by the compiler or editor.

With strict configuration for TypeScript enabled, this will cause TypeScript to display an error for the untyped parameter. The specific configuration setting related to this is `noImplicitAny`, although the same behavior is enforced when using the catch-all `strict` setting.

For example, if we remove the `string` type following the `name` parameter in our `sayHello` function, like this:

```
function sayHello(name): string {
  return `Hello ${name}`;
}
```

We'll then see this error:

```
(parameter) name: any
Parameter 'name' implicitly has an 'any'
type. ts(7006)
```

Figure 7.5: *Implicit 'any' error in Visual Studio Code*

This doesn't mean that we can't manually specify that a parameter has the type **any** if we truly want, the error is just caused by TypeScript *inferring* that the type is **any**, because in this situation we could lose typing for the value inside the function unknowingly.

If we manually set the parameter to **any**, TypeScript will conclude that we know what we are doing and simply stop type-checking the parameter inside the function without showing an error.

TypeScript will infer the return type of a function based on what is actually returned from the function, In the case of our **sayHello** example function, the function is explicitly returning a value of the type **string**, so if we leave off the annotation for the return type, like this:

```
function sayHello(name: string) {
  return `Hello ${name}`;
}
```

TypeScript will still correctly infer the return type of the function to be **string** and prevent us from using the return type incorrectly.

Arrow Functions

Let's also take a moment to look at using the same type annotations as before but with an arrow function. Arrow functions are short-hand function syntax that allows us to do away with some of the boiler-plate code associated with functions, like the **function** and **return** keywords. They also preserve the value of **this** inside the function, unlike regular functions.

A basic arrow function equivalent to the **sayHello** function from earlier looks like this:

```
const sayGoodbye = (name: string): string => `Bye ${name}`;
```

The syntax for an arrow function is basically the parameter list followed by what is called a **fat arrow** – an equals sign followed by a right-angle bracket, and then the body of the function. But notice that we do not use the **function** or **return** keywords anywhere, and because the function body is a single line of code, we don't need curly braces either.

The parameter type annotations are still specified after the parameter name and a colon, and the function's return type is still specified directly after the parameter list, also following a colon, but before the fat arrow.

Another small point to note is that, while the function is stored in a variable called **sayGoodbye**, the function itself does not have an identifier, making it an anonymous function. This makes no difference to how TypeScript sees the function, or how we can use it in our code, I merely point it out as an interesting observation.

A single-line arrow function has an implicit return value, so in the previous example, it will return the displayed string. For a multi-line arrow function, however, we do still need to provide an explicit return (if we want the function to return something), and use curly braces, like this:

```
const sayGoodbye = (name: string): string => {

  // other lines

  return `Bye ${name}`;

};
```

We've assigned the arrow function to a variable called **sayGoodbye**, so we use this variable to invoke the function in the same way that we would invoke a regular function:

```
sayGoodbye('Dan');
```

We get the exact same parameter type and return type checking as we do with regular functions, so again, it is impossible for us to call the function incorrectly.

Type Inference for Arrow Functions

As we saw a little earlier, if we don't specify the types of parameters in a function declaration, the compiler will set their types to **any** automatically, which is usually a situation we want to avoid.

When using arrow functions, TypeScript is usually able to correctly infer parameter types, when it is able to see exactly how the function is going to be called. For example, consider the following example code:

```
const str = 'string';

str.split('').forEach((char) => char.padStart(2, 'X'));
```

What the code in this example actually does is irrelevant, which is fortunate as it does nothing useful whatsoever. What we're interested in is the fact that we can completely avoid specifying the type for the **char** parameter that the arrow function passed to the **forEach** method receives, this part of the code specifically:

```
(char) => char.padStart(2, 'X')
```

In this case, TypeScript knows that the type of the **char** parameter will be **string**, because the method is being called on an array containing string values and so the type of **char** will be correctly inferred as **string** and will not be set to **any** like it would with a regular function declaration. TypeScript also knows that the **padStart** method returns a **string** value.

This is great because we get full type checking for the parameter as a **string** inside the body of the arrow function, and for the return type of the function, without requiring us to manually add the type annotations ourselves.

Optional Parameters

As mentioned a little earlier, in TypeScript, declared function parameters are strictly required. However, it is very easy to make them optional instead, using the same syntax that we used earlier in the book to make object properties optional - by using a question mark character directly after the parameter name:

```
function optional(maybe?: string) {}
```

In this case, the **maybe** parameter will be optional, but if it is provided, it will need to be of the type **string**. This means that we can call the function like this:

```
optional('anyString'); // fine
```

Or, like this:

```
optional(); // also fine
```

In both cases, the editor or compiler will not display any errors.

With optional parameters, TypeScript will always see the parameter as a union of the parameter type, `string` in this example, and `undefined`, so before using it inside the function, we'll need to ensure that it is definitely a string and not `undefined`, like this for example:

```
function optional(maybe?: string) {

  if (!maybe) return;

  // maybe is definitely a string now

}
```

Inside the function, we check if the `maybe` parameter is falsey (meaning `undefined`, `null`, or any value that coerces to `false`), and if it is, we immediately return from the function.

After the `if` statement on the first line, if execution has continued, we know that the `maybe` parameter is definitely of the type string and not `undefined`, so we can use it safely as a string without generating errors in the editor.

Rest Parameters

Rest parameters are used to pass a variable number of arguments to a function. They use the spread operator ... and should appear at the end of the parameter list, following any regular parameters.

Additionally, there can be only one rest parameter per function:

```
function variadic(a: string, ...extra: string[]) {

  // do something with strings

}
```

In this example, we first declare a single parameter called `a` which will be of the type `string`, and then use a rest parameter to have the function receive any number of additional `string` arguments as an array.

Rest parameters allow us to call the `variadic` function like this:

```
variadic('just one string'); // fine
```

Or even like this:

```
variadic('one string', 'and', 'any', 'others'); // also fine
```

Without causing any errors, making these types of functions very flexible indeed.

Rest parameters are always an array type; in this example, we used the shorthand literal syntax, but we could also have used the generic syntax if we wanted, which would look like this:

```
function variadic(a: string, ...extra: Array<string>) {
  // do something with strings
}
```

There is no difference between the two forms.

Rest Arguments

Very similar to rest parameters are rest arguments; the difference between them is that rest parameters appear in function parameter lists, whereas rest arguments are passed to function invocations.

```
function variadic(a: string, ...extra: string[]): string {
  return a.concat(...extra);
}
```

In this evolution of the previous example, we use the **concat** method on the first string passed to the function, the named parameter **a**, to concatenate all of the additional arguments collected by the rest parameter to the end of the first parameter.

We can also specify the return type here, **string** in this case, because the example function is now actually returning a value.

The **concat** method takes a comma-separated list of strings to concatenate onto the end of the target string, but in our case, we don't know how many extra arguments that will be, so we can use a rest argument to expand the array of strings passed as the extra parameters into a comma-separated list, regardless of how many additional arguments were passed to the **variadic** function.

Note that the example function here is using both a rest parameter, and a rest argument.

Another point to note is that while in JavaScript, the **concat** method takes a comma-separated list of strings, when using TypeScript, the editor will always show this method as accepting a rest argument, even if we pass a comma-separated list of strings.

For example, this **return** statement in the example function:

```
return a.concat(extra[0], extra[1]);
```

Will show the following tooltip in Visual Studio Code, which shows the **concat** method accepting a rest argument even though we passed it two individual strings:

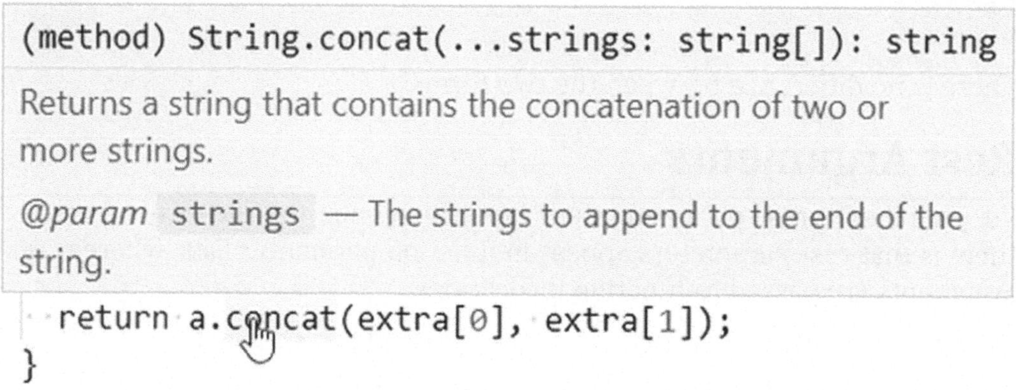

```
(method) String.concat(...strings: string[]): string
```

Returns a string that contains the concatenation of two or more strings.

@param strings — The strings to append to the end of the string.

```
  return a.concat(extra[0], extra[1]);
}
```

Figure 7.6: *Rest argument tooltip for concat method in Visual Studio Code*

Rest parameters and rest arguments are therefore conceptually opposite to each other - rest parameters collect any number of comma-separated values and condense them into a single array, whereas rest arguments take an array and expand them into a comma-separated list of values.

Destructured Parameters

Another type of parameter that should be mentioned is the destructured parameter. In JavaScript, destructuring assignment expressions are used to store the values contained within arrays or objects in individual named variables.

For example, consider the following plain JavaScript:

```
let [height, weight, age] = [180, 70, 44];
```

This expression creates three variables called **`height`**, **`weight`**, and **`age`**, and puts one of each value from the array into each variable, in the order specified on the left-hand of the assignment, so the **`height`** variable on the left side of the expression will take the first value in the array on the right side of the expression, **`weight`** the second, and **`age`** the third.

In the previous example, we wrap the identifiers on the left side in square brackets because we are destructuring an array.

We can also destructure objects, and for this, we wrap the left side of the assignment in curly braces instead of square brackets:

```
let { height, weight, age } = { height: 180, weight: 70, age: 44 };
```

In this case, we would see the exact same result as before. This time, the identifiers on the left side of the expression correspond to property identifiers in the object being destructured on the right side of the expression, and TypeScript will infer the types of the variables being assigned based on the values being destructured, so in this case, the **`height`**, **`weight`**, and **`age`** variables will all have the inferred type **`number`**.

We can use a very similar approach for function parameters, a technique commonly used with configuration objects passed to a function, like this:

```
function showlocation({ lat, lng }): void {

  window.open(`https://www.openstreetmap.org/#map=16/${lat}/${lng}`);

}
```

In this case, the function will be passed an object containing properties called **`lat`** and **`lng`**, but we can destructure them into individual named parameters right there in the parameter list. The function would be invoked like this:

```
showlocation({ lat: '50.9272', lng: '-1.4015' });
```

The only problem we have at this point is that **`lat`** and **`lng`** currently have the inferred type **`any`** and so the function declaration will show errors in the editor with the strict configuration enabled.

We can fix this by adding a type annotation to them, for example:

```
function showlocation({ lat, lng }: { lat: string, lng: string }): void {

  window.open(`https://www.openstreetmap.org/#map=16/${lat}/${lng}`)

}
```

The literal object type shows an object with properties **`lat`** and **`lng`**, both of which are of the type **`string`**.

It is important to note that the type information for destructured parameters must come after the entire destructuring assignment, not after the individual identifiers inside the assignment, and we must specify the individual names of the object properties being destructured.

This results in some duplication, but in this case, it is unavoidable. For objects containing many properties to destructure, it makes sense to use a type alias rather than specifying the full type inline, like this:

```
type location = {

  zoom: string;

  lat: string;

  lng: string

}

function showLocation2({ zoom, lat, lng }: location): void {

      window.open(`https://www.openstreetmap.org/#map=${zoom}/${lat}/${l
ng}`)

}
```

This format is much more readable, and code that is readable is also maintainable, which is something we should always strive for when developing. You should note that although these examples focus on object destructuring with function parameters, we can also use array destructuring here too.

I'd also like to point out that **`window.open`** was used purely to keep things as terse as possible while still conveying a functioning example – this should of course be avoided in production code.

One more thing to be aware of with destructuring in TypeScript is that by default, TypeScript doesn't like values to be unused in the value being destructured, for example, consider the following code:

```
let [height, weight, age] = [180, 70];
```

In this case, TypeScript will complain that the age variable has no matching element in the target array:

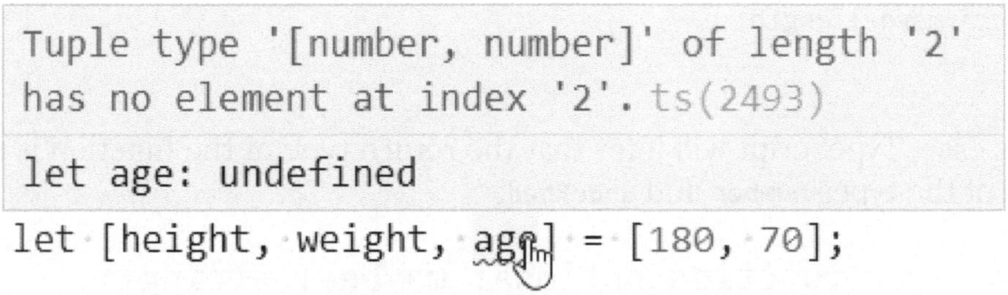

```
Tuple type '[number, number]' of length '2'
has no element at index '2'. ts(2493)

let age: undefined
let [height, weight, age] = [180, 70];
```

Figure 7.7: *No element at index '2' error in Visual Studio Code*

We can fix this common error by simply adding an additional comma after the final value in the target array, like this:

```
let [height, weight, age] = [180, 70,,];
```

This will remove the error in the editor, and the **age** variable will have the value **undefined**.

Void return type

We can use the **void** type as a return type for a function. In fact, that's what TypeScript sees as the **return** value for the **optional** function from an earlier example, since we used the **return** keyword by itself, without returning an actual value:

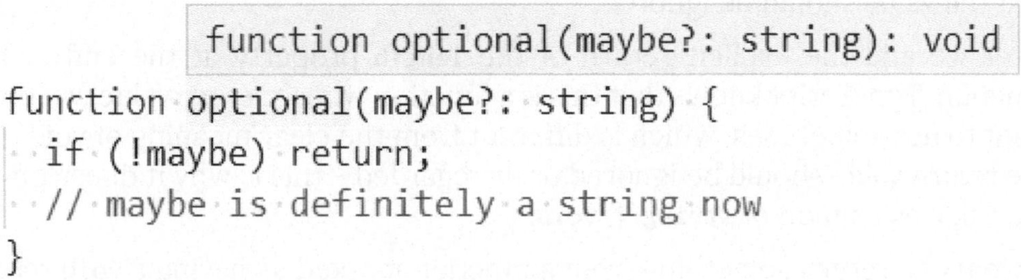

```
function optional(maybe?: string): void

function optional(maybe?: string) {
  if (!maybe) return;
  // maybe is definitely a string now
}
```

Figure 7.8: *Inferred void return type in Visual Studio Code*

In this example, however, the **optional** function might want to return something else if it is passed an argument when invoked, like the length of the parameter perhaps:

```
function optional(maybe?: string) {
  if (!maybe) return;
  // maybe is definitely a string now
```

```
  return maybe.length;
}
```

In this case, TypeScript will infer that the return type of the function is now a union of the types **number** and **undefined**:

```
function optional(maybe?: string):
number | undefined
function optional(maybe?: string) {
  if (!maybe) return;
  // maybe is definitely a string now
  return maybe.length;
}
```

***Figure 7.9**: Union type return tooltip in Visual Studio Code*

The **void** type as a return value from a function implies that the return value of the function should not be used. It does not mean that the return value of the function is **undefined**, even though technically, once compiled down to JavaScript, a function that doesn't return anything will have a return value of **undefined**. Undefined values can still be useful, whereas **void** explicitly means that the value should be ignored.

After we add the explicit return of the **length** property at the end of the function, TypeScript knows that this is a function whose return value we might want to use sometimes, which is different from the clear meaning of void that the return value should be ignored or disregarded - this is why it doesn't infer the value as a union of **string | void**.

If we try to return something from a function marked as having a **void** return type, like this for example:

```
function sideEffect(): void {
  // do something
  return 'oops';
}
```

TypeScript will warn us with the following error:

```
Type 'string' is not assignable to type
'void'. ts(2322)
```

***Figure 7.10**: String is not assignable to a void error in Visual Studio Code*

It is a useful practice to always specify the return type of a function directly rather than letting TypeScript infer the return type, including with functions that don't return a useful value, in which case we should take care to mark them as **`void`**.

Function Type Expressions

As well as parameter types and return types, functions themselves can also have types. A function type expression is a type that describes an entire function. For example, let's imagine that we want to declare a variable that will be used to store a function in; we would give it a type like this:

```
let numberFn: (...nums: number[]) => number;
```

Here, we declare a variable called **`numberFn`** and specify that it will contain a function that can receive any number of arguments that are of the type **`number`**, in an array, and which itself returns a value of the type **`number`**. The function type expression is just the type for the function, which appears after the colon following the variable identifier, it's not the implementation.

Notice that we use a fat arrow to denote the return type of the function and not a colon. This makes function-type expressions look very similar to arrow functions, so be careful not to confuse them with actual arrow functions.

The **`numberFn`** variable can now contain any function that receives zero or more numeric arguments and also returns a number, a function like this for example:

```
numberFn = (...nums: number[]): number => {

  return nums.reduce((prev: number, curr: number) => prev + curr, 0);

}

numberFn(1, 2, 3); // 6
```

In this example, we define a function that uses the **`reduce`** method to sum up all the numbers passed to the function when it is invoked. Notice how similar the actual function is to the function type expression - the only difference is that the actual function specifies the return type in between the parameter list and fat arrow.

As mentioned earlier, any function that meets the specification laid out by the function type expression may be stored in the **numberFn** variable, so a function like this would also work:

```
numberFn = (...nums: number[]): number => {
  return nums.reduce((prev: number, curr: number) => {
    if (!prev) return curr;
    return prev * curr;
  });
}
numberFn(4, 5, 6); // 120
```

The function is very similar to the previous example except that it multiplies all of the numbers passed to the function instead of summing them.

The variable we've created is reusable, and we can store any function inside it that conforms to the function type expression, but the function type expression itself can't be reused. For that we need to use a type alias, like this:

```
type numberFn2 = (...nums: number[]) => number;
```

Now we can use **numberFn2** type anywhere that type annotations can be provided, like as a variable type for example:

```
const addAllTheNums: numberFn2 = (...numbers: number[]) => {
  return numbers.reduce((prev, next) => prev + next, 0);
}
```

As long as the provided function matches the function type expression, we can store it in the variable that has the corresponding type.

Call signatures

In JavaScript, functions are objects and in addition to being callable, they may also have properties – in fact, all functions have a **length** property, which corresponds to the number of named parameters the function may receive.

A function type expression doesn't allow us to specify properties that a function may have in addition to the parameter and types. If we need to do this, we need to use an object type and specify the function's call signature in addition to the properties we want to add, for example:

```
type numberFn3 = {
  operation: string;
  (...nums: number[]): number;
}
```

The type **numberFn3** will require that functions of this type will need to have a property of the type **string** called **operation**. After the property, we specify the call signature for the function, that is, the parameter **names** and **types**, and the return type of the function. Notice that we use a colon here to specify the return type and not a fat arrow as we do with a function type expression.

Now we can create a function that satisfies this type:

```
let myNumberFn3 = ((...nums: number[]): number => {
  return nums.reduce((prev: number, curr: number) => prev + curr, 0);
}) as numberFn3;
myNumberFn3.operation = 'Sum';
```

The actual function declaration itself is very similar to the previous example, so we won't go over it in much detail again. The only real difference is that this time we need to wrap the whole arrow function in another set of parentheses, and then add the type assertion **as numberFn3** after the parentheses.

If we don't do this, we won't be able to then add the **operation** property to the function on the last line without seeing an error in the editor.

Note that as well as using the **as** operator, we could also use the older type-casting syntax, like this:

```
let myNumberFn3 = <numberFn3>((...nums: number[]): number => {
  return nums.reduce((prev: number, curr: number) => prev + curr, 0);
});
```

We should also note that the editor won't show any errors if we don't set the **operation** property on the function after declaring it. But it will show errors if we try to add a different property that isn't specified in the call signature, like this perhaps:

```
myNumberFn3.oops = 'error!';
```

In this case, we would see the following error in the editor:

```
any

Property 'oops' does not exist on type
'numberFn3'. ts(2339)
```

Figure 7.11: *Illegal property addition error in Visual Studio Code*

This is also the error that we would see when trying to add a property to any function that does not have the required object type call signature.

Function Type Interfaces

We looked at interfaces containing method definitions earlier in the book, but we shall revisit them here for clarity. A function-type interface is an interface that describes a function, for example:

```
interface logFn {
  (arg0: string): void;
}
```

As with a regular interface, we begin with the **`interface`** keyword, followed by the identifier and a pair of curly braces. Inside the braces, we define the function call signature specifying only the parameter list, which must have a type for each parameter, and the return type, which is separated from the parameter list by a colon.

Note that if we don't specify a type for each parameter, the parameter type will be inferred as **`any`**, which will cause an error with TypeScript's strict configuration enabled.

Now we can use the **`logFn`** interface when creating an actual function declaration, like this for example:

```
let myLogFn: logFn = (str: string) => console.log(str);
```

The syntax for a function type interface is very similar to the syntax for declaring an object which contains a method, be sure not to get them confused.

This Parameter

Another type of parameter that TypeScript supports is this parameter. This is a special kind of function parameter that allows us to set the type for the value **`this`** inside a function.

In JavaScript, **`this`** is a special value that can be different things in different situations and remains a frequent source of bugs and confusion.

For the next example, let's imagine we have an interface that describes **`user`** objects:

```
interface user {

  name: string;

}
```

These objects will have just a single property called **`name`** which will be of the type **`string`**.

Now let's say we have a constructor function, that is, a function that should be used with the **`new`** keyword and which creates new **`user`** objects:

```
function User(this: user, name: string): user {

  this.name = name;

  return this;

}
```

Notice that we can call the first parameter **`this`** and specify a type. Then inside the function, the **`this`** value will be set to the type that we specified. We also set **`user`** as the return type of the function, as the function will return **`user`** instance objects. Inside the function, we can set the **`name`** property of the **`user`** object, which is available as the **`this`** value, and then also return the **`this`** value.

Using **`this`** inside the function with the strict configuration enabled is only possible because we are using the **`this`** parameter to specify the type of the **`this`** value – without the parameter TypeScript will infer the type **`any`** for it instead, and this will result in errors in the editor and compiler.

Although the previous code is valid TypeScript, we need to make a small modification before we can actually create new **`user`** objects using the **`User`** constructor function.

To create a new **user** object, we need to use a double type-assertion, for example:

```
const user1 = new (User as unknown as user)('Dan');
```

We need to wrap the constructor name in parentheses and cast it to **unknown** and then to our **user** interface. The **name** argument that needs to be passed to the constructor can then be provided in another set of parentheses after the double assertion in the first set of parentheses.

This works because anything can be cast to the **unknown** type. This is also safer than just casting the constructor to **any**, as this would disable further type-checking of the **user1** variable in any following code.

Note that this is not the only way that we could fix this error. An alternative to casting first to unknown and then to our desired type would be to convert the function to a function expression and cast the return type first to unknown and then to the desired type, for example:

```
const User = function(this: user, name: string) {
  this.name = name
} as unknown as { new (name: string): user };
```

We could then use the constructor without any special casting:

```
const user1 = new User('Dan');
```

Which variation you use to overcome this error will depend on where the constructor comes from; if the constructor is from a third party library, we will not be able to change the original function declaration and so the first example will be more beneficial to us.

If we do have full control over the constructor function, we may wish to use the second format. As always, the solution you use going forward will depend on multiple factors including your own preference.

We're almost done, but at this point, the editor will show the following error:

```
This expression is not constructable.
  Type 'user' has no construct
signatures. ts(2351)
```

Figure 7.12: *Expression is not constructable error in Visual Studio Code*

To fix this error, we need to add a construct signature to our **user** interface, like this:

```
interface user {
  name: string;
  new (name: string): user;
}
```

A construct signature is almost identical to a call signature, the only difference being that a construct signature starts with the **new** keyword. Construct signatures are just call signatures for constructor functions!

Since JavaScript now natively supports classes, we probably won't see too many old-style constructor functions like in the previous example, but it's worth being aware of how they can be used in TypeScript just in case we come across one in the wild if we ever need to support a legacy application.

Function overloads

In many object-oriented programming languages, function overloading is the practice of having multiple functions with the same name, but different signatures. JavaScript does not support function overloading at all, but luckily for us, TypeScript does.

Function overloading in TypeScript is a way to declare functions that receive different numbers of parameters, or different types of parameters, and return different values.

We could handle the different types of parameters using a parameter with a union type encompassing all of the types we want to use inside the function, and we could also use a union of types for the return type of the function.

However, if there are many variations in the parameters received or the types of the value returned by the function, we may find it more readable to use function overloading instead. Let's look at a basic example.

Imagine that we want to declare a function that can accept either a **string**, a **number**, or a **string** array and that it may return either a **string** array or a single **string**:

```
function fn(item: string): string[];
function fn(item: number): string[];
function fn(item: string[], separator?: string): string;
```

We overload a function in TypeScript by declaring multiple function signatures, followed at the end by the actual function implementation, although the previous code snippet shows only the signatures - we'll add the implementation in just a moment. All of the signatures should use the same function name, **`fn`** in this example.

Each of the first three lines in the previous code example is a function signature; the first specifies that the function may receive a parameter of the type **`string`** and return a **`string`** array, the second that the function may receive a **`number`** and return a **`string`** array, and the third line specifies that the function may receive a **`string`** array, and optionally a second parameter, also of the type string, and that this time it will return a single **`string`**.

A function overload should always have two or more function signatures.

Following the function signatures, we then need to declare the function implementation:

```
function fn(a: string | number | string[], sep?: string): string | string[]
{
  if (typeof a === 'string') {
    return a.split('');
  } else if (typeof a === 'number') {
    return a.toString().split('');
  } else {
    return a.join(sep ?? '');
  }
}
```

This time the function must declare all possible parameters and return types, so we can use a union type of **`string | number | string[]`** to cover the different argument types of the first parameter the function may receive. We should also mark the second parameter, **`sep`** (short for separator), as optional since only one overload specifies it.

Lastly, we can also use a union type of **`string | string[]`** for the return type, which covers all of the different possibilities of the return types specified by the different overloads.

Inside the function, we can use a **`typeof`** type guard to handle each of the different types that the first parameter, **`a`**, maybe. We'll look at type guards in more detail later in the book, the takeaway here is that they are used to differentiate between different types that a value may be.

In the last branch of the if statement, we don't explicitly need to check for the array type as we already handled the only other possible variations. We'll be looking at type guards in more detail later in the book.

Now we can use the function, and pass it any of the supported arguments, for example:

```
fn(‘test’); // [‘t’, ‘e’, ‘s’, ‘t’]

fn(1234); // [‘1’, ‘2’, ‘3’, ‘4’]

fn([‘a’, ‘b’, ‘c’], ‘|’); // ‘a|b|c’
```

If we try to pass an unsupported argument type when invoking the function, like this for example:

```
fn(true); // error
```

Then we will see a detailed error the in the editor listing all of the different overloads the function supports:

```
No overload matches this call.
  Overload 1 of 3, '(a: string): string[]', gave the following error.
    Argument of type 'boolean' is not assignable to parameter of type 'string'.
  Overload 2 of 3, '(a: number): string[]', gave the following error.
    Argument of type 'boolean' is not assignable to parameter of type 'number'.
  Overload 3 of 3, '(a: string[], separator?: string | undefined): string', gave the following error.
    Argument of type 'boolean' is not assignable to parameter of type 'string[]'. ts(2769)
```

Figure 7.13: *No matching overload error in Visual Studio Code*

This time the error message is extremely verbose and lists all of the variations of the overloaded function.

Overloading Arrow Functions

Arrow functions can't be overloaded in the same way as regular function declarations, but they can still be overloaded. To overload an arrow function, we need to use a type alias or an interface, for example:

```
type fn2 = {
  (a: string): string[];
  (a: number): string[];
  (a: string | number | string[], sep?: string): string | string[];
}
```

In this case, we add a type alias called **fn2** and inside list all of the overload call signatures for the function. Note that we're reusing the exact same overload signatures as we used in the previous section.

Next, we can add the actual implementation for the arrow function:

```
const ol = ((a: string | number | string[], sep?: string): string |
string[] => {
  if (typeof a === 'string') {
    return a.split('');
  } else if (typeof a === 'number') {
    return a.toString().split('');
  } else {
    return a.join(sep ?? '');
  }
}) as fn2;
```

Again, this snippet is almost identical to the implementation in the previous section, just in arrow function format. Note that we wrap the whole arrow function in parentheses and follow it with an assertion, using the **as** operator, to the desired type.

Now we can use the arrow function in the expected way:

```
ol('test'); // ['t', 'e', 's', 't']
ol(1234); // ['1', '2', '3', '4']
ol(['a', 'b', 'c'], '|'); // 'a|b|c'
```

Being an arrow function, it is likely that we will want to pass this function to other functions as an argument, for example:

```
function fn3(callback: fn2): void {
  // do something, then invoke the callback
}
```

We simply use the type alias to annotate the parameter representing the arrow function we wish to use.

Inside the function when we go to use the overloaded arrow function passed in as a parameter, we then get a nice code-completion popup allowing us to see all of the different overloads supported by the function:

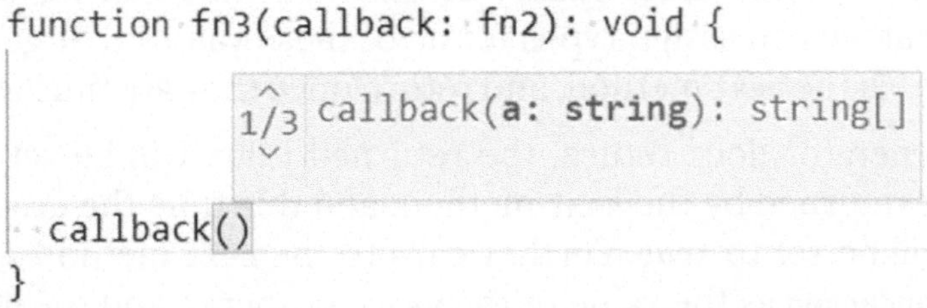

```
function fn3(callback: fn2): void {
                 1/3 callback(a: string): string[]
  callback()
}
```

Figure 7.14: *Overloaded parameter types dialog in Visual Studio Code*

Function overloading gives us a clean and readable syntax for describing complex functions with many different parameters and return types.

Generator functions

Generator functions are a special type of function in JavaScript that can yield multiple values, and have their execution paused and resumed at will. Generator functions work in a slightly different way than regular functions.

Regular functions follow a model called **run to completion** – once the function is invoked, it runs all of the code inside its body, returns a value (which may be undefined if no explicit return is used), and then stops executing. The function will do nothing further unless it is invoked again.

Generator functions use a different model, called **pause and resume**. In this model, the statements inside the function do not all execute at once – the function can be paused, and later, can be resumed to continue executing statements inside its body.

When we invoke a generator function, it doesn't actually invoke the function, instead, it returns an iterator. This iterator is an object that has a **`next`** method, and it is this method that actually invokes the function in the way that a traditional function is invoked.

Each time the **`next`** method is called, it returns an object; this object contains two properties, **`value`** which contains the **`value`** yielded by the function, and **`done`** which is a Boolean that tells us whether the function can be invoked again or not.

We can also pass values to the **`next`** method, and these values will be injected into the function for that call of the method. Generators can also return a final value when they have finished executing and cannot be invoked anymore.

TypeScript doesn't add functionality or enhance the behavior of generators in any way, but we can assign types for all of these values that generators can yield, receive via the **`next`** method, and return once they are finished executing.

When the generator does return, the returned value will be set as the value of the object returned by the **`next`** method, and this time the **`done`** property of the object will be set to **`true`**. Further calls to the **`next`** method will return an object with **`undefined`** as the value of the **`value`** property, and the **`done`** property set to **`true`**.

Let's take a quick look at a basic example to see what level of typing we can expect when using them. Imagine that we want to create a generator function that returns a random integer between **`0`** and **`10`** each time the **`next`** method of its iterator is invoked:

```
function* randomInt() {

  while (true) {

    yield Math.round(Math.random() * 10);

  }

}
```

Generator functions are declared by adding an asterisk directly after the **`function`** keyword. Inside the function, we use a **`while`** loop locked to the value **`true`**, and inside the loop, we use the **`yield`** keyword to output a single-digit random number.

We can now invoke the function to get the iterator, and then call the iterator's **next** method to get a random number:

```
const randomIterator = randomInt();

console.log(randomIterator.next());
```

Each time the **next** method is called, the loop inside the generator will execute a single time, so we can keep on calling the **next** method if we wish, and we will keep getting random numbers.

We haven't added any type annotations to this example code yet, but TypeScript can infer some information about the function:

```
function randomInt(): Generator<number, void, unknown>
```

***Figure 7.15**: Generator function tooltip in Visual Studio Code*

TypeScript knows that it's a generator function and that it yields values of the type **number**, which is the first type parameter in the built-in generic **Generator** type.

The second type parameter is set to **void** by TypeScript because the function doesn't explicitly return a value. The last type parameter is the type for a value passed to the iterator's **next** method, which TypeScript sets to the **unknown** type, which as we know, is safer than using **any**.

One point to note is that even though TypeScript has correctly inferred that the function will yield values of the type **number**, we'll find that if we try to use the value returned by the **next** method as if it were a number, by calling its **toString** method for example:

```
console.log(randomIterator.next().value.toString());
```

Then we'll see an error:

```
any

Property 'toString' does not exist on type
'number | void'.
  Property 'toString' does not exist on type
'void'. ts(2339)
```

***Figure 7.16**: Error when using unguarded union in Visual Studio Code*

The reason the type is a union of **`number | void`** is due to the fact that the value **`property`** of the **`next`** method can be undefined when the function returns, even though that doesn't happen with the example generator because it doesn't use the **`return`** keyword and will just infinitely loop.

Additionally, the **`value`** property of the object returned by the **`next`** method is currently set to **`any`**, which we can also see from the header of the error popup shown in *Figure* 7.16.

Generally, we want to avoid values being inferred as **`any`**, although in this case there will not be an error, the value just won't be type checked.

To fix both of these issues, we can add a type annotation to the generator function:

```
function* randomInt(): Generator<number, number> {
  ...
}
```

We can add the built-in **`Generator`** type and use angle brackets to specify the first and second type parameters that generators can have. Even though the function isn't explicitly returning a number, we need to add both the first and second type parameters in the type annotation to both remove the error from the **`toString`** method and ensure the value is not **`any`**.

Now the error under the **`toString`** method has gone, as we've signaled to TypeScript that the yielded value will always be of the type **`number`**:

```
function randomInt(): Generator<number, number>
```

***Figure 7.17**: Generator type tooltip in Visual Studio Code*

The **`value`** property of the object returned by the **`next`** method will also be correctly typed as a number:

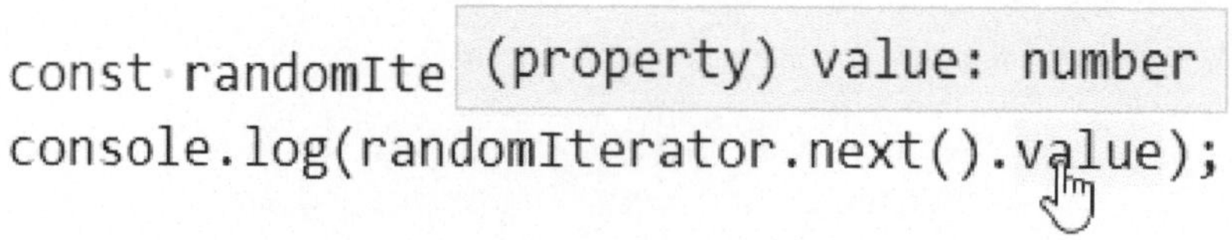

```
const randomIte (property) value: number
console.log(randomIterator.next().value);
```

***Figure 7.18**: Type popup in Visual Studio Code*

As the value **`property`** is correctly typed, the editor will of course warn us if we try to call a method on it that numbers don't have, ensuring we work with the values yielded by the generator in the expected way.

Like regular functions, generator functions can also have named parameters, and we add types for them in the same way as we do for regular functions. Let's update the example so that the generator can receive a limit of the maximum times random numbers can be generated:

```
function* randomInt2(limit: number): Generator<number, number> {
  let currentLimit = limit;
  while (true) {
    if (--currentLimit >= 0) {
      yield Math.round(Math.random() * 10);
    } else {
      return 'Random numbers exhausted!';
    }
  }
}
```

In this case, we added a parameter called **`limit`**, which is of the type **`number`**, that the generator function receives when it is initially invoked. Inside the function, we initialize a counter variable called **`currentLimit`** to the **`limit`** parameter's value.

Inside the **`while`** loop, we can then decrement the **`currentLimit`** variable and check that it's greater than or equal to **`0`**. If it is, we can yield a number as before, but if not, we can instead use a regular **`return`** statement to return a string.

At this point, the editor will show an error on the **`return`** statement because of the function's type. Now that the function is returning a string value, we need to update the second type parameter:

```
function* randomInt2(limit: number): Generator<number, string> {
  …
}
```

Now we can create an iterator, this time passing a number for the limit parameter:

```
const randomIterator2 = randomInt2(1);
```

In this case, the function will return only a single random number when the **next** method is called:

```
console.log(randomIterator2.next().value);
```

The second time the **next** method is called, the **value** property of the object it returns will contain the string that we returned from the generator. This will occur only once; on subsequent calls to the **next** method, the **value** property will be **undefined**.

One point to note here is that the **value** property of the object returned by the **next** method will now be a union type of **number | string**, so we may need to use type-guards to work with the value successfully.

The last type parameter that we can specify is for the type of value that may be passed to the **next** method of the iterator. Let's update the generator one more time to see the implications of using the third type parameter:

```
function* randomInt3(limit: number): Generator<number, string, boolean> {
  let currentLimit = limit;
  const message = 'Random numbers exhausted!';
  while (true) {
    if (--currentLimit >= 0) {
      if (yield Math.round(Math.random() * 10)) {
        break;
      }
    } else {
      return message;
    }
  }
  return message;
}
```

We have updated the type for the generator function to **`Generator<number, string, boolean>`**, adding a third type parameter to the annotation.

Inside the function, we tidy the string returned from the function in some cases to a variable called **`message`** as we are now going to return the message at two different points in the function.

Next, we added an **`if`** statement around the original **`yield`** statement, and when the condition is **`true`**, we use the **`break`** expression to exit from the **`while`** loop. This means that the function may cause a full return if the limit of the loop is reached, or if the value **`true`** is passed to the **`next`** method.

The way that this will work is that if the **`next`** method of the iterator is called without a parameter, the loop will continue and **`yield`** will return a value. But if we pass **`true`** to the **`next`** method, inside the function, the keyword **`yield`** will be *replaced* with the value **`true`**, which in turn will cause the **`if`** expression to exit from the loop immediately with the **`break`** keyword.

We can now use the generator in a similar way that we did before:

```
const randomIterator3 = randomInt3(10);

console.log(randomIterator3.next().value);

console.log(randomIterator3.next().value);

console.log(randomIterator3.next(true).value);      //   Random   numbers
exhausted!

console.log(randomIterator3.next().value); // undefined
```

The only difference is that passing **`true`** to the **`next`** method will cause the function to immediately return, and from that point on, further calls of the iterator will result in a value of **undefined** being returned.

You should also note that in this example, before we pass **`true`** to the **`next`** method, the **`done`** property of the returned object will be **`false`**, but after we pass **`true`**, the **`done`** property will be **`true`**, as the function has no more values to return.

Generic functions

Generic functions are another aspect of generics, similar to the generic objects that we looked at in the previous chapter. Generic functions are functions that can work with any different types, which can be useful when building a library, or some other code, that will be used by other developers, who may wish to use our functions with their own types. Let's take a look at a basic example:

```
function echo<T>(input: T): T {
  return input;
}
```

The function identifier, `echo`, is immediately followed by a type parameter inside angle brackets, which by convention is called `T`. As with generic objects, the parameter `T` acts like a variable for a type, so we can also say that the parameter the function receives is of the type `T`, and the return type of the function will also be of the type `T`.

Inside the function, we merely return the input parameter. The function will simply return whatever is passed to it, but we now get full type-safety when using the function:

```
let oops: string = echo(123);
```

In this case, TypeScript will not let us specify the variable type to be of a different type than the value of the argument we pass to the function when invoking it. The previous line of code will cause the following error in the editor:

```
let oops: string
Type 'number' is not assignable to
type 'string'. ts(2322)
```

***Figure 7.19**: Type not assignable error in Visual Studio Code*

In most cases, the editor's type inference will be sufficient to use the function with confidence, but we can of course specify the type decisively using either the literal:

```
let strTest: string = echo('Test'); // Test
```

Or generic syntax:

```
let numTest = echo<number>(123); // 123
```

We can now use function with any types as long as the type of the variable matches the type of the argument we pass the function. In this basic example, explicitly typing the variable is unnecessary, but is required when using our own custom types.

Generic Function Constraints

Generic functions are useful because we can make them generic so that they work across any type the consumer of the function wishes to use. We can also constrain the types that may be used with generic functions so that they don't operate over any type, but only types that meet some condition.

The concept is best explained with code, so let's look at another basic example. First, we'll need a type with which to make the constraint:

```
interface Item {
  save: (arg0: any[]) => void;
  contents: any[];
  [key: string]: any;
}
```

In this case, we define an interface called **`Item`**, objects of which should have a property called **`save`** which contains a function that accepts an array of **`any`** type of values, and a property called **`contents`**, which can be an array of **`any`** types of value. To make the interface more flexible, we can also add an index signature to say that objects of this type may specify any other additional properties.

Now we can add a generic function that is constrained to work only with objects that match the **`Item`** interface:

```
function save<T extends Item>(item: T): boolean | unknown {
  try {
    item.save(item.contents);
    return true;
  } catch(err) {
    throw new Error('Save failed', err);
  }
}
```

We use the **extends** keyword to add a constraint to the function. It basically says that the function will accept any type of value for the argument, as long as the value meets the **Item** interface, so it must at least contain a property called **save** which is a function, and a property called **contents** which is an array.

What the function does internally is not too important in the context of this example, what we're focused on here is the constraint on the types that may be used with the function, rather than what the function actually does.

In this case, the function can just call the **save** method of the item that was passed to it, passing in the **contents** array, and then return **true**. This logic is wrapped in a **try catch** in case the save fails, in which case we can throw an error. This is why the return type of the function is a union of Boolean and unknown.

When we come to use the **save** function, we will not have any problems as long as the argument we pass to it has at least **save** and **contents** properties of the expected types, for example:

```
const basket: Item = {

  save: () => {

    // save wherever...

  },

  contents: [],

}

save(basket); // fine
```

In this case, the basket object does have **save** and **contents** properties, so we can use it with the **save** function without any errors in the editor.

If we try to use the save function and pass an argument that does not match the **Item** interface, like this perhaps:

```
save('oops');
```

Then we will see an error that the argument is not of the expected type.

Constraints are useful to restrict the types that may be used with a generic function, and still give us all the benefits of type safety when using the constrained function.

Conclusion

In this chapter we have covered functions in TypeScript; functions will make up the bulk of the TypeScript code we write, so it's good to have a solid foundation of the benefits that TypeScript adds when using them.

We've seen how to add types that describe functions and all of the different types of parameters they can accept, from optional parameters and `this` parameters, to rest parameters and destructured parameters, as well as covering some more advanced topics like generator functions, and generic functions with constraints.

In the next chapter, we can move on to looking at classes through the lens of TypeScript.

References

- **https://www.typescriptlang.org/docs/handbook**
- **https://mariusschulz.com/blog/typing-destructured-object-parameters-in-typescript**
- **https://melvingeorge.me/blog/add-properties-to-functions-typescript**

CHAPTER 8

Classes in TypeScript

Introduction

TypeScript has full support for JavaScript's class system, which itself is largely a syntactic sugar on top of JavaScript's prototypical inheritance model. TypeScript also extends JavaScript classes by adding additional features like member visibility, abstract and generic classes, and more.

We will explore all of these TypeScript features in detail over the course of this chapter; all class features of both JavaScript and TypeScript will be discussed in full, but I will draw your attention to particular features where these are TypeScript-only enhancements added on top of JavaScript's existing functionality.

Some popular front-end development frameworks, including Google's Angular (2+), make heavy use of TypeScript classes, so it is a good idea to become very familiar with them and how they work if you plan to use Angular or another TypeScript-based framework. By the end of this chapter, your knowledge of TypeScript classes will be in a class of its own.

Structure

In this chapter we will cover the following topics:

- Class declarations
- Class expressions
- Constructors
- Access modifiers

- Parameter properties
- Getters and setters
- this parameter
- Index signatures
- Implementing an interface
- Static class members
- Inheritance
- Abstract classes and members
- Generic classes
- TypeScript Design Patterns

Class Declarations

Classes in JavaScript/TypeScript are a special kind of construct for creating objects. Classes have a constructor function which is called when objects are constructed via invoking the class using the `new` keyword.

Classes are a simple wrapper for working with object prototypes without having to work with them directly, and do not constitute a new way of working with inheritance or object-oriented development.

Let's start by looking at the anatomy of a basic class in TypeScript. We can then build on this in successive examples as we explore the features of classes:

```
class Shape {
  kind: string;

  constructor(kind: string) {
    this.kind = kind;
  }
}
```

The `class` keyword is used to declare the class, and this is immediately followed by the identifier for the class, `Shape` in this case. In this example, the class has a single property called `kind` which should be of the type `string`.

In this case, the type is explicitly declared, but we could avoid this, especially in the case of simple primitive types like strings. If we don't specify the type explicitly, the type of the property will be inferred based on the value assigned to the property in the constructor.

Following the property, there is a constructor function for the class, which looks like a standard class method except that it is called `constructor`. We'll look at constructors in a little more detail in just a moment.

While the previous code snippet looks very similar to a class in regular JavaScript, TypeScript already diverges subtly. Aside from the obvious type annotations on the `kind` class property and constructor parameter, the fact that we are specifying the property explicitly at all is something we would only do in TypeScript.

In pure JavaScript, the class definition for an equivalent class to `Shape` would look like this instead:

```
class Shape {
  constructor(kind) {
    this.kind = kind;
  }
}
```

One small point to note here is that the `Shape` class in the both the original code snippet, as well as the JavaScript version, is a class declaration.

Class Expressions

As well as class declarations, we can also use class expressions; this is where the statement that defines the class begins with anything other than the `class` keyword, for example:

```
const Shape = class {

  ... // identical to previous example

}
```

This time the class definition is stored in a variable called `Shape` instead of the class identifier being `Shape`, although this makes no practical difference.

As the statement begins with the `const` keyword and not the class `keyword`, it is a class expression as opposed to a class declaration. Aside from this, everything about the class expression is identical to the class declaration.

Constructors

The TypeScript class example in the previous section contained a constructor, which looked like this:

```
constructor(kind: string) {
  this.kind = kind;
}
```

The constructor receives a single parameter called **kind**, which is of the type **string**. With the strict configuration setting enabled, we must specify a type for each parameter passed to the constructor. If we do not do this, the parameter will be inferred as the **any** type, which will produce errors in the editor.

To create a new instance of the **Shape** class, we use the constructor with the **new** keyword, passing any required parameters, like this:

```
const myShape = new Shape('square');
myShape.kind; // square
```

Inside the constructor, the value of the **kind** parameter passed to the constructor is assigned to the class property called **kind**. This is known as property initialization, and it is a necessary step to avoid another error in the editor when the strict configuration is enabled.

If we do not assign a value to all class properties that are not initialized inside the constructor, we will see an error like this instead:

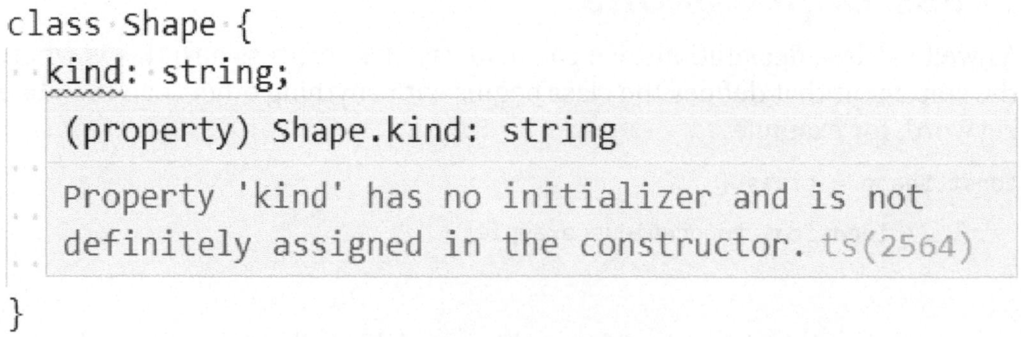

```
class Shape {
  kind: string;
    (property) Shape.kind: string
    Property 'kind' has no initializer and is not
    definitely assigned in the constructor. ts(2564)
}
```

***Figure 8.1**: No property initializer error in Visual Studio Code*

The configuration setting that controls whether this causes an error or not is **`strictPropertyInitialization`**.

NOTE: Class properties are sometimes referred to as fields.

As well as assigning values to class properties inside the **`constructor`**, we can also initialize properties inline, to give them a default value, for example:

```
class Shape {
  kind = 'square';

  constructor(kind: string) {
  }
}
```

In this case, the previous error will now be gone as the property is definitely initialized.

Even if we assign a value to the property directly, as we have here, we will still need to pass a parameter to the constructor for the **`kind`** property., if we don't do this, we'll see an error, for example:

```
const myShape = new Shape(); // error
```

Technically, we can also provide default values for the parameters passed to the constructor, like this for example:

```
class Shape {
  kind: string;

  constructor(kind = 'square') {
    this.kind = kind;
  }
}
```

But in this case, we should still ensure the class property is initialized inside the constructor when using default parameter values. This approach will not cause errors in the editor if we don't pass the parameter to the constructor when creating new instances of the class:

```
const myShape = new Shape(); // fine
```

But we can specify this if we wish:

```
const otherShape = new Shape('hexagon'); // also fine
```

Lastly, **constructor** parameters may also be explicitly marked as optional, for example:

```
class Shape {
  kind: string;
  isEuclidian: boolean | undefined;

  constructor(kind: string, isEuclidian?: boolean) {
    this.kind = kind;
    this.isEuclidian = isEuclidian;
  }
}
```

This time the constructor receives a second parameter which is made optional with the question mark immediately following the identifier.

The type of the optional parameter can be set to just **boolean**, but TypeScript will see it as the union **boolean | undefined**. anyway, so we may as well specify the full union when adding the type for the **isEuclidian** class property, to which the constructor assigns the parameter.

We can use the constructor of the class to create instances of the class, for example:

```
const ball = new Shape('sphere', false);
```

If we try to use the constructor incorrectly, the editor will warn us. If we passed a number as the first argument to the constructor, for example:

```
const wrong = new Shape(123);
```

Then we will see this error in the editor:

```
Argument of type 'number' is not
assignable to parameter of type
'string'. ts(2345)
```

***Figure 8.2**: Argument of wrong type error in Visual Studio Code*

As with regular functions, TypeScript makes it impossible to use a constructor function incorrectly.

Constructor Overloading

Another similarity between constructor functions and regular functions in TypeScript is that constructor functions can be overloaded, just like regular functions. This is another place where TypeScript diverges from plain JavaScript.

To overload a constructor, we provide multiple variations of the constructor, like this for example:

```
constructor(kind: string);

constructor(kind: string, isEuclidian: boolean);

constructor(kind: string, isEuclidian?: boolean) {

  this.kind = kind;

  this.isEuclidian = isEuclidian;

}
```

In this case, we provide a variation of the constructor that receives only a single **string** parameter and a variation where the constructor must receive both **string** and **boolean** parameters.

The last constructor is the actual implementation and contains the function body of the constructor. This constructor must be able to represent all of the variations of the overloads the constructor supports and is unchanged from prior examples in this section.

The syntax is very similar to regular function overloading, except that return types are not specified for each constructor. This is due to the fact that constructors always return instances of the class and never another value.

We can now use the constructor in all of the different ways supported by the overloads, for example:

```
const tile = new Shape('square', true);

const ball = new Shape('sphere');
```

As before, TypeScript will warn us if we try to use the constructor in a way that does not meet any of the overloads and will display errors that should by now be familiar.

Parameter Properties

One more constructor feature of TypeScript is that we can add access modifiers to parameters passed to the constructor, and via this feature, TypeScript gives us an incredibly useful short-cut to avoid having to manually set the value of class properties to the values passed to the constructor. The way that we use this feature is like this, for example:

```
class Shape {

  constructor(public kind: string, public isEuclidian?: boolean) {}

}
```

This time we prefix both of the constructor parameters with the **public** modifier in the parameter list. Notice that we don't have to list properties manually, and we don't have to explicitly set them in the constructor body - TypeScript does this for us automatically.

This technique also works with the **private**, **protected**, and **readonly** modifiers too. When used inside the parameter list, the access modifiers are known as parameter properties. We can still use the class in exactly the same way:

```
const block = new Shape('cube');

console.log(block.kind); // cube
```

This can save time and a lot of repetitive, boiler-plate code when using classes in TypeScript.

Access Modifiers

TypeScript supports a number of different access modifiers that can be applied to class members; access modifiers are used to control whether or not a class member is accessible from outside of the class itself.

There are several different access modifiers that we can use:

- **public**
- **private**
- **protected**
- **readonly**

The first three, **public**, **private**, and **protected** are used to control whether the member is visible outside of the class, whereas the last, **readonly**, controls whether the member can be assigned outside of the class constructor.

The **public** modifier means that the member can be accessed outside of the class, as well as in sub-classes. The **private** modifier means the member can only be accessed within the class, not even by subclasses. The **protected** modifier means that the member can be accessed within the class, or in any subclasses, but not by code outside of the class.

It is possible to make the constructor function, as well as methods of the class, **protected**, although this type of usage is for advanced use-cases where we may wish to have a constructor that is only visible to classes which extend it. We will look at extending classes later in this chapter.

By default, all class members are **public** – members are visible everywhere. The properties in all of the prior examples are all public by default, even though we didn't explicitly specify this. We can also explicitly mark a class member as public if we wish:

```
class Shape {
  public kind: string;
  public isEuclidian: boolean | undefined;
  constructor(kind: string, isEuclidian?: boolean) {
    this.kind = kind;
    this.isEuclidian = isEuclidian;
  }
}
```

In this case, both the **kind** and **isEuclidian** properties are marked as **public**. Some people consider this explicit form to be more readable, while others may consider it overly verbose.

It is legal to add the **private** access modifier to a constructor, but in this case, it will not be possible to create instance objects, for example:

```
private constructor(kind: string, isEuclidian?: boolean) {
  this.kind = kind;
  this.isEuclidian = isEuclidian;
}
const hole = new Shape('circle'); // error
```

In this case, we will see the following error in the editor:

```
constructor Shape(kind: string,
isEuclidian?: boolean): Shape

Constructor of class 'Shape' is private
and only accessible within the class
declaration. ts(2673)
```

***Figure 8.3**: Private constructor error in Visual Studio Code*

This may be the desired behavior if you are implementing the Singleton design pattern, but outside of this, it is fairly unusual to see. We'll look at design patterns in more detail towards the end of this chapter.

One point to note is that properties marked with the **`private`** access modifier aren't private once they become compiled down to JavaScript. TypeScript will prevent us from accessing it, but only in the development stage.

Even in TypeScript, we can still access private class members from outside of the class – we just need to use square bracket notation. Let's take a look at a quick example:

```
class Shape {
  private kind = 'private';
}
```

In this case, we have a version of the **`Shape`** class with only a single property, **`kind`**, which is prefixed with the **`private`** access modifier. If we create a new instance of this class and try to access the **`kind`** property using standard dot notation:

```
const myShape = new Shape();
console.log(myShape.kind); // error
```

Then we'll see an error in the editor similar to the one above. However, we can easily access the private property using square-bracket notation instead:

```
console.log(myShape['kind']); // private
```

In this case, there will be no error in the editor, and if we compile it into JavaScript and run it in a browser, we'll see the private member printed to the console.

Private Members in JavaScript

JavaScript lacked any concept of private members on classes until ECMAScript 2022 when it introduced a new syntax to mark class members as private. In pure JavaScript, the syntax for this is the hash sign **#**.

For reference, we would use the modifier in regular JavaScript like this:

```
class Shape {
  #kind = 'private';
}
```

The symbol is prefixed to the beginning of the property that is to be made private. JavaScript then enforces the same checks as we see when using the private modifier in TypeScript - if we try to use it outside of the class itself, we see an error in the browser's console warning us that the member is not accessible.

Interestingly, if we use this syntax in TypeScript, then we will still see appropriate errors in the editor if we try to access the member outside of the class, just like if we had used the **private** keyword.

Additionally, the syntax will be retained after the TypeScript has been compiled down to JavaScript as long as we are targeting **es2022** or above in the **tsconfig.json** configuration file, so using this now should be quite future-proof for some time to come.

If we are targeting a version lower than es2022, then TypeScript will emulate privacy using a **Set**, and if we try to access it outside of the class, we'll just see **undefined.**

This is very different from using the **private** modifier in TypeScript; even when using the latest (at the time of writing) **es2022** target, the **private** modifier is simply removed, and the "private" member becomes public and accessible, which could expose data that we did not mean to expose.

In order to fully retain the **#** symbol after compilation, right now we need to target **ESNEXT**, but going forward, I expect this to fall into the **es2022** target in some not-too-distant future version of TypeScript, and I would hope that the **private** keyword would also start to be compiled down to **#** rather than using **Set** emulation or losing privacy altogether.

Getters and Setters

Two more access modifiers worth mentioning, and which are supported by both JavaScript and TypeScript in classes, are the **get** and **set** modifiers. These can be applied either singly, or both together, on properties of the class to control how access to those properties works.

These modifiers are used to perform custom operations, like validation for example, when retrieving or assigning to a class property that has them, and are often used to provide limited access to **private** or **protected** properties of the class without exposing those directly to code external to the class.

Let's take a look at a basic example:

```
class Shape {
  private _kind = 'shape';
  private allowed = ['square', 'rectangle'];

  get kind(): string {
    return this._kind;
  }

  set kind(value: string) {
    if (this.allowed.includes(value)) {
      this._kind = value;
    } else {
      console.error('Kind not allowed');
    }
  }
}
```

In this example, the **Shape** class has a private **_kind** property and a public **kind** property with both **get** and **set** modifiers. The getter simply returns the value of the private **_kind** property, providing proxy access to the private property outside of the class.

We can also provide a return type annotation for the getter property, string in this case. It has a second private property called **allowed**, which is an array of strings.

The setter receives a **value** parameter which will be of the type **string** – this will be the value that the consumer is trying to set as the value of the property. We can provide the annotation for the parameter here, but we cannot provide a return type annotation for a setter – setters are not allowed to return a value.

Inside the setter for the **kind** property, we first check whether the value being set is one of the allowed kinds – if it is, we set it as the value of the private **_kind** property. If it isn't, we instead log an error to the console.

We can initialize an instance of this class in the same way as other class examples we've looked at:

```
const shape = new Shape();
```

If we try to set the **kind** property to a value not listed in the **allowed** array, compile the code and run it in a browser, we'll see the error in the browser's console, and the **_kind** property will retain its original value:

```
shape.kind = 'circle'; // error

console.log(shape.kind); // shape
```

When we provide a value that is listed in the **allowed** array, then there will be no error, and the private **_kind** property will be updated as expected:

```
shape.kind = 'square'; // allowed

console.log(shape.kind); // square
```

This allows us to use getters and setters to provide validation logic on properties before they are set or perform any other custom behavior we wish to implement.

This Parameter

In the last chapter, we learned that functions can receive a **this** parameter, which sets the value of the **this** object inside the function. Methods inside classes may also make use of a **this** parameter to set the value of **this** inside the method, which is useful to ensure that the value of **this** inside the function is what we expect it to be.

Consider the following code:

```
class Shape {

  private _kind = 'shape';

  getKind(): string {

    return this._kind;

  }

}
```

This variant of the **Shape** class has a private property called **_kind** which is set to the string **shape**. It also has a method called **getKind** which returns the value of the private property. This is basically an alternative to the getter from the example code in the last section.

If someone is using the class in the expected way, for example:

```
const myShape = new Shape();

console.log(myShape.getKind()); // shape
```

Then, there will be no problems. But if the method is used in a different calling context, then the value of **this** may not be the containing class. For example:

```
const myObj = {

  getKind: myShape.getKind

};

console.log(myObj.getKind()); // undefined
```

In this case, we create a new object called **myObj** and add a **getKind** property, the value of which is the **getKind** method of the **myShape** instance. When we invoke the **getKind** method of **myObj**, the calling context will be **myObj** instead of the **myShape** instance of the class, which will result in **undefined** being returned.

Note also that we see no warnings in the editor for this issue, which could lead to actual errors in the browser at runtime.

We can fix this issue using a **this** parameter in the definition of the method in the class:

```
getKind(this: Shape): string {

  return this._kind;

}
```

We set the **this** parameter to the containing class, which will enforce the value of **this** inside the method, whichever way the method is called. Immediately, we should see an error in the editor warning us that there is an issue with the **myObj** usage of the method:

```
const myObj: {
    getKind: (this: Shape) => string;
}
The 'this' context of type '{ getKind: (this:
Shape) => string; }' is not assignable to
method's 'this' of type 'Shape'.
  Property '_kind' is missing in type '{ getKind:
(this: Shape) => string; }' but required in type
'Shape'. ts(2684)
```

Figure 8.4*: Wrong this context error in Visual Studio Code*

Using a **this** parameter to set the value of **this** to the containing class has a similar effect to using an arrow function for the method implementation, but this technique works in a different way and has different pros and cons.

For example, using a **this** parameter is more efficient in terms of memory usage because there will be only one instance of the method that exists - the one in the class definition. Using an arrow function means that a copy of the method will exist in each instance of the class that gets initialized, which could consume a lot of resource if there are a great number of instances.

NOTE: Getters and Setters cannot use a this parameter.

Index Signatures

Classes in TypeScript can also make use of index signatures, just like object types, which we looked at earlier in the book.

Let's look at a basic example:

```
class Shape {
  [index: number]: string;
```

```
  constructor(public kind: string, public isEuclidian?: boolean) {
    this[0] = crypto.randomUUID();
  }
}
```

The index signature appears in square brackets; it is given the identifier **index** in this example, but this can be anything at all. It is of the type **number** for the index, and the type **string** for the value.

Inside the body of the constructor in this example, we create a random UUID (universally unique identifier) using the **randomUUID** method of the global **crypto** object and assign it to the zeroth index of the class.

NOTE: The global crypto object is a web API built into modern browsers that give access to cryptographic functionality.

Now when we create a new instance of the class, we will be able to access this UUID via its zeroth index:

```
const plate = new Shape('circle');
console.log(plate[0]); // a guid
```

Index signatures aren't commonly used like this with classes, and it can be awkward to add index signatures that are for methods rather than simple properties like in this example.

Implementing an Interface

In TypeScript, we can say that a class should implement a particular interface. Let's say that we want to allow shapes to be placed on a two-dimensional grid. First, let's create a simple interface called **placeable**:

```
interface Placeable {
  left: number;
  top: number;
};
```

We can now define a class that implements this interface, for example:

```
class Shape implements Placeable {
```

```
  left: number;
  top: number;
  constructor(public kind: string, coords: placeable) {
    this.left = coords.left;
    this.top = coords.top;
  }
}
```

We use the **implements** keyword to state that the **Shape** class should include all of the properties specified by the **Placeable** interface. It can also define other members, and indeed, the constructor specifies the **kind** property as a public property with a type of **string**.

In order to meet the requirement of the interface, this version of the constructor for the **Shape** class can also accept an object called **coords** which also meets the **Placeable** interface, that is, it should be an object with **left** and **top** properties of the type **number**. These properties are then initialized in the **constructor** body.

We can now create **Shape** instances and specify placement for them:

```
const tile = new Shape('square', { left: 0, top: 0 });
```

Implementing an interface is a useful way to enforce that classes have particular members.

Note that we can specify both properties and methods of the interface that are optional, for example:

```
interface Placeable {
  left: number;
  top: number;
  zIndex?: number;
  changeZIndex?: (newIndex: number) => void;
}
```

This interface has an optional **zIndex** property which has a type of **number**, and an optional method called **changeZIndex** which accepts a parameter with the type **number** and returns **void**.

Static Class Members

One more class feature that we have not yet looked at, and which is supported by both JavaScript and TypeScript, is the **`static`** modifier. The **`static`** modifier is used to make a property or method existing only on the class itself rather than on object instances of the class.

Let's see how to use them in practice in a basic example; first, we can add a new variation of the **`Shape`** class:

```
class Shape {

  private static shapeInstances: Shape[] = [];

  constructor() {

    Shape.shapeInstances.push(this);

  }

  static getShapes() {

    return Shape.shapeInstances;

  }

}
```

The first member uses both the **`private`** and **`static`** modifiers for a property called **`shapeInstances`**, which will be an array of **`Shape`** objects. This will be used by the base **`Shape`** class in this example to keep track of all instances of the class and is initialized to an empty array.

The constructor for this class adds the new instance of the class (**`this`**) to the **`shapeInstances`** array. It is important to note that in order to refer correctly to the **`shapeInstances`** property, we must access it from the **`Shape`** class directly and not from **`this`**.

Lastly, the class has a **`static`** method called **`getShapes`** which is used to return the **`private static`** member **`shapeInstances`**.

Now, whenever we create new instances of the **`Shape`** class, these instances will be added to the static property **`shapeInstances`**. We can access these instances if we need to via the static **`getShapes`** method, which is invoked on the **`Shape`** class directly rather than on instances of the class, for example:

```
const myShape = new Shape();

const myOtherShape = new Shape();

console.log(Shape.getShapes().length); // 2
```

Note that we call the **`getShapes`** method directly on the **`Shape`** class, rather than on one of the instances like **`myShape`** or **`myOtherShape`**.

Static properties and methods are useful when the information or behavior we wish to use applies to the class itself rather than to individual instances of the class. One point to note is that we would probably only want to collect all instances of a class if we knew in advance that there would be a relatively small number of instances of the class.

Static Blocks

As well as static members, JavaScript and TypeScript also let us define static blocks in classes. These can be used to perform complex initialization of any static properties the class has. Let's see how they are used.

We can start out with a basic class that has a single **`static`** property:

```
class Shape {

  static allowedKinds: string[];

}
```

The class has a static property called **`allowedKinds`** which is an array of strings. Let's change the example to use a static block to initialize this property:

```
class Shape {

  static {

    Shape.allowedKinds = ['square'];

  }

}
```

A static block is created with the **`static`** keyword followed by a block of statements within curly brackets. In this case, we just hardcode an array with a single string value, but in reality, this could be the result of a function call or anything more complex that we need to do.

Finally, we can add a constructor to the class that checks that the instance being created has an allowed kind:

```
constructor(public kind: string) {
  if (!Shape.allowedKinds.includes(kind)) {
    throw new Error(`'${kind}' not allowed`);
  }
  this.kind = kind;
}
```

The constructor accepts a parameter called **kind**, which is of the type **string**, and inside the **constructor** it checks whether the kind is included in the static **allowedKinds** array. If it isn't, we can throw an error in this example.

Now, we can create instances that do have an allowed kind, for example:

```
const shape1 = new Shape('square'); // fine
```

But we'll see an error if we try to use a kind that isn't allowed:

```
const shape2 = new Shape('circle'); // Error: 'circle' not allowed
```

For reference, the complete definition of the class should look like this:

```
class Shape {
  static allowedKinds: string[];
  static {
    Shape.allowedKinds = ['square'];
  }
  constructor(public kind: string) {
    if (!Shape.allowedKinds.includes(kind)) {
      throw new Error(`'${kind}' not allowed`);
    }
    this.kind = kind;
  }
}
```

While the example here is not particularly useful unless the consumer of the class knows in advance which kinds of shapes are actually allowed, the takeaway is that static blocks can be used to initialize static properties where the initialization may be more complex than a simple assignment.

Multiple static blocks can be used in a single class, and where more than one static block is provided, they will be executed sequentially in the order in which they are declared.

Inheritance

In JavaScript, subclasses of a class are created using the **extends** keyword, and in TypeScript, it is no different. Inheritance is a powerful feature of JavaScript that can allow us to create hierarchies of related objects with shared functionality, and this can help us to keep our code modular and organized.

Let's start with a version of the **Shape** class from prior examples:

```
class Shape {
  constructor(public kind: string, public isEuclidian?: boolean) { }
}
```

We can create a more specific subclass of this to represent actual concrete shapes:

```
class Square extends Shape {
  constructor(public sidesLength: number) {
    super('square', true);
  }

  getArea(): number {
    return this.sidesLength ** 2;
  }
}
```

In this case, we define a new class called **Square** and use the **extends** keyword to specify **Shape** as the base class. In the constructor of the subclass, we can receive a new parameter called **sidesLength**, which should be of the type number, and we use a **constructor** property to avoid having to explicitly initialize the new property.

Inside the constructor, we can call the constructor of the base class using the **super** keyword, and here we pass in the appropriate arguments to set the **kind** and **isEuclidian** properties required by the base class.

NOTE: Subclasses are sometimes referred to as derived classes.

As well as adding new properties, subclasses can also add methods, and in the previous example, we add a method called **getArea**, which returns a value of the type **number**. Inside the method, we return the result of using the exponentiation operator ** to raise the **sidesLength** property to the power of two.

Any instances of the **Square** class we create will have all of the properties and methods of both the base and derived class, for example:

```
const myShape = new Square(3);

console.log(myShape.getArea()); // 9

console.log(myShape.kind); // square
```

Additionally, the subclass may override methods on the base class, changing their behavior. Let's add a new method to the base class to illustrate this:

```
class Shape {

  constructor(public kind: string, public isEuclidian?: boolean) { }

  logKind(): void {

    console.log('Base kind: ', this.kind);

  }

}
```

This time we add a method to the base class called **logKind**, which simply logs a brief message to the console and references **this.kind**. Now let's extend that with a simple subclass:

```
class Square extends Shape {

  logKind(): void {

    console.log('Derived kind: ', this.kind);

  }

}
```

In the derived class, we don't need to specifically add a constructor unless we want to accept different parameters. We do add a method to this class with the same name as the method we want to override on the base class – **`logKind`**.

Now let's create some new instances:

```
const generic = new Shape('shape');

const box = new Shape('cuboid');
```

Even though the derived class doesn't even have a constructor, we can still pass it an argument for **`kind`** and that argument will still be set as the **`kind`** property on the class, just as it is with the base class.

When we call the **`logKind`** method of the base and derived class, we should see each message respectively:

```
generic.logKind(); // Base kind: shape

box.logKind(); // Derived kind: cuboid
```

Once the TypeScript for this example has been compiled, when we view it in a browser, we should see the log messages as expected:

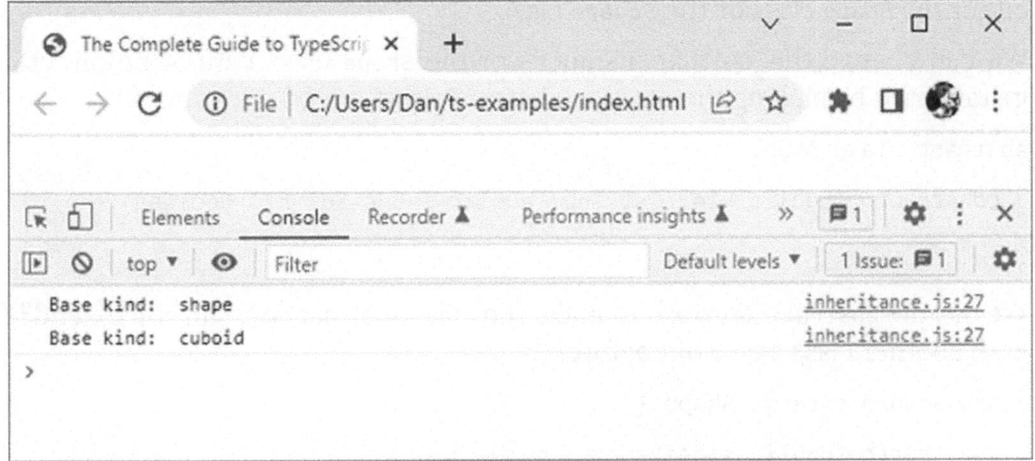

***Figure 8.5**: Compiled output in the Chrome browser on Windows*

In this example, all we did was override the message that gets logged to the console, but in reality, we can do anything that we need to. Classes in TypeScript can both implement an interface and extend a base class simultaneously as well.

Subclasses are inherently polymorphic in TypeScript, as derived classes may each perform their own specialized versions of methods inherited from the parent class. Polymorphism is a feature of many object-oriented languages, and TypeScript is no exception.

Abstract Classes

An abstract class is a class that should not be instantiated directly, instead only instances of derived classes that extend the abstract class should be created.

While JavaScript indirectly supports abstract classes via functions and prototype checking during initialization, JavaScript itself does not implement the **abstract** keyword – this is purely a TypeScript device at this, and for the foreseeable, time.

Abstract classes are useful when we wish to define a common base class with default behavior for a range of classes that extend the base class. Think of an abstract class as a template for other classes to extend and build upon.

In the previous section, we created a subclass of the **Shape** class called **Square** and because the **Shape** class was a regular class, we could create instances of either the **Shape** class or the **Square** class.

We can change this so that instances of the **Shape** class cannot be directly instantiated by making the class an abstract class:

```
abstract class Shape {

  constructor(public kind: string, public isEuclidian?: boolean) { }

}
```

We use the **abstract** keyword to make the class abstract. We can still extend it with another class as we did before:

```
class Square extends Shape {

  constructor(public sidesLength: number) {

    super('square', true);

  }

}
```

Now, we can only create instances of the **Square** class, and not the base **Shape** class. If we try to create a new instance of the **Shape** class, for example:

```
const badShape = new Shape('triangle');
```

Then, we'll see this error in the editor:

```
constructor Shape(kind: string, isEuclidian?:
boolean): Shape

Cannot create an instance of an abstract
class. ts(2511)
```

***Figure 8.6**: Abstract class instance error in Visual Studio Code*

Abstract classes are useful when the base class lacks functionality that is only implemented in extending classes.

Abstract Properties

Abstract classes may also contain abstract properties and abstract methods. These are properties and methods that do not contain a value or implementation themselves, but classes that extend them must initialize them if they are properties, or implement them if they are methods. You cannot use the abstract modifier on a parameter property.

Consider the following code:

```
abstract class Shape {
  abstract kind: string;
  constructor(public isEuclidian?: boolean) { }
}
```

This time we have pulled the **kind** property out of the constructor function and made it an abstract property of the class instead of using the **abstract** keyword.

Now, classes that extend the **Shape** class must initialize a property called **kind** with a string **value**:

```
class Square extends Shape {
  constructor(public kind: string, public sidesLength: number) {
    super(true);
  }
}
```

In this case, we can use a parameter property to initialize the **kind** property for convenience, but we could also initialize it inside the constructor manually if we wished.

One point to note is that only abstract classes may contain abstract properties (or abstract methods).

You should also note that we can use the **abstract** modifier in conjunction with other modifiers like **public** or **private**. In this case, the **abstract** keyword should come after the **public/private** modifier, for example:

```
abstract class Shape {
  public abstract kind: string;
  constructor(public isEuclidian?: boolean) { }
}
```

Note that the same applies when using **private** or **protected**.

Abstract Methods

In addition to abstract properties, we can also apply the **abstract** modifier to methods. For these, we provide only the signature of the method, not the implementation – this is left for subclasses to implement, for example:

```
abstract class Shape {
  constructor(public kind: string, public isEuclidian?: boolean) { }
  abstract getKind(): string;
}
```

In this variation of the **Shape** class, we revert to specifying **kind** as a parameter property rather than defining it as an **abstract** property. We added a single **abstract** method called **getKind** and specified that it should return a value of the type **string**.

We can now extend this class with a new subclass – let's go with a simple **Square** class as in previous examples:

```
class Square extends Shape {
  constructor(public kind: string, public sidesLength: number) {
    super('square', true);
  }
```

```
  getKind(): string {
    return this.kind;
  }
}
```

This class successfully extends the base class because it implements a **`getKind`** method which returns a **`string`** value. If we extend a class and fail to implement any of the base class's abstract methods, we'll see the following error in the editor:

```
class Square
Non-abstract class 'Square' does not implement
inherited abstract member 'getKind' from class
'Shape'. ts(2515)
```

Figure 8.7: *Abstract method does not implement error in Visual Studio Code*

Generic Classes

Like objects and functions, classes in TypeScript can also be generic, allowing them to work over a range of different types. The syntax of generic classes is similar to that of other generics, for example:

```
class Shape<T> {
  constructor(public kind: T) {}
}
```

We specify that the class is generic by providing a type parameter in angle brackets after the class identifier. As before, the convention here is to use **`T`**, but you can use whatever you prefer. We can use this parameter elsewhere inside the class; here a parameter property is used to initialize the **`kind`** property, which will be the type of the type parameter.

We could then have some other classes which corresponded to actual shapes:

```
class Square {
  constructor(public sidesLength: number) {}
}

class Triangle {
  constructor(
    public sidesLength: [number, number, number],
    public angles: [number, number, number]
  ) {}
}
```

In this example, we have a simple **Square** class that has a **sidesLength** property, and a **Triangle** class that has properties for the **sidesLength** and also **angles**. Both of these are tuple types of three numbers.

At this point, we can create concrete shapes like squares and triangles:

```
const mySquare = new Square(3);
const myTriangle = new Triangle([2, 2, 2], [60, 60, 60]);
```

And we can also create new **Shapes** instances which use the actual shapes as types:

```
const myShape = new Shape(mySquare);
const otherShape = new Shape(myTriangle);
console.log(myShape.kind); // Square
console.log(otherShape.kind); // Triangle
```

In this case, the whole kind object will be displayed in the console log messages in the browser's console once the code has been compiled:

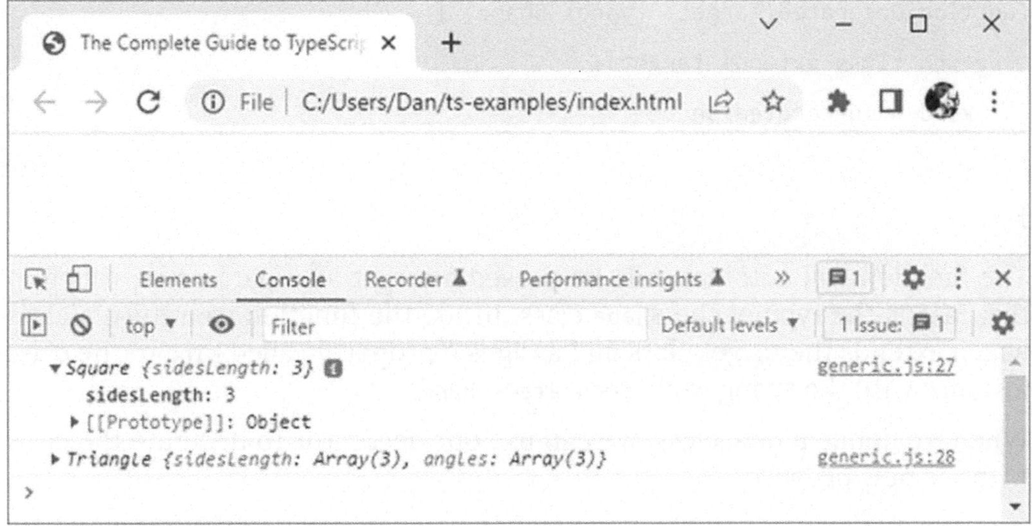

***Figure 8.8**: Kind objects logged to console in the Chrome browser on Windows*

We can also use the **Shape** class for other types, such as arrays containing shapes of any type, or arrays containing only specific types of shapes:

```
const allShapes: Shape<any>[] = [myShape, otherShape];
const allSquares: Shape<Square>[] = [myShape];
```

We can also use generic constraints as we did with generic functions, and the syntax here would be the same.

Decorators

The latest versions of TypeScript (5.0.0 and above) provide support for the upcoming JavaScript decorators syntax. Decorators provide a way of modifying a class, or members of the class, with extra functionality whenever the class is used with the decorator.

For example, we can add a decorator to a class that automatically adds a new property to the class whenever a new instance of the class is created.

A decorator is essentially just a function:

```
function Decorated(target: typeof Shape) {
  return class extends target {
    kind = 'decorated-shape'
  }
}
```

The function will automatically be passed a target as a parameter, which in this case is the type of the **Shape** class. Inside the function we return a class which extends the target class and assigns a property called **kind** to the class instance with the string value **decorated-shape**.

When we define a new class, we can use our decorator to decorate the class with the new property:

```
@Decorated
class Shape {}
```

The decorator we use is specified before the class keyword and must begin with the **@** character. Note that the **Shape** class in this example is completely empty, but as we have decorated it with the **Decorated decorator**, instances of this class will contain a property called **kind** with the value decorated-shape:

```
const myShape = new Shape();
(myShape as any).kind; // decorated-shape
```

Note that we must cast the type of our instance to **any** in order to access the **kind** property.

Stylistically, the decorator may appear on the same line as the **class** keyword if we prefer, and we can use multiple decorators for the same class, so we could do something like this if we wished:

```
function Decorated(target: typeof Shape) {
  return class extends target {
    kind = 'decorated-shape'
  }
}

function DecoratedAgain(target: typeof Shape) {
  return class extends target {
```

```
    special = 'decorated again!'
  }
}


@Decorated
@DecoratedAgain
class Shape {}

const myShape = new Shape();
(myShape as any).special; // decorated again!
```

Note that when using multiple decorators, the decorators are applied in reverse order, so in this case, the **DecoratedAgain** decorator is applied to the class first, followed by the original **Decorated** decorator, and inside the **Decorated** decorator, we would be able to see and operate on the **special** property added by the **DecoratedAgain** decorator. The order of decorators thus becomes important if one of the decorators relies on functionality added by another decorator.

NOTE: At the time of writing, in the tsconfig.json file, the target property must not be set to CommonJS and experimentalDecorators must be set to true for decorators to be used.

TypeScript Design Patterns

Design patterns are a recognized optimal solution to a common problem in software development. They exist for all common programming languages and both JavaScript and TypeScript are no exception.

There are many commonly used design patterns, and they can be the subject of entire books, so we will cover only a single one here as an example of a very commonly used design pattern in TypeScript – the Observer pattern.

The Observer pattern is a design pattern that allows objects to have observers added to them that are notified when the value being observed changes.

This can be a very complex solution indeed – the popular RXJS framework is dedicated to providing observable objects with huge amounts of functionality and specialized behavior. We will look at a much-simplified example here that has only extremely limited functionality in comparison.

The common problem that we would like to solve with the Observer pattern is to be able to respond to changes in a particular object's value. Typically, this is done by allowing observers or subscribers to be added to an object. These observers are functions that will be invoked whenever the value of the object being observed changes.

Let's start by adding an **Observable** class:

```
abstract class Observable<T> {
  private observers: ((update: T) => void)[] = [];

  constructor(public value: T) {}

  observe(observer: (update: T) => void) {
    this.observers.push(observer);
  }
  notify() {
    this.observers.forEach((observer) => observer(this.value));
  }
}
```

We use the **abstract** keyword to prevent this class from being initialized directly, and we make it generic by adding a **T** type parameter so that it can work on different types. The class has a parameter property that initializes a property called **value**, which will be of the **T** type parameter.

The class has a private **observers** property which will contain all of the functions that are registered as observers. These functions will receive a parameter called **update**, which will also be of the generic **T** type and won't return a useful value, so is marked as **void**. This property is initialized to an empty array.

The **observe** method is used to add an observer to the private array of observers. This method receives the function to add to the array of observers, so this has the same type as the observers inside the **observers** array. Inside the method, the observer is pushed into the array.

Lastly, the class has a method called **notify**. This method is used to broadcast to the observers that the value has changed. It uses **forEach** to visit each observer in the array and invokes each of them, passing them the updated **value**.

We can now create other classes that are observable by extending the **Observable** class, for example, we could create an **ObservableString** class:

```
class ObservableString extends Observable<string> {
  updateValue(value: string) {
    this.value = value;
    this.notify();
  }
}
```

This class has a method called **updateValue**, which is used to set the object's **value** property and call the object's **notify** method, which will trigger the broadcast to any observers. We can now create instances of **ObservableString** and observe their values:

```
const myObservableString = new ObservableString('test');
myObservableString.observe((update: string) => {
  console.log(`The value was updated to ${update}`);
});
```

In this case, we create a new **ObservableString** with the value **test**. We then observe the value by adding an observer using the **observe** method. The function that we pass to this method simply logs the new value that was updated to the console.

Now, whenever we update the value of the object using the **updateValue** method, we will see the message from the observer logged into the console:

```
myObservableString.updateValue('new!'); // The value was updated to new!
```

There are many, many design patterns for TypeScript and becoming familiar with them enables you to talk about software development in a common language that many other developers will be able to understand. They can teach you a lot about both TypeScript and application development, so I would urge you to continue learning about them.

Conclusion

In this chapter, we've taken a good look at classes in TypeScript and seen how to use all of their core functionality and leverage TypeScript to make using them as intuitive and safe as possible.

In the next chapter, we'll move on to look to start looking at some of the more advanced aspects of TypeScript, starting with control flow analysis, which is the practice of narrowing types from a wide range of different possible types down to a specific type.

References

- **https://www.typescriptlang.org/docs/handbook**
- **https://blog.jetbrains.com/webstorm/2019/03/write-object-oriented-typescript-polymorphism**
- **https://2ality.com/2021/09/class-static-block.html**
- **https://refactoring.guru/design-patterns/observer/typescript/example**
- **https://compiletab.com/private-constructor-typescript**

CHAPTER 9

Control Flow Analysis

Introduction

In this chapter, we are going to look at some of TypeScript's more advanced concepts and features, things that so far, I may have hinted at when looking at other aspects of TypeScript, but not really covered in full, to avoid detracting from the topic we were covering at the time.

Now that we've covered the basics of TypeScript, it's time to take a deep dive into some additional aspects of how it works to really build that solid foundation of understanding TypeScript. The first of these aspects is something called Control Flow Analysis, which is what the TypeScript compiler uses in order to infer the types that we're using if they aren't explicitly annotated.

Control Flow Analysis uses the process of narrowing to determine the most specific type a value may be, and there are times that we will also need to use narrowing manually with type-guards in our own code in order to satisfy the compiler that we are fully accounting for any of the possible types that a value might have. This occurs mostly when using union types or dealing with optional parameters.

Structure

In this chapter, we will cover the following topics:

- Narrowing
- Widening
- Type guards

- Type predicates
- Discriminated unions
- Assertion functions
- Using as const

Narrowing

Narrowing is the process of removing possible types that a value may have until there is (usually) only a single type left, which should be the most specific type possible. This is most keenly demonstrated with union types; for example, consider the following code:

```
const which: string | number = 'str';

which.concat('a');
```

On the first line, ignore momentarily that we've assigned a string literal value to the **`which`** variable, the type is set to the union type **`string | number`**, and if we hover over the identifier on that line, we'll see the type is definitely the full union type:

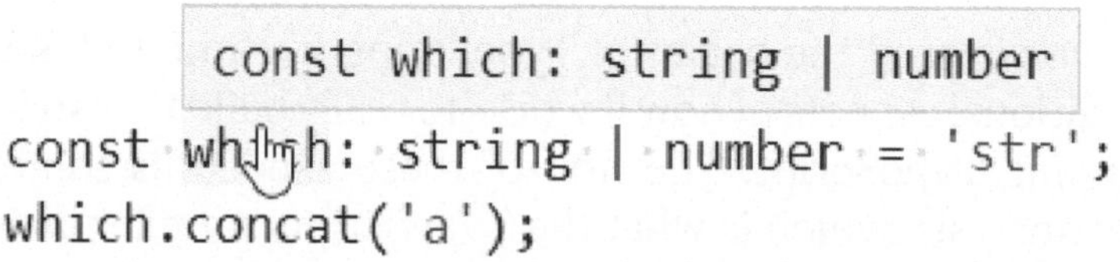

```
const which: string | number
const which: string | number = 'str';
which.concat('a');
```

***Figure 9.1**: Union type tooltip in Visual Studio Code*

On the second line, because we explicitly set the value of the **`which`** variable to an actual string literal on the first line, the compiler can narrow the type down from either **`string`** or **`number`** to just **`string`**. If we hover over the identifier on the second line, we do indeed see that the type is no longer the union type, but a single specific type - **`string`**:

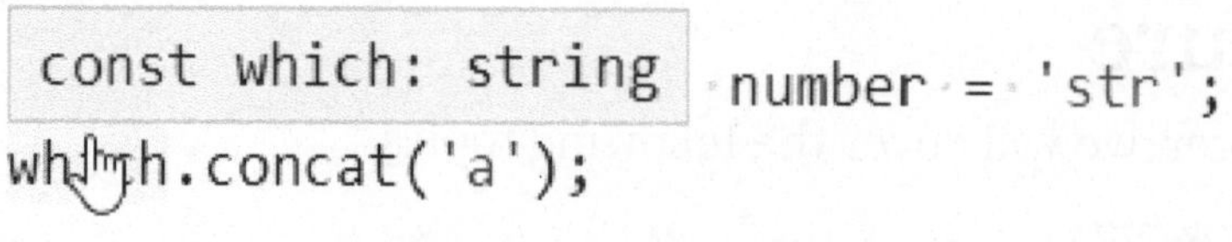

```
const which: string  number = 'str';
which.concat('a');
```

***Figure 9.2**: Narrowed type tooltip in Visual Studio Code*

This is an example of how the compiler narrows types and is the reason we are able to safely call the `concat` string method on the `which` variable without causing the editor to display any errors.

Narrowing is also something we'll need to do ourselves from time to time as well, and we'll look at that in just a moment.

Widening

Widening is the opposite of narrowing - taking a more-specific type and making it less specific. Unlike narrowing, widening is not something we do ourselves in our own code very often at all, and not generally something that we have to worry about or consider, but let's see a very basic example of a kind of widening - literal widening - for completeness' sake.

Let's again consider some very basic code:

```
const num1 = 1;

let num2 = 2;
```

The previous code snippet is just two very simple variable declarations with assignments, we haven't even added any actual type annotations. The key point here is that one of the variables is declared with `const`, and the other with `let`, and it is this which triggers the different treatment of these two variables in TypeScript.

If we hover the mouse on the first line, we'll see that the `num1` variable has been given the literal type `1`:

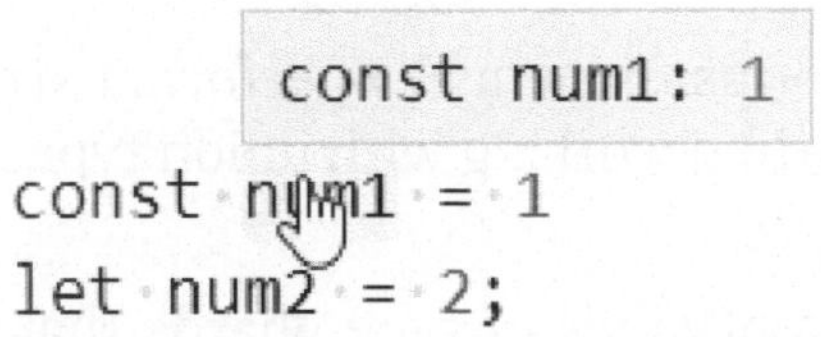

```
const num1: 1

const num1 = 1
let num2 = 2;
```

***Figure 9.3**: Literal type tooltip in Visual Studio Code*

The second line looks almost identical, the only differences are that the variable is declared using `let` this time, and the value assigned is the literal value `2`. The literal value `2` is still the literal type `2`, just like the literal value `1` is the literal type `1`, but if we hover the pointer on the second variable, we'll see that this variable has a different type:

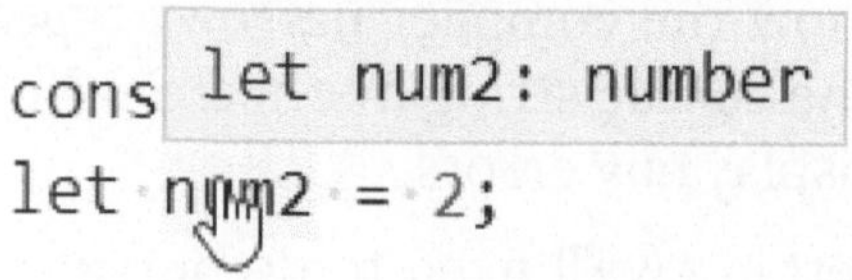

```
cons let num2: number
let num2 = 2;
```

***Figure 9.4**: Widened type tooltip in Visual Studio Code*

This time, the compiler has widened the type from the entirely specific literal type `2` to the less specific type `number`. The reason the second variable is widened is because it's not a constant value, it could change while the program is running and so may no longer be the literal type `2`, it could be any other literal `number` type, so it has to be widened to `number` to account for that.

In addition to numbers, the other primitive types `string` and `boolean` may also be widened by the compiler, and enum members are widened to the type of the enum itself.

This is really all that we need to know about widening – the compiler does it in certain limited situations, but it shouldn't make any difference to how we write our own code unless we take it as a possible sign that variables declared with `const` are preferred over those declared with `let` as they give the compiler slightly less work to do. I'll leave it up to you to decide.

Historically, the types `null` and `undefined` were widened to the type `any`, but in current versions of TypeScript, as long as the configuration is strict, or the `strictNullChecks` option is enabled, this no longer happens.

Type Guards

A type-guard is a way for us to manually perform narrowing in our own code, which we'll need to do when working with union types or optional parameters for example.

There are several different kinds of type guards that we can use, depending on the situation, and all of them are based on using conditional logic, and one of several different operators, to determine and handle the precise type that a value has.

Truthiness Type Guards

Perhaps the simplest type guard we can write is a type guard that uses truthiness to narrow a type. Consider the following example; imagine we have a simple type to represent a wrapper for strings:

```
type Wrapper = {
  contents?: string;
}
```

The **string** property **contents** is optional, therefore its type is actually not just **string** but the union **string | undefined** (another example of the compiler widening a type behind the scenes). This means that if we create an object and set its type to **Wrapper**, if we want to use the **contents** property in some way as if it is a string, like this for example:

```
const myWrapper: Wrapper = {};
''.concat(myWrapper.contents);
```

We will need to narrow the type down from **string | undefined** to just **string**. If we don't do this, we'll see an error in the editor like in the following figure:

```
(property) contents?: string | undefined
Argument of type 'string | undefined' is not
assignable to parameter of type 'string'.
  Type 'undefined' is not assignable to type
'string'. ts(2345)
```

***Figure 9.5**: Undefined is unassignable to string error in Visual Studio Code*

To narrow the type in this example, we can use a simple truthiness type-guard to ensure that the property exists, and is therefore a string:

```
if (myWrapper.contents) {
  ''.concat(myWrapper.contents);
}
```

The **contents** property will have a truthy value as long as it is not an empty string. An empty string, or an **undefined** value if the property doesn't exist, is coerced to the value **false** and is therefore not truthy. We don't even need to use an operator in simple cases such as this.

Now the error shown in *Figure* 9.5 will disappear as we only use the property in a string context when we know that the property exists. If we hover the mouse over the **contents** property inside the body of the **if** statement, we see that it is successfully narrowed down to the type string:

```
if (myWr (property) contents?: string
  ''.concat(myWrapper.contents);
}
```

***Figure 9.6**: Narrowed string type tooltip in Visual Studio Code*

Now let's move on to look at some additional types of narrowing.

Narrowing with Typeof

Another very common form of type guard uses the **`typeof`** operator to check what type a value has. We looked at a basic example of using this operator earlier in the book, but let's look at another quick example.

Let's consider an example where we have a function that may receive either a **`string`** or a **`number`**, and then needs to return the first three digits of whatever it was passed:

```
function getIdPrefix(id: string | number) {
  if (typeof id === 'string') {
    return id.slice(0, 3);
  } else {
    return id.toString().slice(0, 3);
  }
}
```

The **`id`** parameter is a union type of **`string | number`**, so before we can do anything with it inside the **`getIdPrefix`** function, we need to manually narrow the type down to either **`string`** or **`number`**. The **`typeof`** operator returns a string that tells us what is the type of the value that follows the operator.

In this example, we can first check whether **`typeof`** returns the value **`string`**, and if it does, we have narrowed the type down to string, and we can safely call **`string`** methods like **`slice`** on it.

As the union contains only two types, we don't even need to check the return value of **`typeof`** in the **`else`** branch - if the value returned by **`typeof`** is not **`string`**, then it must logically be **`number`**, as these are the only members in the union, so in the else branch, we can safely call **`number`** methods, like **`toString`**, on the value without seeing any errors.

We aren't restricted to using an **`if`** statement for a type guard, we could equally use a **`switch`** statement instead for the same effect:

```
switch (typeof id) {
  case 'string':
    return id.slice(0, 3);
  case 'number':
    return id.toString().slice(0, 3);
}
```

While entirely valid, it does seem overkill to use a switch statement when working with a union of only two types, so the recommendation would be to only use it in cases where there are three or more members in the union.

Handling null Values

One thing to be aware of with regard to the **`typeof`** operator is how it treats **`null`** values. The string **`'null'`** is the only primitive representation that the **`typeof`** operator doesn't return, instead, it returns the string **`'object'`** when it encounters **`null`**. This is because JavaScript also exhibits the same behavior since it was initially created so TypeScript mirrors this behavior to avoid confusion.

TypeScript will warn us if we are working with an object that might be **`null`**. For example, consider the following code:

```
type Rocket = { launch: () => void };
function attemptLaunch(rocket: Rocket | null) {
  rocket.launch();
}
```

In this case, we specify a type called **`Rocket`**, which is for objects that have a **`launch`** method. We then have a function called **`attemptLaunch`** which receives a single parameter that might be a **`Rocket`** object, or it might be **`null`**.

Immediately, inside the **`attemptLaunch`** function, TypeScript will highlight the use of the **`rocket`** parameter as an error, and display a message that the object might be **`null`**, like in the following figure:

```
(parameter) rocket: Rocket | null
'rocket' is possibly 'null'. ts(18047)
```

***Figure 9.7**: Object is possibly a null error in Visual Studio Code*

The solution is to narrow the value down to the type that we think it is when trying to use the **launch** method, like this:

```
if (rocket !== null) {
  rocket.launch();
}
```

We just need to check that the parameter is not equal to **null**. Now the error will go away as we have satisfied the compiler that the object has the expected type before trying to call methods on it.

Note that we could also use a truthiness check here instead:

```
if (rocket) {
  rocket.launch();
}
```

The behavior here would be the same.

Narrowing with Instanceof

As well as using the **typeof** operator to narrow types, we can also use the **instanceof** operator to check that an object is of the expected type. This time, imagine we have a couple of classes:

```
class Employee {
  work = () => console.log('Working');
}
class Manager {
  manage = () => console.log('Managing');
}
```

Each class has a single method, either **work** for the **Employee** class or **manage** for the **Manager** class. Now consider a function that receives an object which may be an instance of either of these two classes:

```
function work(emp: Employee | Manager) {
  // do something with emp
}
```

TypeScript won't let us call any of the **emp** parameter's methods until we narrow the type down to one of the two union members, if we try to call the **work** method, for example, we'll see a familiar error that the property does not exist on the union type of **Employee | Manager** because it doesn't exist on **Manager**:

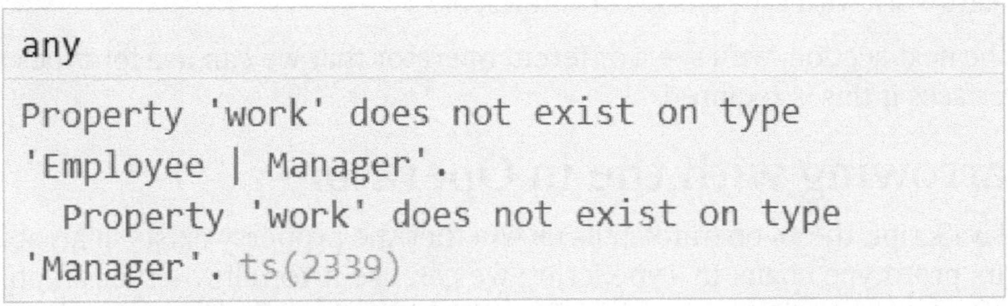

```
any
Property 'work' does not exist on type
'Employee | Manager'.
  Property 'work' does not exist on type
'Manager'. ts(2339)
```

***Figure 9.8**: Property does not exist on type error in Visual Studio Code*

We can't use the **typeof** operator here because we are working with custom classes which the **typeof** operator will not return strings for. Instead, we can use the **instanceof** operator, like this:

```
if (emp instanceof Employee) {
  emp.work();
} else {
  emp.manage();
}
```

We can use the **instanceof** operator to check whether the **emp** object is an instance of the **Employee** class, and if it is, we can safely call the **work** method. If it isn't the **Employee** class, it must be an instance of the **Manager** class, and we can instead call the **manage** method.

If we hover over the object in each branch, we can see that the union type is successfully narrowed down to a single type:

```
function work(emp: Employee | Manager) {
  if (parameter) emp: Employee {
    emp.work();
  } else {
    emp.manage();
  }
}
```

Figure 9.9: *Narrowed instance tooltip in Visual Studio Code*

One point to note is that the **instanceof** operator only works with classes, it doesn't work with type aliases or interfaces.

In the next section, we'll see a different operator that we can use for types and interfaces if this is required.

Narrowing with the in Operator

In JavaScript, the **in** operator tells us whether the property exists in an object or its prototype chain. In TypeScript, we can use it to tell whether an object confirms to a specific type or interface. Consider the following example code:

```
type SaveLocally = {

  saveInLocalStorage: () => boolean;

};

type SaveRemotely = {

  sendToApi: () => boolean;

};
```

We define two type aliases, one called **SaveLocally**, which has a method called **saveInLocalStroage**, and another called **SaveRemotely**, which has a method called **sendToApi**.

For a function that receives an object which may be one of the previous two types, we can use the **in** operator to narrow the type down to a specific member of the union:

```
function save(item: SaveLocally | SaveRemotely): boolean {
  if ('saveInLocalStorage' in item) {
    return item.saveInLocalStorage();
  } else {
    return item.sendToApi();
  }
}
```

In the first branch of the `if` statement, we check whether the method `saveInLocalStorage` exists in the `item` object using the `in` operator. If it does, we can call the method safely. As the union has only two types, we can use the `else` block to call the `sendToApi` method if the `in` operator in the first branch returns `false`.

You should note that we can also use the `in` operator with interfaces and classes, not just types as we did in this example.

Narrowing with Type Predicates

A type predicate is a special kind of return type that makes use of the TypeScript-only `is` operator. We can use a type predicate to create a custom type guard that can test that an object is of the expected type so that we can call the methods on it that we expect it to expose.

For this example, imagine we are writing software for a factory that can produce different types of machines, and that we have a union type that represents the different types of machines the factory can produce:

```
type MachineKind = 'robot' | 'drone';
```

We might also have an `interface` that represents generic machines:

```
interface Machine { kind: MachineKind; }
```

Then we might have a series of different classes for the specific kinds of machines that may be produced:

```
class Humanoid implements Machine {
  kind: MachineKind = 'robot';
  walk() { /* do walking */  }
}
```

This class is for **Humanoid** machines, which implement the **Machine** interface and has a **kind** property of the **MachineKind** type that was defined first, the value of which is set to the string **robot**. Now we can create instances of the **Humanoid** class:

```
const terminator: Machine = new Humanoid();
```

This instance will be of the type **Machine**. We would expect this instance to have a **walk** method given that we know the **Humanoid** class defines one, however, if we try to call the method, like this:

```
terminator.walk();
```

TypeScript won't let us, and will display an error in the editor instead:

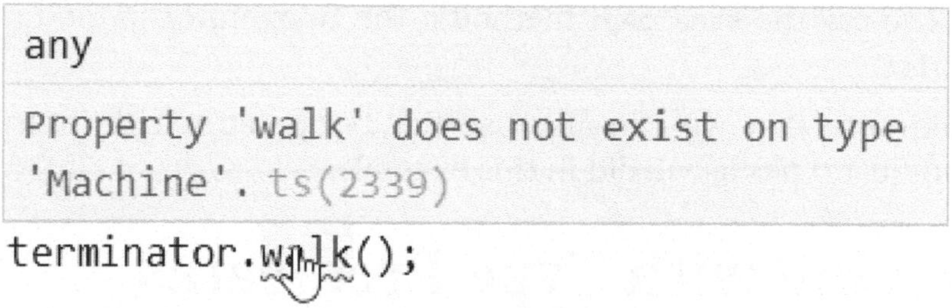

```
any
Property 'walk' does not exist on type
'Machine'. ts(2339)
terminator.walk();
```

***Figure 9.10**: Property does not exist error in Visual Studio Code*

In this case, because the **Humanoid** class implements the **Machine** interface, but this interface doesn't specify the **walk** method, TypeScript can't be certain that the object will contain a method called **walk**.

We can create a custom type guard which uses a type predicate to convince TypeScript that the **walk** method can safely be invoked:

```
function machineIsHumanoid(machine: Machine): machine is Humanoid {
  return machine.kind === 'robot';
}
```

We know that **Humanoid** instances have a **kind** property, which comes from the **Machine** interface, and that this will be set to the literal type **robot** for machines that have a **walk** method, so the type guard can simply return **true** if the **kind** property of the machine it is passed is equal to the string **robot**.

The type predicate is the return type of **machine is Humanoid.** – an assertion of the type the parameter is. On the left of the **is** operator is the parameter passed to the function, and on the right side is the thing we want to match, the

Humanoid class in this example. The left side must match an argument passed to the function.

Note that we don't have to verify the object is of the expected type by checking an internal property matches a particular union member, we can perform any kind of check that we like.

For example, inside the **machineIsHumanoid** function, we could check for the existence of the **walk** method instead of comparing the **kind** property with the **MachineKind** type:

```
function machineIsHumanoid(machine: Machine): machine is Humanoid {

  return 'walk' in machine;

}
```

This would make no difference to the overall example or how it works. Now, we can wrap the usage of the **walk** method in a simple conditional that uses the **machineIsHumanoid** function to determine the type of object we are working with:

```
if (machineIsHumanoid(terminator)) {

  terminator.walk();

}
```

This will satisfy TypeScript that the object is of the expected type. Outside of the **if** statement, the **terminator** variable has the type **Machine**, but inside of it, the type is narrowed to **Humanoid**.

You should also note that the example in this section would work equally as well using **instanceof** narrowing instead of a type-predicate, and lead to exactly the same type being narrowed, but the thing to remember is that type predicates give us much more control over how the type is narrowed, and so become more useful in more advanced scenarios.

Discriminated Unions

A discriminated union is a special type of union where each member of the union has a unique value for a property that is shared by all members of the union. The unique property is known as the discriminator. We can use these to make checking for a particular type within the union easier.

Consider an application that deals with vehicle rentals for different types of vehicles. We may have interfaces representing each type of vehicle:

```
interface Car {
  drive: () => void;
}
interface Truck {
  haul: () => void;
}
interface Plane {
  fly: () => void;
}
```

Each **interface** specifies a different method. We may also have a general type that is a union of all of the interfaces:

```
type Vehicle = Car | Truck | Plane;
```

In an all too familiar scenario, we might have an object of the type **Vehicle**, but then try to interact with that object as if it were a narrowed type rather than a union type:

```
const myJet: Vehicle = {} as any;
myJet.fly();
```

In this case, TypeScript will complain about the use of the **fly** method on the **myJet** variable because some members in the **Vehicle** union don't have a **fly** method and will show the same 'property ... does not exist on type ...' error that we saw in *Figure* 9.10 in the last section.

In this example, the object literal assigned to the **myJet** variable uses **as any** to avoid having to define the **fly** method - if we do add a **fly** method, then TypeScript will narrow the type of **myJet** to **Plane** based on the fact that the object has a **fly** method and so must be of the type **Plane**. As previously mentioned, in production code, we should avoid using the **any** type wherever possible to avoid bugs creeping into our code.

We can improve the union by making it a discriminated union. To do this, we need to add a discriminator - the shared property that each interface in the union contains, but each with its own unique value:

```
interface Car {
  drive: () => void;
  kind: 'car';
```

```
}
interface Truck {
  haul: () => void;
  kind: 'truck';
}
interface Plane {
  fly: () => void;
  kind: 'plane';
}
```

Now, each member of the union has a **kind** property that contains a unique literal type. When we create an object and use the **Vehicle** type, we are now forced to add a **kind** property matching one of the literal types of the union members:

```
const myJet: Vehicle = {
  kind: 'plane',
  fly: () =>  { /* do flying */ }
};
myJet.fly();
```

TypeScript can now discriminate between the different members of the union based on the **kind** property that we assign to our object – we don't have to use conditional logic here to check the type of object before calling its methods – TypeScript will already know.

Note that we can no longer get away with giving the object the type **any** – if we want to call the **fly** method, not only does the object have to be discriminated to the type **Plane**, but it also must have a **fly** method to call.

NOTE: The MachineKind example from the previous section is also a type of discriminated union.

Assertion Functions

Assertion functions are very similar to custom-type guards and are equally as powerful and expressive. One of the main differences between type guards and assertion functions is their return values or lack thereof.

As we learned earlier, a custom type guard returns **`true`** if the value being checked is of the expected type, or **`false`** if it is not. Assertion functions on the other hand, only return if the value being checked is of the expected type. If the value is not of the expected type, they should instead throw an error.

There are two different variations of assertion function in TypeScript; the first kind is a simple condition-assert, let's take a look at this kind first.

Imagine we have some similar but fundamentally different types:

```
type User = { name: string; getName?: () => string; }

type Artifact = { id: string, getId?: () => string; }
```

Both of the types have a **`string`** property, and both have a method that takes no parameters and returns a **`string`**. This is where the similarities end however as the property and method in each type have different identifiers.

Now consider creating an object that may be one of either of these two types:

```
const mightBeUser: User | Artifact = {

  name: ‘test’,

  getName: () => ‘test’,

};
```

Although the object is of the type **`User | Artifact`**, it certainly looks like it's a **`User`** object – it has a **`name`** property which is a string, and it has a **`getName`** property which returns a string. However, if we try to call the **`getName`** method of the **`mightBeUser`** object, we'll see an error in the editor informing us that the method may be undefined (the method is optional after all).

```
(property) getName?: (() => string) | undefined
Cannot invoke an object which is possibly
'undefined'. ts(2722)
View Problem (Alt+F8)   No quick fixes available
mightBeUser.getName();
```

***Figure 9.11**: Object is possibly an undefined error in Visual Studio Code*

We can use a condition-assert assertion function to overcome this issue:

```
function assertIsUser(test: any): asserts test {
  if (!test) throw new Error('Not a valid user');
}
```

The `assertIsUser` function receives a test condition that it should assert and has the special return type `asserts test` – the part after the `asserts` keyword is the thing being asserted, the test or condition to evaluate. This return type is known as an assertion signature, and in this example, is asserting that the `test` argument is not null or undefined – it's not asserting that the argument is specifically of the type `User`.

Inside the function, if the test fails, we simply throw an error; we don't need to add a `return` statement if the test being asserted does pass, we just need to throw an error if it doesn't.

Now, before trying to call the `getName` method, we just need to assert that the method exists, for example:

```
assertIsUser(mightBeUser.getName !== undefined);
```

The test we want the function to perform is a simple check that the `getName` method does not equal `undefined`.

Now, as long as we only try to call the `getName` method after the line where we call the assertion function, we can avoid errors in the editor, and if we pay attention to the type of the `mightBeUser` object at different points in the code, we can see that prior to the assertion, the type is the union type:

```
const mightBeUser: User | Artefact
const mightBeUser: User | Artefact = {
  name: 'test',
  getName: () => 'test',
};
```

***Figure 9.12**: Union type tooltip in Visual Studio Code*

But after the assertion is made, the type is successfully narrowed to `User`:

```
assertIsUser(mightBeUser.getName !== undefined);

const mightBeUser: User
mightBeUser.getName();
```

***Figure 9.13**: Narrowed type tooltip in Visual Studio Code*

In the preceding example, we weren't explicitly confirming the type of anything, only that some condition, that the object had a method called **getName**, evaluated to **true**.

The other form of assertion function uses a slightly different form of assertion signature to confirm the actual type of something, let's see it in action.

We can stick with the same types we used in the previous example, but this time, let's make the **getName** and **getId** methods mandatory in both of the types:

```
type User = { name: string; getName: () => string; }

type Artifact = { id: string, getId: () => string; }
```

Now, this time imagine we have a function that receives an object which may be one or the other of the two types:

```
function getName(obj: User | Artifact) {

  return obj.getName();

}
```

As you might have expected, TypeScript won't let us call the **getName** method at this point, because it can't guarantee that the object has this method. We can use an assertion function to check:

```
function assertIsUser(maybeUser: any): asserts maybeUser is User {

  if (maybeUser.name === undefined || maybeUser.getName === undefined) {

    throw new Error('Not a valid user');

  }

}
```

This time, the assertion signature uses the **is** operator to assert that the parameter **maybeUser** is of the type **User**.

Inside the function, we can perform a test that the object passed to the function has all of the expected properties and that they are not **undefined**, and if either of them is **undefined**, then it throws an error. Again, we don't need to use a **return** statement, we simply throw an error if either of the properties is equal to **undefined**.

Now inside the function, as long as the **assertIsUser** function doesn't throw, we can safely use methods from the **User** type:

```
function getName(obj: User | Artifact) {
  assertIsUser(obj);
  return obj.getName();
}
```

We should now see no errors in the editor after the line that invokes the **assertIsUser** assertion function, and that will be the same throughout the current scope, which in this example is inside the **getName** function.

Using as const

Earlier in this chapter, we looked at widening and saw that this is something that TypeScript does in some situations when inferring types, and means that a type is changed from a more specific type to a less specific type.

One of the things that we can do with **as const** is to prevent this widening from happening, for example:

```
let num2 = 2 as const;
```

This line of code is identical to the line of code that we looked at earlier, except that we add as **const** to the end of the statement. Now, even though we used **let** instead of **const** to declare the variable, the type will remain the literal type **2**:

```
let num2: 2
let num2 = 2 as const;
```

***Figure 9.14**: Un-widened value tooltip in Visual Studio Code*

Now TypeScript will treat the variable as if it had been declared using the **const** keyword, and we will be unable to assign a new value to it. If we try to do this, like this for example:

```
num2 = 3; // error
```

Then we'll see any error like in the following figure:

```
let num2: 2

Type '3' is not assignable to type
'2'. ts(2322)
```

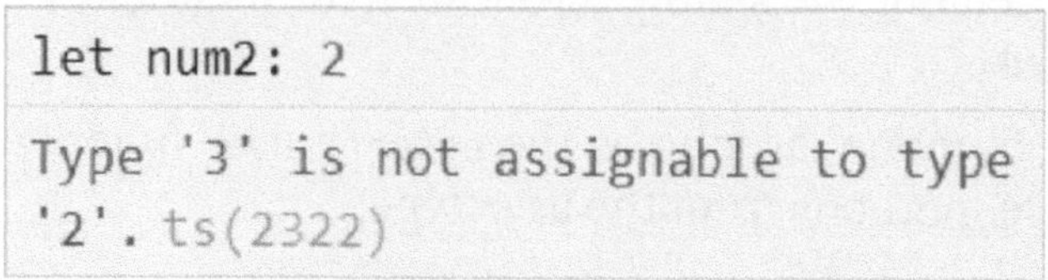

Figure 9.15: *Literal type is not assignable to a different literal type error in Visual Studio Code*

This leads nicely on to the other usage for **`as const`** – making objects and their members, completely immutable.

In JavaScript, and indeed TypeScript, even if we declare an object using **`const`**, we can still make changes to the properties inside that object, and this includes arrays, for example:

```
const mutable = [];

mutable.push('yay'); // Fine
```

Even though the **`mutable`** variable was declared with **`const`**, we can still push new elements into it or call any other methods that might mutate the array in some way.

We can change that behavior using **`as const`**:

```
const immutable = ['constant'] as const;
```

Now the array contained in the **`immutable`** variable is completely immutable, and we cannot change it, or the elements inside of it at all. As you can see in the following figure, the type gains the **`readonly`** modifier:

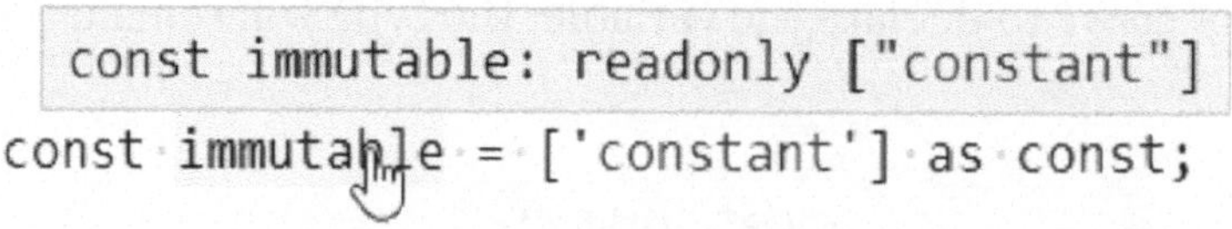

```
const immutable: readonly ["constant"]
const immutable = ['constant'] as const;
```

Figure 9.16: *Read-only array type tooltip in Visual Studio Code*

Additionally, if we read the first and only item in the **`immutable`** array and inspect its type, in this example it will be the literal string type **`'constant'`**:

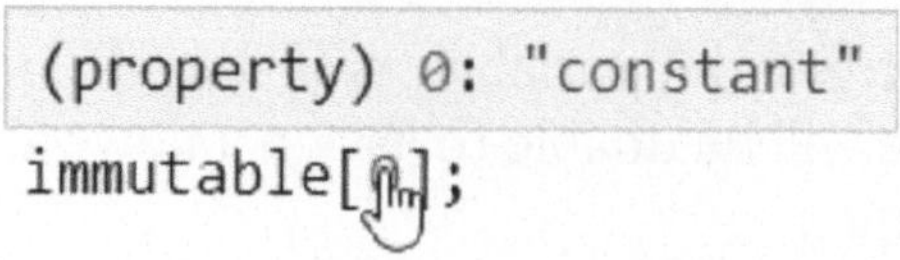

```
(property) 0: "constant"
immutable[0];
```

Figure 9.17: *Literal string type tooltip in Visual Studio Code*

From this point on in the code, we cannot **push** new items into the array, or **pop** items from it, if we try, we'll see an error that the method doesn't even exist:

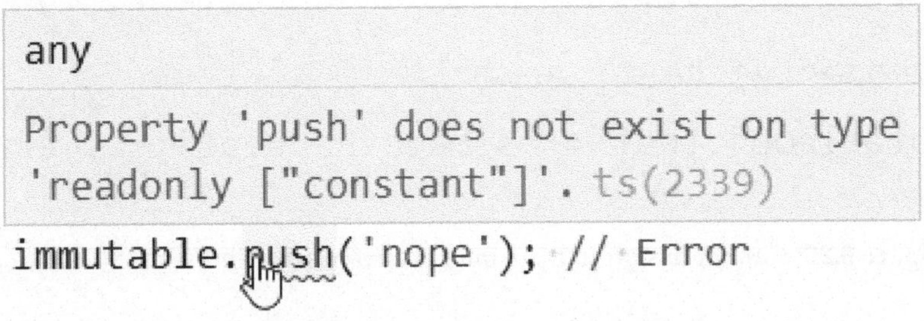

```
any
Property 'push' does not exist on type
'readonly ["constant"]'. ts(2339)
immutable.push('nope'); // Error
```

***Figure 9.18**: Property push does not exist on read-only array error in Visual Studio Code*

We are also prevented from changing any of the existing elements inside the array in any way:

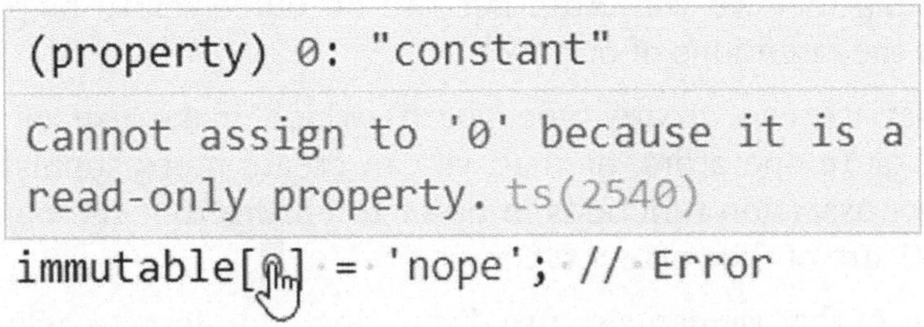

```
(property) 0: "constant"
Cannot assign to '0' because it is a
read-only property. ts(2540)
immutable[0] = 'nope'; // Error
```

***Figure 9.19**: Cannot assign to read-only element error in Visual Studio Code*

These concepts apply to all objects, not just arrays, and this is really the main use of **as const**; to make objects truly immutable. For example, a regular object, even when declared as a **const** variable, allows the values of any properties to be changed:

```
const mutableObj = { test: 'anything' };

mutableObj.test = 'something else'; // fine
```

Using **as const** after the declaration prevents this occurring:

```
const immutableObj = { test: 'anything' } as const;

immutableObj.test = 'something else'; // error
```

Now we cannot modify the value of the **test** property, and the error message we see is the same as that for arrays, except that the name of the property will be referenced in the error message instead of the index as it was for the array example:

```
Cannot assign to 'test' because it is a read-
only property. ts(2540)

c (property) test: any
immutableObj.test = 'something else'; // error
```

Figure 9.20: *Cannot assign to read-only property error in Visual Studio Code*

Conclusion

In this chapter, we have learned about control flow analysis and narrowing, specifically that it is something the compiler itself does when inferring types, and something that we will often need to do ourselves to help TypeScript understand the intentions of our code.

We saw that we can create type guards which make use of the `typeof`, `instanceof`, or `in` operators, or that we can create more sophisticated type predicates or assertion functions in order to ensure that the objects we are working with are of the correct type.

Let's not forget that we can also use discriminated unions to help TypeScript differentiate easily between union members, or that we can create truly immutable read-only objects and arrays using `as const`.

In the next chapter, we are going to move on to take a more detailed look at how we can manipulate types.

References

- **https://www.typescriptlang.org/docs/handbook**
- **https://sandersn.github.io/manual/Widening-and-Narrowing-in-Typescript.html**
- **https://css-tricks.com/typescript-discriminated-unions/**
- **https://blog.logrocket.com/assertion-functions-typescript**

CHAPTER 10

Manipulating Types

Introduction

In this chapter, we are going to focus on the different ways that we can manipulate types to get the maximum benefit from using them.

Some of the concepts discussed in this chapter rely on generics, so we'll start by refamiliarizing ourselves with what generics are and see some basic examples of how they can be used.

Many of the techniques discussed in this chapter can be used together to create powerful ways of expressing new types; we can use template literal types, conditional types, or one of TypeScript's built-in utility types when writing mapped types for example.

We'll finish off with a good look at all of TypeScript's aforementioned built-in utility types, which we can use to transform one type into another type. Let's get started.

Structure

Over the course of this chapter, we will cover the following topics:

- Generics
- Conditional types
- Indexed access types
- Mapped types
- Template literal types
- Utility types

Generics

We've already looked at different kinds of generics in different chapters throughout this book, but the topics that we are going to look at throughout this chapter make heavy use of generics, so let's pull what we've looked at so far together and have a quick refresher on them as a single topic as a foundation for the rest of the chapter.

Generics are a way of creating structures that work over a range of different types, rather than being constrained to a single type, which allows us to write code that is more reusable and more future-proof to the range of types the structures our applications can use.

We can create generic functions, generic interfaces, generic types, and generic classes. Generics use type variables (also referred to as type parameters) as placeholders in our code and are treated like variables but for types, as opposed to the more familiar variables for values that we are used to working with.

Generic Interfaces

Generic interfaces are possibly the most basic kind of generic in TypeScript, for example:

```
interface Identifier<Id> {
  value: Id;
}
```

In this example, the **Identifier** interface accepts a type parameter called **Id**, and specifies a single property called **value**, the type of which will also be the generic type **Id**, whatever type that happens to be. This means that we can create objects of the type **Identifier** with any type of value – a string, a number, or even a symbol:

```
const stringId: Identifier<string> = { value: 'abc123' };
const numberId: Identifier<number> = { value: 123 };
const symbolId: Identifier<symbol> = { value: Symbol() };
```

When we set the type to **Identifier**, we also need to set the type parameter to a concrete type, such as **string**, **number**, or **symbol**, using angle brackets.

> **NOTE: Generic interfaces are sometimes referred to as generic object types.**

Generic Types

As well as generic interfaces, we can also create generic type aliases, and the principle is really the same as with interfaces, in fact, the previous example could be easily rewritten to use a type alias instead:

```
type Identifier<Id> = { value: Id };

const stringId: Identifier<string> =  { value: 'abc123' };

const numberId: Identifier<number> =  { value: 123 };

const symbolId: Identifier<symbol> = { value: Symbol() };
```

This example is exactly equivalent to the generic interface example except that it uses a type alias.

Generic Classes

As well as generic type aliases and generic interfaces, we can also create generic classes using the same angle-bracket syntax as before:

```
class Shape<Kind> {

  constructor(public kind: Kind) {}

}
```

Here we declare a **Shape** class with a type parameter called **Kind**. Inside the constructor, we can initialize and assign a property called **kind** which is of the type passed in as the type parameter.

We could then declare other shape classes and use these as the **Kind** parameter passed to the **Shape** constructor, for example:

```
class Square {

  constructor(public sidesLength: number) {}

}

const myShape: Shape<Square> = new Shape(new Square(5));

console.log(myShape.kind); //  Square: { "sidesLength": 5 }

console.log(myShape.kind.sidesLength); // 5
```

Using generics makes the class easier to use with a range of different types, minimizing any changes that are required if more types are added to your application in the future.

Generic Functions

Generic functions can both receive generic argument types, as well as return generic types. Consider the following example; first, let's define some similar but subtly different types:

```
type Email = {

  to: string;

};

type Sms = {

  to: number;

};
```

Here we have two types, both with a **to** property, but in the first type, **Email**, this **to** property is a **string**, and in the second, **Sms**, the property is a **number**. Now we can define a generic function that can handle both of these types:

```
function send<T extends object>(item: T): T {

  if ('to' in item && typeof item.to === 'string') {

    // send email

  } else if ('to' in item && typeof item.to === 'number') {

    // send sms

  }

  return item;

}
```

The **send** function is made generic by virtue of the type parameter specified within angle brackets directly after the function identifier. In this case, the type parameter **T** also uses a constraint to tell TypeScript that although this function can receive almost any type, the type that it receives must extend the **object** type.

Note also that the **item** parameter the function receives is also of the type parameter **T** and that the function will return a value of this same type **T**. We don't have to call the type parameter **T**, but conventionally **T** is used as shorthand for *Type*.

The actual inner workings of the function are not too important in the context of this example but note that as the parameter the function receives is generic, and could be any type that extends **`object`**, we need to do some checks inside the function to determine what type the parameter actually is before we can use the **`item`** object safely.

In this example, in the first branch of the **`if`** statement, we use the **`in`** operator to check that the item has a property called **`to`**, and then that the type of this **`to`** property is a **`string`** - if it is, we know we're working with a value of the **`Email`** type and can send the item accordingly. The second branch of the **`if`** statement also needs to check that the object has a **`to`** property, but this time, checks that the property type is **`number`**.

Conditional Types

Conditional types are a way of assigning a type based on whether a type or interface extends another type/interface or not. They are the TypeScript version of a JavaScript ternary expression and use a very similar syntax. Let's look at a basic example.

Let's say that we have some interfaces, one of which extends to one of the others:

```
interface BaseType { a: string }

interface SubType extends BaseType { b: number }

interface OtherType { c: boolean }
```

Later on, we might want to create a new type based on whether the type we are working with extends the **`BaseType`** interface:

```
type conditionalType = SubType extends BaseType

  ? string

  : number;
```

In this case, **`conditionalType`** will end up being of the type **`string`** because **`SubType`** does indeed extend **`BaseType`**:

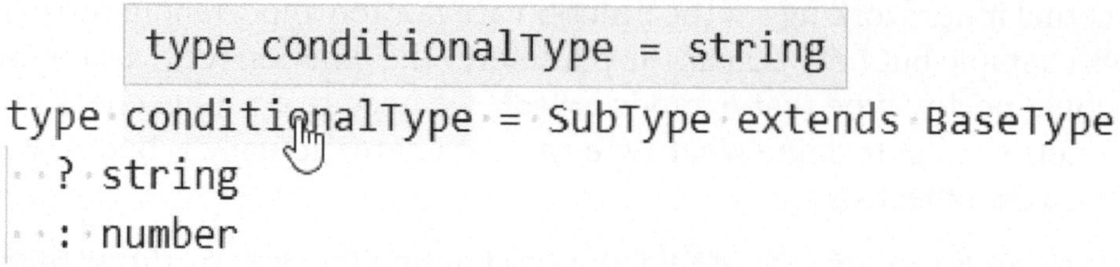

```
type conditionalType = string
```

```
type conditionalType = SubType extends BaseType
  ? string
  : number
```

***Figure 10.1**: Condition is true, the resulting type is string tooltip in Visual Studio Code*

Conversely, if we were working with the **`OtherType`**, the second clause of the conditional would be used and the **`conditionalType`** would end up being the type **`number`**:

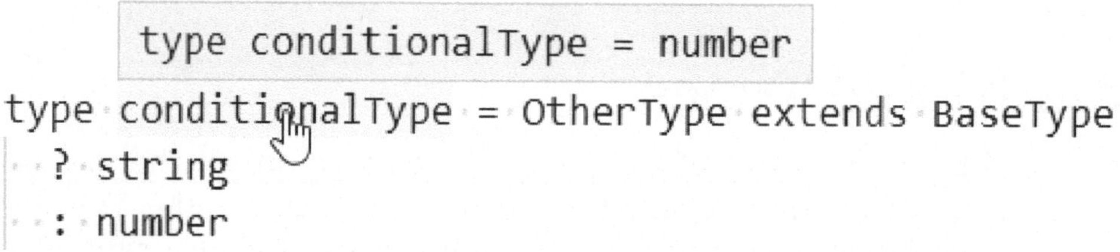

```
type conditionalType = number
```

```
type conditionalType = OtherType extends BaseType
  ? string
  : number
```

***Figure 10.2**: Condition is false, resulting type is number tooltip in Visual Studio Code*

If the type on the left side of the **`extends`** keyword is assignable to the type on the right side, the expression will be **`true`** and the type following the question mark will be used. If not, the expression will be **`false`** and the type following the colon will be used instead.

Indexed Access Types

An indexed access type is a way that we can look up a type property, in a similar way to how we can use square-bracket notation in JavaScript to read the value of an object literal property.

Let's say that we have an object type with several property types inside it:

```
type User = {
  id: string | number;
  email: string;
};
```

To pull out the type of one of the **User** type's properties, we can use an indexed access type, like this for example:

```
type Id = User[‘id’]
```

In this case, the **Id** type will be the union type **string | number**, as this is the type of the **id** property within the **User** type.

The part within square brackets is known as the indexing type; in this example, the indexing type is a string literal type matching one of the properties in the **User** type, but we can use other types here as well, such as union types, like this for example:

```
type IdOrEmail = User[‘id’|’email’];
```

In this case, the **IdOrEmail** type would be the union type **string | number** as these are the types found in both the **id** and **email** types inside the **User** type. The end result is that the **IdOrEmail** type is a union of all matching types inside the type whose properties are being indexed.

We can also use multiple indexing types for nested types, for example, imagine we have an **Email** type that has a **subject** and an **attachment**, and **attachment** is itself an object type with sub-types:

```
type Email = {
  subject: string;
  attachment: {
    filename: string;
    size: number;
  };
};
```

We can then look up one of the **attachment** type's properties like this:

```
type AttachmentSize = Email[‘attachment’][‘size’];
```

In this case, the **AttachmentSize** type will be of the type **number**:

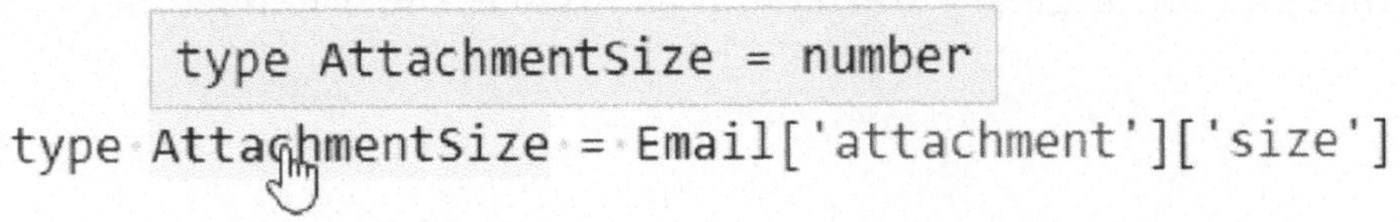

```
type AttachmentSize = number
type AttachmentSize = Email['attachment']['size']
```

***Figure 10.3**: Type tooltip in Visual Studio Code*

Mapped Types

Mapped types are a powerful way to create new types based on other types by transforming individual type properties within the target type.

Let's look at a basic example; imagine we have a type where all of the properties of that type are the literal Boolean type `false`:

```
type FalseType = {
  a: false;
  b: false;
}
```

We can easily create a mapped type where all of the properties are of the literal type `true` instead:

```
type TrueType<T> = {
  [P in keyof T]: true;
}
```

Mapped types are generic; in this case, the `TrueType` type takes a single type parameter, which conventionally is called `T`.

Inside the type, we use square brackets for the property name, just like with indexed access types, and inside these, we iterate each property inside the input type using the `in` and `keyof` operators. By convention, we use `P` for property, and `T` is the input type whose properties will be iterated.

We also specify that each property in the resulting type will be set to the literal type `true`. We don't have to set this to be a Boolean, by the way, we could map each property in the input type to any other valid type.

Now we can create a completely new type using nothing but the `TrueType` mapped type that we just created:

```
type NewType = TrueType<FalseType>;
```

All of the inner property types inside the new type will be the literal type `true` even though they originally started out as `false` in the original type:

```
type NewType = {
    a: true;
    b: true;
}
type NewType = TrueType<FalseType>;
```

***Figure 10.4**: Mapped type output tooltip in Visual Studio Code*

Adding and Removing Property Modifiers

Type object properties can use read-only or optional modifiers to control whether the property can be written to, or whether it can be substituted with undefined in the resulting type.

When mapping property types to other types, we can also add or remove these modifiers as required. For example, imagine we wanted to create a mapped type that takes an input type and makes all of the inner properties read-only:

```
type MakeReadonly<T> = {
  +readonly [P in keyof T]: T[P];
}
```

In this case, the **`MakeReadonly`** type takes a single type parameter **`T`**, and adds the **`readonly`** modifier to all properties within the type using the **`+`** character before the modifier, but note that when adding modifiers, this plus symbol is optional. The type for each property is the existing type of each property in the input type, which we access using an indexed access type of **`T[P]`**.

At this point, we can start with a completely writable type:

```
type WritableType = {
  [key: string]: string;
}
```

And end up with a type containing only read-only types using our mapped type:

```
type NonWritableType = MakeReadonly<WritableType>;
```

As well as adding modifiers with the `+` character, we can also remove them with the `-` character. For example, let's say we have a type where all of the properties are optional:

```
type CompletelyOptional = {
  a?: string;
  b?: number;
}
```

We can create a mapped type that removes the `?` modifiers like this:

```
type NotOptional<T> = {
  [P in keyof T]-?: T[P];
}
```

Inside the **`NotOptional`** type we again use the **`[P in keyof T]`** expression but this time append **`-?`** immediately after it. This will serve to remove any optional modifiers that the property being mapped may have.

Now, we can create a brand new type using the **`NotOptional`** mapped type:

```
type Mandatory = NotOptional<CompletelyOptional>;
```

Now, when using the **`Mandatory`** type, all of the optional properties in the original **`CompletelyOptional`** type are made mandatory and are no longer optional, as shown in the following figure:

```
type Mandatory = {
    a: string;
    b: number;
}
type Mandatory = NotOptional<CompletelyOptional>;
```

***Figure 10.5**: Optional modifier removed in type tooltip in Visual Studio Code*

You should note that this example was purely for illustrative purposes. TypeScript already includes the **`Required`** utility type, which functions in the exact same way – you should use the built-in utility instead. We'll be looking at this utility later in this chapter.

Remapping Property Keys

We can use the **as** operator to remap the names of keys in mapped types. For example, consider a type with several named properties:

```
type NamedProps = {

  a: string;

  b: number;

}
```

When creating objects with the **NamedProps** type, we would have to add properties called **a** and **b**, but not any other properties:

```
const rigid: NamedProps = { a: '', b: 1, c: 'oops' };
```

In this case, the editor will highlight the property with the identifier **c** as an error.

We can remap the key names **a** and **b** so that any **string** names can be used instead:

```
type AnyProps<T> = {

  [P in keyof T as string]: T[P];

}
```

Inside the **AnyProps** type, we use the same **[P in keyof T]** syntax as before, but this time we also use the **as** operator followed by the **string** type. The result of this is that we can take a type that mandates the use of specific named properties, and convert it to a type that allows for any property names to be used:

```
type Flexible = AnyProps<NamedProps>;
```

With the **Flexible** type, we can create objects with any property names instead of having to use only **a** and **b**, like this for example:

```
const flexible: Flexible = { a: '', b: 1, c: 'works' };
```

We can see in the tooltip in the editor when we hover over the **Flexible** type that the type will accept any **string** property names and that the value types will be a union of **string | number** because the original **a** and **b** properties in the input type were string and **number** respectively:

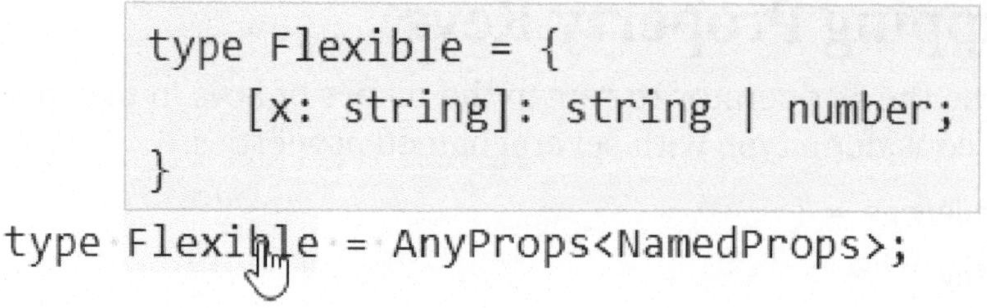

```
type Flexible = {
    [x: string]: string | number;
}
type Flexible = AnyProps<NamedProps>;
```

Figure 10.6: *Remapped property keys tooltip in Visual Studio Code*

Template Literal Types

Template literal types are similar conceptually to template literal strings in JavaScript, and use the same familiar syntax, making them a powerful, but relatively straightforward technique to pick up for anyone who has worked with template literals in JavaScript, although in TypeScript they work with types instead of values.

Template literal types are used to create literal string types, and can concatenate them together to produce new literal string types, for example:

```
type Template = ‘template’;

type Literal = `${Template} literal`;
```

Here we have a type alias called **template**, which is the literal string type **literal**. In the next line, we have another type alias, this time called **literal**. Note the use of back-ticks in the second expression, and that we use the exact same template syntax (**${}**) as we do in regular JavaScript.

The result is that value of the second type is the literal value of the first type alias and the **literal** string literal concatenated together, as we can see if we hover the mouse pointer on the second type alias:

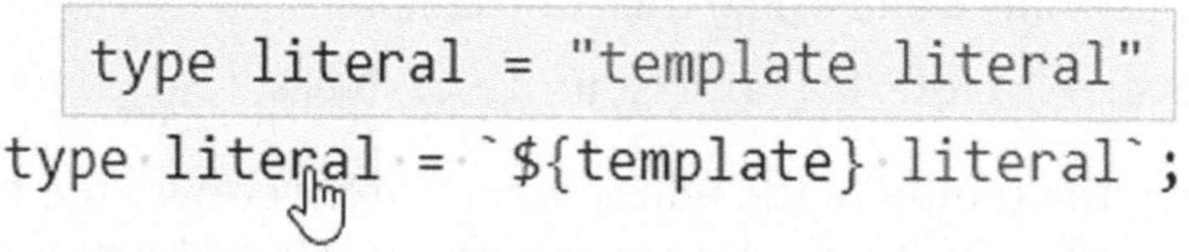

```
type literal = "template literal"
type literal = `${template} literal`;
```

Figure 10.7: *Template literal type tooltip in Visual Studio Code*

As well as literal **string** types, we can also use unions of literal **string** types. In this case, the resulting type will consist of all of the types in all of the unions combined, in all possible combinations, for example:

```
type versions = ‘1.0’ | ‘1.1’ | ‘1.2’;

type names = ‘alpha’ | ‘beta’ | ‘gold’;

type releases = `${versions}-${names}`;
```

This time there are two type aliases which are both unions of literal string types, one called **versions** and one called **names**. The third type, **releases**, is a union type consisting of all nine variations of the combinations of the first two types:

```
type releases = "1.0-alpha" | "1.0-beta" |
"1.0-gold" | "1.1-alpha" | "1.1-beta" |
"1.1-gold" | "1.2-alpha" | "1.2-beta" |
"1.2-gold"
type releases = `${versions}-${names}`;
```

Figure 10.8: *Combinations of literal string types in Visual Studio Code*

TypeScript also provides a number of string literal utilities that we can use to automatically perform certain transformations of literal string types, let's look at these now.

Capitalize

The **Capitalize** template utility takes a literal string type as input and returns the same literal string but capitalized, for example:

```
type input = ‘input’;

type result = Capitalize<input>;
```

The type parameter, **input** in this case, passed in angle brackets after the **Capitalize** identifier, is the input string that the utility will operate on. We can see from the result that the output is the same string in the capitalized format:

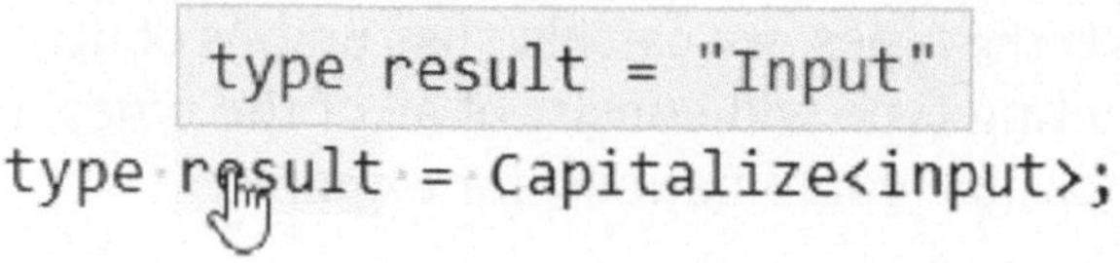

```
type result = "Input"
type result = Capitalize<input>;
```

***Figure 10.9**: Output of the Capitalized utility in Visual Studio Code Lowercase*

The **`Lowercase`** utility takes an input type in literal string format, and returns the same string with all characters converted to lowercase. It is basically the inverse of the Capitalize utility. The usage is very similar to the previous example:

```
type input = 'INPUT';

type result = Lowercase<input>;
```

This utility again takes an input string as a type parameter and returns a type consisting of the same literal string but with all of the characters in lowercase:

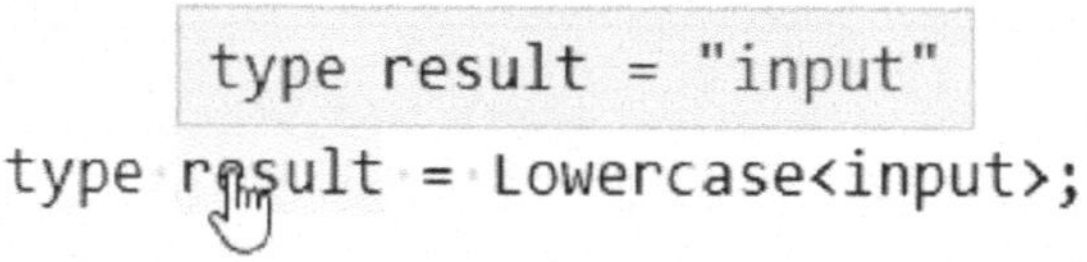

```
type result = "input"
type result = Lowercase<input>;
```

***Figure 10.10**: Output of the Lowercase utility in Visual Studio Code*

Any uppercase character anywhere in the string will be affected.

Uncapitalize

The **`Uncapitalize`** utility takes a literal string type as input and returns the same string with the very first letter in lowercase, for example:

```
type input = 'Input';

type result = Uncapitalize<input>;
```

We can see that the output type consists of the same input string, but with a lowercase first character:

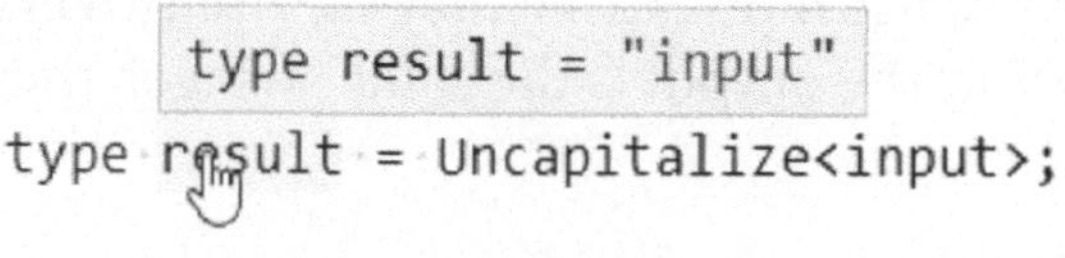

```
type result = "input"
type result = Uncapitalize<input>;
```

***Figure 10.11**: Output of the Uncapitalize utility in Visual Studio Code*

The difference between this utility and the **`Lowercase`** utility is that with this utility, only the very first character in the string will be converted to lowercase - uppercase characters that appear later in the string will remain unchanged. The utility will do nothing if the first character of the string is already lowercase.

Uppercase

The last string literal utility is the **`Uppercase`** utility, which is used to convert an input string literal type from lowercase to uppercase:

```
type input = 'input';

type result = Uppercase<input>;
```

The result in this case is the input string in capitals:

```
type result = "INPUT"
type result = Uppercase<input>;
```

Figure 10.12: *Output of the Uppercase utility in Visual Studio Code*

Utility Types

In addition to the literal string type utilities that we've already covered in the last section, TypeScript also provides a wide range of built-in general utility types that we can use to create new types using existing types. Think of them as predefined mapped types that we can use as coding shortcuts.

Awaited

The **`Awaited`** utility is used to get the unwrapped type from inside a promise, for example, imagine we have a type that represents a simple response from an API:

```
type ApiResponse = {
  data: string;
}
```

In its most basic usage, the **`Await`** utility will unwrap a promise that contains **`ApiResponse`** objects:

```
type unwrappedApiResponse = Awaited<Promise<ApiResponse>>;
```

In this case, the actual type of the **unwrappedApiResponse** type will be the same as the **ApiResponse** type – an object that has a property called **data**, as you can see in the following figure:

```
type unwrappedApiResponse = {
    data: string;
}
type unwrappedApiResponse = Awaited<Promise<ApiResponse>>;
```

Figure 10.13: *Output of the Awaited utility in Visual Studio Code*

We can also use it to get the unwrapped return type of a function that returns a promise. Consider the following function:

```
async function getApiResponse(): Promise<ApiResponse> {
  return { data: 'test'};
}
```

The **getApiResponse** function uses the **async** keyword, so this function will automatically return a promise as per the ECMAScript specification. We specify a promise containing the **ApiResponse** type as the return type of the function, and inside the function, we can just return an object containing a **data** property with a string value as an example. In real code, this is where we would likely make an HTTP request to get the required data from the server.

We can then use the **Awaited** utility to extract the unwrapped return type of the **getApiResponse** function:

```
type RespType = Awaited<ReturnType<typeof getApiResponse>>;
```

We need to use the **typeof** operator with **getApiResponse** here because **getApiResponse** is a function, but we want the type returned by the function, which is **Promise<ApiResponse>**, rather than the function itself.

Note that we also need to use the **ReturnType** utility to get the return type of the function, which the **Awaited** utility will then unwrap. We'll be looking at the **ReturnType** utility a little later in this section.

ConstructorParameters

The **ConstructorParameters** utility creates a tuple type based on the parameters accepted by a class's constructor function type.

We can pass the utility a constructor function and it will extract the parameters that the function accepts as a tuple, for example:

```
type ConstructorParams = ConstructorParameters<ObjectConstructor>
```

In this case, the **type** parameter passed to the **ConstructorParameters** utility is the built-in **ObjectConstructor** interface. This means that the tuple produced by this utility has an optional **value** parameter of the type **any**:

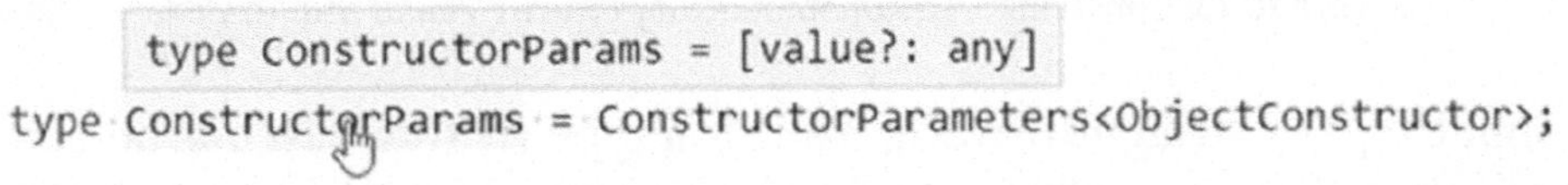

Figure 10.14: *Tuple type returned by the ConstructorParameters utility in Visual Studio Code*

As well as passing a constructor function type to the utility, we can also pass it as a reference to a class and use the **typeof** operator to get the constructor function's type, for example. We can pull out the parameters passed to the class constructor as a tuple just as if we had passed a literal function type to the utility:

```
class Car {

  constructor(public model: string) {}

}

type CarConstructorParams = ConstructorParameters<typeof Car>
```

In this case, we have a very simple **Car** class with a constructor that accepts a single parameter called **model** and is of the type **string**. We can see if we hover on the **CarConstructorParams** type that it is a tuple containing a single string:

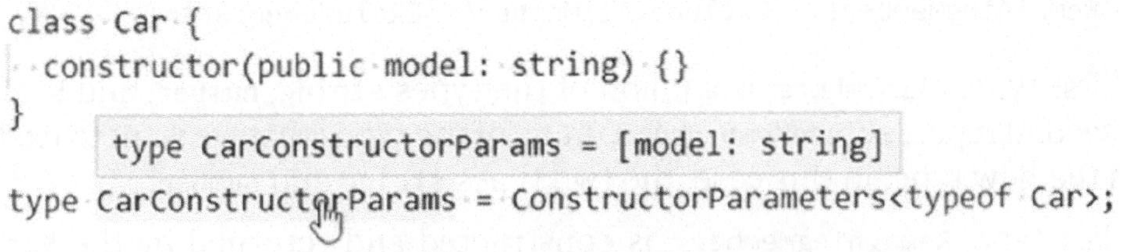

Figure 10.15: *Second tuple type returned by the ConstructorParameters utility in Visual Studio Code*

The internal workings of this type are a little more complex than some of the other utilities we've looked at, so let's go through it in detail:

```
type ConstructorParameters<T extends abstract new
(...args: any) => any> = T extends abstract new
(...args: infer P) => any ? P : never
```

Obtain the parameters of a constructor function type in a tuple

```
ConstructorParameters<typeof Car>;
```

***Figure 10.16**: ConstructorParameters utility type in Visual Studio Code*

The input type is straightforward, it's just a type (`T`) that extends an abstract newable function (a constructor function) type that takes any number of parameters of the type `any` and returns `any` type of value (`extends abstract new (...args: any) => any`).

In terms of output, this utility is using a conditional type to return either the parameters of the input type if the input type is a constructor function, or the `never` type if it is not a constructor function (`T extends (...args: infer P) => any ? P : never`).

Exclude

The `Exclude` utility creates a new type by excluding certain types from a specified union of types. This utility is passed two union types and omits any types from the first type that also appear in the second type.

Let's look at a brief example:

```
type AllMembers = string | number | boolean;

type ExcludeMembers = string | number;

type RemainingMembers = Exclude<AllMembers, ExcludeMembers>;
```

The first type, `AllMembers`, is a union of the types `string`, `number`, and `boolean`. The second type, `ExcludeMembers` is a union of the types that we want to exclude from the new type, in this case, the two types `string` and `number`.

The last type, `RemainingMembers`, is constructed and returned by the `Exclude` utility, and consists of the remaining types left in the `AllMembers` union after excluding any matching members from the `ExcludeMembers` union, which in this case will be just the single type **boolean**:

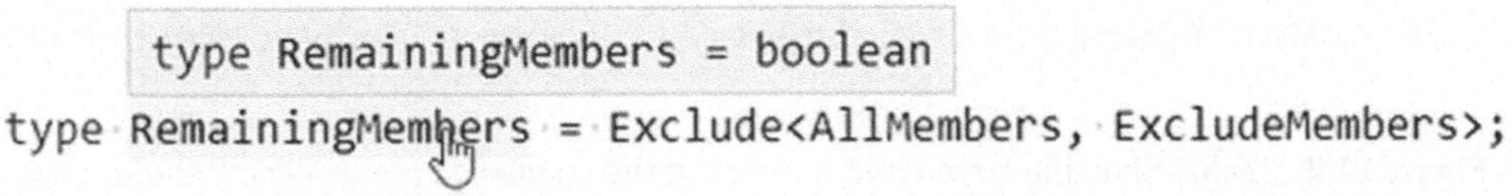

```
type RemainingMembers = boolean
type RemainingMembers = Exclude<AllMembers, ExcludeMembers>;
```

***Figure 10.17**: Tooltip showing boolean as the only remaining type in Visual Studio Code*

To see how this utility works internally, we can hover on the **Exclude** utility itself like with other utilities:

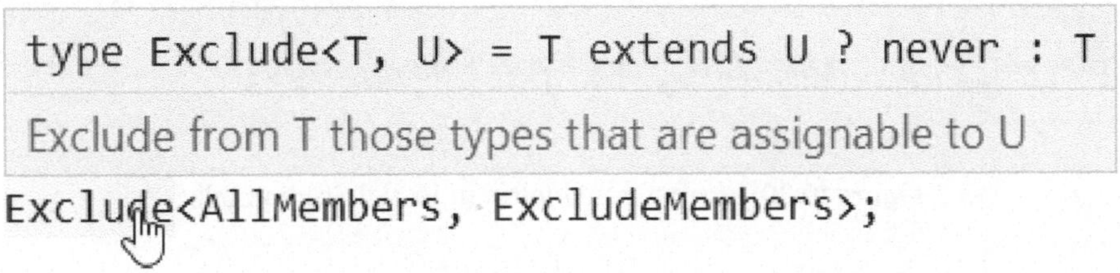

```
type Exclude<T, U> = T extends U ? never : T
Exclude from T those types that are assignable to U
Exclude<AllMembers, ExcludeMembers>;
```

***Figure 10.18**: Exclude type tooltip in Visual Studio Code*

As far as inputs go, **Exclude** is entirely straightforward; it just needs to be passed two types (**T** and **U**). To construct the new type the **Exclude** utility internally uses a conditional type to either return the **never** type if the first type extends the second type or the type itself if it doesn't (**T extends U ? never : T**).

Extract

The **Extract** utility is basically the inverse of the **Exclude** utility; this utility also accepts two types as a type parameter, but this time it constructs a new type that retains only those types from the first type parameter which are also specified in the second type parameter.

Consider the following code for example:

```
type AllMembers = string | number | boolean

type ExtractMembers = string | number

type RemainingMembers = Extract<AllMembers, ExtractMembers>
```

As the types **string** and **number** appear in both input types, **AllMembers** and **ExtractMembers**, the resulting type, **RemainingMembers**, will consist of the union **string | number**:

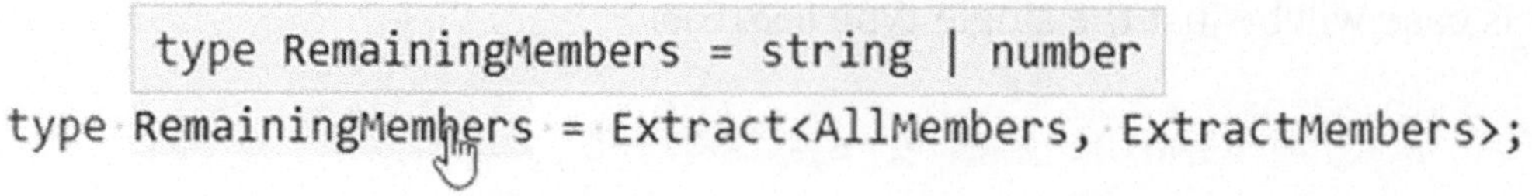

```
type RemainingMembers = string | number
type RemainingMembers = Extract<AllMembers, ExtractMembers>;
```

Figure 10.19: *Tooltip showing string and number in the resulting type in Visual Studio Code*

Again, we can inspect the utility to learn more about it:

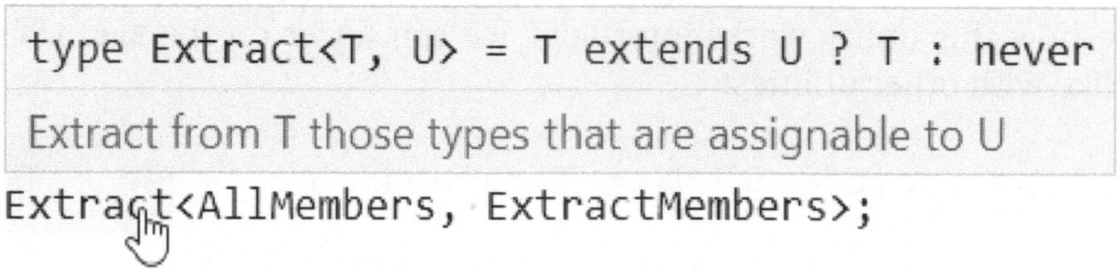

```
type Extract<T, U> = T extends U ? T : never
Extract from T those types that are assignable to U
Extract<AllMembers, ExtractMembers>;
```

Figure 10.20: *Extract type tooltip in Visual Studio Code*

This utility takes two types as inputs (**`T`** and **`U`**) and also uses a conditional type, but this time includes the type in the output type only if it appears in both input types, otherwise, it returns the **`never`** type (**`T extends U ? T : never`**).

InstanceType

The **`InstanceType`** utility is used to extract the type returned by a constructor function. This is very similar to another utility for regular functions called **`ReturnType`**, which we'll look at in more detail later in this section.

This utility is often used with classes; let's see a basic example. First, we will need some classes:

```
class Cat {
  constructor(public name: string) {}
  meow() { console.log('Meow') }
}
class Dog {
  constructor(public name: string) {}
  bark() { console.log('Woof') }
}
```

Now let's add a factory function that can be passed either one of these classes and construct an instance of them:

```
function PetFactory<T extends new (...args: any[]) => any>(pet: T, n: string): T {
  return new pet(n);
}
```

The `PetFactory` function is a generic function and takes a type `T` which should contain a constructor function (remember, `new (…args: any[]) => any` is a construct signature as it uses the `new` keyword). This constructor function can accept any arguments and return any type of value.

The factory function also takes two parameters, the first is a `pet`, which is of the generic `T` type, and the second parameter is called `n` which is of the type `string`. We can initially have the function return the generic type `T` also, as this is probably what we would think to do first based on what we know about generics.

Now let's try to create an instance of the `Cat` class using the factory:

```
const kitty = PetFactory(Cat, 'fluffy');
console.log(kitty.name); // fluffy
```

So far, so good – we can create a new `Cat` instance using the `factory` function, and we can even log out of the `name` property without any issues. However, if we try to call a method unique to the `Cat` class, like `meow`:

```
kitty.meow(); // error
```

Then we'll see an error in the editor:

```
any
Property 'meow' does not exist on type
'typeof Cat'. ts(2339)
```

***Figure 10.21**: Property does not exist on type error in Visual Studio Code*

To fix this, we can change the return type of the `PetFactory` function to use the `InstanceType` utility instead of just returning the generic type:

```
function PetFactory<T extends new (...args: any[]) => any>(pet: T, n: string): InstanceType<T> {
  return new pet(n);
}
```

Now the error will go away because TypeScript will be able to understand that the `kitty` object is of the type `Cat`.

Let's inspect the utility to understand how it works internally:

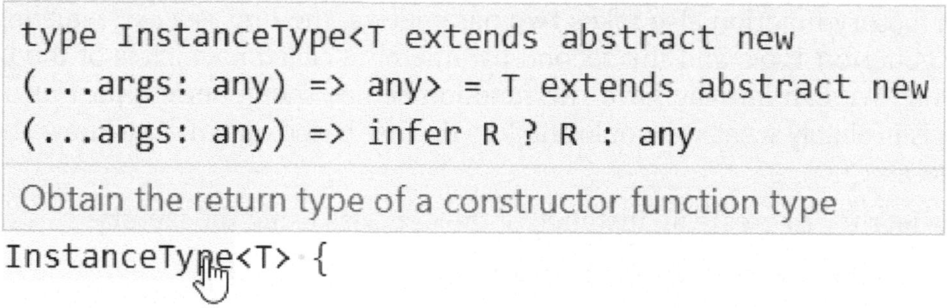

```
type InstanceType<T extends abstract new
(...args: any) => any> = T extends abstract new
(...args: any) => infer R ? R : any
```

Obtain the return type of a constructor function type

```
InstanceType<T> {
```

***Figure 10.22**: InstanceType utility tooltip in Visual Studio Code*

Here we can see that the input type is a type that contains a constructor function (a function used with `new`) that takes an array of `any` parameters and returns `any` value (`T extends abstract new (…args: any[]) => any`).

The output type is a conditional type that infers the type returned by the constructor function. If the input type does have a constructor function, the utility returns the inferred return type of the constructor (`R`). If the input type doesn't have a constructor function, then it returns the type `any`.

NonNullable

The `NonNullable` utility type can be used to strip out any `null` or `undefined` types from a union type:

```
type CannotBeNull = NonNullable<string | null | undefined>
```

In this case, the resulting **CannotBeNull** type will simply be the type string, not the original union **string | null | undefined**. This works exactly the same if we use the union **string | null** or **string | undefined**.

The definition of this type is very straight-forward, we can see it by hovering the mouse pointer on the utility itself:

```
type NonNullable<T> = T & {}
Exclude null and undefined from T
NonNullable<string | null | undefined>
```

***Figure 10.23**: NonNullable type tooltip in Visual Studio Code*

The utility takes a type (**T**) and returns a type that is an intersection of the original type and an empty type (**T & {}**). This works because an empty type can be assigned any type of value, except for null or undefined, for example:

```
type NotNull= {};

const notNull1: NotNull = 1; // Fine

const notNull2: NotNull = 'Not empty!'; // Fine

const notNull3: NotNull = true; // Fine

const notNull4: NotNull = ['anything']; // Fine

const notNull5: NotNull = { a: null }; // Fine

const notNull6: NotNull = null; // Error

const notNull7: NotNull = undefined; // Error
```

We could do the same thing as the **NonNullable** utility does manually if we wanted to, the original example at the start of this section could have been written like this instead:

```
type CannotBeNull2 = (string | null | undefined) & {}
```

This would work in exactly the same way, with the type **CannotBeNull2** ultimately only being able to accept values of the type **string**. However, I find the **NonNullable** utility to be more readable as it better signals the intent of the code to other developers.

One thing to note is that this utility cannot strip **null** or **undefined** from within types, so this code does not cause any errors in the editor:

```
type HasNull = { a: string | null }

type CanContainNull = NonNullable<HasNull>

const someObj: CanContainNull = { a: null };
```

The utility does not remove the **null** type from the union of **string | null** for the **a** property in the **CanContainNull** type.

Omit

The Omit utility allows us to specify a source type and a union of a subset of the property keys from that type, and create a new type that contains all of the keys of the original type minus the ones specified in the union.

Let's see a basic example of how we can use this utility:

```
interface Operations {

  create: () => void;

  read: () => void;

  update: () => void;

  delete: () => void;

}

type WriteOps = 'create' | 'update' | 'delete'

type ReadOnlyOps = Omit<Operations, WriteOps>;
```

First, we define an interface called **Operations** which defines some CRUD operations as methods. To keep things simple these are all just empty methods that don't receive any parameters and don't return any useful values.

Next, we define a union type called **WriteOps**, which contains literal strings matching some, but not all, of the methods specified in the **Operations** interface.

Last of all, we create a type called **ReadOnlyOps** which uses the **Omit** utility to filter out all of the write operations in the new type. The original type is passed to the utility as the first type parameter, and the union of key names that we want to omit from the new type is specified in the union passed to as the second type parameter.

When we use the new type constructed by the `Omit` utility, we cannot specify any of the property names that were omitted from the original type, so in this case, that means any objects using the `ReadOnlyOps` type can only contain a single method called `read`:

```
const read: ReadOnlyOps = {
  read: () => undefined,
}
```

This utility acts as a filter to remove keys from the original type that we do not require in the transformed type.

To really get a feel for what this utility is doing under the hood, we can inspect the type definition for it by hovering the mouse pointer on it:

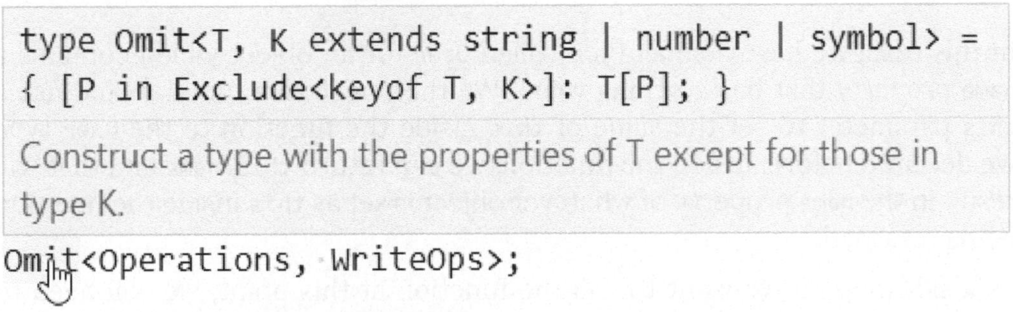

```
type Omit<T, K extends string | number | symbol> =
{ [P in Exclude<keyof T, K>]: T[P]; }
```

Construct a type with the properties of T except for those in type K.

```
Omit<Operations, WriteOps>;
```

Figure 10.24: *Omit type tooltip in Visual Studio Code*

It looks a little intimidating at first, so let's break it down into bite-sized chunks. On the input side, we can see that it takes a type (`T`) and a union of key names constrained to the types `string`, `number`, or `symbol` (`K extends string | number | symbol`). On the output side, the constructed type is using the remaining property names of the input type (`[P in`) after excluding all of the key names specified in the input union (`Exclude<keyof T, K>]`) using the built-in Exclude utility. The original value types of the input type are retained in the output type (`T[P]`).

This utility type is one of the few built-in types that make use of other built-in types internally.

OmitThisParameter

Earlier in the book, we learned that we can use a special parameter called this parameter in a function to set the value of the **this** object inside the function. The **OmitThisParameter** utility can be used to remove a **this** parameter from a function type. Consider the following example:

```
type User = {

  name: string;

};

function getUserName(this: User): string {

  return this.name;

}
```

In this case, we have a small type called **User** for an object which contains a **name** property that has a **string** value. We then declare a function and use a **this** parameter to set the value of **this** inside the function to the **User** type we declared before. Inside the function, we can return **this.name** and that will result in the **name** property of whatever object is set as **this** inside the function being returned.

As a side-note, if we want to call the function at this point, we will need to use one of JavaScript's **Function** methods which allows the **this** object to be specified, such **bind** for example:

```
const userName = getUserName.bind({ name: 'Bill' });
```

In any case, if we inspect the **getUserName** function at this point, we will see that its type clearly contains the **this** parameter:

```
function getUserName(this: User): string
function getUserName(this: User): string {
  return this.name;
}
```

Figure 10.25: *Function type with this parameter tooltip in Visual Studio Code*

To create a new type based on the **getUserName** function type but without reference to the **this** parameter, we can use the **OmitThisParameter** utility:

```
const fnWithoutThisParam: OmitThisParameter<typeof getUserName> =
  getUserName.bind({ name: 'Fred' });
```

The **OmitThisParameter** utility takes a single type parameter which is the function containing the **this** parameter we want to remove. As with some of the other utilities we've looked at, we need to use the **typeof** operator to extract the type of the **getUserName** function.

If we inspect the type of the **fnWithoutThisParam** function, we can see that it contains no **this** parameter:

```
const fnWithoutThisParam: () => string
```

***Figure 10.26**: Function type without this parameter tooltip in Visual Studio Code*

Let's look at how this utility transforms the type, as we have with other utilities that we've looked at:

```
type OmitThisParameter<T> = unknown
extends ThisParameterType<T> ? T : T
extends (...args: infer A) => infer R ?
(...args: A) => R : T
Removes the 'this' parameter from a function type.
```

***Figure 10.27**: OmitThisParameter type tooltip in Visual Studio Code*

We can see that the input type is a simple type (**T**) and that the output is a complex nested conditional type; the condition uses another utility, which we'll look at shortly, called **ThisParameterType** to extract the this parameter from the type (**ThisParameterType<T>**) – if this has the type **unknown** it means there is no **this** parameter, and the utility returns the original type.

If the type does have a **this** parameter, the utility checks whether the type is a function and if so, infers the arguments and the return type of the function and returns this return type (**R**). If this second nested condition fails, the utility again just returns the input type (**T**).

Partial

The **Partial** utility type transforms a regular type where all properties are required, to a type where all of the properties are optional. Consider the following code:

```
type Mandatory = {

  required: string;

}

const mustHaveRequired: Mandatory = {

  required: ‘’,

}
```

In this case, there is a type called **Mandatory** which defines a single property called **required** which should be of the type **string**.

Following the type definition, a new **const** variable called **mustHaveRequired** is declared, with the type set to the **Mandatory** type. This object therefore must have a **required** property with a string value in order to conform to the **Mandatory** type.

The mandatory type can be transformed using **Partial** like this:

```
type NonMandatory = Partial<Mandatory>;

const mightHaveRequired: NonMandatory = {};
```

A new type called **NonMandatory** is declared using the **Partial** utility type with the **Mandatory** type passed as the type parameter in angle brackets. When we create values that conform to this type, we do not have to specify a required property with a string value, although we can if we want to.

If you hover the mouse pointer on the type annotation, you will see that all of the original properties from the original type have been made optional:

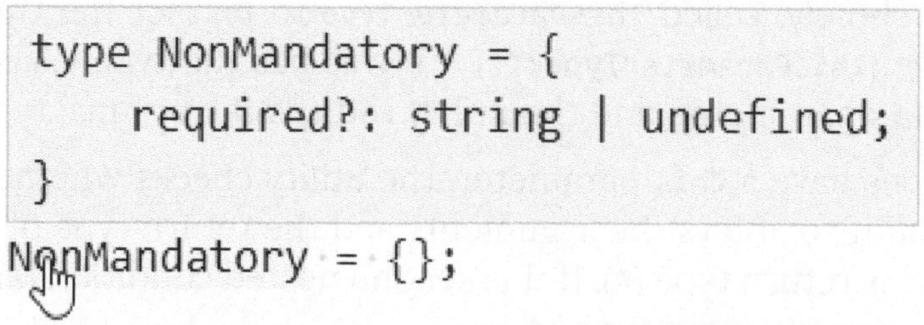

```
type NonMandatory = {
    required?: string | undefined;
}
NonMandatory = {};
```

***Figure 10.28**: Optional property type tooltip in Visual Studio Code*

The way that this utility works can be seen if you hover the mouse pointer over the **Partial** keyword itself:

```
type Partial<T> = { [P in keyof T]?:
T[P] | undefined; }
Make all properties in T optional
```

Figure 10.29: *Partial type definition tooltip in Visual Studio Code*

We can see that this utility is using the **keyof** operator to map every property (**P**) in the original type (**T**), to a union of **T[P] | undefined**.

Parameters

The **Parameters** utility creates a tuple type based on the parameters accepted by a function type passed to the utility. This utility is very similar to the **ConstructorParameters** utility that we looked at earlier.

We can pass the utility a function and it will extract the parameters it accepts as a tuple, for example:

```
type FnParams = Parameters<(a: string, b: number) => void>
```

In this case, the type parameter passed to the **Parameters** utility is a function type, which describes a function that accepts two parameters - the first a **string**, the second a **number**.

The return type is **void** in this example, although that makes no difference to the example as the **Parameters** utility disregards the return type entirely. For a utility dedicated to return types, see the **ReturnType** utility a little later in this section.

We can see in the editor that the type returned by **Parameters** will be a tuple consisting of a **string** followed by a **number**:

```
type FnParams = [a: string, b: number]
```

Figure 10.30: *Tuple type returned by the Parameters utility in Visual Studio Code*

As well as passing a function type to the utility, we can also pass a function reference and use the **`typeof`** operator to get the function's type. Consider the following function:

```
function myFn(a: boolean, b: string): void {}
```

We can pull out the parameters passed to this function as a tuple as if we had passed a function type to the utility:

```
type FnParams2 = Parameters<typeof myFn>
```

We can see that in this case, the tuple produced consists of a **`boolean`** followed by a **`string`**:

```
type FnParams2 = [a: boolean, b: string]
```

***Figure 10.31**: Second tuple type returned by the Parameters utility in Visual Studio Code*

This utility works in almost the exact same way internally that the **`ConstructorParameters`** utility works except that it works with regular functions instead of constructor functions:

```
type Parameters<T extends (...args: any) => any> =
T extends (...args: infer P) => any ? P : never
```

Obtain the parameters of a function type in a tuple

***Figure 10.32**: Parameters utility type in Visual Studio Code*

Pick

The **`Pick`** utility allows us to pick selected key names and value types for an object type from another type. The signature for this utility is **`Pick<T, K>`** where **`T`** is the type to pick from, and **`K`** is the key from that type to use in the transformed type. This utility is basically the opposite of the **`Omit`** utility that we looked at a little earlier.

Let's see an example of this utility in action. We can use the same example here as we did for the Omit utility so that we can contrast their output:

```
interface Operations {
  create: () => void;
  read: () => void;
  update: () => void;
  delete: () => void;
}
type WriteOps = 'create' | 'update' | 'delete'
type Write = Pick<Operations, WriteOps>;
```

Again, we first define an interface called **Operations** which defines the standard CRUD operations as methods.

Next, we define a union type called **WriteOps**, which contains literal strings matching some, but not all, of the methods specified in the **Operations** interface.

In the last line of the previous code snippet, we created a new type called **Write** which uses the **Pick** utility to pick only those properties from the **Operations** type that are in the **WriteOps** union. We can now create an object using the **Write** type created by the Pick utility:

```
const write: Write = {
  create: () => undefined,
  update: () => { undefined },
  delete: () => { undefined },
}
```

Again, for conciseness, the actual method implementations are left empty. The key point is that we need to specify only those properties that are specifically mentioned in the **WriteOps** union in the object using the **Write** type.

We can inspect the **Pick** utility itself by hovering the mouse pointer on it to see how it works internally:

```
type Pick<T, K extends keyof T> = { [P in K]: T[P]; }
From T, pick a set of properties whose keys are in the union K
```

***Figure 10.33**: Pick type tooltip in Visual Studio Code*

In terms of input, the utility takes a type (**T**) as the first type parameter, and a union that is constrained by the keys within that type (**K extends keyof T**) as the second type parameter. We can also see that the output of this utility is a type comprised of the original keys that are specified (**[P in K]**), using the original value types of the picked keys (**T[P]**).

Readonly

The **Readonly** utility type is used to transform a type whose properties are both readable and writable, to a type whose properties are read-only and cannot be written to after initialization.

We did already look at this utility earlier in the book, but let's go over it again here so that this section remains a complete guide to the built-in utility types.

Consider the following code:

```
type Writable = {
  canBeWritten: string;
}
const notReadonly: Writable = { canBeWritten: 'yes' };
notReadonly.canBeWritten = 'new!';
```

In this case, a type called **Writable** is created, which contains a single property called **canBeWritten**, which is of the type **string**. We can initialize this property when we declare a variable to be of the **Writable** type, and we can later reassign that value to any other **string** value.

The **Readonly** partial can transform the **Writable** type to a type where all of the properties, the **canBeWritten** property in this example, are made **readonly**:

```
type NotWritable = Readonly<Writable>;
const readonly: NotWritable = { canBeWritten: 'no' };
readonly.canBeWritten = 'nope'; // Error
```

We use the **Readonly** utility and set the type parameter to the type whose properties we wish to make **readonly**. We can initialize the **canBeWritten** property when declaring a variable of the **NotWritable** type, but we cannot then later assign a new value – if we try, like in the previous code snippet, we'll see an error in the editor that the property is read-only.

We can see in the tooltip when we hover on the **NotWritable** type, that all of the properties inside the type are prefixed with the **readonly** modifier:

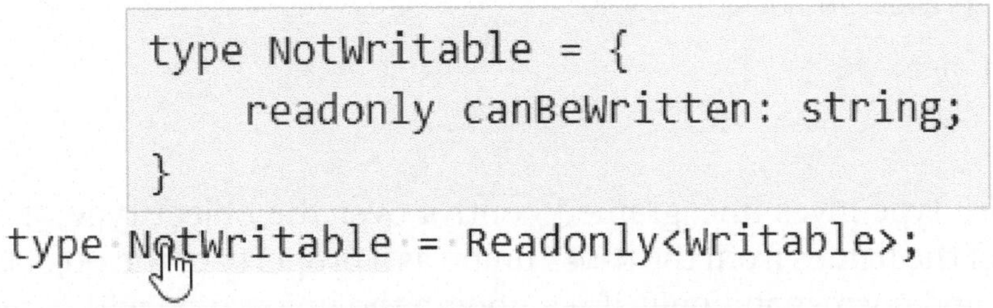

```
type NotWritable = {
    readonly canBeWritten: string;
}
type NotWritable = Readonly<Writable>;
```

***Figure 10.34**: Readonly property tooltip in Visual Studio Code*

If we inspect the **Readonly** utility itself, we can see that it works in a similar way to some of the other utilities like **Partial** and **Required**:

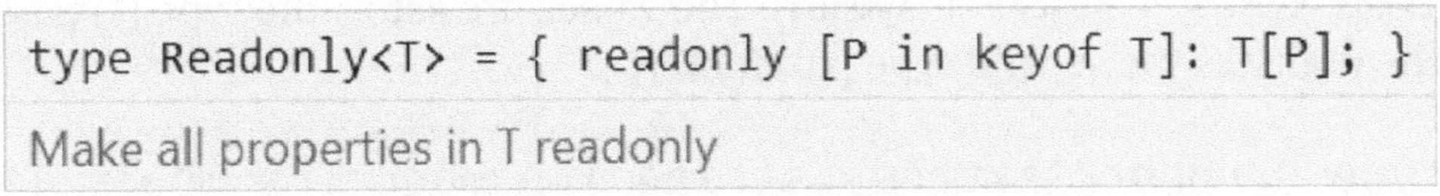

```
type Readonly<T> = { readonly [P in keyof T]: T[P]; }
Make all properties in T readonly
```

***Figure 10.35**: Readonly utility type tooltip in Visual Studio Code*

The utility adds the **readonly** prefix to all properties (**P**) in the type (**T**) and uses the existing value types (**T[P]**) for the transformed values.

Record

A **Record** is used to declare an object type of key-value pairs. The signature for this utility is **Record<K, T>** where **K** is the type for the keys in the object type, and **T** is the type of the values in the object. Consider the following code:

```
interface Person { age: number }
type Names = 'roger'|'dave'
type Guitarists = Record<Names, Person>
```

We start with a simple interface called **Person** which specifies a single property called **age** that should be of the type **number**. Next, we have a simple union type called **Names**, which consists of the literal strings **roger** and **dave**.

On the last line, we create a type called **Guitarists** and use the Record utility, passing in the **Names** type as the first type parameter, and the **Person** interface as the second type parameter. This means that an object of the type **Guitarists** must have the keys **roger** and **dave**, and that each of these properties contains an object that has an **age** property which is a number, like the following example:

```
const pf: Guitarists = {
  roger: { age: 79 },
  dave: { age: 76 },
};
```

The **Record** type gives fine-grained control over the object type; if we fail to add one of the names from the **Names** union as a property of the object, we'll see an error, and correspondingly, if we update the union type with a new name, we'll also see an error.

If we hover the mouse pointer on the **Record** utility, we can see that it uses a constraint on the key value (**K**) to constrain the key values of the type passed to the utility as the first type parameter to either string, number, or symbol types (**extends string | number | symbol**). The values are set to the type (**T**) passed to the utility as the second type parameter:

```
type Record<K extends string | number | symbol, T>
= { [P in K]: T; }
```

Construct a type with a set of properties K of type T

***Figure 10.36**: Record type tooltip in Visual Studio Code*

One point to note is that we don't have to use a union type as the first type parameter, and we don't have to use an interface for the second type parameter – something as simple as the following code snippet is also perfectly acceptable:

```
type Example = Record<string, number>
```

In this case, the keys in objects of the **Example** type can be any string value, and the values may be any number type, like this:

```
const ex: Example = { a: 1 };
```

A follow-up point is that while perfectly acceptable, it would be more common to use an index type instead of a record in this case, like this:

```
type Example2 = { [key: string]: number }
```

In this case, any **string** key identifier is acceptable, and any **number** is acceptable for a value. Ultimately, using a union of string literals as the first type parameter passed to the **Record** utility allows us to limit the identifiers that can be used as keys.

Required

The **Required** utility is essentially the diametric opposite of the **Partial** utility that we looked at a little earlier in this section. This type transforms a type with optional properties into a type where all of the properties of the type are mandatory.

Consider the following code:

```
type NonMandatory = {
  optional?: string;
}
const mightHaveOptional: NonMandatory = {};
```

A type called **NonMandatory** is defined, which contains a single optional property called **optional**, which, if specified, should be of type **string**. Objects declared with this type may or may not specify a property called **optional**.

To transform this type into a type where all properties are required, the **Required** utility can be used:

```
type Mandatory = Required<NonMandatory>;
const mustHaveOptional: Mandatory = {
  optional: '',
};
```

A new type is defined called **Mandatory** which uses the **Required** utility type, with the type parameter set to the **NonMandatory** type. Types created with this type must now define all properties from the original type.

The tooltip shown when we hover over the transformed **Mandatory** type shows that there are no optional modifiers after any of the properties in the type:

```
type Mandatory = {
    optional: string;
}
type Mandatory = Required<NonMandatory>;
```

***Figure 10.37**: Required properties tooltip in Visual Studio Code*

The definition of the **Required** utility is the opposite of that of the **Partial** utility from earlier:

```
type Required<T> = { [P in keyof T]-?: T[P]; }
Make all properties in T required
```

Figure 10.38: *Required type tooltip in Visual Studio Code*

This utility type also uses the **keyof** operator to map any optional properties (**P**) in the original type (**T**) minus the optional modifier (**-?**) to the property type (**T[P]**).

ReturnType

The **ReturnType** utility is used to create a new type based on the return type of a function:

```
type fnReturn = ReturnType<() => boolean>;
```

In this case, we pass an **arrow** function type with a return type of **boolean** to the **ReturnType** utility as a **type** parameter; the **fnReturn** type will therefore be **boolean**:

```
type fnReturn = boolean
type fnReturn = ReturnType<() => boolean>;
```

Figure 10.39: *Boolean type tooltip in Visual Studio Code*

We can also pass a function reference to the utility by using the **typeof** operator to extract the return type of the function, for example:

```
function myFn(arg0: string): number { return 1; }

type alsoFnReturn = ReturnType<typeof myFn>;
```

The **myFn** function is annotated with a return type of **number**, so in this case, the **alsoReturnFn** type will be number as well:

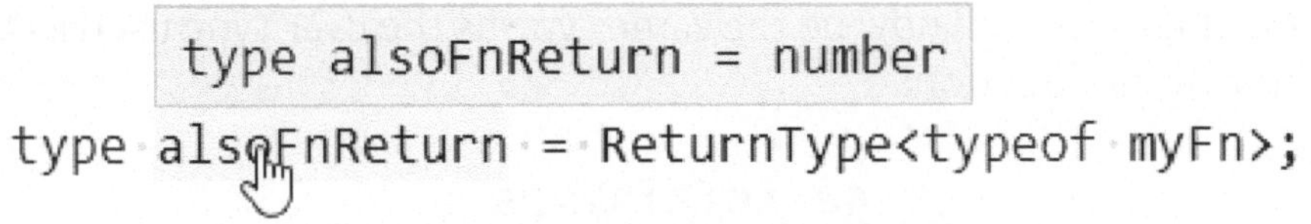

```
type alsoFnReturn = number
type alsoFnReturn = ReturnType<typeof myFn>;
```

***Figure 10.40**: Number type tooltip in Visual Studio Code*

Let's see how this utility works internally by hovering over the **`ReturnType`** utility itself:

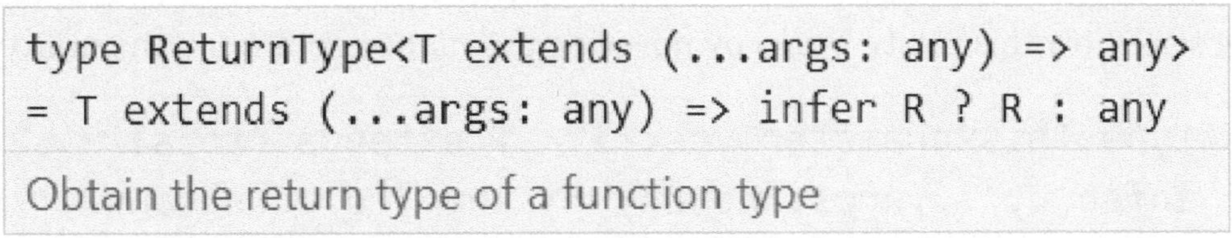

```
type ReturnType<T extends (...args: any) => any>
= T extends (...args: any) => infer R ? R : any
Obtain the return type of a function type
```

***Figure 10.41**: ReturnType tooltip in Visual Studio Code*

We can see that the input type is a function that takes any number of arguments of the type **`any`** and returns **`any`** value (**`T extends (...args: any) => any`**), and that the output type is either the inferred return type of the function or the type **`any`** if the return type could not be inferred (**`T extends (...args: any) => infer R ? R : any`**).

ThisParameterType

The **`ThisParameterType`** utility can be used to extract the **`this`** parameter type from a function type. It was mentioned briefly when we covered the **`OmitThisParameter`** utility, but let's take a moment to see its action, we can use the same **`User`** type and **`getUserName`** function from earlier in this section:

```
type User = {
  name: string;
};
function getUserName(this: User): string {
  return this.name;
}
```

In order to create a new type consisting of the **`this`** type of the **`getUserName`** function, we can use the **`ThisParameterType`** utility:

```
type fnThisType = ThisParameterType<typeof getUserName>;
```

The **fnThisType** type will now be the same type as the **User** type used as the this parameter of the function:

```
type fnThisType = {
    name: string;
}
```

Figure 10.42: *Output of the ThisParameterType in Visual Studio Code*

Let's see how this utility works by hovering the mouse pointer on the utility:

```
type ThisParameterType<T> = T extends (this:
infer U, ...args: never) => any ? U : unknown
```

Extracts the type of the 'this' parameter of a function type, or 'unknown' if the function type has no 'this' parameter.

Figure 10.43: *ThisParameterType utility tooltip in Visual Studio Code*

We can see that the utility takes a single input type (`T`), and uses a conditional type to check whether the function has a **this** type, while ignoring any other parameters (**T extends (this: infer U, ...args: never)**), if it does, the conditional returns the this type (**U**), and if it doesn't, it returns **unknown**.

ThisType

Unlike the rest of the utilities that we have looked at, the **ThisType** utility is not used to transform one type into another type or to extract some piece of information from a type.

Instead, it can be used to set the **this** value inside a function; it's essentially an alternative to **this** parameters, for situations where it is not possible to use **this** parameters.

Let's look at a basic example:

```
type libCore = {

  version: '1.2'

};

type lib = {
```

```
  helperFn: Function
} & ThisType<libCore>
```

In this example, we have a small type called `libCore` which just has a `version` property with a literal string value of some version number, `1.2` in this case. Next is a type for a `lib` object which contains a property called `helperFn`, which should be of the type `Function`.

The `lib` type is also an intersection with the `ThisType` utility, which we pass the `libCore` type to. This has the effect of setting the `libCore` object as the value of `this` inside the `helperFn` function:

```
const myLib: lib = {
  helperFn: function() { return this.version }
}
```

Inside the `helperFn` function, we can safely use the `version` property of `this` thanks to the `ThisType` utility. TypeScript will correctly set the value of `this` inside any objects with the type `lib` to the `libCore` object:

```
const myLib: lib = {                          this: libCore
  helperFn: function() { return this.version }
}
```

***Figure 10.44**: libCore type tooltip for lib object in Visual Studio Code*

Conclusion

Throughout this chapter, we have looked at a variety of powerful tools for manipulating or transforming types. We also learned about the wide range of different built-in utility types that we can use to perform common type transformations.

As I mentioned at the start of the chapter, all of these features can be combined together to create our own custom utility types that we can use to promote reuse and code-sharing throughout the applications we create.

We'll continue on the theme of reuse in the next chapter by looking at TypeScript's module system.

References

- **https://www.typescriptlang.org/docs/handbook**
- **https://fjolt.com/article/typescript-parameters-utility-type**
- **https://bobbyhadz.com/blog/typescript-get-constructor-parameters-type**

CHAPTER 11

TypeScript Modules

Introduction

Modular JavaScript is an essential component when building large-scale but maintainable applications. They allow us to break our applications up into smaller, more manageable pieces and promote reusability as these pieces can be shared and reused in many places.

TypeScript has supported modules since very early in its history and can support a wide variety of different module formats, depending on whether the application is targeting browsers or the Node.js platform.

In this chapter, we'll take a deep dive into modules and look at the different types of modules we can use and the differences between them, in order to import and export code throughout our applications.

Structure

In this chapter, we will cover the following topics:

- Modules in TypeScript
- Importing and exporting modules
- Type-only imports and exports
- Module-related configuration options
- Module resolution
- Compiler directives
- Barrel files
- Augmenting modules

Modules in TypeScript

A module, as far as JavaScript or TypeScript are concerned, is a self-contained unit of functionality with its own execution scope; unlike regular JavaScript or TypeScript files, variables defined outside of a function don't become global throughout the application when declared inside a module.

A module's internal functionality is exported out of the file, and this can then be imported into other files in order to be used. Modules are incredibly useful because they allow us to structure our applications into smaller, more manageable pieces that can be reused in order to prevent duplication, but they haven't always been a part of the official specification.

Modules in JavaScript have a less than straightforward history; an official specification was missing from the language for a long time so numerous 3rd party solutions were devised, but no single one specification was adopted everywhere.

Asynchronous Module Definition, or AMD, was the module format used in browsers and was supported by frameworks like RequireJS. Node.js on the other hand used a different format called CommonJS. Another format called Universal Module Format was able to support both AMD and CommonJS.

Since ES2015, JavaScript has contained an official specification for modules, but it still took browsers some years before a module loader was natively supported. TypeScript supports all of these different module formats and can generate code for each of them based on configuration.

Let's get started with some of the basics, like how to import and export modules in TypeScript.

Importing and exporting modules

Code can be exported out of a module using an `export` declaration. For example, consider that there are two files in the same directory called **module1.ts** and **module2.ts**. Let's export some code from **module1.ts**:

```
export type Answer = {
  score: number;
  correct: boolean;
};
```

We can export simple **Answer** type-alias for the purposes of this demonstration, but interfaces can also be exported, like this for example:

```
export interface Exam {
  questions: string[];
  answers: Answer[];
}
```

We can also export regular values like functions, classes, or variables, for example,

```
export class MathExam implements Exam {
  questions: string[] = [];
  answers: Answer[] = [];
}

export function getScore(exam: MathExam): number {
  return exam.answers.reduce((prev, curr) => {
    return (curr.correct) ? prev + curr.score : 0;
  }, 0);
}

export const stduent1Score = getScore({
  questions: [],
  answers: [],
});
```

In order to import code into another module, we use an **import** declaration. Add the following code to **module2.ts**:

```
import { Exam } from './module1';
```

In this case, we import the **Exam** interface by specifying it within curly brackets after the **import** keyword. There are different types of imports that we can do depending on whether the module has a default export, but let's not worry about that for now.

After the curly brackets, we have the `from` keyword followed by the relative path to the file that contains the thing we want to import. Absolute paths can also be used, although this is not recommended for portability reasons. This string containing the path to the module is known as a module specifier.

Note that we do not need to specify the **.ts** extension in the file path, in fact we should not – the compiler assumes we want to import a TypeScript file.

In TypeScript, any file that contains either an `import` or an `export` declaration is considered to be a module. Modules are self-contained and values declared inside them are only accessible to other modules if they are exported.

Type-only imports and exports

TypeScript also supports a special type of import and export called a type-only import or export. This feature was added to support the popular transpiler Babel and ensure that Babel is able to remove all type-only codes correctly, and other advanced use-cases involving working directly with TypeScript's `transpileModule` API; so, it's not a feature that you'll need to make use of very often, but it's useful to know that the feature exists.

In order to declare a type-only import, we add the `type` keyword directly after the `import` keyword. We can add this code to **module2.ts**:

```
import type { Exam } from './module1';
```

In this case, the `Exam` interface will be imported into the module and be useable in exactly the same way as a regular import. The purpose is really to signal to the compiler or Babel, that this imported entity is only used as a type and is safe to discard during the compilation process.

In most cases, provided we are using the `Exam` interface purely as a type, we wouldn't need to explicitly mark the import as a type-only import as the compiler would know from the usage within the module that it was safe to remove, but this is not always the case when using Babel for example, as Babel is only a transpiler, it is not a full TypeScript compiler like TSC is.

We declare a type-only export in the same way as a type-only import. For example, we could also export the `Exam` interface from **module2.ts** as a type-only export:

```
export type { Exam }
```

The time the **type** keyword comes directly after the **export** keyword, and for all intents and purposes, behaves in the same way as a regular export.

We would only use this syntax if we wanted to re-export the **Exam** interface. We can't export an interface or type alias as a type-only export directly, but we can re-export them after importing them into an intermediary module. It is in this scenario that the **type** keyword should be used to signal to the compiler that the exported entity is just a type and can be safely removed during compilation.

Compiled modules

We can compile the two example modules by running the **tsc** command in a command prompt focused on the directory containing them. The accompanying companion project already has a **tsconfig.json** file, so in this case, only the **tsc** command is required. In other scenarios, if there is no **tsconfig.json** file, the files to compile can be specified after the command, like this for example:

```
tsc module1.ts module2.ts
```

After running the command in the project folder, the result should be two JavaScript files in the **dist/chapter 11** directory called **module1.js** and **module2.js**. As the **module** configuration option in the **tsconfig.json** file for the accompanying project has the setting **ES2022**, the compiled modules will be standard ES Modules. The compiled JavaScript version of **module1.ts** should look like this:

JS module1.js ×

dist > chapter 11 > JS module1.js > ...

```
export class MathExam {
    questions = [];
    answers = [];
}
export function getScore(exam) {
    return exam.answers.reduce((prev, curr) => {
        return (curr.correct) ? prev + curr.score : 0;
    }, 0);
}
export const stduent1Score = getScore({
    questions: [],
    answers: [],
});
```

Figure 11.1: *Compiled output of an example module in Visual Studio Code*

As one would expect, all of the type information has been stripped out of the file during the compilation process, so the type alias and interface are completely gone. The class, function, and variable all still exist, but these too have had any references to types removed.

There is nothing particularly special about a module after it has been compiled, compared to a regular TypeScript file after it has been compiled. The only difference is for modules that only export types or interfaces.

The **module1.ts** file contains a range of exported entities but consider the situation where a module only exports interfaces or type aliases. As these are removed during the compilation process, you may wonder what the contents of the compiled file would be.

As a quick example, comment out everything except the exported `Answer` type alias in **module1.ts** and compile the module again.

If the resulting JavaScript file doesn't contain either an `import` or `export` declaration, it will not be considered a module and will therefore not be treated as one by the browser, which would break any other modules that were trying to import from this module. So, in order to preserve its status as a module and prevent other code from potentially throwing an error, TypeScript will insert an `export` for an empty object:

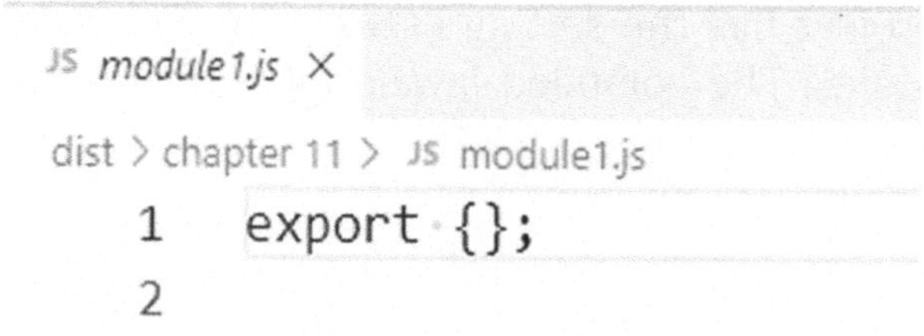

JS module1.js ×

dist > chapter 11 > JS module1.js

```
export {};

```

Figure 11.2: *Compiled type-only module*

Now let's move on and look at some of the configuration options in the **tsconfig.json** file that are related to modules.

Module-related configuration options

TypeScript has a wide range of different configuration options that can be used in the `compilerOptions` section of the **tsconfig.json** file, in order to change how modules, work. Let's take a look at some of the most commonly used options.

Module

The companion project for this book has the **module** configuration property set to **ES2022**, so the emitted JavaScript is compatible with the very latest version of the JavaScript module specification.

We can also set this option to other notable (in terms of module support) versions of EcmaScript including **ES2020** and **ES2015**. To get the very latest version, whatever that happens to be, we can also use **ESNEXT**. However, TypeScript supports more than just ES versions.

If we set the **module** property to **AMD**, the output will use a syntax familiar to users of RequireJS, for example, the following figure shows the output of **module2.ts** after being compiled:

```
define(["require", "exports"], function (require, exports) {
    "use strict";
    Object.defineProperty(exports, "__esModule", { value: true });
    exports.mathExam = void 0;
    exports.mathExam = {
        questions: [],
        answers: [],
    };
});
```

Figure 11.3: AMD-compatible compiler output

For compiled code compatible with Node.js, we can use either the value **Node16** or **NodeNext** for the **module** option:

```
"use strict";
Object.defineProperty(exports, "__esModule", { value: true });
exports.mathExam = void 0;
exports.mathExam = {
    questions: [],
    answers: [],
};
```

Figure 11.4: *Node-compatible compiler output*

The only difference here is that the **define** method, which is part of the AMD specification, is not used. Another supported value for the **module** option is **System** for SystemJS, another more recent module loader:

```
System.register([], function (exports_1, context_1) {
    "use strict";
    var mathExam;
    var __moduleName = context_1 && context_1.id;
    return {
        setters: [],
        execute: function () {
            exports_1("mathExam", mathExam = {
                questions: [],
                answers: [],
            });
        }
    };
});
```

Figure 11.5: *SystemJS-compatible compiler output*

Additionally, the **module** option supports the value **UMD** for Universal Module Definition, which can support either AMD or CommonJS at runtime depending on where the code is being used:

```
(function (factory) {
    if (typeof module === "object" && typeof module.exports === "object") {
        var v = factory(require, exports);
        if (v !== undefined) module.exports = v;
    }
    else if (typeof define === "function" && define.amd) {
        define(["require", "exports"], factory);
    }
})(function (require, exports) {
    "use strict";
    Object.defineProperty(exports, "__esModule", { value: true });
    exports.mathExam = void 0;
    exports.mathExam = {
        questions: [],
        answers: [],
    };
});
```

Figure 11.6: *UMD-compatible compiler output*

TypeScript is able to output all the most common module formats so TypeScript can be used with many different module environments.

Module resolution

The **moduleResolution** property is used to control how the compiler resolves modules given a module specifier. By default, the compiler uses the **classic** setting, although this is intended for legacy versions of TypeScript prior to 1.6 and is not recommended for use with more recent versions of TypeScript.

The preferred setting for this option is **node**, which means that the compiler looks up and resolves modules in the same way that Node.js does with CommonJS modules.

Module support in Node.js changed in Node.js version 16, and we can use the module resolution strategy from this version of Node.js by using the value **node16** for the **moduleResolution** property. To get the latest support, we can also use **nodenext**.

As well as the **moduleResolution** configuration property, we're also going to look at module resolution as a process a little later in this chapter.

Base URL

The **baseUrl** configuration property is used to set a directory as the root directory from which the compiler can resolve modules with non-relative imports. Relative imports are resolved relative to the file making the import, but we can also use non-relative imports as well.

In the example project, the two modules we created earlier are in the **chapter 11** directory, and currently, **module2.ts** is importing the **Exam** interface from **module1.ts** in the same directory using a relative path:

```
import { Exam } from './module1';
```

The path is relative because it begins with a period.

If we set the **baseUrl** configuration property to **chapter 11**, we can then change the import statement in **module2.ts** to a non-relative path:

```
import { Exam } from 'module1';
```

This time the path does not begin with a period and so is not relative.

Paths

We can use the **paths** configuration option to map one path to another path; think of them as aliases for **import** paths. This property takes an object where the keys are the names of the aliases we wish to use in module specifiers, and the value is an array of paths to the actual modules the alias is for.

The paths to the modules are relative to the `baseUrl`, or if this is not set in the **tsconfig.json** file, paths are relative to the **tsconfig.json** file itself. Let's keep that set to `chapter 11` for this example as well. We can add the following configuration for the paths option in the **tsconfig.json** file:

```
"paths": {
  "a": ["module1"]
},
```

We use `a` for the alias and map this to path module1. Now in the **module2.ts** file, we can import the `Exam` interface from the alias:

```
import { Exam } from 'a';
```

The `paths` option can be very useful for simplifying imports in large projects, or projects with lots of third-party dependencies that need to be imported.

Rootdirs

The `rootDirs` property is used to configure a series of different directories that the compiler will treat as if they were a single directory for the purposes of module resolution. For example, consider a project that has several different folders where components are stored (you should recreate this structure inside the **chapter 11** directory if you have been building up the example project manually throughout the book):

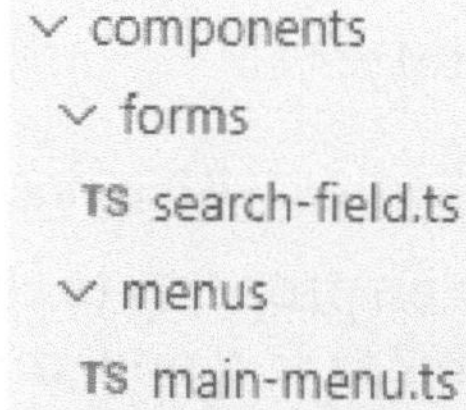

Figure 11.7: *Separate directories for different types of modules*

We can add entries for the two directories `forms` and `menus` using the `rootDir` property in the **tsconfig.json** file like this:

```
"rootDirs": [
  "components/forms",
  "components/menus"
],
```

The paths are relative to the directory containing the **tsconfig.json** file.

Now, for example, inside the **main-menu.ts** module, we can import something from the **search-field.ts** module as if they were located in the same directory:

```
import { SearchField } from './search-field';
```

This configuration option can be useful if the directories specified in `rootDirs` are combined as a result of a build process.

Type roots

When using third party TypeScript packages, the declaration files containing the type information for these packages are usually installed in your project in the directory **node_modules/@types**; all of the files within this directory, and all of its subdirectories, will be available throughout your project without requiring any special configuration.

The `typeRoots` property allows us to specify one or more alternative directories for these declaration files to be resolved from. For example, let's say that we keep all of the declaration files for our project in a directory called **declarations**, which contains two subdirectories called **internal** and **external**.

We can instruct TypeScript to look in these folders for declaration files instead of the **node_modules/@types** folder using this `typeRoots` configuration:

```
"typeRoots":

  "declarations/internal",

  "declarations/external"

],
```

The paths used in the array are relative to the **tsconfig.json** file for the project. Note also that with this configuration enabled, the compiler will not look for types in the **node_modules/@types** directory.

Module suffixes

When trying to resolve modules, TypeScript will look for more than just a matching **.ts** file – depending on the configuration, it may look for **.ts**, **.tsx**, **.d.ts**, and perhaps even **.js** files. The `moduleSuffixes` property allows us to add new suffixes to this list for the compiler to look for when resolving modules.

For example, if we add this configuration to the **tsconfig.json** file:

```
"moduleSuffixes": [".preferred", ""],
```

Then in this case, the compiler will look for ***.preferred.ts** files before it looks for ***.ts**, ***.d.t.s**, and so on. The empty string at the end is required for TypeScript to fall back to the default if it cannot find a module with a matching suffix.

Note however that this will not cause TypeScript to rewrite any module paths in import statements – we cannot use this as a shortcut to avoid typing common suffixes when adding import statements to our files.

This option is useful when using third party loaders or bundlers like Webpack for example and helps TypeScript understand which files should be type-checked. In some cross-platform native application frameworks, TypeScript files have an extension that matches the targeted platform, like **app.android.ts** and **app.ios.ts**.

When building an application for Android for example, we would not want the ***.ios.ts** files to be type-checked as this would waste time and resources. So, the `moduleSuffixes` configuration option is used to support that kind of scenario. It will often be set by the framework in use, so it's not an option that you'll need to manually configure frequently.

Resolve JSON module

By default, TypeScript will not allow you to import directly from JSON files, but JSON files are very often used to store configuration for web applications. We can enable importing from this type of file with the `resolveJsonModule` option.

For example, imagine we have a simple **config.json** file that looks like this:

```
{
  "enableFeature": true
}
```

By setting `resolveJsonModule` to `true` in the **tsconfig.json** file, we can then import the **config.json** file into TypeScript modules as if the JSON file was a TypeScript file with a default import:

```
import config from './config.json';
```

Now, throughout this module, we would get full typing for the `config` token, as if it had been declared as a TypeScript module, for example:

```
const enable = config.enableFeature; // fine
```

One thing to note about this option is that it can only be used when the `moduleResolution` option in the project's **tsconfig.json** file is enabled (uncommented) and set to `node`, and the `allowSyntheticDefaultImports` option is enabled and set to `true`.

Module resolution

Module resolution is the process of the compiler looking up modules to load when following an `import` statement. Loading relative module specifiers is easy for the compiler – the paths to these modules are always relative to the file making the import and always point to a single specific location.

Non-relative imports are different however, and the compiler will look for modules to load in a specific range of different locations, and this range of locations is different depending on the value of the `moduleResolution` configuration option, which we looked at a little earlier in this chapter.

Remember that this option is not configured by default, so the compiler will use the `classic` resolution strategy unless this setting is uncommented in the **tsconfig.json** file and configured to another supported value like `node`. We'll look at the `node` module resolution strategy in just a moment, but first, let's understand the `classic` strategy.

Imagine that we are trying to load the popular and ubiquitous jQuery library using an import like this:

```
import jquery from 'jquery';
```

The specifier here isn't a relative path, because it doesn't start with at least one period, so the module can't be found by starting at the current location and following the path.

The process the compiler will use to try to resolve non-relative imports using the `classic` strategy is as follows. It will attempt to resolve the module by looking for a range of different files from each of these locations in the following order:

1. Look in the current directory for a module called **jquery.ts**.
2. Look in the current directory for a module called **jquery.tsx**.
3. Look in the current directory for a module called **jquery.d.ts**.
4. Keep looking for the previous three module types (**jquery.ts**, **jquery.tsx**, **jquery.d.ts**) in all parent directories until one of the module types can be found, or the root of the file system is found (note that this process

will continue beyond the root of the project regardless of the setting of the `rootDir` or `baseUrl` TypeScript configuration options).

5. Look in the current directory for a **node_modules** folder.
6. Keep navigating up the project file system until it finds a **node_modules** folder.
7. Once, and if, the **node_modules** directory is found, look for a file called **jquery.d.ts** in **node_modules/@types**.
8. Look in the **package.json** file for a property called `typings`, which may contain instructions on how to load modules.
9. Look in the **package.json** file for a property called `types`, which may contain instructions on where to find type declaration files.
10. Look in the current directory for a file called **jquery.js**.
11. Look in the current folder for a file called **jquery.jsx**.
12. Keep looking for a **.js/.jsx** module in all parent directories until one of the modules can be found or the root of the file system is reached.

If the module is not found at this point, assume it is not present and stop trying to resolve it.

The process seems quite long and convoluted but the compiler is basically searching for a range of several different applicable file types that it could load the module from in all parent directories, working its way up the file-system tree until it finds an appropriate module or runs out of places to search.

The above process will stop as soon as the compiler is able to locate an appropriate target file, so the full process described earlier will not happen in all cases.

The preferred `moduleResolution` strategy is `node`; with this setting, look-ups for non-relative modules using the same `import` statement as above will be carried out as follows:

1. Look in the current directory for a directory called **node_modules**.
2. Look in the parent directory for a directory called **node_modules**.
3. Keep looking in parent directories for a **node_modules** folder.
4. Once **node_modules** is located look for a **package.json** file inside **node_modules** and see if it has a `typesVersions` property configured.
5. Look for a module called **jquery.ts** in **node_modules**.
6. Look for a module called **jquery.tsx** in **node_modules**.

7. Look for a module called **jquery.d.ts** in **node_modules.**
8. Check if the **package.json** has a **typings** property configured.
9. Check if the **package.json** has a **types** property configured.
10. Check if **package.json** has a main property configured which points to **dist/jquery.js**.
11. Look for **jquery.ts** in **node_modules/jquery/dist**.
12. Look for **jquery.tsx** in **node_modules/jquery/dist**.
13. Look for **jquery.d.ts** in **node_modules/jquery/dist**.
14. Look for **index.ts** in **node_modules/jquery**.
15. Look for **jquery.ts**, **jquery.tsx**, or **jquery.d.ts** in all parent directories of **nodule_modules/jquery/dist** until **node_modules** is reached.
16. Look for **jquery.d.ts** in **node_modules/@types**.
17. If no **.ts**, **.tsx**, or **.d.ts** files are found at this point, the compiler will use the **jquery.js** that it found in *Step* 10 and use that as the module.

The process for Node.js style look-ups is similar to classic mode, but it will use the first **node_modules** directory that it finds as the root of module look-ups, and it will also look for **index.ts** files in directories, which are known as barrel files (we'll look at these shortly).

If we want to see the exact process the compiler is using to try to load a module, we can add the --traceResolution compiler flag and it will output the full resolution process that was used.

Compiler directives

Compiler directives, also known as triple-slash directives, are an older way of telling the TypeScript compiler how to load dependencies for the current file. They date back to before the adoption of widespread support for ES Modules, and their use is now discouraged everywhere except declaration files.

Compiler directives must be used at the very top of any files they are used in – if they do not appear before any other statements, the compiler will treat them as regular comments and ignore them completely. Compiler directives must point to a file that exists, and cannot point to the same file they are used in.

There are a number of different compiler directives which serve different purposes, but all of them begin with a triple slash `///`. You should note also that these triple-slash compiler directives are completely ignored but the compiler when the **noResolve** configuration option is enabled.

Let's take a quick look at each of the different types of triple-slash directives.

Reference path

Reference paths are (or were when they were more commonly used) the most commonly-used compiler directive and are used to tell the compiler that the file containing the directive depends upon another file. The syntax is as follows:

```
/// <reference path="path/to/file">
```

The `path/to/file` is relative to the file containing the directive, and the compiler will resolve the module found in the path and include it in the compilation. But remember, `import` statements are the preferred means of including other modules in your module, and compiler directives cannot import actual code, only type declarations.

Let's see a basic example. Imagine we have a folder called **declarations**, which contains two subfolders, **internal** and **external**. The **internal** folder contains a file called **lib1.d.ts**, and the **external** folder contains a file called **lib2.d.ts**, like this:

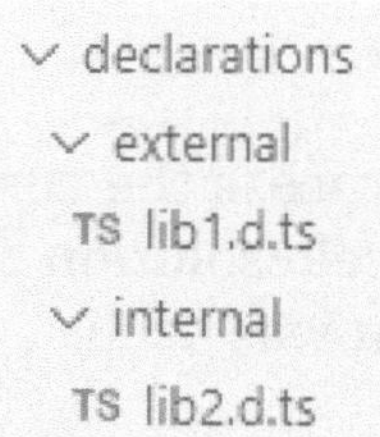

Figure 11.8: *Example folder structure in Visual Studio code*

In the **lib1.d.ts** file, we just declare an `interface` called `Test`:

```
declare interface Test {
  questions: string[];
}
```

We can reference this interface in **lib2.d.ts** using a reference path directive, like this:

```
/// <reference path="../external/lib1">
```

Now we can use the **`Test`** interface inside this file, perhaps like this:

```
const myTest: Test = {
  questions: [],
}
```

Without the compiler directive, the editor would mark **`Test`** as **`any`**.

Reference types

Another common compiler directive is reference types, which is similar to reference paths except that you specify the name of a set of types as opposed to the path to a specific file.

For example, if our own declaration file depends on the types from a package in the **node_modules@types** directory, we could use the following directive in our own declaration file to include them:

```
/// <reference types="node">
```

You should note that we should not need to do this in practice, however, as types from the **node_modules@types** directory are automatically included. These directives date back to a time before this mechanism existed.

Reference lib

The reference lib directive is similar to reference types, except that it is used to include one of TypeScript's built-in library files as opposed to types that we can explicitly install into the **node_modules@types** directory.

For example, if we want to use the types for the Reflect API from ES2015, we can include this with the following directive:

```
/// <reference lib="ES2015.Reflect">
```

No default lib

By default, TypeScript contains a declaration file called **lib.d.ts**, which is known as the default lib. To exclude **lib.d.ts** from the compilation, you can use the **`no-default-lib`** directive in your own ***.d.ts** file, like this:

```
/// <reference no-default-lib="true"/>
```

This directive has the same effect as setting the **`noLib`** configuration property in the **tsconfig.json** file.

AMD module

Depending on the module loader in use in your project, for example, when working with legacy projects that use RequireJS, it may be necessary to specify names for your AMD modules. This can be done using the AMD module directive:

```
/// <amd-module name="MyAmdModule"/>
```

AMD dependency

The last compiler directive is called AMD dependency and used to be used to tell the compiler about a non-TypeScript dependency that was needed by an AMD module, however, this directive is now deprecated and should not be used; regular **import** statements should be used instead.

Barrel files

Barrel files are a way that we can simplify imports by collecting all of the exports from a series of files and making them available via a single file, the barrel file.

> **NOTE: In order to use barrel files, the moduleResolution property in the tsconfig.json file should be set to node.**

For example, imagine a project has a **root** directory called lib with sub-directories **api** and **ui**, each containing one or more TypeScript files, like this:

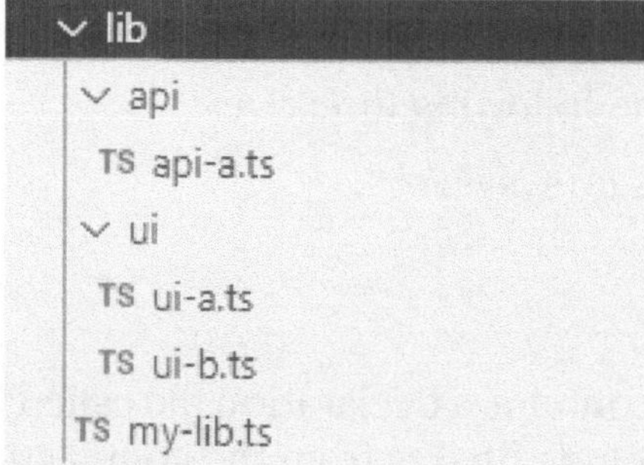

Figure 11.9: *A simple project structure with sub-directories*

The root **lib** folder also contains a file called **my-lib.ts**. Each of the **ui-a.ts** and **ui-b.ts** files export a single and very simple interface, which is as follows:

ui-a.ts:

```
export interface UiA {
  aProp: string;
}
```

ui-b.ts:

```
export interface UiB {
  bProp: number;
}
```

Now let's imagine that we want to import both of these interfaces into the **api-a.ts** file. Without a barrel file, we would have to import each of them individually:

```
import { UiA } from '../ui/ui-a';
import { UiB } from '../ui/ui-b';
```

To simplify these imports and import both interfaces in the same statement, we could add a file to the **ui** directory called **index.ts**, which simply re-exports the exports from **ui-a.ts** and **ui.-b.ts** respectively:

```
export * from './ui-a';
export * from './ui-b';
```

The **`export * from './ui-a`** syntax basically just says *export everything which is exported from module ui-a.ts*. We can also export specific dependencies if we wish, like this for example:

```
export { UiB } from './ui-b';
```

Now in **api-a.ts**, instead of importing both the interfaces from their individual files, we can import them both at the same time from the **index.ts** barrel file, like this:

```
import { UiA, UiB } from '../ui';
```

The **index.ts** file is treated as a default module for the directory it is inside, so we can import anything this file exports from the directory itself rather than having to go down to an individual file.

Nested barrels

We can even nest barrel files in order to create a simplified import structure for our entire project. This time consider that the **api-a.ts** file also exports some kind of interface:

```
export interface Api {

  apiA: string;

}
```

And that the containing **api** directory also contains a barrel file, also called **index.ts**, which contains the following:

```
export * from './api-a';
```

Now let's add a new barrel file inside the top-level lib folder:

```
export * from './api';

export * from './ui';
```

This barrel file simply re-exports everything from the barrel files inside `api` and `ui` folders. Now, for example, we can import all of the example interfaces in the **my-lib.ts** file from this top-level barrel file, like this:

```
import { UiA, UiB, Api } from './';
```

Now we are importing everything from the top-level **index.ts**, which itself re-exports everything from the nested **index.ts** files inside the **api** and **ui** subdirectories respectively.

Barrel files are useful and can simplify imports when we need to import many things from the same locations. But they should be used with caution, especially in larger applications, for several reasons.

First of all, they can easily lead to circular dependencies in an application, where two different modules depend on each other. This is bad because there is no way for the compiler to know which of these modules needs to be loaded first. Barrel files make it easy to introduce circular dependencies unknowingly.

Secondly, with some configurations, unused code cannot be removed from your application when importing from barrel files, which can lead to more code being included in your application than is necessary. This has performance implications for production applications as your users will need to download more code and can lead to development issues like slow-running units and integration tests.

Augmenting modules

Module augmentation is the process of adding new type information to existing modules. We can declare a module that contains an interface with the same name as an existing class, and TypeScript will merge the two together, allowing us to use properties and methods from both.

This can be especially useful if we are working with third party code or files that for some reason we cannot change directly. Let's look at a quick example; imagine we have the following basic class in a file called **customer.ts**:

```
export class Customer {
  constructor(public name: string) {}

  public updateName(name: string): void {
    this.name = name;
  }
}
```

The class has a single public property called **`name`**, which is of the type **`string`**, and we can give it a simple method called **`updateName`** which can update the **`name`** property.

Now, in another file called **customer-social.ts**, we can import this class and declare a new module with the same path:

```
import { Customer } from './customer';

declare module './customer' {
  interface Customer {
    socialMediaName: string;
    updateSocialMediaName(name: string): void;
  }
}
```

Inside the module we can add an interface with the same name as the class from the module being augmented and can add any new properties or methods that we want, in this case, we can just add a single new property called **`socialMediaName`**, and a single new method called **`updateSocialMediaName`**.

So now we can create new instances for the **`Customer`** class and we'll be able to add a **`socialMediaName`** property to those objects as if the property had been added to the original **customer.ts** module, like this for example:

```
const mySocialCustomer: Customer = new Customer('Jon Doe');

mySocialCustomer.socialMediaName = '@jondoe';
```

Remember, the interface we added in the redeclared **`Customer`** module only contains the type for the **`updateSocialMediaName`** method, not the implementation. If we wanted to add this method to all instances of the **`Customer`** class alongside the **`updateName`** method from the class itself, we would have to add this via the prototype, like this for example, which we could add to the **customer-social.ts** file:

```
Customer.prototype.updateSocialMediaName = function (name: string) {

  this.socialMediaName = name;

}
```

Although in this example the module being redeclared is in the same directory as the file that redeclares it, this doesn't have to be the case, as long as the paths match it doesn't matter.

NOTE: We can only augment classes with interfaces, we can't use other classes or type aliases.

Conclusion

Modules are an essential part of modern front-end development because they allow us to break an application up into many small components instead of a single huge monolith, and also promote code reuse and maintainability.

Modules are very easy to use, as we have seen over the course of this chapter, and the compiler supports all of the common module formats in use today, including the very latest ES2022 specification.

In the next chapter, we are going to focus on creating declaration files.

References

- **https://www.typescriptlang.org/docs/handbook/modules.html**
- **https://www.typescriptlang.org/docs/handbook/module-resolution.html**
- **https://www.typescriptlang.org/tsconfig#module**
- **https://www.typescriptlang.org/docs/handbook/triple-slash-directives.html**
- **https://www.digitalocean.com/community/tutorials/typescript-module-augmentation**

CHAPTER 12

Creating Declaration Files

Introduction

In this chapter we will look at how to manually write a TypeScript declaration file; this isn't necessarily a task that you'll undertake too often, given that almost all popular JavaScript libraries have publicly available type packages that provide type information in the editor, and that we can generate declaration files using the compiler. But for those rare occasions where it may be necessary, you'll want at least a grounding in the basics.

There are several different general types of JavaScript libraries that are commonly used, so there are several subtle variations in how we need to create the declaration file, depending on what type of library it is for.

As well as looking at the different kinds of JavaScript libraries that we could be working with, we can also see how to publish our declaration files to the Definitely Typed repository so that they can be installed by anyone via NPM.

Structure

In this chapter, we will cover the following subjects:

- Creating declaration files
- Declaring global libraries
- Enhancing Intellisense with JSDoc
- Declaring global functions and variables
- Augmenting built-ins

- Declaring modular libraries
- Declaring default exports
- Declaring classes
- Declaring CommonJS modules
- Publishing declarations

Creating declaration files

The type of JavaScript library that we are writing the declaration file for will determine how we write the declaration file itself. Generally, there are two main ways that JavaScript libraries are consumed by other developers in browsers; either they are manually linked to using a `script` element in an HTML page, or they are imported into the developer's code as some kind of module. Outside of the browser, JavaScript libraries may also be used in Node.js applications.

Generally, in the browser, the `script` element approach is used by older libraries, like the popular jQuery library for example, which adds an object that contains the API of the library to the global `Window` object, and developers interact with this object in order to use the library.

Declaring global libraries

Let's consider a very small and basic JavaScript library of the kind that adds an object into the global namespace for this example. The accompanying project contains this code in a file called **str-global.js** in the **global** folder, which in turn is in **chapter 12** folder:

```
(function () {
  if (window && !window.str) {
    window.str = {
      version: '1.0.0',
      lastChar: function(word) {
        return word.slice(-1);
      },
      ordinalize: function(dayOfMonth) {
        const d = '' + dayOfMonth;
```

```
            if (!d || !parseInt(d, 10)) return '';
            return str.lastChar(d) === '1'
              ? `${dayOfMonth}st`
              : str.lastChar(d) === '2'
                ? `${dayOfMonth}nd`
                : str.lastChar(d) === '3'
                  ? `${dayOfMonth}rd`
                  : `${dayOfMonth}th`;
        },
      };
    }
}());
```

The whole library is enclosed within an immediately invoked function expression, and inside this, the library first checks to see whether the **window** object exists, just in case the code is running in an environment outside of the browser, and that it doesn't already contain a property called **str**. As long as both of these conditions are true, the library proceeds to add an object called **str** to the **window** object.

This object, the API of the library essentially consists of a property called **version** which contains a hard-coded string, and a couple of small utility methods called **lastChar** and **ordinalize**. Both of these methods return **string** values in all cases.

The first method accepts a **string** parameter called **word** and returns the last character of this string. The second method may receive a parameter called **dayOfMonth**, which may be either a string or a number, and returns the same string with an appropriate ordinal suffix, so passing the string or number **2** would result in the string **2nd** being returned, for example.

This library could be something that you've written yourself, something created by a co-worker and used in an old project at work, or anything in between.

It's clear that this is a global library because it adds to the global **window** object, and it's clear how the method parameters and return types should work, so writing a declaration file for this library shouldn't be too difficult.

The declaration file for this library will be very small because the file will only provide type information - the implementation already exists in the form of the library itself, and the type information should be fairly straightforward.

We can create a basic declaration file for the example library as follows. In the example project, this file is called **str-global.d.ts** and sits alongside the JavaScript file it describes:

```
declare namespace str {

  const version: '1.0.0';

  function lastChar(word: string): string;

  function ordinalize(dayOfMonth: number | string): string;

}
```

We use the `declare` keyword to tell TypeScript that a namespace, or object, called `str` exists. Next, we describe the `version` property and assign it the literal string type `1.0.0`. To ensure the property is read-only, we declare it using `const`.

We could also have used `let` or even `var` here instead for a property that can be written to. As you can see, object properties are declared just like a regular variable declaration, but with type information instead of a value.

To describe methods, we use the `function` keyword, followed by the method identifier and parameter list. As mentioned earlier, the first method, `lastChar`, take a single string parameter called `word`. Last of all we provide the return type, which is string for both of the methods. The parameter for the second method should be a string or number.

This is all we need for our simple global library, but there's one more thing we need to do in order to get Intellisense when using the library in our own TypeScript files. In the **tsconfig.json** file in the root of the project, we should use the `include` top-level option to include this declaration file in the compilation. Nothing imports the file, so if we don't do this, the editor won't recognize the declarations inside it.

In the example project, the declaration file is contained within the **chapter 12** directory, so we can just add the path to that directory relative to the **tsconfig.json** file in an array for the `include` option:

```
"include": ["./chapter 12"]
```

This configuration will tell the compiler to include any **d.ts** files in the listed directories. We should now see that we can use the **`str`** object as a global object in our TypeScript files and receive full type information as expected:

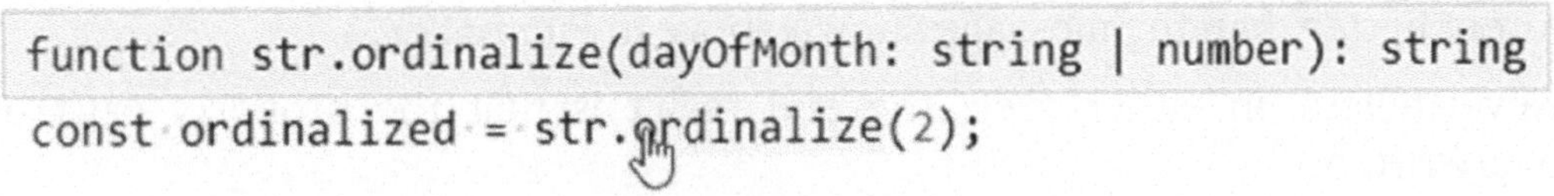

```
function str.ordinalize(dayOfMonth: string | number): string
const ordinalized = str.ordinalize(2);
```

Figure 12.1: *Type tooltip for a global JavaScript library in Visual Studio Code*

We will also see a warning if we try to use the library incorrectly; if we try to assign to the **`version`** property for example, we'll see a warning that the property is read-only and cannot be assigned to:

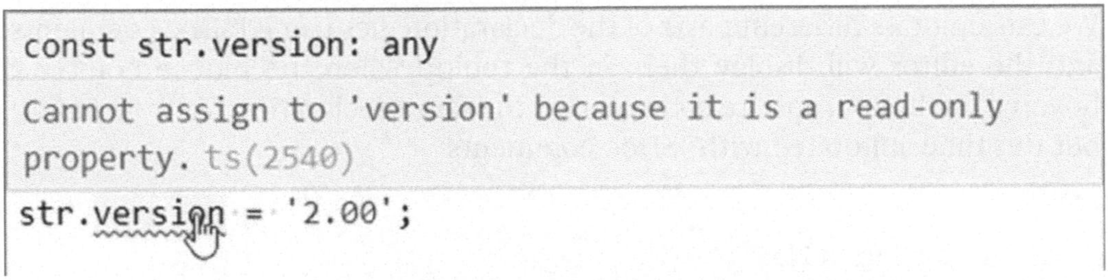

```
const str.version: any
Cannot assign to 'version' because it is a read-only
property. ts(2540)
str.version = '2.00';
```

Figure 12.2: *Assigning to read-only property error in Visual Studio Code*

One point to note in the above figure is that the header of the tooltip is showing the type **`any`** for the **`version`** property, which is probably not what we would expect – we would perhaps expect it to have the literal string type of **`1.0.0`**.

To fix this, we can use **`let`** (or **`var`**) to declare the property in the declaration file. Since we used a literal string for the property type, the property will still be effectively read-only because the property can only equal the literal string:

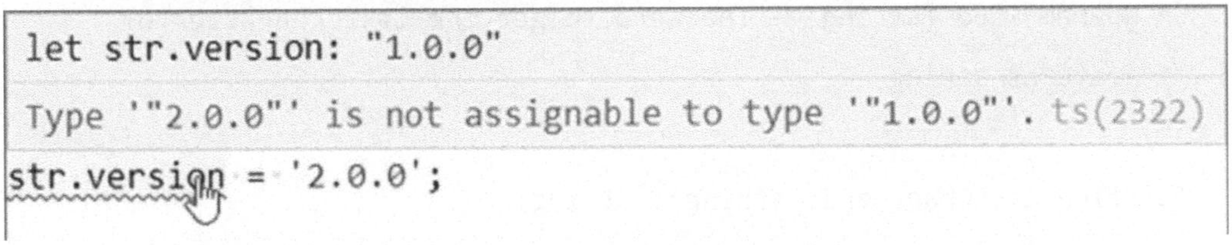

```
let str.version: "1.0.0"
Type '"2.0.0"' is not assignable to type '"1.0.0"'. ts(2322)
str.version = '2.0.0';
```

Figure 12.3: *Error with the correct property type in Visual Studio Code*

This time the property has the correct **type** information, but personally I feel the actual error message from the earlier **const** version is more explanatory as it better signals the intent of the original code - the intent was for the property to be read-only, and the first tooltip in *figure* 12.2 communicates that intent better than the message shown above in *Figure* 12.3.

Nevertheless, in either case, the end result is that the property can't be overwritten.

Enhancing Intellisense with JSDoc

In addition to the standard Intellisense that shows how a given piece of code works, we can also add supplementary information to the tooltips displayed in the editor using JSDoc comments.

We can annotate different parts of the declaration files using JSDoc comments, and the editor will display them in the tooltip when the mouse pointer is hovered on the appropriate code. Here is the same declaration file from before, but this time annotated with JSDoc comments:

```
/**
 * Simple string utils
 * @license MIT
 */
declare namespace str {
  const version: ‘1.0.0’;

  /**
   * lastChar
   * @param word {string} - The word to get the last character of
   * @returns string
   */
  function lastChar(word: string): string;

  /**
   * ordinalize
  * @param {number|string} dayOfMonth - the day of the month to ordinalize
```

```
   * @returns {string}
   */
  function ordinalize(dayOfMonth: number | string): string;
}
```

In this case, we've added the name and license at the top of the whole file, and descriptions for both of the methods exposed by the library. Now in the editor, if we hover over the global object the library adds to the **`Window`** object, we'll see the top-level JSDoc:

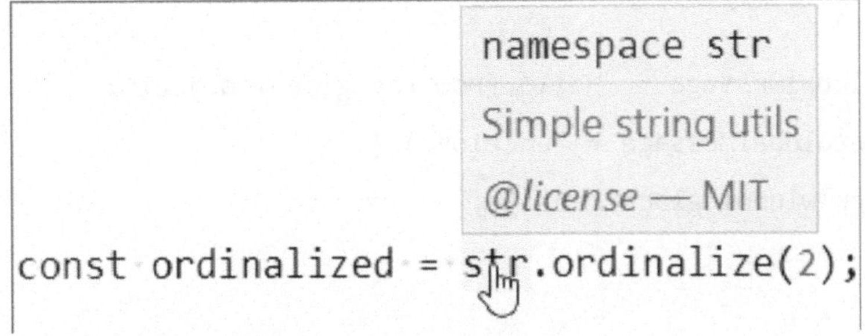

Figure 12.4: *Top-level JSDoc comment in Visual Studio Code*

Whereas, if we hover over one of the methods, we'll see the JSDoc for that specific method:

```
function str.ordinalize(date: string | number): string
ordinalize
@param date — the date to ordinalize
const ordinalized = str.ordinalize(2);
```

Figure 12.5: *Method-level documentation in Visual Studio Code*

In this example, we used the JSDoc tag **`@license`** to briefly mention the license for the file. JSDoc supports a wide range of different tags to convey rich information about the code. You can learn more at **http://jsdoc.app**.

Declaring global functions and variables

In the previous section we saw how to describe a JavaScript library available as a global object containing properties and methods, not unlike some very popular JavaScript libraries of the not-too-distant past that are still very widespread out in the wild.

We can also describe purely global variables and functions if necessary. Consider an example JavaScript library which adds a property and a method directly to the global **window** object:

```
(function () {

  window.globalMessage = 'Hello from the global object';

  window.getGlobalMessage = function() {

      return window.globalMessage;

  }

}());
```

To keep things concise, this small example doesn't check for the existence of the **window** object, or the property or method before trying to add them. For reference, this code is also in the **str-global.d.ts** file in the accompanying project. To describe them, we just need to use the **declare** keyword with a variable or a function declaration:

```
declare const globalMessage: string;

declare function getGlobalMessage(): string;
```

They can be declared at the top level of the declaration file without needing to be wrapped in a namespace.

As before, we will now get type information in the editor for both the global property and the global function:

```
function getGlobalMessage(): string
window.getGlobalMessage();
```

Figure 12.6: *Global method tooltip in Visual Studio Code*

There's one more global kind of library that we might need to write a declaration file for – a library that modifies a built-in global. Let's take a look at this next.

Augmenting built-ins

Although less common today than at one point, another global kind of library is one that modifies a built-in object, like when adding new methods to string objects for example. This is generally considered a bad practice today, so you probably won't see this kind of JavaScript library in practice very often at all now.

This time let's consider a small JavaScript library that augments the prototype of the existing built-in `String` constructor with a new method:

```
(function () {

  if (!String.prototype.reverse) {

    String.prototype.reverse = function() {

      return this.split('').reverse().join('');

    }

  }

}());
```

This snippet of code uses `this` inside the function – the method will be called on literal string instances, and `this` inside the function will refer to the `string` instance the method is being called on. It would be used like this:

```
'test'.reverse(); // tset
```

To declare this new method, we use the same approach as earlier when augmenting modules:

```
interface String {

  reverse(this: string): string;

}
```

We simply redeclare the object we are augmenting using an `interface` and then add the definition for the new method being added to the object. We use a this parameter to specify that the type of the `this` value will be a `string`.

This is an example of interface merging, which we looked at earlier in the book.

Declaring modular libraries

The other main kind of library that we might use in JavaScript is a modular library which exports code to be imported and used in other modules. A modular version of the **str** library that was the basis of earlier examples in this chapter might look like this:

```
export const str = {
  version: '1.0.0',
  lastChar: function(word) {
    return word.slice(-1);
  },
  ordinalize: function(dayOfMonth) {
    const d = '' +dayOfMonth;

    if (!d || (!parseInt(d, 10)) return '';
    return str.lastChar(d) === '1'
      ? `${ dayOfMonth}st`
      : str.lastChar(d) === '2'
        ? `${ dayOfMonth}nd`
        : str.lastChar(d) === '3'
          ? `${ dayOfMonth}rd`
          : `${ dayOfMonth}th`;
  },
}
```

The functionality is identical to earlier examples, it just uses the **export** keyword to export the **str** object rather than attaching it to the global **window** object, and additionally, isn't wrapped in an immediately invoked function expression which isn't needed because modules are always executed. This code is in the file called **str-module.js**, in a folder called **module**, which in turn is in the **chapter 11** directory in the example project.

To create a declaration file for the above module, we can use an almost identical declaration file to the one we used for the global version of the library in the previous section, except that this time we need to use the **`export`** keyword to mark the declaration file as a module – exactly the same as using the **`export`** keyword in a regular TypeScript (or JavaScript) file to signify that the file is a module:

```
/**
 * Simple modular string utils
 * @license MIT
 */
export declare namespace str {
  const version: '1.0.0';
  function lastChar(word: string): string;
  function ordinalize(dayOfMonth: number | string): string;
}
```

I've added a slightly different JSDoc to the top of this file to distinguish it from the previous declaration file, but I haven't explicitly annotated the methods this time to keep the example shorter – they would be exactly the same as before. This code is in a file called **str-module.d.ts** alongside the previous JavaScript file.

Aside from the **`export`** keyword and lack of JSDoc comments for the methods, the file is identical to the previous declaration file.

We can now import our library into another TypeScript file (in a file called **my-module-app.ts** in the module folder):

```
import { str } from './str-module';
```

We will then get full type information for the imported library when we use it:

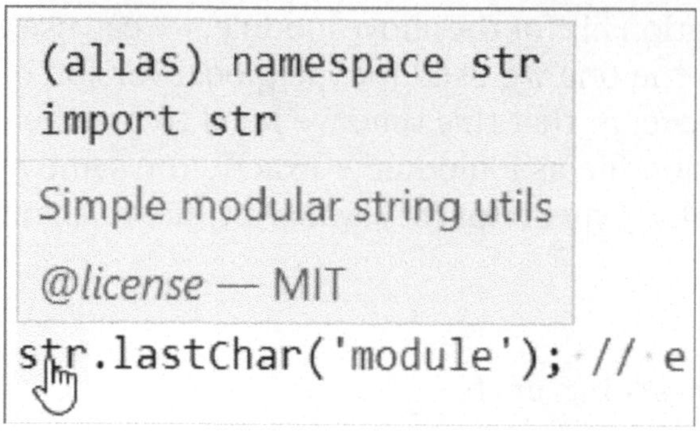

```
(alias) namespace str
import str
Simple modular string utils
@license — MIT
str.lastChar('module'); // e
```

Figure 12.7: *Tooltip for a modular library in Visual Studio Code*

NOTE: Since module declaration files are used via import statements, they do not need to be included in the compilation using the top-level include configuration option in the tsconfig.json file.

Declaring default exports

As well as exporting any number of named exports, JavaScript modules can also export a default export. This is more common with modern JavaScript libraries that export a large API for working with the library.

Imagine that the module version of our example **str** library also contains a default export to export a function (this code can also be found in the **str-module.js** file):

```
export default reverse = function(word) {
  if (!word) return '';
  return word.split('').reverse().join('');
}
```

As well as the **export** keyword, the default export also uses the **default** keyword. Aside from that, the rest is fairly inconsequential. The **import** statement for the default export differs slightly from that of the named export. To use the **reverse** function in another module, we would import it like this:

```
import reverse from './str-module';
```

Note the lack of curly braces around the imported identifier for the function. However, if we try to use this function before we have declared it, we will see an error in the editor complaining that the expression is not callable:

```
import reverse

This expression is not callable.
  Type 'typeof import("c:/Users/Dan/ts-examples/chapter
12/module/str-module")' has no call signatures. ts(2349)

reverse('test'); // tset
```

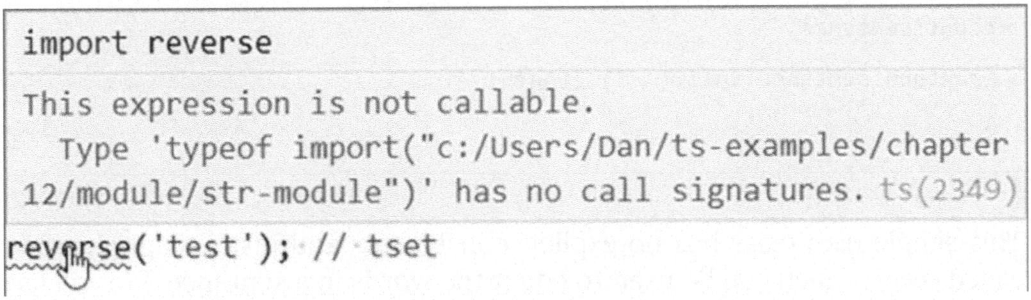

Figure 12.8: *Expression not callable error in Visual Studio Code*

To fix this, we can declare the function in the declaration file and also use the **`default`** keyword to tell TypeScript that this is the default export:

```
export default function reverse(word: string): string;
```

Now the error will disappear in the editor, and we will get type information for the method:

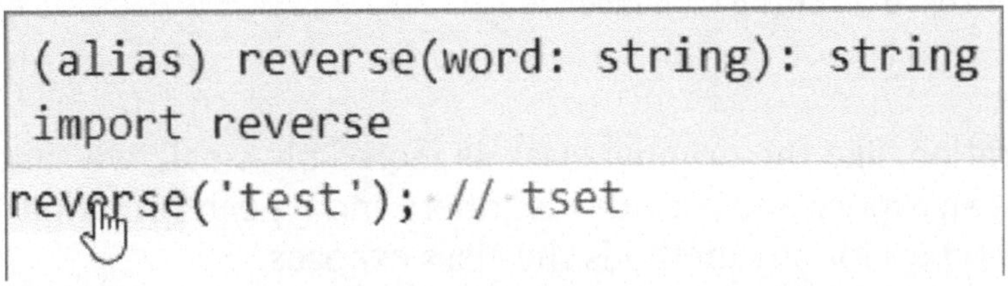

```
(alias) reverse(word: string): string
import reverse

reverse('test'); // tset
```

Figure 12.9: *Full default export type tooltip in Visual Studio Code*

This time the method is not called on literal instances of strings like the previous incarnation of the **`reverse`** function. This time the function itself is imported, so we use it like a regular function.

Declaring classes

As well as exporting values or functions, JavaScript libraries may also export whole classes. In this case, the constructor for the class would be imported, and the functionality of the library would be exposed through instances of the class created in the consuming modules.

Consider the example modular **str** JavaScript library that we've worked with so far also exports a basic class (again, this code is in the file **str-module.js**):

```
export class Word {

  count(sentence) {

    return sentence.split(' ').length;

  }

}
```

This simple **Word** class has no explicit constructor and just a single method called **count**, which can be used to count the words in a sentence. We will use the class in our modules (for example in the **my-module-app.ts** file) like this:

```
import { Word } from './str-module';

const word = new Word();

const wordcount = word.count('Lorem ipsum'); // 2
```

However, before we are able to use it, we need to tell TypeScript about it. To do that, we just need to add a declaration for it to the **str-module.d.ts** file:

```
export declare class Word {

  count(sentence: string): number;

}
```

The declaration, like the original class, is incredibly small; we simply declare the class as an export, and provide identifiers and type information (parameter and return types) for any methods the class exposes.

Declaring CommonJS modules

Another popular module format for JavaScript libraries is CommonJS. For this example, consider that our **str** library is in CommonJS format. The code for this example is in the file called **str-common.js** in the **module** folder:

```
module.exports = {

  version: '1.0.0',


  lastChar: function(word) {

    return word.slice(-1);
```

```
  },
  ordinalize: function(dayOfMonth) {
    const d = '' + dayOfMonth;

    if (!d) return '';
    if (!parseInt(d, 10)) return '';

    return str.lastChar(d) === '1'
      ? `${dayOfMonth}st`
      : str.lastChar(d) === '2'
        ? `${dayOfMonth}nd`
        : str.lastChar(d) === '3'
          ? `${dayOfMonth}rd`
          : `${dayOfMonth}th`;
  },
};
```

CommonJS modules use **`module.exports`** to export values from the module. In this case, the value is the object containing the properties and methods of the library. To declare CommonJS modules, we just need to export the properties and methods that the library object exposes:

```
export const version: '1.0.0';
export function lastChar(word: string): string;
export function ordinalize(dayOfMonth: string | number): string;
```

This code is in a file called **str-commonjs.d.ts** in the **module** folder. To consume the library in another module, we need to import it using the global **`require`** function:

```
import str = require('./str-commonjs');
```

Now we get full type information in the editor when working with the imported library:

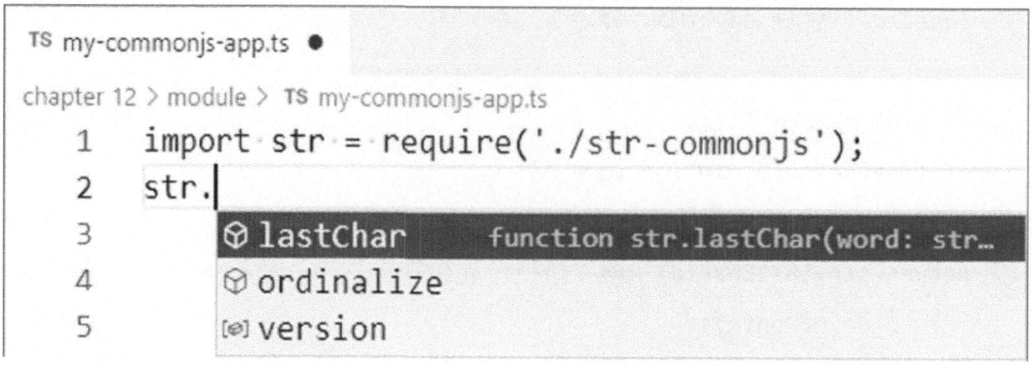

```
TS my-commonjs-app.ts ●
chapter 12 > module > TS my-commonjs-app.ts
1   import str = require('./str-commonjs');
2   str.
3       lastChar      function str.lastChar(word: str…
4       ordinalize
5       version
```

Figure 12.10: Intellisense for CommonJS module in Visual Studio Code

Note that to avoid errors for the `require` function, the types for Node.js should be installed. To install them, run the following command in a Terminal or command line application at the root of the project:

```
npm install @types/node
```

This will install the types for Node.js into the **node_modules/@types** folder. You will also need to remove the `include` option that we added earlier from the **tsconfig.json** file before this example will work as expected.

Declaring UMD modules

Modules written in UMD are also very common and declaring types for them is extremely easy. A UMD version of our example `str` library, in a file called **str-umd.js**, looks like this:

```
(function (root, factory) {
  if (typeof define === 'function' && define.amd) {
      define([], factory);
  } else if (typeof module === 'object' && module.exports) {
      module.exports = factory();
  } else {
      root.str = factory();
```

```
  }
}(typeof self !== 'undefined' ? self : this, function () {
  return {
    version: '1.0.0',
    lastChar: function(word) { },
    ordinalize: function(dayOfMonth) { },
  };
}));
```

The **lastChar** and **ordinalize** methods are exactly as before, so I have not duplicated them again. This code is almost exactly the same as the module version of the library, it just has an extra wrapper around it that checks for the existence of various module loaders in order to support different environments.

In this case, code has an outer anonymous function which accepts two parameters, one called **root** which will be the **window** object in a browser, and one called **factory**, which is the **factory** function that will be invoked when this file is run.

Inside this function is an **if** statement that first checks for the existence of a global function called **define** and that this function has a property called **amd**. When a loader that supports AMD is running the code, these will be **true** and the **define** function will then be invoked, passing an empty array (or any dependency names) and the **factory** function.

If **define** does not exist, the next branch of the **if** statement checks to see if there is a global object called **module**, and if so whether it has a property called **exports**. If these are both **true** it means the **module** is in CommonJS format and is being used in NodeJS, and in this case, the **factory** function is invoked, and the result is assigned to **module.exports**.

The last branch of the **if** statement is for when neither AMD or CommonJS are used and in this case, it simply assigns the return value of the **factory** function to a property of the **root** object (which will be the **window** object in a browser) called **str**, the name of the example library.

The first function is immediately invoked and passed the two expected parameters. The first parameter is obtained by checking for a global object called **self**, which will be present in NodeJS or Webworker contexts. This object is passed in if it exists, and if not, **this** is passed instead, which will refer to the **window** object in browsers.

The **factory** function is the function that is passed into the first function as the second argument, this function simply returns the actual **str** library itself.

The declaration file for this variation of the library, in a file in the **module** folder in the example project called **str-umd.d.ts**, is like this:

```
/**
 * Simple UMD string utils
 * @license MIT
 */
export declare namespace str {
  const version: '1.0.0';
  function lastChar(word: string): string;
  function ordinalize(dayOfMonth: number | string): string;
}
```

The UMD version of the declaration file is exactly the same as the regular module version, making it very easy to support UMD. Using this library in our own TypeScript files is also incredibly easy.

We can either **import** the library as a module as we did with other versions:

```
import { str } from './str-umd';
```

We then use the **str** object in the normal way, like this for example:

```
str.lastChar('umd'); // d
```

Or, we can access the library via the **window** object, like this:

```
window.str.lastChar('also works!') // !
```

Of course, we get full type information in the editor even for the version of the library accessed via the **window** object:

```
namespace str
Simple string utils
@license — MIT
window.str.lastChar('also works!') // !
```

Figure 12.11: *Tooltip for UMD module in Visual Studio Code*

Now that we know how to create declarations for the most common scenarios, let's move on to see how we can share those declarations with others by publishing them.

Publishing declarations

There are two main ways to publish declaration files for a library; we can include the declaration files with the library so that when the library is installed, the types are installed with it. Or alternatively, we can publish the types to the Definitely Typed public repository.

Publishing with the library

Publishing the declaration with the library is the most common approach; if you're creating a JavaScript library using TypeScript today, there's no reason not to include the types with it, which TypeScript can usually generate for us in any case.

If we were publishing a JavaScript library to NPM, we would have a **package.json** file for the library, containing some basic information about it. If we were publishing the example simple string utilities library from earlier in this chapter, for example, we might have a **package.json** file similar to this:

```
{
  "name": "str",
  "version": "1.0.0",
  "description": "Simple modular string utils",
  "license": "MIT",
  "main": "./str.js",
  "types": "./str.d.ts"
}
```

We can use the `types` configuration property to specify the path to the declaration file. In this example, the library itself is contained in the file **str.js**, and the declaration file is **str.d.ts**.

When published to NPM and installed by a consumer of the library, the types are installed within the library and no further configuration is required.

Publishing to Definitely Typed

Packages installed from the Definitely Typed repository are installed in a directory inside the **node_modules** folder called **@types** and are picked up by the editor automatically from this directory.

Publishing to the Definitely Typed repository will require some knowledge of using Git and GitHub, as you will first need to clone the Definitely Typed repository to your local computer and create a new branch in Git for your development to be done in.

Describing these processes in full is beyond the scope of the book, but you can find out more about both Git and GitHub on the Git website at **http://git-scm.com**.

More information about the Definitely Typed repository can be found on GitHub at the URL **https://github.com/Definitely Typed/Definitely Typed**.

Once you have a copy of the Definitely Typed repository locally, the first task is to create a new directory inside the **types** directory with the name of the library you are creating types for, for example:

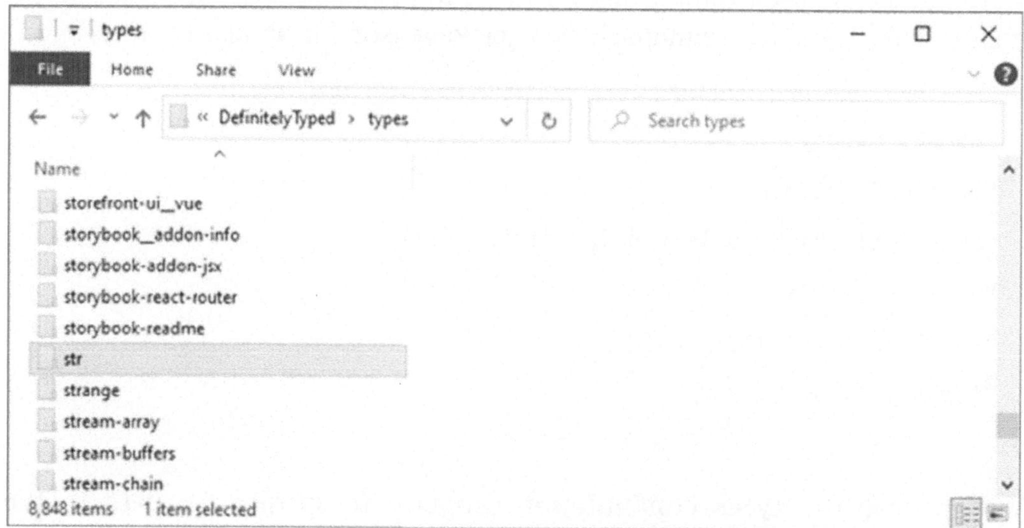

Figure 12.12: *New directory inside Definitely Typed/types in Windows Explorer*

Once this new directory is created, you should add at least the following set of files at a minimum:

- **index.d.ts**
- **[package-name].tests.ts**

- **tsconfig.json**
- **tslint.json**

We can generate this set of files automatically using an application called `dts-gen`. Using the `npx` command here means that we can use the `dts-gen` application without installing it first.

With a Terminal or command line focused on the Definitely Typed repository, we can run the following command to generate the files:

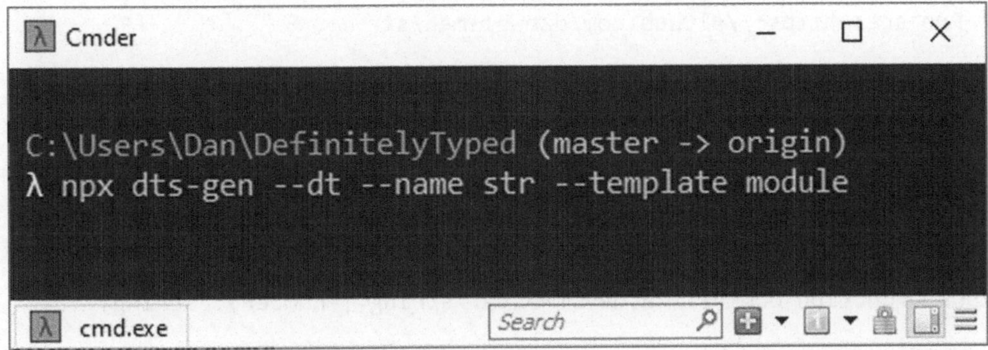

Figure 12.13: *Command to generate the required files for Definitely Typed in a Terminal window*

It is recommended to use this tool when creating types for Definitely Typed.

Consider that we want to publish declarations for a library called `str`, our directory will initially appear like this when running the above command, with the str directory being created for us automatically:

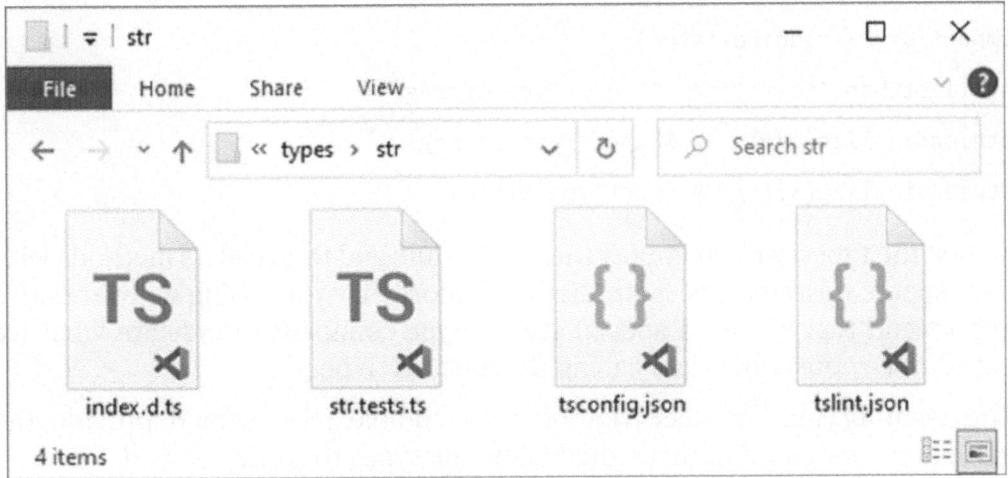

Figure 12.14: *Initial directory layout for Definitely Typed package in Windows Explorer*

The **index.d.ts** file contains the declarations for the library we are adding types for. If you generated the files using the `dts-gen` program, as shown above, this file will contain some example code to get you started for the type of template that we specified in the command. We can remove all of this except for the header, which should remain in place.

In this example, we can use the exact same CommonJS format declarations from the previous example in the **index.d.ts** file:

```
// Type definitions for str 1.0

// Project: https://github.com/danwellman/str

// Definitions by: Dan Wellman <https://github.com/Definitely Typed>

// Definitions: https://github.com/Definitely Typed/Definitely Typed


export const version: '1.0.0';

export function lastChar(word: string): string;

export function ordinalize(dayOfMonth: string | number): string;
```

Note that there are four comments at the top of the file and these should strictly be in the format shown to allow this file to be correctly tested.

Declarations for Definitely Typed can support any of the kinds of modules that we've looked at over the course of this chapter, so take care to ensure that the types reflect the type of library they are written for.

The **str.tests.ts** file is where we show the types we've added work in the expected way. In this example, the file would look as follows:

```
import str = require('str');

str.lastChar('test'); // $ExpectType string

str.ordinalize('2'); // $ExpectType string

str.ordinalize(3); // $ExpectType string
```

To test the types, we can import the `str` module and then call its methods with the expected parameters. Note that we import the types using a non-relative import and that we use a special `$ExpectType` comment to indicate what we expect the return type from calling the method to be.

The **tsconfig.json** file need not be very complex; we should provide the minimum configuration that would allow the types to work:

```
{
    "compilerOptions": {
        "module": "commonjs",
        "strict": true,
        "baseUrl": "../",
        "typeRoots": [
            "../"
        ],
        "noEmit": true,
        "forceConsistentCasingInFileNames": true
    },
    "files": [
        "index.d.ts",
        "str-tests.ts"
    ]
}
```

Note that this is slightly trimmed down compared to the version of the file that is generated but should still be acceptable.

We are just providing the definitions when using Definitely Typed, which will ultimately be used by another developer in another project, which will have its own build process. For this reason, nothing needs to be compiled in this project, so we can use the `noEmit` option to ensure no output is created by this package.

The `forceConsistentCasingInFileNames` option is used to make sure the package is cross-platform in terms of whether the file system is case-sensitive or not.

In order to tell TypeScript which files to include in this package, we use the `files` property and specify both the **index.d.ts** declaration file and the test file. Once this file is saved, the error in the test file should go away. This file is prepopulated when you use `dts-gen`.

The last file **tslint.json** is used to configure Ts Lint, which is a tool that scans TypeScript files and checks them for common code style issues and errors. This file should in most cases simply extend the existing **tslint.json** configuration file as follows:

```
{
  "extends": "@Definitely Typed/dtslint/dt.json"
}
```

This file is also prepopulated when using the **dts-gen** application.

Testing types

To ensure that we have done everything correctly, we can run the **test** or **lint** commands shown in the **package.json** file at the root of the Definitely Typed repository like this and this will run the included type testing and linting program called **dtslint**:

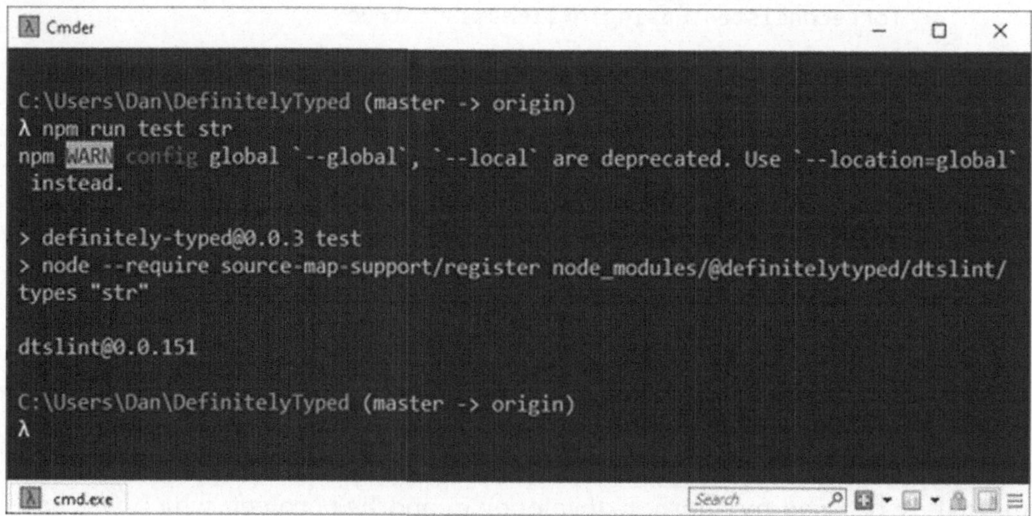

Figure 12.15: *Output of the test command in the terminal window*

Note that we specify the name of the package that we want to test at the end of the command, **str** in this case. As long as there are no errors or lint issues in the declaration file or tests file, there will be no output from the command after displaying the name and version of the linter (**dtslint@0.0.151** in this example).

If there is an error in the declaration or tests file, it will be displayed when running the **test** command; for example, if we change the **$expectType** comment after the **lastChar** method to say that we expect a **boolean**, like this:

```
str.lastChar('test'); // $ExpectType boolean
```

Then the test will fail:

```
dtslint@0.0.151
Error: C:/Users/Dan/DefinitelyTyped/types/str/str-tests.ts:3:1
ERROR: 3:1  expect  TypeScript@5.1 expected type to be:
  boolean
got:
  string
```

Figure 12.16: *A failed type test in the terminal window*

Once the tests are passed, it is time to raise a pull request in the repository on GitHub in order to have your types published and available for consumers of your library to install and use.

Conclusion

In this chapter, we've covered the basics of writing declaration files manually to support the most common types of JavaScript libraries that might be used including traditional libraries which add objects, properties, or methods to the global scope, or more modern modular libraries, including those written to run on Node.js using the popular CommonJS format.

We also looked at how to publish the type declarations we've written ourselves to the industry standard Definitely Typed repository and saw how we can test our types for correctness using the tools included in the Definitely Typed repository.

In the next and final chapter, we will consolidate everything we've learned throughout the book so far and put that knowledge to use in order to build a real application. We'll use the latest version of the popular Angular framework, which is itself written in TypeScript to build a fully functioning TypeScript web application. This will provide practical examples of TypeScript in action that we can use to deepen our understanding of the language.

References

- **https://www.typescriptlang.org/docs/handbook/declaration-files/introduction.html**
- **https://www.typescriptlang.org/docs/handbook/declaration-files/dts-from-js.html**
- **https://www.skovy.dev/blog/contributing-to-definitely-typed-for-first-time**
- **https://github.com/umdjs/umd/blob/master/templates/returnExports.js**

CHAPTER 13

Building a Conference App with Angular and TypeScript

Introduction

In this final chapter of the book, we will put some of the knowledge that we've acquired throughout the book into practice and build a small example web application.

The application that we'll be building will be a small conference companion app that will let us add conferences that we are attending and provide some basic information about the conference.

Production web applications are usually comprised of both back-end and front-end parts, with the front-end dealing with the visible UI and some level of application logic, and the back-end handling things like secure authentication and access control, data storage and retrieval, and any intensive business logic that requires more processing power than is generally available on the client. For this example, we will focus on the front-end part of the application only.

As well as TypeScript, we'll be using Angular, the popular web application framework created by Google, which itself is written in TypeScript. Let's get started!

Structure

In this chapter, we will cover the following topics:

- Getting started
- Running build tasks
- Building the application shell

- Adding views
- Data handling
- Unit testing

Getting started

While the companion code for the example application includes the full source for the application we are about to build, I would recommend that you follow the steps in building the application yourself to create the application manually, as well as get some experience in using the development tools used in the industry, such as Git and Node.js.

We can use the Angular CLI tool to create the project and scaffold a minimal Angular web application. To install the CLI globally, use the following command in your terminal:

```
npm install -g @angular/cli
```

Once the command has finished successfully, you can verify that the CLI was installed correctly using the **`version`** command:

```
ng version
```

You should see some output similar to the following figure:

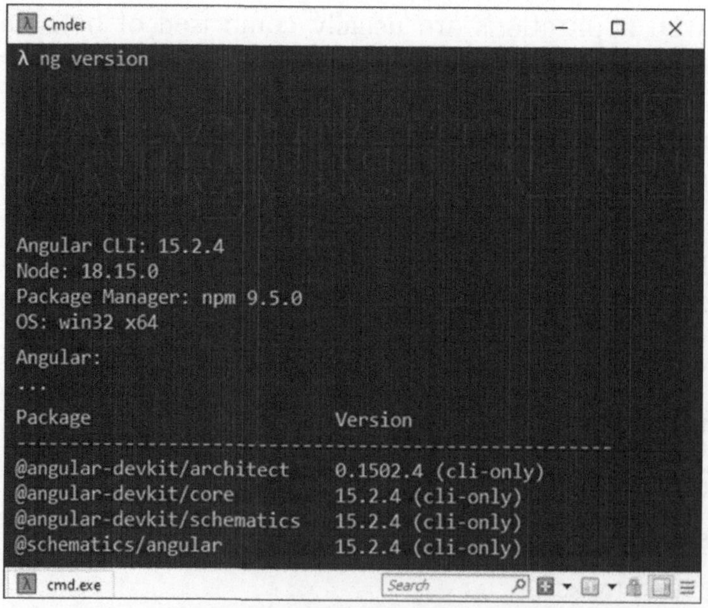

```
Cmder
λ ng version

Angular CLI: 15.2.4
Node: 18.15.0
Package Manager: npm 9.5.0
OS: win32 x64

Angular:
...

Package                          Version
---------------------------------------------------------
@angular-devkit/architect        0.1502.4 (cli-only)
@angular-devkit/core             15.2.4 (cli-only)
@angular-devkit/schematics       15.2.4 (cli-only)
@schematics/angular              15.2.4 (cli-only)
cmd.exe
```

Figure 13.1: *Angular CLI version command output on Windows*

As you can see in the Figure 13.1, the current major version of Angular is 15 at the time of writing, although this is certain to change in the near future so you may see a different version when running this command on your own system. If the application doesn't work for you, try specifically installing the version shown in Figure 13.1 after the **`package.json`** file has been created in the next step.

Now we can use the CLI to create a brand-new Angular application for us. To do that, make sure your terminal application is focused on the directory you would like the project to be stored in, and run the following command:

```
ng new conferences-app
```

This command will initiate the creation process, and the CLI will ask a series of questions to gather some information about the type of project you'd like to create.

Answer the prompts with the following:

- Would you like to add Angular Routing? Yes
- Which stylesheet format would you like to use? SCSS

The command will take some time to complete, but the end result will be a new directory in the location the project was created called **`conferences-app`**, which will also be the name of the application.

Let's take a moment to review the starter files that the Angular CLI has generated inside the project:

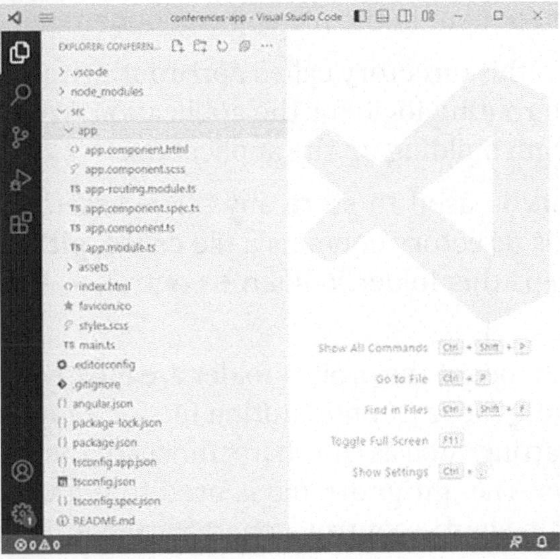

Figure 13.2: *Contents of the generated project directory in Visual Studio Code*

Aside from the folders and files are shown in the previous figure, the project directory will also contain a hidden **.git** folder, making the project ready to be used with the most popular version control system, Git.

The **.vscode** folder, which will be created automatically as soon as you open the project in Visual Studio Code, contains some configuration specific to this editor, and the **node_modules** folder contains all of the third-party packages used by the application.

The **src** directory contains the source code for the application and contains generic items like an **index.html** page, a favicon, and an SCSS stylesheet; SCSS is a variant os the SASS CSS preprocessor, which adds many powerful features to CSS. The entry-point for the application is called **main.ts**, which Angular uses to bootstrap the application.

The **src** folder also contains a directory called **app**, which contains the root application module **app.module.ts**. In Angular, modules are used as containers for components, services, and other modules.

These modules are distinct from TypeScript modules in that they are a feature of the Angular framework but note that many of the files used throughout the project are also modules in the TypeScript sense and are used to import and export our code.

Components in Angular are usually comprised several files; for example, the logic for the App component is in the **app.component.ts** TypeScript file, the HTML template for this component is in a file called **app.component.html**, and the styling for it is in the file called **app.component.scss**. There is also a simple unit test for the component in the file **app.component.spec.ts**.

There is also a file in this directory called app-routing.module.ts, which will be used to contain the routing logic for the application. We will add the routes a little later as we begin building up the application.

The **assets** directory is used to store any static assets, like images, used in the application. This directory contains a file called **.gitkeep**, which is used to ensure that Git keeps this folder in source control, as Git won't store empty directories.

The loose files at the root of the project folder are mostly various configuration files; the **.editorconfig** file is a configuration file for a range of popular editors that specifies formatting such as the character set of the files and indent styles among other things. The **.gitignore** file is used to tell Git about files that we don't wish to track in source control, generally things like artifacts generated by the build process.

The **angular.json** file is the Angular project configuration file and contains metadata for the project, and some preconfigured build tasks such as running the unit tests, running development or production builds for the project, and working with internationalization.

There are also some Node/NPM configuration files - the **package.json** and **package-lock.json** file which both manage the third-party dependencies and project-level metadata such as the project name, project website, author, and so on.

There are three separate configuration files for TypeScript here too; the base **tsconfig.json** file sets the general TypeScript configuration for the project as a whole. We then have two additional configuration files, one for the application and one for the unit tests, called **tsconfig.app.json** and **tsconfig.spec.json** respectively. These both extend the main **tsconfig.json** file and then set additional config relevant to either the app or the tests.

Running build tasks

Angular comes pre-configured with a number of build tasks, including a development build and a production build, and a task for running the unit tests. Let's take a quick look at running the unit test and lint tasks.

Unit tests

By default, there is a configured task for running the unit tests for the application and we know already that the default app skeleton includes a unit test for the app component, which gives us a solid foundation for adding our own unit tests during development.

To run the default unit test, make sure the terminal is focused on the root directory of the application, and then use the following command in the terminal:

```
ng test
```

By default, Angular comes preconfigured with Jasmine for writing the unit tests, and Karma for running them. Once we run the test command, Angular will build the application and open up a browser to show the test output.

At this point, the application should contain three individual unit tests, all of which should pass. The browser output should appear like this:

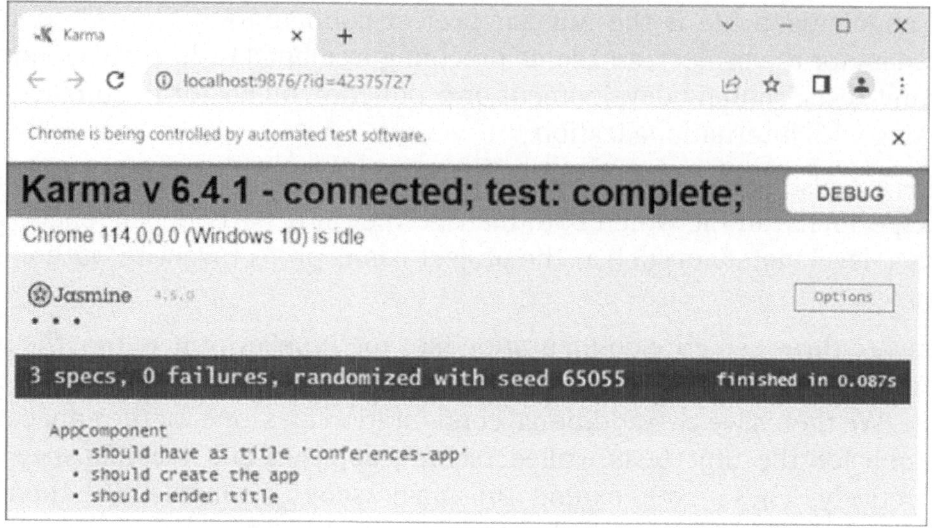

Figure 13.3: *Successful unit test output in the Chrome browser on Windows*

The unit tests will keep running in the background and will automatically rerun the tests any time we change any of the application files. To see an example of a failing test, open up the app.component.ts file and change the title of the application to a different string such as **`"oops app is running!"`**.

As soon as the file is saved, the browser output should change to show us the failing test:

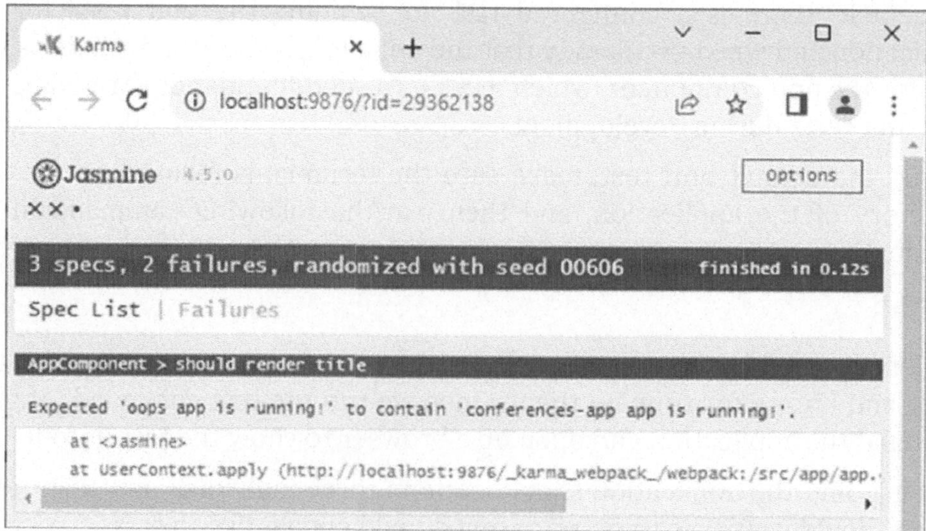

Figure 13.4: *Failing unit test output in the Chrome browser on Windows*

Be sure to revert the change to the application title so that the tests are passing once more. To stop the unit test task, use *Ctrl* + C in the terminal.

Linting

Linting is a common task for JavaScript or TypeScript projects and is an automated process where a special tool scans all of our script files looking for common issues with our code that can lead to bugs.

The linting tool will be configured using a wizard process similar to when we generated the initial application the first time we use the lint command. To start this configuration process, we can use the following command in the terminal:

```
ng lint
```

The wizard will first prompt us to ask whether we want to allow usage data to be shared with the Angular team, you can choose yes or no for this question – it will not impact your development at all, although it will add a new configuration section to the **angular.json** file if you choose `yes`.

Next, the wizard will ask us if we want to use a tool called `ESLint`, which is the de facto linting application for modern web-based projects; we should answer `yes` at this prompt, and then yes again when the CLI asks if we would like to use the latest ESLint schematic.

The CLI will now install the required packages and add some new configurations for the lint task to the **angular.json** file. It will also generate a new configuration file at the root of the project called **.eslintrc.json** which contains all of the lint rules that we would like our project to observe.

This configuration file sets some general lint rules and some Angular-specific rules that are commonly required by Angular projects. We can also provide our own project-specific lint rules if we wish and disable or enable any of the supported rules. We will stick with the defaults for our example application. You can see all of the rules supported by ESLint at `https://eslint.org/docs/latest/rules/`.

To run the linter on the TypeScript files in the application, we can again use the `ng lint` command in the terminal. By default, there should be no lint errors. The successful output will look like this:

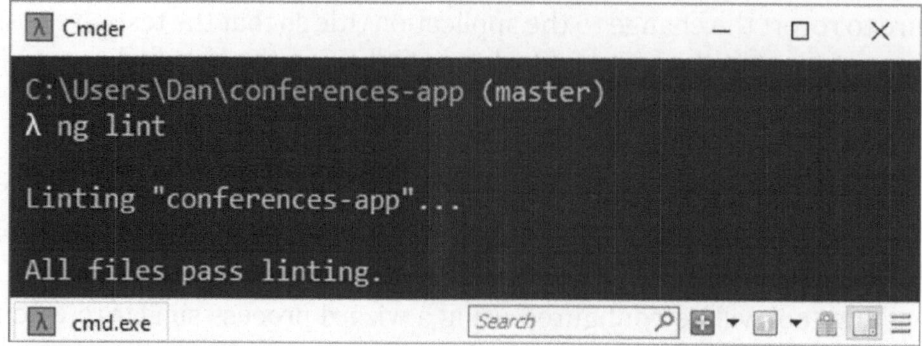

Figure 13.5: *Successful linting output in the terminal on Windows*

To see an example of a lint error, open up the **app.component.ts** file, and on line 4, change the selector string from `app-root` to just root. Now run the `ng lint` command in the terminal again.

This time you should see output like this in the terminal:

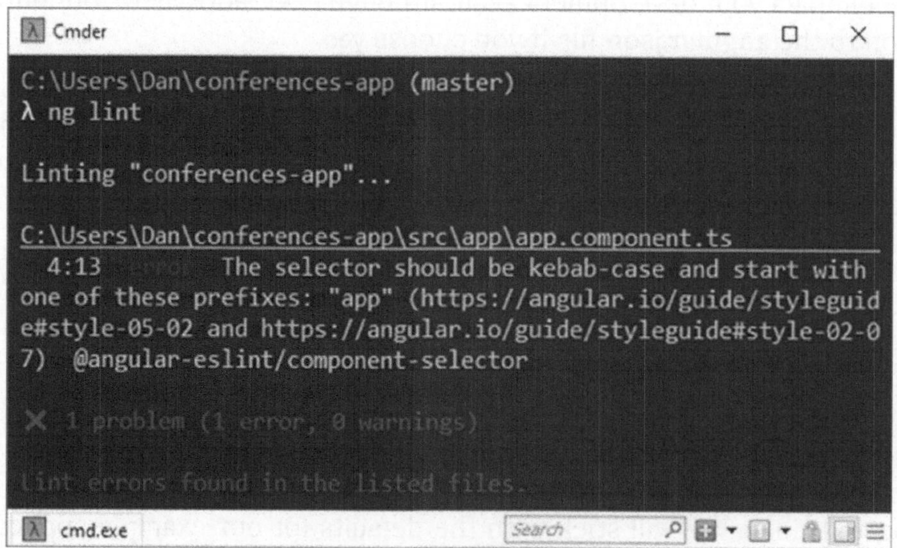

Figure 13.6: *Failing linting output in the terminal on Windows*

Unlike the unit test command, the lint command does not continue running in the background. We will need to manually run it each time we want to check the application for issues. As before, be sure to revert to the change that caused the lint task to fail.

As well as manually running the lint command from the terminal, it is also possible to integrate it directly into the code editor using a plugin or extension, depending on which editor you are using. In visual Studio code, you can open up the extensions tab, search for ESLint, and install the extension, like this:

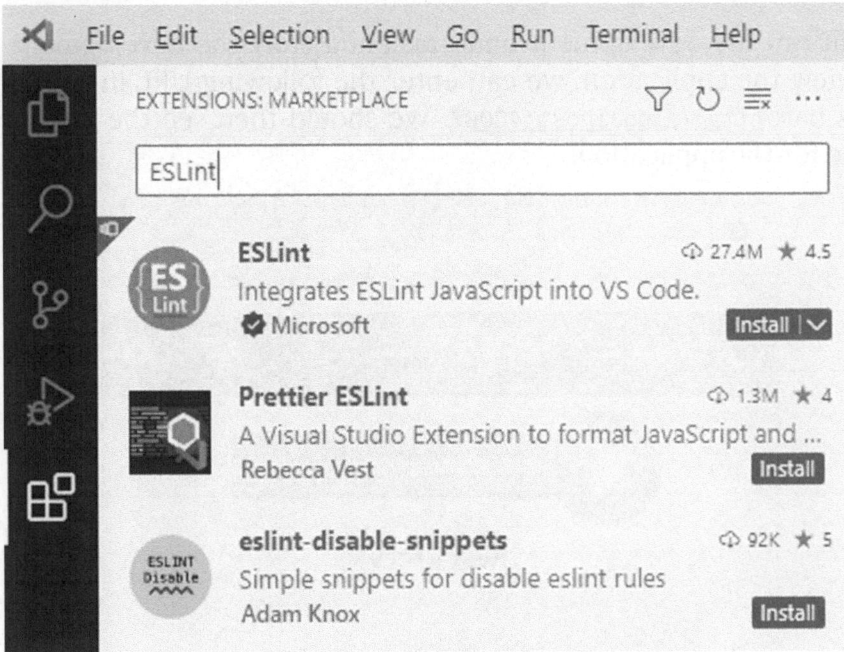

Figure 13.7: *ESLint extension in Visual Studio Code*

Once this is done, the editor will use your project's **.eslintrc.json** configuration file to automatically lint your code as you write it.

Serving the application

During development, we will frequently want to run our application in a browser to check that it is functioning in the way that we expect. Angular comes with a built-in local server for development so that we can build the front-end without having a true back-end in place - any data we require during this phase of application development can be provided by local mocks.

Note that the server provided by Angular is just intended for internal development of the application, we should never rely on it for a production application as it is missing many of the basic security aspects of a true public-facing web server.

In order to run the application using this development server, we can use the serve task. To start this task, use the following command in the terminal:

```
ng serve
```

This will run the development build task and start the development server. To preview the application, we can enter the following URL in the browser's address bar: `http://localhost:4200/`. We should then see the default **index.html** file for the application:

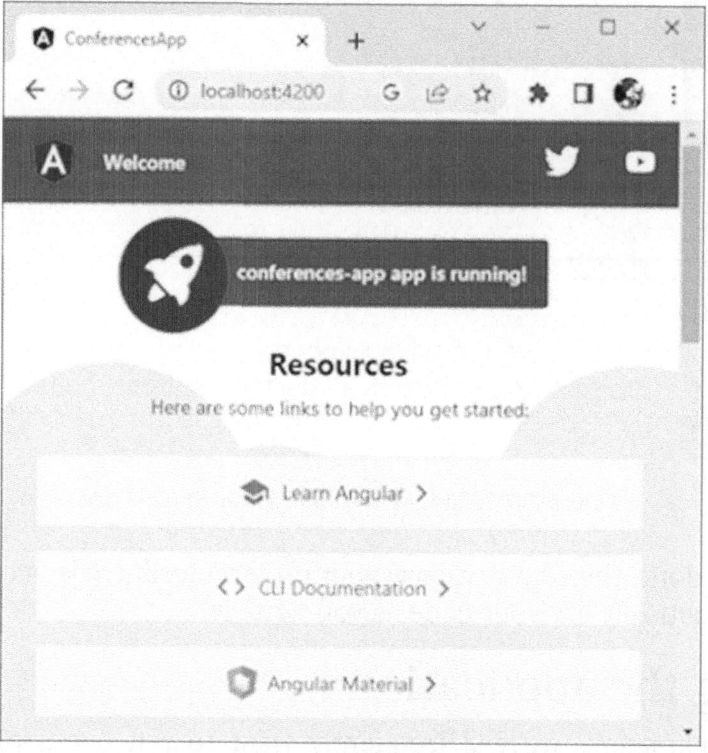

***Figure 13.8:** The default Angular application landing page in the Chrome browser on Windows*

By default, the serve command will continue to run in the background and like the unit tests command, will rebuild the relevant parts of the application any time we make a change to a file and save it. To stop serving the application, we can again use *Ctrl* + C in the terminal.

Creating the application shell

Now that we are familiar with the commands that we will need to run to build and test the application, we can begin development.

We can start with the template and styling; the **app.component.html** file already contains a lot of styling and mark-up and while we can reuse some of it to get us up and running quickly, a lot of it can be deleted. The file contains a lot of styling, some specific to the app component directly, and some that is more generic and applies across the whole application.

Let's create a new file in the app folder called **base.scss** - this file should contain the following code, which can be copied almost verbatim from the **app.component.html** file:

```
html {
   font-family: -apple-system, BlinkMacSystemFont, "Segoe UI", Roboto, Helvetica, Arial, sans-serif, "Apple Color Emoji", "Segoe UI Emoji", "Segoe UI Symbol";
  font-size: 14px;
  color: #333;
  box-sizing: border-box;
  -webkit-font-smoothing: antialiased;
  -moz-osx-font-smoothing: grayscale;
}
h1,
h2,
h3,
h4,
h5,
h6 {
  margin: 8px 0;
}
p {
  margin: 0;
```

```
}
.spacer {
  flex: 1;
}
```

The only change we need to make is to change the `:host` selector originally used in the **app.component.html** file to html in order to apply to all the text in the application. We won't focus on the styling here in detail, and we aren't using any SCSS features here, but in the same way that all JavaScript is also valid TypeScript, all CSS is also valid SCSS.

Next let's create another new file called **layout.scss**, also in the app directory. Again, we can copy all the following stylings from the **app.component.html file**. The new file should contain the following code:

```
.content {
  display: flex;
  margin: 82px auto 32px;
  padding: 0 16px;
  max-width: 960px;
  flex-direction: column;
  align-items: center;
}
.card-container {
  display: flex;
  flex-wrap: wrap;
  justify-content: center;
  margin-top: 16px;
}

.card {
  all: unset;
  border-radius: 4px;
  border: 1px solid #eee;
```

```
  background-color: #fafafa;
  margin: 0 0 16px;
  padding: 16px;
  display: flex;
  flex-direction: row;
  justify-content: start;
  align-items: center;
  transition: all 0.2s ease-in-out;
  line-height: 24px;
}

.card-container .card:not(:last-child) {
  margin-right: 0;
}
```

Some of the styles for the `.card` selector is changed so ensure the code looks as in the previous snippet. For example, the `height` and `width` styles have been removed, and the `margin` and `justify-content` have been changed.

This will give us a simple layout that we can build on. In order to include these new files in the application, we just need to import them into the styles.scss file in the **src** directory:

```
@import 'app/base.scss';
@import 'app/layout.scss';
```

There is already an **app.component.scss** file in the app directory, but it's currently empty; we can also move some of the styles there as well. Copy the following code from the **app.component.html** file into it. New styles are shown in bold:

```
.toolbar {
  position: absolute;
  top: 0;
  left: 0;
```

```
  right: 0;
  height: 60px;
  display: flex;
  align-items: center;
  background-color: #1976d2;
  color: white;
  font-weight: 600;
  padding-left: 2rem;
}

footer {
  margin-top: 8px;
  display: flex;
  align-items: center;
  line-height: 20px;
}

footer a {
  display: flex;
  align-items: center;
}
```

After copying the code to the new location, be sure to add the `padding-left` to the `.toolbar` selector – this isn't part of the default styling but is needed by our application.

At this point, all the styles we haven't copied from the **app.component.html** file can be deleted. We can also remove a lot of the existing HTML. Change the file so that it contains only the following mark-up:

```
<div class="toolbar" role="banner">
  <span>Conferences App</span>
  <div class="spacer"></div>
```

```
</div>
<div class="content" role="main">
  <div class="card-container">
    <button class="card card-small" tabindex="0">
      <span>Card</span>
    </button>
  </div>
  <router-outlet></router-outlet>
  <footer></footer>
</div>
```

Note that the **`router-outlet`** element will need to be moved into the main content container from the bottom of the file. This element is where Angular will render other components, once we have added some more, based on the application's routing, which we'll add shortly.

Creating a data model

The application functionality revolves around the concept of a conference, so we will need a data model that represents many aspects of a conference. We would expect a conference to have many attributes, like a title, a logo, a start and end date, and start and end times for each of the days the conference is operating.

Additionally, we would expect a conference to be composed of a series of talks, and these talks would need to be represented also and would have attributes such as the name of the speaker of the talk, its own title, and perhaps a short description of the talk. Some conferences might have multiple tracks, with multiple talks occurring at the same time, but this example application will not consider this.

Even for a very small application such as this, you can see there are a lot of different objects and attributes that the data model will need to account for. Before we start building components of our own, let's create some interfaces that will represent the different objects we'll be working with throughout the remainder of this chapter.

In the **app** directory of the project, create a new file called model.ts. First of all, add the following interface to the new file:

```
export interface Talk {
  speaker: {
    name: string;
    avatar?: string;
  };
  title: string;
  duration: string;
  description: string;
  day: number;
}
```

We've added an exported **`interface`** called **`Talk`**, which will represent an individual talk within a conference. The interface defines some simple **`string`** properties like a **`title`**, **`duration`**, and **`description`**, and a more complex property called **`speaker`** which itself comprises the **`string`** properties **`name`** and **`avatar`**, the latter of which is optional. Each talk also has a numerical **`day`** property to show on which day of the conference the talk will occur.

Next, we can add the interface for a conference to the same file:

```
export interface Conference {
  id: number;
  logo?: {
    src: string;
    title?: string;
  },
  title: string;
  startDateTime: string;
  endDateTime: string;
  shortDescription?: string;
  description: string;
  talks?: Talk[];
}
```

Each conference will have a unique `id` number, and an optional `logo` object containing `src` and `title` properties, which are both `string` properties. The `title` property is optional.

The `Conference` interface will share some similarities with the `Talk` interface such as a string `title` and `description`, although conferences also have an optional `shortDescription` property to display a shorter description for when there is a list of conferences.

A conference also has `string` properties for the date and time of the start of the conference, and the date and time of the end of the conference, as a conference may span multiple days. In an application that worked heavily with dates, we would probably want to use actual `Date` objects, but as we will mostly just be displaying the dates, we can use strings to keep things simple.

Lastly, the conference has a `talks` property, which will be an array of objects implementing the `Talk` interface. For this demo application, we'll need to mark this property as optional.

Thinking about the structure of the different objects used by the application at this stage and designing our types to suit those objects will help us to build the application in a cleaner and less error-prone way - as we are building the different views, we already know which objects and properties each component will have available to work with and display.

If we build the application organically, without considering the data structures now, we could end up with a confused data model where different components all work with slightly differently named properties or similar, and we would have to go back and align the views later on in the development process.

Adding views

The application will have a number of different views, or screens, which show different parts of the application, or allow different functionality. We already have the shared app component, which will serve as a container for the rest of the application, but we will also need to add the following views:

- A home view which will be the landing screen for the application and display a list of upcoming conferences
- An add conference view that will allow users to enter the details of an upcoming conference they are attending
- A conference view which will display all the information associated with a conference

The individual conference will be the largest and most complicated view, so we'll add this one last; for now, let's start out by adding the home view.

Home view

The initial screen of the application will list any upcoming conferences that the user is attending, or if there are none, it should allow the user to add an upcoming conference. We can add a new component for the home view using the following command in the terminal, with the terminal focused on the root directory of the project:

```
ng generate component home
```

This command will invoke an Angular schematic (a kind of blueprint or template) which automatically creates the specified component for us. The command tells the CLI to create a new component called `home`, which will automatically put the new component in the **app** directory. It will create a new HTML template, a stylesheet, a TypeScript file, and a test file, as well as update the app module to import and load the new component. The CLI will show output confirming the creation of the new files:

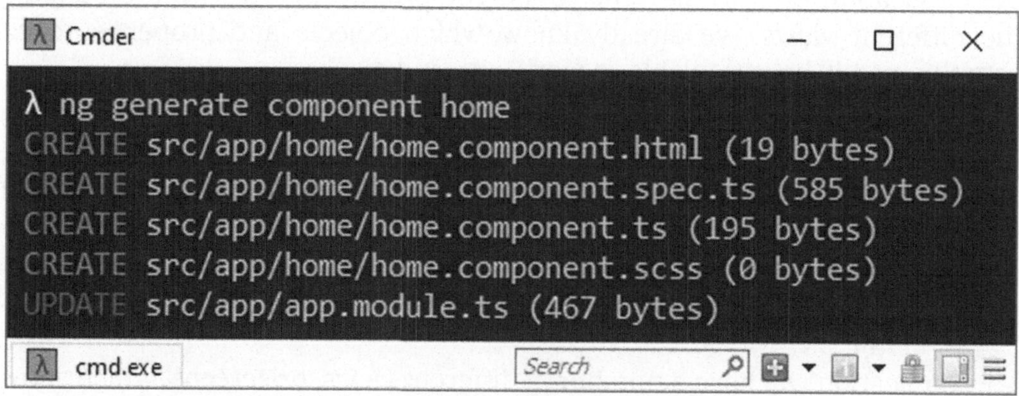

Figure 13.9: *Generate schematic output in a terminal on Windows*

> **NOTE: The command shown in figure 13.8 can be shortened to ng g c home for convenience.**

The template and the stylesheet are practically empty – the template just contains a single paragraph that says the component is working. The TypeScript file contains just the shell of a component. Let's open it up and take a quick look before we add any code.

The **home.component.ts** file initially contains just the following code, which is added by the CLI automatically whenever it generates a new component:

```
import { Component } from '@angular/core';

@Component({
  selector: 'app-home',
  templateUrl: './home.component.html',
  styleUrls: ['./home.component.scss']
})
export class HomeComponent {
}
```

The file imports a decorator from Angular called `Component`; this is used to provide Angular with some metadata about the component, including the selector for the component, which we will need to use in order to render it, and the paths to the HTML template and the SCSS stylesheet. The decorator will be executed when the file is initially loaded and is used internally by Angular to create all of the required components during the initial bootstrapping of the application.

Lastly, the file exports a class called `HomeComponent`, which is initially empty, but is where we will add all the logic required by the component shortly.

Now let's add some code, first of all, we can move the element with the class `card-container` out of the **app.component.html** file into the new template for the home component in the file **home.component.html**, replacing the example `p` element.

The file should now look like this:

```
<div class="card-container">
  <button class="card card-small" tabindex="0">
    <span>Card</span>
  </button>
</div>
```

Next, let's replace the `button` element with something that will display a list of upcoming conferences or display a message if there are no conferences to display. We can change the button so that it can be used to add a new conference.

Update the template so that it looks like this:

```
<div class="card-container" *ngIf="confs?.length; else noConfs">
  <ul>
    <li class="card" tabindex="0" *ngFor="let conf of confs">
      <img *ngIf="conf.logo" [src]="conf.logo.src" [title]="conf.logo.title" />
      <h1>{{ conf.title }}</h1>
      <div class="desc">
        <p>{{ conf.shortDescription }}</p>
        <time>{{ conf.startDateTime }} - {{ conf.endDateTime }}</time>
        <a routerLink="/view-conference/{{ conf.id }}">View</a>
      </div>
    </li>
  </ul>
</div>
<ng-template #noConfs>
  <div class="no-confs">
    <h1>You aren't attending any upcoming conferences!</h1>
  </div>
</ng-template>
<button (click)="addConference()">Add conference</button>
```

We've kept the outer container `div` from the original mark-up with the `card-container` class but have also added a `*ngIf` directive on it. This is one of many Angular-specific template features that allow us to control the visibility or state of HTML elements based on the state of the component.

In this case, the expression is bound to the `length` property of an object from the component called `confs`. We haven't added this yet, so the editor will flag it as an error at this point, you can ignore that for now. We can also use the optional chaining character (`?`) here to avoid errors if the `confs` object is `undefined` or `null`.

The `*ngIf` also has an else clause that points to the `ng-template` element near the end of the previous code snippet, we'll look at this in more detail in just a moment, for now just understand that if there is a `confs` object in the component with a positive `length` property, then Angular will display the first `div` element, and if there isn't a `confs` object, or its `length` property is falsey, it will display the `ng-template` instead.

Inside the `div` we've added a `ul` element. There is a `li` element which has another Angular directive on it; this time we use the `*ngFor` directive in order to repeat the `li` element and its contents for each item in the `confs` object – as you can probably tell at this point, this object will be an array. This `*ngFor` directive is analogous to a for loop in TypeScript or JavaScript.

In the template, we use the `let conf` part of the expression to define a template variable that will be set to the corresponding object within the `confs` array and allows us to refer to the different properties that this object will contain within the template, and this is what we do for each of the elements inside the `li` element. We then use the `of confs` part of the expression to link this part of the template to the `confs` array in the component.

Inside the `li` element, we've added an `img` to show a small image for the conference, an `h1` element to display the title of the conference, a `p` element that will contain a description of the conference, a `time` element to display the start and end dates and times of the conference, and an `a` element to open up another view, which again we haven't yet added but will get to soon.

The `img` element has `src` and `title` attributes, but these have square brackets around them – this is how we make these attributes dynamic in Angular, and both are linked to properties of the `conf` object provided by the `*ngFor` loop.

Most of the remaining elements use a different syntax for the template bindings; when a binding forms the content of an element instead of an attribute of the element, we use double curly braces instead to reference properties of the `conf` object.

The final element in the `li`, the `a` element, uses an Angular directive called `routerLink` – this directive allows us to work with Angular's routing system and provides a hyperlink to another component and its associated view – this expression specifies a path of `view-conference/` and then curly braces to add a unique `id` to the end of the path after the forward-slash, which will also be obtained from the `conf` object.

After the first **div** element, we use a special element called **ng-template**. This allows us to add part of the template that Angular will only display under certain situations, in this case, when there are no conferences to display.

This element has an identifier of **noConfs** which must be preceded by a hash sign (**#**) for Angular to recognize it. Inside this part of the template, we just have a simple container with a message to say that there aren't any conferences yet.

Last of all is a **button** element that we can use to add a new conference. This will be another view that'll be adding shortly.

The **button** has a binding for the **click** event; to add an event handler to a template in Angular, we use parentheses around the event name and set the value of the attribute to the name of the event handler, **addConference** in this case.

At this point, we should update the component to account for the **confs** property used by the template, and the **addConference** event handler used by the button. The button will be used to change the route to the add conference component, but instead of using the **routerLink** directive in the template as we did previously, we'll use Angular's router programmatically from the class instead to demonstrate usage from code.

Open up the **home.component.ts** file and import the Angular Router at the top of the file:

```
import { Router } from '@angular/router';
```

We'll also need to import the **Conference** interface from the **model.ts** file that we added earlier:

```
import { Conference } from '../model';
```

Now update the existing but currently empty **HomeComponent** class so that it appears like this instead:

```
export class HomeComponent {
  protected confs: Conference[] = [];

  constructor(private router: Router) {}

  public addConference(): void {
```

```
    this.router.navigateByUrl('/add');
  }
}
```

We've added a new property to the component called **`confs`** and used the **`protected`** access modifier so that it can't be changed by any external classes that don't extend this class. This still allows us to use the property in the component's template, as the template is a conserved part of the class. We set the type of the array to the **`Conference`** interface we imported from the model – **`Conference[]`**.

Angular's router is an injectable class, which means that it is managed by Angular's Dependency Injection system. Using this system we can inject instances of injectable classes into other classes without having to instantiate and manage them ourselves.

In this case, we can add it to the constructor for the class and will be able to use it inside our component; it won't be used outside of this file so we can automatically initialize it by giving it **`private`** access modifier and setting it as the type of property called **`Router`**.

Lastly, we define the **`addConference`** method that will be invoked when the add button is clicked. We mark the method **`public`** and specify a **`void`** return value. Inside the method, we can use our reference to the router to change to another view. The router has a method called **`navigateByUrl`**.

This method allows us to pass a string which corresponds to a route of our application and Angular will load this route in the browser whenever the method is invoked. Here we pass the value **`/add`** – we don't yet have a route for this but will add it shortly when we add the new component that will be used to add a new conference to the app.

We can also add some basic styling for the home view; open up **home.conference.scss** and add the following code:

```
ul { padding-left: 0; }

img { margin: 0 1rem 1rem 0; }

h1 { align-self: baseline; }

a { display: block; }
```

This should be all we need.

Adding routing

At this point, we still can't see the home component in the browser, because even though the app module is loading the component, it isn't actually being used anywhere.

In Angular we can display a component in multiple ways, using a selector in a template, or by using a component with a router-outlet. In this example, we'll be using the Angular router to load our components based on the address in the browser's address bar.

We will use the router-outlet in the **app.component.html** template file which we looked at earlier to load most of our components in the example application.

Open up the file called **app-routing.module.ts.** which was one of the files the Angular CLI created for us when we created the application. It initially contains the following code:

```
import { NgModule } from '@angular/core';

import { RouterModule, Routes } from '@angular/router';


const routes: Routes = [];

@NgModule({

  imports: [RouterModule.forRoot(routes)],

  exports: [RouterModule]

})

export class AppRoutingModule { }
```

This file is a module, in the Angular sense as well as the TypeScript sense, so it imports the **`NgModule`** decorator. It also imports the **`RouterModule`**, and a type-alias called **`Routes`**. The file then declares a variable called **`routes`** which uses the imported **`Routes`** type and initializes it to an empty array – this is where we will add the routes for the application.

Finally, the file exports a class called **`AppRoutingModule`**, which is decorated with the **`NgModule`** decorator. The decorator is passed an object which is used to provide any **`imports`** required by the module and its **`exports`**.

In this case, the module imports the **RouterModule** and also exports the **RouterModule** so that it can be used in other parts of the application. In the **import** field, the **forRoot** method of the **RouterModule** is used to load the routes array.

All we need to do at this point is add some basic routes for the application. Each individual route will correspond to a path in the browser's address bar and will map to an individual component.

First of all, we'll need to import our home component into the routing module. We can add the following import after the existing ones:

```
import { HomeComponent } from './home/home.component';
```

Now we can update the routes array in the preceding code so that it appears like this:

```
const routes: Routes = [
  { path: 'home', component: HomeComponent },
  { path: '',   redirectTo: '/home', pathMatch: 'full' },
];
```

We've added two new **Route** objects; the first is for the path **home** and will load the imported **HomeComponent**. The second object specifies an empty path and uses the **redirectTo** property to redirect an empty path to the **/home** route.

This means that the home component will be displayed in both cases where the URL **/home** is used or if no path is specified after the host name.

The main **app.module.ts** file already imports and consumes the **AppRoutingModule** that we just updated, so we shouldn't need to do anything else at this point in order to see the home component in the browser (as long as the **ng serve** command is running – if it isn't running, start it up now!):

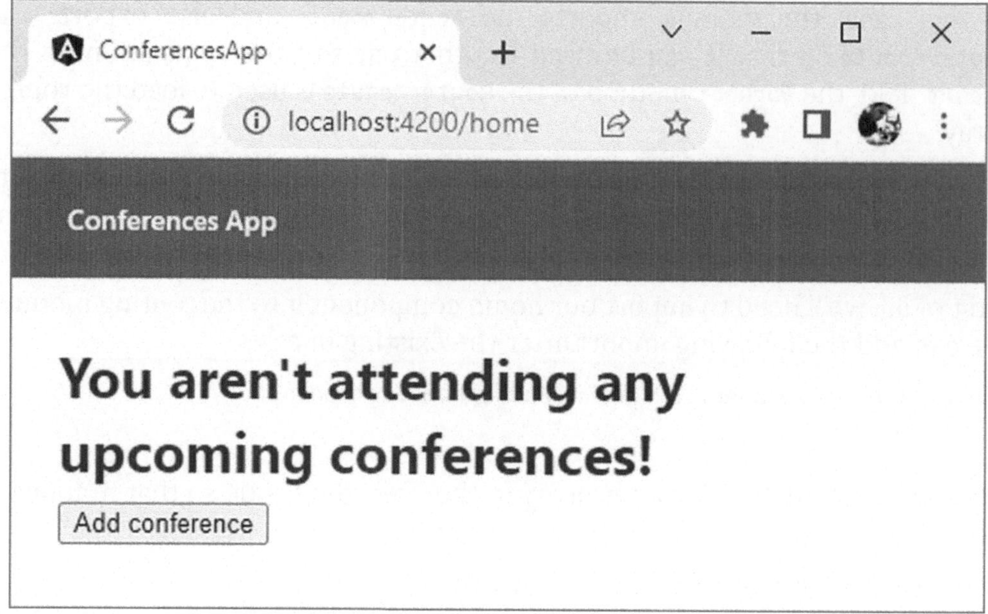

Figure 13.10: *The routed home component*

We should find that our routing is working as expected, and the **`HomeComponent`** is displayed in the router-outlet element inside the **`AppComponent`**.

We should also see that even if we enter the URL **`http://localhost:4200`** in the browser's address bar, we are redirected to **`http://localhost:4200/home`** automatically.

At this point, we just see the message that you aren't attending any upcoming conferences because we haven't added any conferences yet. Let's add the view that will allow us to add a conference next.

Building the add-conference view

Next, let's add a view which will present a form to the user to allow them to add the details for a conference they are attending. We can use the CLI to scaffold out the new component as we did when creating the home component.

Enter the following command in your terminal, ensuring the terminal is focused on the root folder of the project:

```
ng g c add-conference
```

The CLI will create a new folder in the **app** directory called **add-conference**, and inside this folder add the template, stylesheet, class, and test files for the new component, and update the **AppModule** to load the new component. The CLI output should reflect these changes:

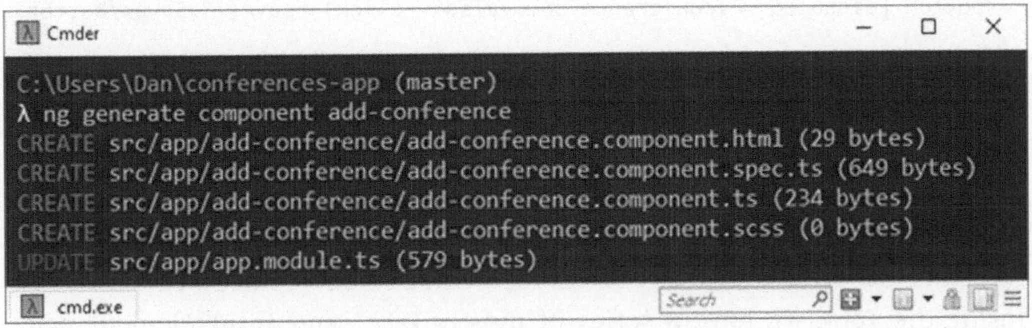

```
Cmder
C:\Users\Dan\conferences-app (master)
λ ng generate component add-conference
CREATE src/app/add-conference/add-conference.component.html (29 bytes)
CREATE src/app/add-conference/add-conference.component.spec.ts (649 bytes)
CREATE src/app/add-conference/add-conference.component.ts (234 bytes)
CREATE src/app/add-conference/add-conference.component.scss (0 bytes)
UPDATE src/app/app.module.ts (579 bytes)
cmd.exe
```

Figure 13.11: *CLI output of the ng generate command on Windows*

First of all, let's update the new template. Open up the **add-conference.component.html** file inside the new **add-conference** directory, and replace the default contents with the following code:

```
<h1>Add New Conference</h1>

<form [formGroup]=”conferenceForm”>

  <label for=”name”>Conference name<sup>*</sup>:</label>

  <input id=”name” formControlName=”name”>


  <label for=”img”>Logo:</label>

  <div class=”logo-container”>

    <img *ngIf=”logoDataSrc.length” [src]=”logoDataSrc”>

   <input #logo type=”file” accept=”image/*” (change)=”uploadLogo(logo)”>

  </div>


  <label for=”startDate”>Start date<sup>*</sup>:</label>

  <input type=”datetime-local” formControlName=”startDateTime”>


  <label for=”endDate”>End date<sup>*</sup>:</label>

  <input type=”datetime-local” formControlName=”endDateTime”>


  <label for=”desc”>Description<sup>*</sup>:</label>
```

```
  <textarea id="desc" formControlName="desc"></textarea>

  <button [disabled]="!conferenceForm.valid" (click)="save()">Save</button>
</form>
```

We start with a **h1** element for the title of the form. Following the heading is a form element containing an Angular form directive called **formGroup**. This directive is used to link a form in a template with a form object in a class. We haven't added this yet, so expect an error in the editor on this line to begin with - we'll add the required TypeScript next.

Inside the **form**, we have a series of mostly **label** and **input** element pairs. For accessibility, each of the labels is associated with its corresponding form control with the **for** attribute, which matches the **id** of the form control it is paired with.

Most of the input elements, as well as the **textarea**, but not the image upload control, have an attribute called **formControlName**. This is another special Angular directive that links each of the individual form controls with an **UntypedFormControl** object inside the **UntypedFormGroup** object, again, we'll add these in the class file shortly.

The image upload input element, used to upload a logo for the conference, is a little different; it has a template reference variable **#logo**, and instead of using the **formControlName** directive, it instead binds to the change event.

We also provide an **img** element and use the ***ngIf** directive to control whether the element appears in the DOM or not. If the **logoDataSrc** property of the component class, which will be a string, has a length, the element will appear, and if not, it won't. We can also bind the **src** attribute of the image to this same **logoDataSrc** property. Both the **image** and the **input** are wrapped in a container div for styling purposes.

The **handler** function that the change event will be handled by is called **uploadLogo**, and the handler function will be passed a reference to the **input** itself - we can use the template reference variable here but note that we do not use the hash symbol when passing it to the method.

The last item in the form is a **button** that will be used to submit the form. This element also binds to an event - the **click** event and attaches a handler called **save**. We can also add a binding for the **disabled** attribute so that the button is only clickable when the form is considered valid.

Let's move on now to add the logic for this component. Open up the **add-conference.component.ts** file in the editor. It will have the standard component boilerplate added by the CLI during creation.

First, we'll need to import a couple of things from Angular in order to work with forms. Add the following code immediately after the `Component` import on the first line of the file:

```
import { UntypedFormGroup, UntypedFormControl, Validators } from '@
angular/forms';
```

We need to import the `UntypedFormGroup` and `UntypedFormControl` classes so that we can build the required objects that will store the values from the form on the page.

We also import the `Validators` class from Angular's forms module, which provides a range of common validation functions to make it easier to add form validation on the front-end, which is often a complex and error-prone task to do manually.

Now let's create the form and form controls used by the template. Add the following code inside the `AddConferenceComponent` class:

```
protected logoDataSrc = '';

protected conferenceForm = new UntypedFormGroup({

    name: new UntypedFormControl('', Validators.required),

    logo: new UntypedFormControl(''),

    startDateTime: new UntypedFormControl('', Validators.required),

    endDateTime: new UntypedFormControl('', Validators.required),

    desc: new UntypedFormControl('', Validators.required),

});
```

The first property, which is marked as `protected` so that it can be accessed by the template but can't be changed from outside of the `AddConferenceClass` component or any classes that extend it, is the `logoDataSrc` property that is used by the `img` element of the upload control.

We can initialize this with an empty string, which is why we used the `length` property of this string to control whether the image is visible or not - this empty string initializer will not cause the image to appear before it has been updated with a proper value. We can avoid specifying a type of `string` here as TypeScript will be able to infer it from the assignment.

We've also added another protected property to the class called **conferenceForm** and initialized it using the **UntypedFormGroup** constructor that we imported from the Angular **forms** module.

This constructor takes an object where each of the keys in the object matches the name of a form control in the template, and the value of each is an object created with the **UntypedFormControl** constructor, which we also imported from Angular.

This constructor takes two parameters in most cases; the first parameter is the initial value of the control, which in most cases can be an empty string, to begin with. If we were loading a partially completed form, we could pre-populate the values of these controls with any values the user had previously entered, although we don't need to cater for that here.

The second parameter of the **UntypedFormControl** constructor, which we pass for each of the controls except the upload control, is the **required** property of the **Validators** class, which we also imported from Angular.

This tells Angular that each of these form controls is required and must be completed for the form to be considered valid. When the form is in this state, the button in the template to save the conference will become enabled.

Next, we should add the change event handler for the logo upload control. To handle user uploads fully, a back end is needed to process and store uploaded files. We aren't working with a back end, so we won't be fully handling this process. Instead, we will convert the image to a base64 encoded string and simply show whatever image the user chooses.

Inside the **AddConferenceComponent** class, after the code that we have already added, add the following method:

```
public uploadLogo(input: HTMLInputElement): void {
  const files: FileList | null = input.files;
  const firstFile: File | null = (files instanceof FileList)
    ? files[0]
    : null;

  const reader: FileReader = new FileReader();
  reader.addEventListener('load', (event: ProgressEvent<FileReader>) => {
    if (event.target?.result) {
      const value = event.target.result as string;
```

```
      this.conferenceForm.patchValue({
        logo: value,
      });
      this.logoDataSrc = value;
    }
  });
  if (firstFile) {
    reader.readAsDataURL(firstFile);
  }
}
```

The **uploadLogo** method is passed a parameter called **input** which will be of the type **HTMLInputElement**. The method doesn't have a useful return so we can mark it as **void**.

Inside the method, we first try to get the list of files stored in the **files** property of the **input** parameter. The type of this variable will be either a **FileList** object or null, so we use a union type of these two possible values.

Next, we try to extract the first file from the list of files that we obtained in the previous line. As the **files** variable may be **null**, we need to check whether the variable has the expected type, so we use a ternary expression that checks whether **files** is an instance of the **FileList** class. If it is, we can store the first file in the **files** array using **files[0]**, and if it isn't, we can store the value of **null**. This makes the type of this second variable, **firstFile**, another union, this time a union of **File | null**.

Next, we create another variable called **reader**. This will be of the type **FileReader** and is created using the **FileReader** constructor. We then add a handler to the file reader using the **addEventListener** method; the first argument to this method is the event we want to handle, load in this case. The second argument is a **callback** function that will be invoked whenever the event occurs.

This callback function will receive a single argument called **event**, which will be an event object. In order to access the correct properties of an event object triggered by a file reader, we need to set the type of the parameter passed to the callback function to the generic type **ProgressEvent<FileReader>**.

Inside the callback function, we can first check whether the event has a **target** property, and if so, whether the **target** property has a property called **result**. We use the optional property chaining operator (**?**) here to avoid errors if the **target** property does not exist for some reason.

If the **target** and **result** properties do exist, we first store the value in a variable called **value**. Because this **result** property may be one of several types, including a string, we use the **as** operator here to explicitly mark the variable as having the **string** type.

Once we have the value, we can update the logo **UntypedFormControl** in the **conferenceForm** object using Angular's **patchValue** method, which is available in all **UntypedFormGroup** instances. This method takes an object where we can set the value of the inner **UntypedFormControl** objects, by specifying the name of the control as a key in this object, and the value to set, although in this case we just want to update the logo control.

We can also manually set the value of the **logoDataSrc** property of our component using the same value that we patched into the form. Remember, this value will be a base64 encoded string representation of the image the user selected in the file selection dialog that appears when the **Choose file** button is clicked.

Last of all in the **uploadLogo** method, we can check whether the **firstFile** variable has a truthy value, and if so, we can call the **readAsDataUrl** method of the file reader and pass it to the **File** object stored in the **firstFile** variable. This will trigger the load event to be fired by the file reader, and this in turn will trigger the callback function we passed to the **addEventListener** method will be invoked.

Now we need to add the **save** method, which will be invoked when the **Save** button on the page is clicked. This button will become enabled when all of the required fields in the form have been completed.

Add the following method after the **uploadLogo** method inside the **AddConferenceComponent** class:

```
public save(): void {

  console.log('form', this.conferenceForm.value);

}
```

We've added a new public method called **`save`** and set the return value to **`void`**, as the method won't be returning a useful value. We could also use protected here to allow the method to be visible to the template but safe from being overwritten accidentally by another class.

At this point, we don't have any facility really to deal with the storage and retrieval of data. For now, let's just log the values from the form to the console – we'll add a very simple data handling mechanism a little later and then come back and fix up this method once this mechanism is in place.

All **`UntypedFormGroup`** objects in Angular have a **`value`** property, and as long as the form has been completed, it will contain an object with keys for each control in the group, where each key contains the values entered into each field.

We can also add some very basic styling to this component, just to lay the form controls out nicely. Open up the empty **add-conference.component.scss** file and add the following code:

```
label, input, textarea { width: 100%; }

input, textarea {

  box-sizing: border-box;

  margin: 0.5rem 0 1rem;

  padding: 0.25rem 0.75rem;


  &[type="file"] { padding-left: 0; }

  &.ng-touched.ng-invalid { border: 1px solid red; }

}


.logo-container {

  display: flex;


  img {

    width: 4rem;

    height: auto;
```

```
    margin-right: 0.5rem;

    & + [type="file"] { padding-top: 0.5rem; }
  }
}

button {
  display: block;
  margin-top: 1.5rem;
}
```

We won't focus on this aspect of the example too deeply, but most of the styling added here should be quite self-explanatory. The only styles that really warrant discussion are the styles for **`input`** elements or **`textarea`** elements that have both the special Angular classes **`ng-touched`** and **`ng-invalid`**.

These are classes that Angular will maintain in the HTML template for us automatically based on the state of the controls. The form controls will all start out with the **`ng-invalid`** classes, which will remain on the elements until the fields have been completed because the fields are marked as required in the class file.

The **`ng-touched`** class will only be added once the field has been focused by the user, so requiring both **`ng-touched`** and **`ng-invalid`** classes to be present ensures the error styling is not applied before the user has even interacted with the form controls.

There are just a couple more things we need to do before we can see this new component in the browser. There are two types of forms in Angular, template-driven forms, and reactive forms. Both have their strengths and weaknesses, but in this example, we used reactive forms. Therefore, we will need to import the **`ReactiveFormsModule`** into our app module.

Open up **app.module.ts**. First, we should add the import to the top of the file, directly after the existing Angular imports:

```
import { ReactiveFormsModule } from '@angular/forms';
```

We can then add the imported item to the **imports** array in the **NgModule** decorator:

```
imports: [
  BrowserModule,
  AppRoutingModule,
  ReactiveFormsModule,
],
```

Lastly, we need to add the route for our new component. Open up the **app-routing.module.ts** file and import the **AddConferenceComponent** at the top of the file:

```
import { AddConferenceComponent } from './add-conference/add-conference.
component';
```

Now we need to add a new route object to the **routes** array. It should go before the object with the empty path as it's a more specific route:

```
{ path: 'add', component: AddConferenceComponent },
```

At this point, we should have everything in place to view the new component in the browser:

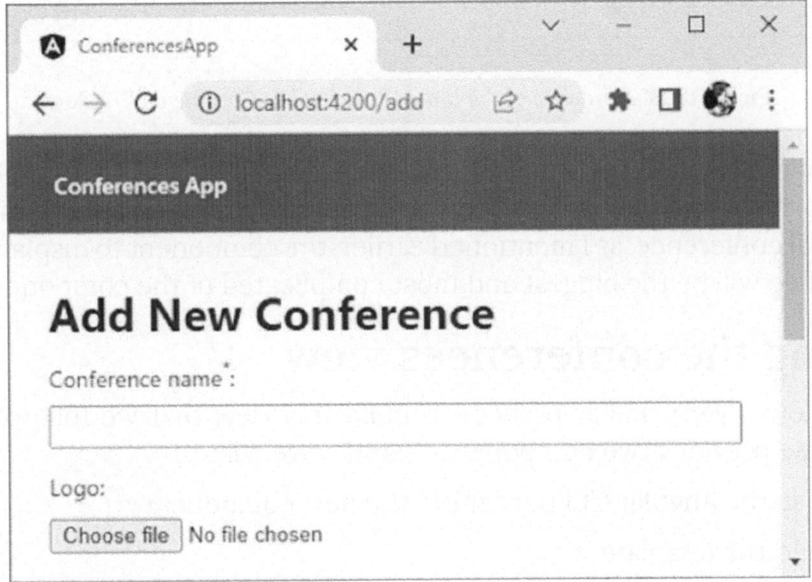

Figure 13.12: *Part of the add conference view in the Chrome browser on Windows*

We should find that once we've completed all the required fields, the **save** button becomes enabled.

If we focus on one of the fields but don't enter anything and then focus on another field, the error styling should appear around the field that was left uncompleted. We should also find that when we click the **Save** button, the form values are posted to the console.

The logo control should allow us to select an image from our computer and then display whatever image was selected to the left of the **Choose file** button:

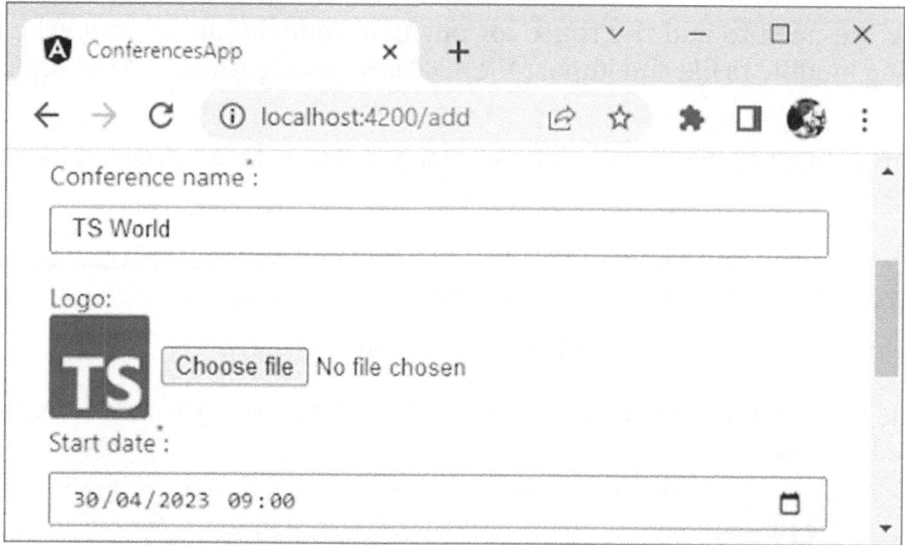

Figure 13.13: *A preview of the image to upload in Chrome on Windows*

The application now has the home view to display a list of all conferences, and a form-based view to add conferences. Let's now add the view for an individual conference, as I mentioned earlier, the component to display a single conference will be the biggest and most complicated of the components.

Adding the conferences view

We'll follow a very similar process to build this view that we followed when adding the previous two components, namely we will:

1. Use the Angular CLI to scaffold the new component
2. Add the template
3. Add the component class

4. Add the styling
5. Add the routing and any additional app-wide tweaks that may be necessary

We can start the process of creating the new component by scaffolding it out using the Angular CLI so that all the required files are created for us in the correct locations automatically. Run the following command in the terminal, ensuring the terminal is focused on the project directory:

```
ng g c view-conference
```

As before, the CLI output will list the created and updated files, and the end result will be a new directory in the **app** directory called **view-conference**, which contains new HTML, SCSS, TS, and Spec files ready for us to start customizing.

As before, we can add the new component's template first of all. Open up the newly created **view-conference.component.html** file and replace the default contents with the following new code:

```
<div class="card-container">
  <header>
   <img *ngIf="conf.logo" [src]="conf.logo.src" [title]="conf.logo.title" />
    <h1>{{ conf.title }}</h1>
    <time>
      {{ conf.startDateTime | date: 'short' }} -
      {{ conf.endDateTime | date: 'short' }}
    </time>
  </header>
  <article>
    <div>{{ conf.description }}</div>
    <div *ngFor="let day of [].constructor(days); let i = index">
      <h1>Day {{ i + 1 }}</h1>
      <section *ngFor="let talk of conf.talks">
        <div *ngIf="talk.day === i + 1">
          <h1>{{ talk.title }}</h1>
```

```
        <time>{{ talk.duration }}</time>
        <div class="speaker">
          <h2>{{ talk.speaker.name }}</h2>
          <img *ngIf="talk.speaker.avatar">
        </div>
        <p>{{ talk.description }}</p>
      </div>
    </section>
  </div>
</article>
</div>
```

For the outer container, we use a simple **div** and reuse the **card-container** class to pick up our basic layout styles. Inside this, we have a **header** element which contains the logo for the conference, the title of the conference, and a time element for the start and end dates and times.

Each of the **startDateTime** and **endDateTime** template bindings also makes use of an Angular formatting tool called a **pipe**. In this case, we are using the built-in date pipe: **| date: 'short'**, which formats the date to a more readable form. We don't need to do anything special to use this pipe as it's one of Angular's built-in ones, however, by default the **date** pipe uses the locale **en-US**. We'll see how to change this to another locale shortly. After the header is an article element which contains the description of the conference.

Following the description, we use a **div** that makes use of Angular's ***ngFor** directive to repeat the **div** and its contents *n* times based on the condition within quotes. Although we've used this directive before, this is the most complex example of this directive that we've seen so far.

This component will have a numerical property called **days**, which specifies how many days the conference runs. In order to iterate this number as if it were an array, we can use the **constructor** method of an array literal and pass in the numerical **days** property of the component to the constructor. This will give us a temporary array with a length that matches the number of days the conference is on.

This expression also uses a special property of the **`*ngFor`** directive called **`index`** – we capture a template variable called **`i`** and set it to the current value of **`index`**, which means that inside this block of markup, **`i`** will indicate the current day of the conference. We add **`1`** to this number because arrays begin at the index zero, so if we didn't do this, the first day of a conference would be day **`0`**.

Inside the outer **`*ngFor`** block we have a heading for the current day, and then we will use a repeated section element for each talk on that day of the conference. This time the **`*ngFor`** loop is based on the **`talks`** property of the conference.

Inside the inner **`*ngFor`** we added a **`div`** element that uses the **`*ngIf`** directive to only display a talk if the day property of the talk matches the current **`i`** template variable of the **`index`** of the outer **`*ngFor`**. This will ensure that any talks with a day value of **`1`** will be displayed under day **`1`**, and so on and so forth for each of the talks. Inside each talk, we then render the **`title`**, **`duration`**, **`description`**, and **`speaker`** information.

Now let's move on and add the TypeScript. For this component, we are going to need to install a third-party utility to work with dates called **`date-fns`**. We can install this from NPM using the terminal, let's do that now. Enter the following command in your terminal:

```
npm install date-fns
```

Next, open up the class file **view-conference.component.ts.** In this example, we will be using one of Angular's life-cycle methods called **`ngOnInit`** to automatically call some initialization code when this component is created. We should add an interface called **`OnInit`** to the first **`import`** statement in the file:

```
import { Component, OnInit } from '@angular/core';
```

Next, we need to import a class from Angular called **`ActivatedRoute`**:

```
import { ActivatedRoute } from '@angular/router';
```

Next, we can import a utility function from the **`date-fns`** package we just installed:

```
import { differenceInCalendarDays } from 'date-fns';
```

We also need to import the **`Conference`** interface from our model file:

```
import { Conference } from '../model';
```

Now we need to update the class to specify that the component uses the **OnInit** interface that we imported from Angular. Change the class declaration so that it appears like this:

```
export class ViewConferenceComponent implements OnInit {
}
```

Now let's add the properties and methods required by the class, starting with the properties. Add these inside the class:

```
protected confs: Conference[] = [];
protected conf: Conference = {} as unknown as Conference;
protected days = 0;
```

We have a **protected** property called **confs**. This will be used to store all the conferences the user has added, and will be of the type **Conference[]** - an array of objects that implement the **Conference** interface. We can initialize this to an empty array to begin with.

Following this is another protected property called **conf**. This will be of the type **Conference** as it will just be a single conference, and will be used to display the correct conference based on the path in the URL.

We can initialize this property to an empty object, but because the type is specified as **Conference**, we can't just use an empty object without creating an error in the editor. We can instead cast the empty object first to the type **unknown**, then to the type **Conference** and this will keep the compiler happy until we can set this properly.

Lastly, we have the **protected** property **days** which will indicate how many days the conference runs. We can initialize this to the value **0**. Again, we will set this property in just a moment.

In order to make the **ActivatedRoute** class that we imported from Angular available for us to use inside our component class, we need to add a **constructor** to our own class and use it to inject the imported class:

```
constructor(private route: ActivatedRoute) {  }
```

An instance of the **ActivatedRoute** class will be available under the private **route** property inside the class.

Next, we need to perform some setup for our component when it is initially created. We can do this using the **ngOnInit** lifecycle method:

```
public ngOnInit(): void {
```

```
  const confId = Number(this.route.snapshot.paramMap.get('id'));
  const conf = this.confs.find((conf) => conf.id === confId);
  this.days = this.calculateDays();
}
```

The method has to be **public** as it will be called by Angular when the component is created. It also doesn't have a useful return, so we mark it as **void**.

Inside the method, we first get the **id** parameter from the path in the browser's address bar. When navigating to this view from the list of conferences on the home component, the URL in the browser's address bar will look like this:

```
/view-conference/1
```

The **/1** at the end corresponds to the **id** property of the conference that was clicked in the list on the home component.

We need to know what this parameter is so that we can display the correct conference. We can get the value from the instance of the **ActivatedRoute** class in the property **route**. This object will have a property called **snapshot** which contains a snapshot of the current URL. The **paramMap** property of the snapshot contains all the route parameters and we can get a parameter by **name** using the **get** method. In this case, that would give us the string value of **1**. The **confId** variable has a type of **number**, however, so we can convert this string value to a number using the **Number** constructor.

Once we have the **id** of the conference to display stored in the **confId** variable, we can then set the **conf** property of the class to the correct **Conference** object by filtering the **confs** array where all the conferences are stored by the **confId** variable. The **filter** method returns a new array of all the matching items, but as long as the conferences all have unique Ids, there should only be one object in the returned array, so we can extract this item using square-bracket notation directly after the **filter** method.

Once we have the correct **Conference** object in the **conf** property, we can then calculate the number of days the conference is running for and set the **days** property of the class, which is used by the template. We do this using the return value of the **calculateDays** method. Let's add this method next:

```
private calculateDays(): number {
  const start = new Date(this.conf.startDateTime);
  const end = new Date(this.conf.endDateTime);
```

```
  return differenceInCalendarDays(end, start) + 1;
}
```

The **calculateDays** method doesn't need to be accessed outside of the class so we can mark it as **private**. The return type is set to **number**. Inside the method, we first create two variables, **start** and **end**, and assign new **Date** instances from the **startDateTime** and **endDataTime** properties of the **Conference** object stored in the **conf** property of the class.

We can then return the value returned by the **differenceInCalendarDays** function that we imported from the **date-fns** library. However, we need to add **1** to this value, the reason for this is that otherwise, if a conference only ran for one day, the **differenceInCalendarDays** method would return zero, or for a conference that started on one day and ended the next day, the function would return 1. So, we always need to increment this value by 1 to obtain the correct number of days.

In order to see the view working in the browser, we'll need to have some **Conference** objects stored somewhere to use, but we don't yet have any data in place to display. Just so we have some initial data to display, we can push a fake object into the **confs** array using the empty **constructor**.

It's best to avoid using the constructor in Angular components as we don't have any control over when it gets called, but as we are just using this for some temporary data, we can go ahead and update the **constructor** body of the class so that it appears like this:

```
this.confs.push({
  id: 1,
  title: 'TypeScript Conference',
  startDateTime: '2024-05-04T09:00:00Z',
  endDateTime: '2024-05-05T17:00:00Z',
  description: 'A fun-filled weekend of pure TypeScript...',
  talks: [
    {
      title: 'Keynote with Anders Hejlsberg',
      speaker: { name: 'Anders Hejlsberg' },
      duration: '2 hours',
```

```
      day: 1,
      description: 'An incredible keynote speech on the future of TypeScript',
    },
    {
      title: 'Latest TypeScript features',
      speaker: { name: 'Daniel Rosenwasser' },
      duration: '1 hour',
      day: 2,
      description: 'All the latest TypeScript features you can use today',
    }
  ]
});
```

We've added a single conference that consists of two talks, one on day one of the conference, and the second on day two. It isn't much, but it should be enough just to test that everything is working as expected.

Now we need to add some basic styling for the component, just to make the view presentable, and so the elements are laid out in a sensible order rather than being all over the place.

Open up the **view-conference.component.scss** file and add the following code:

```
h1 { font-size: 3rem; }

header, article { width: 100%; }

header {
  img {
    float: left;
    margin: 0 1rem 0.5rem 0;
  }

  time {
    display: block;
```

```
    margin-bottom: 0.75rem;
  }
}

article {
  clear: left;

  & > div:not(:last-of-type) { margin-bottom: 1rem; }
}

section {
  h1 { font-size: 2.5rem; }
}
```

We're intentionally keeping the discussion of styling to a minimum, and as before, there isn't anything too complex going on with the styling for this component, so we won't dwell on the specifics here.

All that is left to do at this point is for us to add the new routing for this component. In **app-routing.module.ts**, first import the new `ViewConferenceComponent` at the top of the file:

```
import { ViewConferenceComponent } from './view-conference/view-conference.component';
```

Now add the following new route object, making sure to add it above the route object with the empty path:

```
{ path: 'view-conference/:id', component: ViewConferenceComponent },
```

As with other routes, we have added, the route object consists of a string path, which corresponds to the path part of the URL in the browser's address bar, and a `component` to load when that route is matched.

This time however, we are using a route parameter of `:id` to specify that the path will end with a dynamic conference id so that the correct component will be loaded, depending on which conference in the list on the home component was clicked.

Changing the default locale

I mentioned earlier that although we don't have to do anything special to use Angular's date pipe, it will be locked to the default en-US locale. We can very easily change the default locale of the whole application using Angular. Let's do that now quickly.

Open up the **main.ts** file in the src folder of the project. At the top of the file, we need to import a special token called `LOCALE_ID` from the Angular core:

```
import { LOCALE_ID } from '@angular/core';
```

Now we can override this by passing a configuration object as the second parameter to the `bootstrapModule` method. Change the call to this method so that it appears like this:

```
platformBrowserDynamic().bootstrapModule(AppModule, {

  providers: [{provide: LOCALE_ID, useValue: navigator.language }]

})

.catch(err => console.error(err));
```

The configuration object has a key called `providers` which takes an array of objects. Each object in this array has a key called `provide`, which is set to the `LOCAL_ID` token we imported, and a key called `useValue`. This second key is where we set the locale ID that we would like to use in our application. In this case, we can use `navigator.language` to use whatever locale the user's browser is set to.

What we are saying to Angular here basically is, wherever the token `LOCALE_ID` is used, use the value specified in the `useValue` key of the object. There are various parts of Angular which use this `LOCALE_ID` token internally, such as the date pipe we used in the **view-conference.component** template.

We should now have everything in place to see the view-conference component in the browser. With the `ng serve` command running, enter the following URL in the browser's address bar:

```
http://localhost:4200/view-conference/1
```

Remember. The `/1` on the end of the path needs to match the `id` property of one of the `Conference` objects in the view-component class. In this case, it matches the test object we added to the constructor.

We should now see the test data displayed in the component:

Figure 13.14: *The view-conference view in the Chrome browser on Windows*

However, if we try to access a conference that doesn't exist, by trying to access the URL **http://localhost:4200/view-conference/2** at this point for example, we'll see an empty page with some errors in the browser console. We can handle this scenario by detecting when a conference doesn't exist and redirecting to a page-not-found component.

Adding a page not found component

Let's add the new **not-found** component first. We can do that by entering the following command in the terminal, as we have done when creating other components:

```
ng generate component not-found
```

This will generate all the new files for the new component inside a folder called **not-found** in the **app** directory.

First, we can update the template; open the file **not-found.component.html** and replace the existing code with the following:

```
<h1>Page Not Found!</h1>

<p>The conference you are trying to view could not be found.</p>

<p>Please check the address you entered into your browser.</p>

<p>Try returning to the <a routerLink="/home">home</a> page.</p>
```

We can keep the template very simple and just display a simple heading and a short message indicating that the page could not be found. We can also include a link back to the home page; here we use the **routerLink** directive that we have used elsewhere.

The component won't have any special behavior, so we don't need to update the class file for this component at all. It also doesn't require any custom styling, so we won't need to update the stylesheet for the component at all either.

Instead, we can move straight on to adding the new routing required for this component to work as expected and be displayed at the appropriate time.

Open up the **app-routing.module.ts** file and first import the new **NotFoundComponent** so that we can route to it:

```
import { NotFoundComponent } from './not-found/not-found.component';
```

Now add the following new object directly after the object with an empty path (instead of directly before it, as we've done previously):

```
{ path: '**', component: NotFoundComponent },
```

This type of route, with the path set to a double asterisk, is known as a wildcard path. Angular will match this route any time a route not known to Angular is requested. You can think of it as a fallback route that will be used when no valid route is matched. This is why it needs to come last, after all the other routes.

Now we can handle an unknown conference being requested via the URL's address bar back in the **view-conference.component.ts** file. Inside the file, we need to update the existing import for `ActivatedRoute` - update it so that it appears as follows:

```
import { ActivatedRoute, Router } from '@angular/router';
```

We will also need to import the `Router` class from Angular, and we will need to inject it into the constructor of our class in order to use it.

Update the constructor on line 18 so that it appears like this:

```
constructor(private route: ActivatedRoute, private router: Router) {
```

Now an instance of the `Router` class will be available inside our component in the `router` property.

Finally, change the `ngOnInit` method so that it appears like this:

```
public ngOnInit(): void {

  const confId = Number(this.route.snapshot.paramMap.get('id'));

  const conf = this.confs.filter((conf) => conf.id === confId)[0];

  if (!conf) {

    this.router.navigateByUrl('/not-found');

  } else {

    this.conf = conf;

    this.days = this.calculateDays();

  }

}
```

We've changed the method so that the value returned from the **filter** method is saved to a variable called **conf** instead of being set directly as the **conf** property of the class. If this variable is undefined, we can use the **navigateByUrl** method of the router to navigate to the path **/not-found**. As we don't have a route object for this route, it will trigger the wildcard route and Angular will display the not-found component.

If the variable is defined, we can go ahead and save the variable to the property of the class and calculate the number of days the conference spans as we did previously.

We should now find that we are redirected to the not-found component if we try to access a conference that doesn't exist:

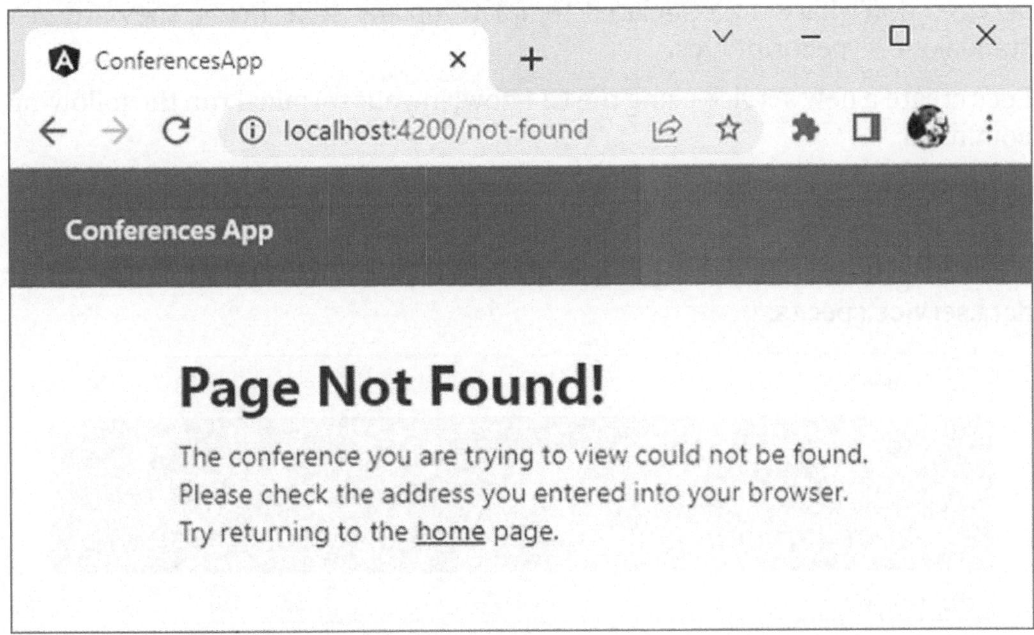

Figure 13.15: *The not-found component in Chrome on Windows*

Handling unexpected situations, such as when the user requests a URL that doesn't exist, is key to keeping the application running and being able to respond to the need of the user.

At this point, all of our components are now in place. At the moment, though, we don't have any real data to use, as the add view doesn't save the conference after it is added, and the home and view-conference views aren't getting the real conferences to display. Let's finish up this practical example by wiring things up so that any conferences added by the user can be saved, and these saved conferences can be loaded in the required places.

Handling data

We need a simple way to store and retrieve data in the example application. Typically, this would involve making HTTP requests to the back end, which would return the appropriate data from the database. We don't have a back-end, or a database, but we can still create a service in our application to handle the data that we will be using.

In Angular, a service is an injectable class containing functionality that is intended to be shared and used by multiple components. Unlike components, services don't have an associated template or any stylesheets, they are just standalone TypeScript files.

Let's create a new service using the CLI now; in your terminal run the following command:

```
ng generate service data
```

This will create two new files in the **app** directory of the project - a file containing the actual service called **data.service.ts**, and a unit test file called **data.service.spec.ts**:

Figure 13.16: *Output of generating a service in the terminal on Windows*

Open up the **data.service.ts** file in the editor.

The file initially contains just a small amount of Angular boiler-plate. Most notable is the `Injectable` decorator imported from Angular. This decorator is used to make the service injectable to any other component in the application, as it will be provided in the root module of the application.

Aside from the decorator, this file just defines a class called **`DataService`**, containing just an empty constructor. We won't be using the constructor as we don't need to inject any other dependencies into the service, so go ahead and remove the **`constructor`**.

We'll also need to import a class from RXJS. RXJS is a third-party library for creating reactive code that makes working with asynchronous code easier and which is included with Angular by default. It is based on the concept of Observables - special objects that we can subscribe to in order to receive a stream of updates to a particular value.

Observables are similar to Promises conceptually, but offer significantly more functionality, and they are often used in places where previously a Promise would be used, such as when making requests to the back-end for data.

Add the following code to the top of the file after the existing **`import`** statement:

```
import { Subject } from 'rxjs';
```

We can also import our **`Conference`** interface, which we'll also be making use of inside the service:

```
import { Conference } from './model';
```

For our simple data storage and retrieval needs here, we will use the browser's **`LocalStorage`** API, so will add methods to the class to handle getting data from local storage or saving it to local storage.

First of all, the class will need some properties. Add the following code inside the **`DataService`** class:

```
public getConferences$: Subject<Conference[]> = new Subject();

public setConferences$: Subject<void | Error> = new Subject();
```

We create two new **`public`** properties called **`getConferences$`** and **`setConferences$`** - these properties are observable so it's a convention to add a dollar sign to the end of the name. Each of these will contain an instance of the **`Subject`** class we imported, and we can use this as a generic type as well.

The type for the first property, **`getConferences$`**, has an inner type of **`Conference[]`**, that is, it will be a **`Subject`** containing an array of **`Conference`** objects. The type for the second property, **`setConferences$`**, has an inner type of the union **`void | Error`** because when this observable is triggered, the next handler doesn't need to receive a value - we're using it to signal something has happened, not fetch data. The **`Error`** type is included in the union in case an error occurs as subscribers will be passed an error in this case.

Now add the following method after the two properties:

```
public getConferences(): void {
  const confs = localStorage.getItem('conferences');
  if (confs) {
    this.getConferences$.next(JSON.parse(confs));
  } else {
    this.getConferences$.next([]);
  }
}
```

The method is marked as **public** and has a return type of **void**. We first attempt to get a property of the **localStorage** global object called **conferences** using the **getItem** method. This method will either return the string value contained in local storage or **null** if the key was not found.

If the **confs** variable is truthy, we can call the **next** method of the subject stored in the **getConferences$** property of the class, passing the result of using **JSON.parse** to parse the string returned by **localStorage** into an array.

If the **confs** variable is falsey, we can just pass an empty array to the subject, which will in turn result in any subscribers to this observable receiving an empty array. This should be all we need to do to handle the retrieval of data.

Lastly, add the following method after the one we just added:

```
public setConferences(conferences: Conference[]): void {
  const confs = localStorage.getItem('conferences');
  if (confs) {
    localStorage.removeItem('conferences');
  }
  try {
    localStorage.setItem('conferences', JSON.stringify(conferences));
    this.setConferences$.next();
  } catch (err) {
```

```
    this.setConferences$.error(err);
  }
}
```

The **setConferences** method is also public and also has a **void** return, but this method will also be passed an array of **Conference** objects as a parameter called **conferences**.

Inside the method, we also try to get anything stored in the conferences key of the **localStorage** global object, but this time, if the key does exist and contains a string value, we delete it using the **removeItem** method of **localStorage**.

We then use a **try catch** statement to try to set a value to **localStorage** using the **setItem** method, which takes the name of the key to set and the string to set as the value. We can get the string to save using **JSON.stringify** to convert the array of **Conference** objects into a string. After storing the data, we then call the next method of the **setConferences$** subject and pass it the value **true** to indicate success.

The **catch** block will pass an error and here, we can call the **error** method of the subject, and pass in the error received by catch. The **catch** block may be invoked if, for example, the user has run out of space in local storage, or has local storage disabled in the browser.

At this point, we're ready to start using the service. The first place we need to use it is in the **HomeComponent**, so open the file **home.component.ts** and first of all, import the **DataService** after the import for **Conference**:

```
import { DataService } from '../data.service';
```

Now we can inject the service into the component in the same way that we injected the **Router**. Update the **constructor** so that it appears like this:

```
constructor(private router: Router, private dataService: DataService) {}
```

We store an instance of the **DataService** in the private property **dataService**, making it available inside the class.

We also need to import a class from RXJS called **Subscription** as we will be subscribing to the observable properties of the data service. Add the following import to the top of the file:

```
import { Subscription } from 'rxjs';
```

In this component, we will want to try to get the data as soon as the component is loaded, so we'll want to make use of the **ngOnInit** method as we did earlier. This time we will also use another life-cycle method, the **ngOnDestroy** method. We should import both of these things from the existing **@angular/core** module. Change the **import** statement on the first line of the file so that it looks like this:

```
import { Component, OnInit, OnDestroy } from '@angular/core';
```

Now we need to specify that the class implements these interfaces. Update the class declaration so that it appears like this:

```
export class HomeComponent implements OnInit, OnDestroy {
```

Now we need to add a new property to the class, and add it before the constructor:

```
private subs: Subscription[] = [];
```

We define a private property called **subs** with a type of **Subscription[]**, and initialize it with an empty array.

Now we can add the **ngOnInit** method:

```
public ngOnInit(): void {

  this.subs.push(

   this.dataService.getConferences$.subscribe((conferences: Conference[])
=> {

       this.confs = conferences;

    })

  );

  this.dataService.getConferences();

}
```

The **getConferences$** observable object of the **dataService** has a method called **subscribe** which returns a **Subscription** object, which we add to the **subs** array using the **push** method. The **subscribe** method takes a callback function which will be passed the value emitted by the observable object, so inside this callback function, we can just set the received conferences to the **confs** property.

After subscribing to the **getConferences$** observable, we then need to actually try to get the data by calling the **getConferences** method of the service.

Now let's add the **ngOnDestroy** method, which we need to use to unsubscribe from the **getConferences$** observable, otherwise, we could cause a memory leak. Add the following method:

```
public ngOnDestroy(): void {
  this.subs.forEach((sub) => sub.unsubscribe());
}
```

We can use the **forEach** method of the **subs** array to call the **unsubscribe** method of each subscription. In this example, we only have a single subscription, but this technique scales well for larger components that may be subscribing to numerous observables.

Now let's look at saving data using the data service. One place we need to do this is in the add component. Open up **add-conference.component.ts**. In this file, we need to import the **OnInit** and **OnDestroy** interfaces from Angular:

```
import { Component, OnInit, OnDestroy } from '@angular/core';
```

We also need the **Subscription** class from RXJS again:

```
import { Subscription } from 'rxjs';
```

And, we'll need the **DataService**:

```
import { DataService } from '../data.service';
```

As well as the **Conference** interface:

```
import { Conference } from '../model';
```

Now that we've added all the required new imports, we next need to mark the class as implementing the **OnInit** and **OnDestroy** interfaces:

```
export class AddConferenceComponent implements OnInit, OnDestroy {
```

As with the home component, we can also add a **private subs** property to store observable subscriptions in:

```
private subs: Subscription[] = [];
```

Let's also add a new private property to the class to store the existing conferences, if there are any:

```
private confs: Conference[] = [];
```

This class doesn't have a constructor, so we'll need to add one in order to inject the **DataService**. Add the following code before the **uploadLogo** method:

```
constructor(private dataService: DataService) {}
```

We can use the **ngOnInit** method to subscribe to both the **getConferences$** observable that we added to the home component and the **setConferences$** observable of the **DataService**.

We'll need to use the **setConferences$** observable to save the data, but in order to generate the next **id** for the conference being added, we'll need to get the list of existing conferences to see what the last **id** that was used was.

```
public ngOnInit(): void {
  this.subs.push(
   this.dataService.getConferences$.subscribe((conferences: Conference[])
=> {
      this.confs = conferences;
    }),
    this.dataService.setConferences$.subscribe({
      next: () => this.resetForm(),
      error: (error) => console.log(error),
    })
  );
  this.dataService.getConferences();
}
```

The method is similar to the version we used in the **home** component, except that this time we pass an object to the **subscribe** method with **next** and **error** keys containing callback functions to be invoked when the observable emits a value or throws an error. We can use the **next** method to call a new method called **resetForm**, which we'll add shortly. We can also add a simple error handler that logs any errors to the console for debugging purposes, as this observable has the capability to emit errors.

Now we can add an **ngOnDestroy** method to handle unsubscribing from any observables. It's identical to the previous **ngOnDestroy** method:

```
public ngOnDestroy(): void {
  this.subs.forEach((sub) => sub.unsubscribe());
}
```

At the bottom of the file is a **save** method. Update this method so that it appears like this:

```
public save(): void {
    const lastId = this.confs.pop()?.id ?? 0;
    const logo = this.conferenceForm.get('logo')?.value || undefined;
    const desc = this.conferenceForm.get('desc')?.value ?? '';
    this.confs.push({
      id: lastId + 1,
      title: this.conferenceForm.get('name')?.value ?? '',
      startDateTime: this.conferenceForm.get('startDateTime')?.value ?? '',
      endDateTime: this.conferenceForm.get('endDateTime')?.value ?? '',
      description: desc,
      shortDescription: (desc.length > 150) ? desc.slice(0, 150) : desc,
      logo: (logo) ? { src: logo } : undefined,
    });

    this.dataService.setConferences(this.confs);
  }
```

Inside the method, we first try to get the **id** property of the last **Conference** object in the **confs** array using the **pop** method. If the array is empty, we use the nullish coalescing operator to set the variable to **0**.

We then get the **value** property of the **UntypedFormControl** called **desc**. **UntypedFormGroup** objects have a method called **get** to get a particular **UntypedFormControl** by name.

Even though we know this field will have some kind of value in order for the **Save** button to become enabled in order to call the method in the first place, we still need to use the optional chaining operator after the **get** method just in case the method returns **undefined**, and the nullish coalescing operator to set the variable to an empty string just in case the **value** property is **undefined.**

We then try to get the **UntypedFormControl** called **logo**. This form field doesn't have the required validator attached to it, and therefore may actually be **undefined**. If it has a value, we get the value, and if it doesn't, we set the variable to **undefined** instead.

At this point, we can push a new **Conference** object into the **confs** array. We pass the **push** method on an object and map the values of the form controls in the form to the correct property names in the object.

We can create the **shortDescription** property of the object by using the **slice** method to get the first 150 characters of the **desc** variable if its **length** is greater than 150 characters, or we can just reuse the whole variable if it is less than 150 characters.

If the **logo** variable has a value, we can create an object with an **src** property, as this is the format required by the **Conference** interface, or we can use the value undefined as the property is optional.

Lastly, we can call the **setConferences** method of the **dataService** and pass it to the **confs** array, which will trigger one of either the next or error handlers that we passed to the observable.

Our last task in this file is to add the **resetForm** method to the class that I mentioned earlier:

```
private resetForm(): void {

  this.conferenceForm.reset();

  this.logoDataSrc = ‘’;

}
```

All we need to do is call the **reset** method of the **UntypedFormGroup**, which will clear the fields and reset the state of the form, and set the **logoDataSrc** property of the class back to an empty string;

At this point, we should be able to go to the add view, fill out the add conference form, and see that an array of **Conferences** is stored in local storage under the domain **localhost**:

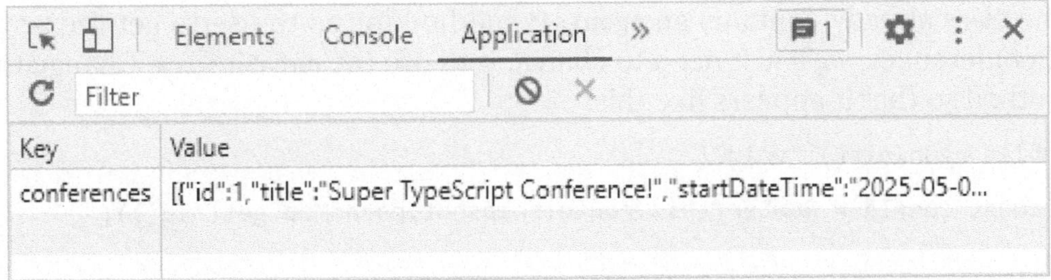

Figure 13.17: *LocalStorage area in the Chrome browser on Windows*

There's one more place where we need to use the **DataService**, and that is in the view conference component, which at the moment is using a fake conference object that we added in the constructor.

Open up the **view-conference.component.ts** file and first of all, let's import the **DataService** and Subscription class from RXJS:

```
import { DataService } from '../data.service';

import { Subscription } from 'rxjs';
```

We should also import the **OnDestroy** interface from Angular to handle cleaning up the subscription we now need to make:

```
import { Component, OnInit, OnDestroy } from '@angular/core';
```

Once **OnDestroy** is imported, we should add it to the list of classes that this class implements, Change the class declaration on line 15 so that it appears like this:

```
export class ViewConferenceComponent implements OnInit, OnDestroy {
```

We'll also need the usual **subs** property to store the observable in:

```
private subs: Subscription[] = [];
```

Next, remove the code inside the **constructor**, and inject the **DataService**. It should end up looking like this:

```
constructor(

  private route: ActivatedRoute,

  private router: Router,

  private dataService: DataService,

) {}
```

The class already contains an **ngOnInit** method for us to use to get the array of conferences, we'll just need to change it to use the **dataService**. Change the method so that it appears like this:

```
public ngOnInit(): void {
  const confId = Number(this.route.snapshot.paramMap.get('id'));


  this.subs.push(
   this.dataService.getConferences$.subscribe((conferences: Conference[])
=> {
      this.confs = conferences;
      const conf = this.confs.filter((conf) => conf.id === confId)[0];
      if (!conf) {
        this.router.navigateByUrl('/not-found');
      } else {
        this.conf = conf;
        this.days = this.calculateDays();
      }
    })
  );
  this.dataService.getConferences();
}
```

It's very similar to what was there before except we've added the same subscription to **getConferences$** that we used in the home component.

Inside the **handler** passed to the **subscribe** method, we can store the returned conferences in the **confs** property and do all of the same things that we were doing before – handling an unknown conference **id** and calculating the number of days the conference is on for.

Now we just need to add an **ngOnDestroy** method to tidy up the subscription. It can be identical to the other usages of the method:

```
public ngOnDestroy(): void {
  this.subs.forEach((sub) => sub.unsubscribe());
}
```

Now we should be able to go to the route **`view-conference/1`** and see the component stored in local storage. If a component isn't displayed, you can add one using the form in the add view but note that the form does not capture any data for the talks in a conference at this point, so no talks will be displayed for the conference.

Now that we have a data service, we can go ahead and remove the temporary data that we pushed into the **`confs`** array earlier in the chapter from the constructor of the **`ViewConferenceComponent`** class.

We should also find at this point that if we visit the home route of the application again now, we can see the conference from local storage displayed instead of the message that no conferences have been added:

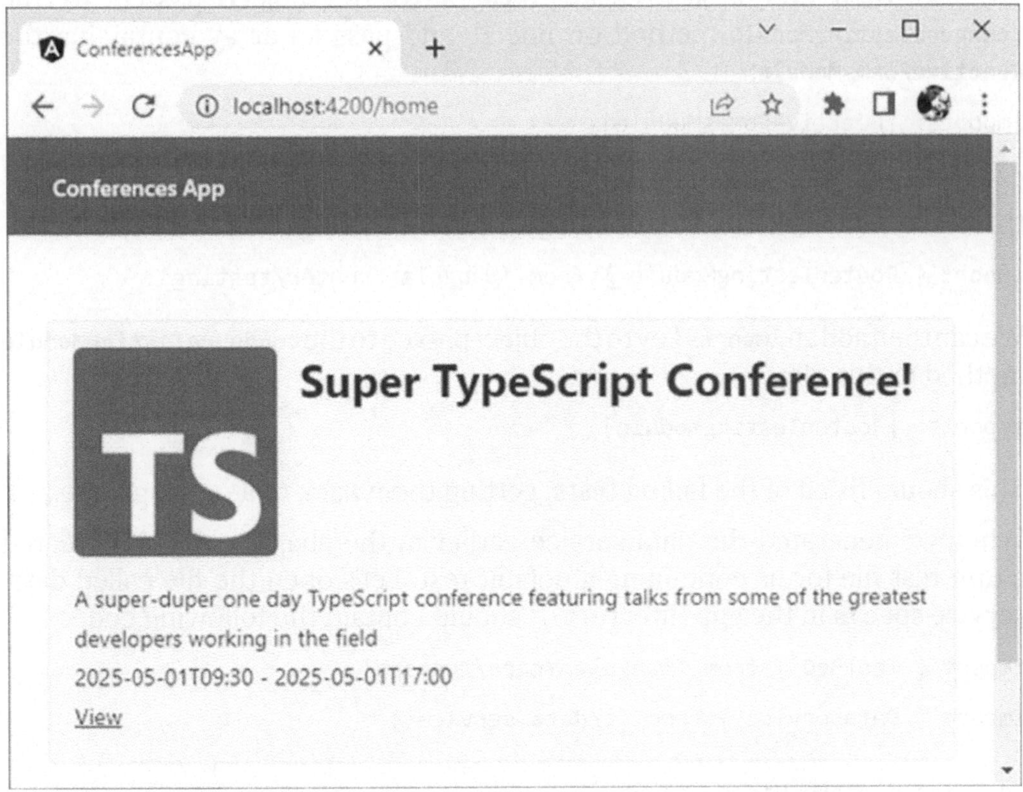

Figure 13.18: *The completed Home screen in Chrome on Windows*

Unit testing

As we've made many changes to the application, the initial unit tests are no longer passing. We should fix these up.

The tests for the app component are looking in the template of the component for a span element containing the text "**`conferences-app is running`**!", but this is one of the elements we removed from this template right back at the start of building the app. We can go ahead and remove the test with the description "**`should render title`**" from the file **app.component.spec.ts.**

In the file **add-conference.component.spec.ts**. there is one issue that needs to be fixed. In the add conference component, we are using some Angular forms features, so in this test file, we will also need to import the **`ReactiveFormsModule`** from Angular:

```
import { ReactiveFormsModule } from '@angular/forms';
```

We can then add a key called **`imports`** to the object passed to the **`configureTestingModule`** method on line 11, and pass an array containing the **`ReactiveFormsModule`**:

```
imports: [ReactiveFormsModule],
```

Finally, in the file **view-conference.component.spec.ts**, we will need to import the **`RouterTestingModule`** from Angular:

```
import { RouterTestingModule } from '@angular/router/testing';
```

We can then add an **`imports`** key to the object passed to the **`configureTestingModule`** method in this file:

```
imports: [RouterTestingModule],
```

This should fix all of the failing tests, getting them back to a passing state.

When we generated the data service earlier in the chapter, the CLI created a unit test file for us containing a default test. Let's open the file called **data.service.spec.ts** in the **app** directory. It should contain the following code:

```
import { TestBed } from '@angular/core/testing';

import { DataService } from './data.service';

describe('DataService', () => {
```

```
  let service: DataService;

  beforeEach(() => {
    TestBed.configureTestingModule({});
    service = TestBed.inject(DataService);
  });

  it('should be created', () => {
    expect(service).toBeTruthy();
  });
});
```

The file imports the **TestBed** utility from Angular, and the actual **DataService** so it can be tested. The test framework in use in this project is Jasmine, so the test is wrapped in an outer describe function which is passed a string describing the thing being tested, and an arrow function that will be invoked when the test is run. The describe function is basically a container for one or more individual tests.

Inside the arrow function we first create a variable called **service** to contain an instance of the service and then use a function called **beforeEach**, which will be invoked before each test is run and which we can use to perform any setup that may be needed.

In this case the **configureTestingModule** method of the **TestBed** class is used to create an empty Angular module for testing purposes and assigns an instance of the **DataService** to the service variable using the inject method of the **TestBed**.

Individual tests in Jasmine are create with the **it** function. This function also takes a string as the first parameter, which describes what is being tested, and an arrow function which will be invoked to run the test. In this file, which was generated by Angular, it is just testing that the service variable has a truthy value using the expect function and the **toBeTruthy** matcher. We can remove this test from the file and add one that actually tests one of the methods in the data service. Delete the whole **it** function from the file.

First of all, we can import the **Conference** interface as the top of the file:

```
import { Conference } from './model';
```

Now we can add a new describe function as a container for the tests relating to the **getConferences** method:

```
describe('getConferences()', () => {

    let fakeConferences: Conference[];

});
```

We can add the method name as the test description, and inside the arrow function we can declare a new variable called **fakeConferences** and specify it is of the type **Conference[]**. Now, directly after the **fakeConferences** variable, inside the arrow function, add the following code:

```
beforeEach(() => {

    fakeConferences = [{ id: 'test' }] as unknown as Conference[];

    spyOn(service.getConferences$, 'next');

    spyOn(localStorage, 'getItem')

      .and.returnValue(JSON.stringify(fakeConferences));

});
```

Inside the **beforeEach** arrow function we first assign the **fakeConferences** variable with an array containing a single object that has a single property called **id**. To avoid adding all of the properties required by the **Conference** interface to this test object, we can double-case it first to **unknown** and then to the **Conference[]** type that we want to use.

Next we use Jasmine's **spyOn** function to record all calls to the next method of the service's **getConferences$** observable. We can then use the **spyOn** function again to spy on on the **getItem** method of **localStorage**, but this time we can also use the **and.returnValue** function to control what the **getItem** method returns. In this case, we can use **JSON.stringify** to produce a string version of the **fakeConferences** array.

Now we can add the test itself:

```
it('calls the next method of the getConferences$ observable', () => {

    service.getConferences();

    expect(service.getConferences$.next)
```

```
    .toHaveBeenCalledWith(fakeConferences);
});
```

We use the **it** function and describe what is being tested in the first parameter. Inside the arrow function we can call the **getConferences** method of the service and then use the expect function in conjunction with the **toHaveBeenCalledWith** matcher to check that the next method of the **getConferences$** observable was called and that it was passed the **fakeConferences** array.

We can now run the tests for the project using the **ng test** command in the terminal, and we should find that the test passes and that the method we tested is behaving in the expected way.

Continuing with the example application

You should now have a fully functional, but very small, reference application, but there are many improvements or new features that could still be added to it. In order to continue applying what you have learned about TypeScript, and Angular, why not try adding one or more of the following features:

- A slick new theme – the styling for the example application is minimal, as this is a book about TypeScript rather than SCSS. There are many styling improvements that could be made, including a better color palette, an improved layout, or some better imagery.
- Update the form in the add component to capture all the required information for a conference, including all the talks that will be taking place.
- Break out some of the nested interface objects from the examples, such as the **speaker** object from the **Talk** interface or the logo object from the **Conference** interface, into their own interfaces or type aliases.
- Consider incorporating new interfaces to describe different kinds of data structures in the app. For example, consider adding an interface for speakers that includes properties like avatar, name, experience, etc.
- Improve the test coverage for the application by adding additional unit tests in the existing spec files for each component we created during this chapter.
- Extend the application so that it can support conferences with multiple tracks. The talks for each track should be grouped accordingly, and the UI updated to display the different tracks - a typical tabbed interface could work well here.

Conclusion

In this final chapter of the book, we have seen how to put some of the information we have learned into practice by building a fully functioning, entirely front-end example application. We've seen how the Angular framework naturally leads to TypeScript development as the framework itself is written in TypeScript. The framework also gives us fully functional build tools that let us build, test, and lint the applications we build, making Angular a great choice for modern professional web application development.

Although this is the end of the book, it will not be the end of your TypeScript journeys. As you read these words, the latest version of TypeScript is being created and prepared for release, with an ever-growing feature-set, and no sign of disappearing, you are sure to be learning about TypeScript for some time to come.

References

- **https://angular.io/guide/router**
- **https://angular.io/guide/reactive-forms**
- **https://developer.mozilla.org/en-US/docs/Web/API/Window/localStorage**

Index

B

C

D